DATE DUE

CAMBRIDGE SOUTH ASIAN STUDIES

THE SWATANTRA PARTY AND INDIAN CONSERVATISM

CAMBRIDGE SOUTH ASIAN STUDIES

These monographs are published by the Syndics of Cambridge University Press in association with the Cambridge University Centre for South Asian Studies. The following books have been published in this series:

Gopal, S., *British Policy in India, 1858–1905*
Palmer, J. A. B., *The Mutiny Outbreak at Meerut in 1857*
Obeyesekere, G., *Land Tenure in Village Ceylon*
Das Gupta, A., *Malabar in Asian Trade, 1740–1800*

THE SWATANTRA PARTY AND INDIAN CONSERVATISM

BY

HOWARD L. ERDMAN

Assistant Professor of Government
Dartmouth College, U.S.A.

CAMBRIDGE
AT THE UNIVERSITY PRESS
1967

Published by the Syndics of the Cambridge University Press
Bentley House, 200 Euston Road, London, N.W.1
American Branch: 32 East 57th Street, New York, N.Y. 10022

Library of Congress Catalogue Card Number: 67-27128

Printed in Great Britain
at the University Printing House, Cambridge
(Brooke Crutchley, University Printer)

TO MY PARENTS

CONTENTS

PREFACE

This book is about the background, emergence, and growth of one Indian political party which came into existence in mid-1959 and which, at the time of writing, had by no means reached the stage where an epitaph was in order. Counsels of prudence might, therefore, have dictated a postponement in the writing and publication of this volume, until more data were available and the dust had settled somewhat. Still, some students of politics rush in where historians fear to tread; but there seems considerable justification for such apparent rashness. For one thing, nothing of any consequence has been written about the Swatantra Party, one of the major political forces in India from 1959 to 1966, at least; and for another—and more important—very little has been written on the general subject of conservative politics in India. By providing considerable background material and by emphasizing factors more enduring than who happens to be second vice-president at a particular time, an attempt has been made to give this book more 'staying power' than it might seem to have at first glance. Readers, and time, will tell.

This being said, it is still true that since this book was first drafted, a distressingly large number of Swatantra luminaries have died or left the party, requiring some substantial revisions of the text. At some points—as in the creation of the new states of the Punjab and Haryana—insufficient material could be mustered, and the text was allowed to stand, despite new developments. Only benevolent intervention from on high could assure that the final text, as it last left the typewriter, would in most substantial respects be up-to-date at the time of publication. The reader's indulgence is begged if he has to keep current *Times of India* cuttings inside the cover of the book.

Under these circumstances, it may only be an embarrassment to those whose help is appreciated to have their names mentioned here. Still, I should like to express my deepest gratitude to Professors Lloyd and Susanne Rudolph (now of the University of Chicago) and to Dr Barrington Moore, Jr., who painstakingly and affectionately—but with often distressingly honest criticism—directed the Harvard University dissertation upon which this book is based; and these same people have been involved subsequently in its wholesale revision. Thanks are due also to Professor Myron Weiner, Massachusetts Institute of Technology, who read the manuscript *in toto* and who rendered valuable criticism as well as encouragement and who generously made available some pertinent manuscript material of his own; and to my Dartmouth colleagues, Professors Henry Ehrmann, Kalman Silvert, and Vincent Starzinger, who have given valuable aid and encouragement at various important junctures. Debts of gratitude are also due to Harvard University and the Fulbright Foundation for jointly sponsoring a year of research in India in 1962–3; to Professor R. Bhaskaran of the University of Madras, who was of much help during that year; to the Comparative Studies Center, Dartmouth College, for support of research time in 1964–5 and for supplementing a grant from the American Institute of Indian Studies, to make possible a second trip to India in 1966–7, when much up-dating was undertaken.

In India, too, splendid co-operation was forthcoming from officials and members of the Swatantra Party, too numerous to mention to the last man here. I would be remiss in my duty, however, if I did not thank Mr M. R. Masani, General-Secretary of the Swatantra Party, for authorizing the opening of certain party files for my benefit; his able executive assistant, Mr S. V. Raju, for steering me through those files and for providing much valuable information both while I was in the United States and in India; Mr A. P. Jain of the Swatantra parliamentary office, for similar assistance; Mr Noorul Arfin, personal assistant to the Raja of Ramgarh, for keeping a steady stream of information about Bihar and Orissa affairs flowing to me; and Major Thakur Raghubir Singh of Bissau, not only for similar help but also for his kindness in allowing me to use his Jaipur home as research headquarters and residence for six hectic weeks. I know that much that I have already written on Swatantra has not met with the approval of many party members who were generous with their time and help, and this book will doubtless be cause for further distress. I only hope, at least, that I have not abused their confidence in any way.

Thanks are also due to the editors of *Asian Survey*, *Pacific Affairs*, and the *Journal of Developing Areas* for allowing me to reproduce material from my articles which appeared earlier in their publications; and to the Hutchinson Publishing Group, Ltd., for allowing me to reproduce the tables from Professor W. H. Morris-Jones' *Government and Politics of India.*

Finally, as research assistant-critic-typist-indexer, my wife Joan, and my young daughter Karen, deserve affectionate mention. The former, in addition to her work, has submitted twice to travelling almost ceaselessly throughout India, while at the same time being something of a book-writer's widow. The latter invariably brought good humour into sundry oppressively serious offices, to good advantage. And this book is dedicated to my parents, whose many sacrifices made my education possible.

Baroda, India H. L. E.
December 1966

ABBREVIATIONS USED IN THE TEXT

AIAF	All-India Agriculturalists' Federation
AICC	All-India Congress Committee
COC	Central Organizing Committee (of the Swatantra Party)
CPI	Communist Party of India
CSP	Congress Socialist Party
DK	Dravida Kazagham
DMK	Dravida Munnetra Kazagham
FFE	Forum of Free Enterprise
FICCI	Federation of Indian Chambers of Commerce and Industry
INDC	Indian National Democratic Congress
IPLP	Independent Progressive Legislature Party
KLP	Krishikar Lok Paksh
MLA	Member of (state) legislative assembly
MP	Member of Parliament
PEPSU	Patiala and Eastern Punjab States Union
PSP	Praja Socialist Party
RRP	Ram Rajya Parishad
RSS	Rashtriya Swayamsevak Sangh
UP	Uttar Pradesh

CHAPTER I

COMMENTS ON CONSERVATISM

The formation of the Swatantra Party in 1959 represented an effort on the part of some of India's most distinguished public figures to build a 'non-leftist' opposition to the ruling Congress Party. This book is intended, first and foremost, to describe in detail the background, genesis, and subsequent development of Swatantra. It is, to use some current terminology, a study of 'interest aggregation' in India.[1] In addition, however, this study will also define what type of non-leftist party Swatantra has or is likely to become. To be more specific, the relationship of Swatantra to Indian conservatism is used as the principal focal point. Other approaches could easily have been taken, but this one seemed the most fruitful, given the present state of the literature on Indian politics.[2]

CONSERVATISM: COMMON USAGE AND COMMON PROBLEMS

The term conservatism is, however, sufficiently ambiguous that some mention must be made of its usage here. To be sure, conservatism (as etymology suggests) denotes a response to a challenge, a response which seeks to preserve, conserve, sustain, etc. It is evident, too, that the frame of reference must be that which actually exists—otherwise the idea of conserving would not be relevant. Thus, Huntington, emphasizing the doctrinal aspect, defines conservatism as 'the ideological justification of established social and political institutions' in response to 'a clear and present danger to the institutions'.[3] Granting that defenders of established institutions generally do advance some ideological justification, we shall not insist upon this here; nor shall we employ a distinction between traditionalism (non-ideological) and conservatism (ideological) as is sometimes done.[4]

These minor points do not, however, get to the heart of the difficulty in using the term conservatism. Huntington's definition is intended to cover any group which defends any established institutions, no matter how divergent these groups or institutions may be. This is akin to Michels' 'technically political' usage of conservatism, which 'means a tendency to maintain the status quo regardless of what that may be'. In this sense, the word is 'devoid of philosophical content, and one may logically designate as conservative the most disparate parties and factions'.[5] As Friedrich puts it, 'conservatism shows very diverse forms in different countries at different times, for it is by definition concerned with maintaining the existing order...Hence the programmatic viewpoint, the ideal objectives of conservatives are variable in the extreme'.[6] Oakeshott insists that conservatism is not 'connected with any particular beliefs about the universe, about the world in general or about human conduct in general', and he adds further that 'what is esteemed is the present; and it is esteemed not on account of its connections with a remote antiquity [*pace* Burke], nor because it is recognised to be more admirable than any possible alternative, but on account of its familiarity...'[7] One logical corollary of such views, with Michels, is that 'a party conservative in this sense may in the past have been revolutionary and without any change of theoretical position...may have become technically conservative on the successful completion of the revolution'.[8]

Needless to say, the implications of such an approach have troubled many writers; and even some of those just cited have provided alternative approaches which restrict the meaning of conservatism somewhat. Mannheim would limit its use to the ideological response of one class (the aristocracy) at one point in time.[9] Others are less restrictive and less precise but also strive for limitation. Michels talks of a second approach to conservatism in which it has a 'philosophical use and meaning' and 'in which case it implies a particular Weltanschauung'; [10] Oakeshott insists that 'to be conservative is to be disposed to think and behave in certain manners; it is to prefer certain kinds of conduct and certain conditions of human existence to others; it is to be disposed to make certain kinds of choices';[11] and Viereck cites distinctive attitudes toward 'human nature, history, tradition, and the tempo of change'.[12] In general, a conservative is seen to prefer stability and prefers change which is gradual and which maintains continuity; he will himself decline to be an important innovator and will place the burden of proof on those who favour change; he will be sceptical of the power of reasoning even among a given society's best talents and he will be sceptical of the reliability of the 'masses', unless properly led; and he will, to use Viereck's words, engage in 'spiritual arithmetic', calculating the moral price paid for material progress.[13] This narrows the scope of conservatism, along the lines of current usage, but it does not establish a precise definition in terms of which this study can be easily and unambiguously located.

Whatever the ultimate merits of alternative approaches may be, it will have to suffice for present purposes to indicate the approach taken here. First, conservatism is primarily (if not exclusively, with Mannheim) associated with the aristocratic defence of the feudal-agrarian *ancien régime*. Secondly, conservatism has also come to refer to middle-class resistance to more radical, lower-class demands. This, for example, follows Friedrich's view that conservatism 'is primarily compounded of the groups and interests who happen to be "in possession", the "haves"...'.[14] This does not mean that all individuals at a given social level and at a given point in time resort to the same actions or doctrinal formulations; nor does it mean that only those 'in possession' are relevant to a study of conservatism. It means only that historically the two principal manifestations of conservatism have been associated in gross terms and in terms of leadership with the aristocracy on the one hand and propertied middle-class interests on the other.

Put somewhat differently, we shall follow the lines suggested by Silvert, who said that it may safely be assumed that 'groups which have would like to keep what they have' but that before we can translate this into meaningful terms, we need to know 'what they think they will permit themselves to do toward that end..., how much real power they have relative to other social groups..., and the actual state of the competitive situation in which they find themselves'.[15] Moore's seminal work and the best of the Marxist literature certainly proceed along these lines;[16] and only through an examination of such issues can the nature (e.g. the intensity, cohesion, substance, effectiveness, latent potential) of a given conservative response be fully intelligible. Thus, the present study will locate certain key groups 'in possession' and it will examine in some historical detail the process of challenge and response as it has affected these groups and the manner in which they interact.

This having been said, there are still certain problems. What if divergent traditions exist within the same country, and what if different social and political institutions exist side-by-side, on a territorially segmented basis? What if an aristocracy is not fully supplanted by a middle-class group and a more radical movement arises to challenge both? Are the defenders of diverse traditions within the same political unit equally conservative, or can we differentiate among them? Are all opponents of radical régimes on the same footing, or can we differentiate among them?

Many of the sources already cited reflect this problem. Huntington states that the French middle classes 'had to face in two directions' and 'expounded liberal ideas against the aristocrats and conservative ideas against the masses'.[17] Similarly, Friedrich states that the liberals, after challenging the *ancien régime*, found that 'the more radical socialist elements' were becoming 'the effective opposition'; and at that point, the liberal movement 'begins to adopt a defensive attitude, and insofar as it does, it becomes conservative'.[18] These writers surely do not mean that the views of the aristocratic and middle-class interests were identical, yet at least in some situations both groups are termed conservative. Viereck takes a perhaps more helpful line by stating only that conservatives and liberals may join hands for certain purposes, while they 'will continue to differ about human nature, history, tradition, and the tempo of change'.[19] Certainly if both aristocratic and middle-class interests exist side-by-side, sometimes in opposition to one another and sometimes associated in resisting radical demands, we must maintain some distinction between them. And even if one privileged class seemingly abandons its claims against another, in pursuit of a common effort against radical demands, we must surely emphasize the element of latent conflict, which, under changed circumstances, could become manifest. Such an approach is indispensable, if we are to make sense out of the Indian case.

Another area of ambiguity concerns the possibility of divergent approaches by the same individual or group to change in social, economic, and political spheres. What, for example, if an aristocrat mechanizes previously traditionally farmed estates or establishes modern industrial enterprises, while still insisting on the divine right of aristocrats to dominate society? Is such an aristocrat conservative or not? One could attempt to define some 'average' or general tendency, embracing all public views, but this would obscure much that is important. Alternatively, one could emphasize a single factor, as, for example, the overall power relationships among major social groups. Such an approach seems more satisfactory than the previous one, but it has deficiencies of its own, viz. it might fail to point up adequately the differences between technologically progressive traditional élites and those who were not, and between those who were 'Tory democrats' and those who were not. An approach which did not specify such distinctions would be of limited value; and it would seem more useful to indicate views on social, economic, and political matters, indicating both departures from and adherence to tradition in each area, with due attention to the impact on the overall pattern of power relationships.

Implicit in many of the preceding remarks is one final problem which must be noted here in preliminary fashion: the use of conservative and often allied terms such as reactionary and rightist. Huntington, for example, states that 'in France...aristocratic thought, once conservative, rapidly became reactionary and eventually became radical'.[20] Viereck, referring to differences between Burke and Maistre, argues that 'the former is evolutionary; the latter counter-revolutionary. Both favor traditions against the innovations of 1789, but their traditions differ...The latter...is often called not "conservative" but "reactionary".' Agreeing substantially with Huntington in this respect, Viereck adds that the reactionary

> sometimes seems just as radical against the existing present as the radical Jacobin or the Marxist, only in the opposite direction. The Burkean, in contrast, does come to terms with the reality of inevitable change. But he does so without the liberal's optimism and faith in progress...But that distinction (between conservative and reactionary) must not be over-simplified or over-applied. Many conservatives do not fully lend themselves to neat pigeon-holing in either category but overlap...[21]

Finally, Michels notes that his 'philosophical conservative' often 'tends to desert his ideology if changes are brought about despite him, and to take on a new attitude favouring change (change in a backward direction, i.e. reaction)...'.[22] Even a cursory reading of Rogger and Weber's *The European Right* will indicate the considerable difficulties in defining the 'radical right' and in relating it to conservatism and reaction.[23] We may ask, for example, if a reactionary in Huntington's sense is not *ipso facto* radical as well, as Michels suggests? If so, how does a reactionary differ from a right radical? How does one decide when a conservative is transformed into a reactionary or a right radical? These are not easily answered questions.

Acknowledging these difficulties, we shall still employ these various terms in the study of Swatantra. The term rightist or right wing will be used broadly to cover all people, parties, and doctrines categorized more specifically as conservative, reactionary, and right radical. The term reactionary will refer to efforts to re-establish some system which actually or substantially existed at one time but which has been (largely) displaced. The term right radical will denote efforts which tend strongly to be authoritarian, chauvinistic, and militant, which seek to establish mass-mobilization régimes through the use of religio-cultural symbols, charisma, and the like, and which tend strongly toward fascism. The term conservative will refer to efforts to sustain some more or less stable, ordered system which in fact exists at a given historical moment (or which very recently existed), by contrast with both reactionary and right radical efforts which will be critical of such a system. Whatever the abstract merits or universal applicability of such a classification may be, it works tolerably in the Indian case. More important is the fact that we are, in any event, more interested in analysing certain major political developments in India than we are in quibbling over the words used to refer to them.

CONSERVATISM: THE INDIAN CASE

The Indian case presents us with much that is familiar, but it presents some important, distinctive features as well. There is no difficulty, for example, in locating an indigenous aristocracy (the so-called native princes—maharajas, rajas, nawabs, etc.—and landed nobles—*jagirdars*, *taluqdars*, *zamindars*, etc.) whose response to challenges will satisfy the search for aristocratic conservatism. However, the absence of stable, indigenous, macro-political institutions and the absence of broad class identifications and cohesion have meant that there was no *national* focal point for aristocratic conservatism. The latter was at best regional; and often it formed around antagonistic individual rulers. The absence of a cohesive body of 'lords temporal' is paralleled on the religious side, where we find no cohesive body of 'lords spiritual'—the latter meaning that Hinduism has no organized 'church'—to serve as a focal point for religious conservatism. All of this is part of the more general problem of social fragmentation in India, to which countless writers have referred.[24]

Moreover, in about half of India, princely polities were swept aside by the British, and different institutions and values and new social classes came to the fore, ultimately to lead to parliamentarism. In the rest of the country, princely polities were nominally retained, but became atrophied. Are the defenders of princely India and of British Indian institutions both conservative and on a par, or is the princely tradition more authentically Indian and its defenders more authentically conservative? Are the surviving aristocrats to be called conservative, if they defended their patrimonies which were at least nominally retained; or are they to be called reactionary, because the social order which they represented had been largely displaced, *de facto*, if not *de jure*? In this study, aristocratic conservatism will be accorded higher 'status' than that relating to British India, and the defenders of the princely régimes will be called conservative, unless they argue for a more or less complete restoration of such régimes along pre-British lines.

There is yet another complication. The historic weakness of India's macro-political institutions, the instability of the princely polities and the fate which befell them, and the pro-British stand ultimately taken by most leading aristocrats combined to lead many Indians to hold that the 'real' India had nothing whatever to do with the princely states. For them, the real India was to be found in the three pillars of the 'self-regulating' Indian society—the joint family, caste, and village—which enabled India to withstand instability in the broader polity and which, rather than the much-vaunted Indian Civil Service, deserve to be called the 'steel frame' of India. At this level, conservatism exists without monarchs and landed nobles, without the pomp and flourish of the courts of the *ancien régimes*. It was, in fact, usually unconcerned with and often opposed to conservatism at 'higher' levels. Furthermore, the caste system, often portrayed as totally inflexible, contained within itself a profoundly conservative mechanism of change (now generally termed 'sanskritization'), which helped to avoid frontal attacks on the system and hence diminished the need to articulate defences of it.[25]

The village order ultimately came to have its Burkes and Maistres, as disintegration set in, in the wake of British rule and as a result of the entering wedge of industrialism. The defence of the old order (itself considerably idealized by many) often revealed a fusion of conservatism with local variants of utopian socialist and Luddite postures. This renders hazardous a characterization of this response as conservatism plain and simple, but its ample conservative component must be set forth in any study of Indian conservatism.

India's urban, and to a much lesser extent rural propertied middle classes looked in two directions; and this was particularly but not exclusively true of those in British India. Many landed peasants were at least happy to contemplate the demise of the aristocracy; but in terms of major social transformations, this is not in any sense decisive, as the village-based, agrarian order remains to be dealt with.[26] More important is the view of the urban industrial-professional classes, which was critical of both aristocratic conservatism and villagism. However, the rise of more radical movements helped to blunt this challenge, which was not, in any event, of massive strength to begin with.

Finally, the British presence affected the outlook of diverse classes, as well as the pattern of inter-class relationships. Many of the forces of change were often traced to the British, and conservative responses were often merged with more broadly anti-imperalist positions. Needless to say, many non-conservatives were associated with the latter.[27] Groups which favoured the types of changes brought about (consciously or unconsciously) by the British ran the risk of being labelled as anti-national, which also helped to blunt anti-traditional efforts. To put the matter differently, we may ask: in what ways was the 'dialogue' between east and west also a dialogue between conservatism and liberalism, and in what ways did conservatism (and class and doctrinal matters more generally) take on new dimensions, because of the colonial setting? The picture which emerges is quite complex, indeed, but one central feature is certainly this: as the nationalist movement progressed in the twentieth century, a wedge was driven between the aristocracy (increasingly alined with the British) and the urban industrial and professional elements (increasingly alined with the Congress), forestalling, if not precluding a fascist-type alliance between them in the face of more radical demands. The present state of the relationship between these two broad classes must be examined in any study of Indian conservatism.

In India, then, we shall find aristocratic conservatives; village-oriented groups which rejected both the aristocratic order and British institutions and values; village-oriented groups which accepted parliamentarism but which wanted the new political institutions to be used in defence of village India; and others who, in varying ways and degrees, were more fully committed to transform India socially, economically, and politically along western lines. For a long time these groups functioned in a colonial setting which further complicated already complex interrelationships. This study is intended to lay bare some basic perspectives and some of these complex interrelationships, many of which exist in microcosm in the background, genesis, and subsequent development of the Swatantra Party. Conservatism will receive the bulk of the attention; but the analysis of Swatantra will be set against the backdrop of *rightist* politics more generally.

CHAPTER 2

DIMENSIONS OF INDIAN RIGHT-WING POLITICS: SOCIAL AND DOCTRINAL ASPECTS

It has been part of the conventional wisdom about Indian politics that right-wing political activity has been extremely ineffectual. Certainly, few writers, apart from Marxists, have argued to the contrary. Thus, two leading students of Indian affairs have commented on reactionary activity in the following fashion: 'It is one of the paradoxes of Indian politics that India's *ancien régime*, surely one of the oldest and most deeply rooted in the world, produced no reaction... Only a few minor local parties today stand for a full return to the rule of Brahmins and *kshatryas* according to the precepts of dharma or traditional duty, and they are ineffectual.'[1] In a more general vein, another scholar has argued: 'Nehru once observed... "Who says that opposition forces are weak in India? The opposition we have to fight is obscurantism and inertia of the people." The Prime Minister had in mind mass lethargy and ignorance: but the record of both the religious and secular Rightist parties is a sad commentary on this maxim.'[2] The last remark misses Nehru's basic point that the resistance of those attached to the *ancien régime* is passive, not active; but the judgment about the weakness of rightist parties is none the less evident here.[3] The situation was such that one writer could announce, after the first two general elections in India (1951–2 and 1957), 'the almost complete eclipse of our so-called rightist parties'.[4] No one denied that there existed privileged classes with a vested interest in maintaining the *ancien régime*, but they seemed quiescent; and the passivity and inarticulateness of these groups were paralleled, ostensibly, in the case of the modern élites in land and industry.

The weakness of conservatism more specifically was noted before independence by a maharaja who commented that 'it must seem strange in a country whose ways of life are so dominated by custom and tradition as India, there should be no political party which calls itself conservative'. Events seem to have falsified this same man's prediction that with growing emancipation from

British tutelage 'a strong party of experienced and responsible politicians will emerge, which will call itself the Conservative Party...'.[5] The 'almost complete eclipse' of rightist parties, conservative or otherwise, seemed to be an obvious, yet puzzling feature of Indian political life.

Were these judgments sound? If so, why? If not, why were so many capable observers misled? What were the problems and prospects of a strong, explicitly rightist—and more specifically, conservative—force in India? These in brief are the important but unanswered questions which account for the focus selected for this study and for which some answers will be sought through an examination of India's Swatantra Party.

SOCIAL BASES: CHALLENGE AND RESPONSE

On 15 August 1947 India gained her independence from British rule. There was no doubt that the mantle of power would fall to the Indian National Congress, but at the time this alone must have seemed clear. Fundamental problems which had plagued India through her long centuries would have to be confronted anew, and there was no assurance that the Congress or any other political force in the country would be adequate to the challenge. Could a united country be created out of the diverse religions, linguistic and caste groups, and out of the former British provinces and the congeries of princely states? Could the weight of centuries of tradition be overcome sufficiently to allow India to develop the dynamism required for desperately needed progress on many fronts? These were but two of the critical questions for which no confident answers could be provided.

From the standpoint of India's conservative elements, as for all others, the future was clouded. Over the years of British rule, traditional India had confronted numerous challenges. Many princely polities had been annexed, and those remaining had atrophied considerably. Conscious efforts at social, legal, educational, and other reforms, as well as changes flowing from the advent of rail-roads, modern communications, new forms of industry, and the like, seemed to many to strike at the roots of Indian society. Over wide areas, erosion, if not sudden destruction, seemed to threaten indigenous institutions and values, and at least from the time of Ram Mohun Roy in the early nineteenth century, there were always articulate Indians who also advocated changes, some modest, some drastic, in traditional India. It remained to be seen what the 'new India' held in store.

Uppermost in the minds of many conservative Indians in 1947 was the knowledge that Jawaharlal Nehru would probably dominate the political scene, and this generated considerable anxiety. From the late 1920s onward, Nehru had explicitly identified himself with the more radical elements in the country and had inveighed against the princely order, the landed aristocracy, the capitalist class, the defenders of socio-religious orthodoxy, the general stagnation of rural India, and the like.[6] Shortly before independence, Gandhi warned the princes that 'Pandit Jawaharlal Nehru will have no patience with you',[7] but the princes were by no means alone in their need to be apprehensive. A government acting responsively to Nehru could have provided a formidable threat to a number of important privileged social groups.

Nehru did, of course, tower over the Indian political scene after independence, until his death in 1964, and in varying degrees each of the groups against whom he had inveighed did confront challenges during his tenure as Prime Minister. The princes had their states 'integrated' into the Indian Union, and thus they lost their residual political power, their status suffered, and their economic position deteriorated badly, where it did not completely collapse. The same was true of the great landed aristocrats, both in the former princely states and in former British India, who were eliminated as 'intermediaries' between the peasant and the state. The middle peasantry came ultimately to confront pressure for heavier taxation, ceilings on land holdings, a vague threat of collectivized agriculture, and a variety of efforts designed to improve the general position of the lowest strata of the rural population, in whose continued exploitation the higher caste Hindus had a deep and abiding vested interest. The business communities were confronted by a wide range of restrictive legislation, including prohibitions on entry into certain fields which were reserved for state-sponsored enterprises; limitations on expansion in other areas; quotas and excises, particularly in the textile field, intended to make hand-woven cloth more competitive; attacks on the 'managing agency' system which had structured Indian enterprise since the nineteenth century; heavy corporate and personal taxation; and occasional intimations of nationalization or at least rather drastic circumscription of the private sector. Legislation intended to reform Hindu family relations, inheritance, and other aspects of traditional private law challenged the orthodox of whatever status or occupation.[8]

Each of these moves produced adverse responses, but for the most part these responses were isolated efforts which did not develop into a cohesive force. Some princes refused, at the outset, to accede to the Government of India and made what amounted to declarations of independence; one or two resorted to military resistance; and in 1951 some former rulers and landed aristocrats attempted to form a 'Rulers' Union', to agitate against the integration of the native states and the decline of the aristocracy more generally. The landed aristocracy, often in consort with former princes, took their fight against land reforms to the courts, where in some cases they were temporarily successful; and in some isolated instances they resorted to banditry as a form of protest against the effects of government policy. Non-aristocratic landed groups worked through many channels, including caste associations and such groups as the All-India Agriculturalists' Federation (1958); while at the village level the attempted rise of depressed groups was countered in a variety of ways, including attrition in prolonged court battles, boycotts of village councils on which they sat and schools which they attended, refusal to respect elections which they might have won and taxes which their representatives might have been instrumental in levying, and a whole spectrum of more or less coercive measures, including the burning of homes and crops, the destruction of cattle, physical assault, and so on. On the national level, the late President of the Republic, Rajendra Prasad, steadfastly opposed certain provisions of the social reform legislation and threatened to withhold his assent, or to resign from office, unless modifications were forthcoming. The business communities, having tried to anticipate and to undercut Congress planning efforts by advancing a development plan of their own in 1944, betrayed a crisis of confidence in the régime immediately after independence, and periodically thereafter they displayed anxiety over Congress policies, especially whenever there seemed to be a move toward 'Soviet' style planning. The frequent complaints of various individuals and business groups, and the creation of a small but vocal organization called the Forum of Free Enterprise (1956) testify to business opposition to diverse government measures. These will suggest the range of responses to Congress policies during the years 1947–59.[9] Efforts along party lines will be discussed below.

Many of these challenges were, thus, acutely felt and many of the responses thereto were certainly conservative; yet there was no coherent, explicitly conservative response at the party level during the first decade after independence. There are many reasons for this, but the brief catalogue of challenge and response during the Nehru era suggests one important factor: the diversity of the social forces involved. In addition to major inter-group cleavages, however, there were also intra-group cleavages, based in large part on the historic social fragmentation of Hindu society; and these also worked against the formation of a cohesive opposition force.

A brief glance at the historical record will show that even within a given group, viz. the aristocracy, landed peasantry, business communities, etc., unity was at best a remote possibility. With respect to the princely order, for example, it is clear that at almost every critical juncture in its history, it was beset by internal cleavages which seriously impaired its collective position. The story is told that sometime before the rebellion of 1857 a leading Indian ruler looked at a standard British map of the sub-continent, with 'British India' coloured red, princely India yellow, and commented, 'one day it will all be red'.[10] Yet this sentiment was either not widely shared or else it did not matter, because at no time did the native rulers act on the maxim that it would be better to hang together than to hang separately. The disunity of the princes in 1857—notwithstanding certain ultra-nationalist fantasies about projected 'United States of India' and kindred visions—is obvious. While some rulers were engaged in a life-and-death struggle (to be counted among the major manifestations of conservatism in India) with the British *raj*, other rulers stood apart or actively assisted in the suppression of the revolt. Subsequently, in the constitutional deliberations of the 1920s and 1930s, the princes once again found it impossible to present anything resembling a united front. Pre-eminent rulers held aloof from the Chamber of Princes and looked upon its activities with scorn; lesser princes who were excluded from the Chamber resented their demotion and demanded equality, which the more prestigious rulers were unwilling to concede. Even as 'doomsday' approached, disunity was prevalent.[11]

Prior to independence, the great landed nobles of British India were virtually compelled to be better united, because they had to function within a somewhat more 'open' and more reformist environment. Over the years, the *zamindars* had organized themselves, at least locally, to petition the *raj* and eventually to elect representatives to the legislative councils, in which they had reserved seats. They amply demonstrated their conservatism by proclaiming and defending their élite status and by steadfastly opposing almost every significant piece of land reform legislation introduced by the British to ameliorate the conditions of the actual tillers of the soil. Throughout the years of the British *raj*, however, differences between big and small *zamindars* were evident; each group, as in the case of the princes, was beset by religious and caste animosities; and, for example, the first 'All-India Landholders' Conference', dominated by the great *zamindars*, was not convened until 1938, which was rather late in the game from the standpoint of the self-interest of the landed aristocracy. Furthermore, the political division of India into British and princely areas inhibited the development of associations which would bring together the *zamindars* and their closest counterparts in the princely states, the *jagirdars*.[12]

The state of Rajasthan provides a good case study of the multiple cleavages which beset the aristocratic classes even on a regional level, in the post-independence era. The great Rajput princes were not particularly solicitous of or fully trusted by, the lesser ones. The non-Rajput rulers, like the Jat family of Bharatpur, were often treated with scorn by the Rajputs, great and small alike. The Rajput *jagirdars* themselves, reasonably well united for a short time in the early years after independence, came ultimately to be split along economic lines, between big and little *jagirdars*. An interesting footnote to this is provided by the manifestly preposterous assertion of some *jagirdars* that they would have treated the people better, had it not been for the presence of the princes who ruled the area.[13]

Thus, while sharing many interests and aspirations *vis-à-vis* more democratic tendencies, the aristocratic classes never formed a cohesive opposition force, either on the national or the state level, either under the British or after 1947. Both the aristocrats and the defenders of religious orthodoxy might be eminently conservative but their activities were inevitably fragmented.[14] To appreciate the significance of this one need only ask how different India's political development might well have been had, say, the Rajputs been the dominant aristocratic group throughout India, or had the Chitpavan Brahmins been similarly dispersed as a religious élite group. Indian conservatism, if not India as a would-be modern, constitutional, democratic polity, has certainly suffered because this was not the case.

Many intra-group conflicts are evident as well among the landed peasant groups and the business communities. In some areas the Rajput-Jat split is evident at this level, as well as within the aristocracy, the Kshatrya-Patidar conflict in much of Gujarat is well known, and the Kamma-Reddy conflict in Andhra has been well documented.[15] Historically organized along family and community (i.e. Parsi, Marwari, Chettiar, Bohra, etc.) lines, Indian business has only partially progressed toward the creation of a broad, more or less national business class. The Parsis, who were Zoroastrians by religion and many of whom were highly Anglicized, were, for example, poles apart from the Hindu and Jain Marwari community, itself quite orthodox religiously; and while this might be the most extreme case, it is not the only one. Certain business organizations and individual firms were intercommunity ones, but others, like the Marwari Chamber of Commerce in Calcutta, were largely or even exclusively confined to one community. Certain 'peak' organizations such as the Federation of Indian Chambers of Commerce and Industry (FICCI) have helped to bring these together, as, significantly, have certain challenges to the position of business in general, viz. the threat of Congress planning which led to the formulation of the 'Bombay Plan' and the attack at a later date on the managing agency system of business organization. All of this notwithstanding, it will be quite a long time before comparably placed businessmen from different communities can be spoken of as one reasonably cohesive business class, even for relatively limited purposes and even after due allowance is made for different sectors of industry and for large- versus small-scale enterprises. This is a specific aspect of Weber's more general view that social cleavages in India virtually precluded the emergence of an urban 'brotherhood' comparable to those which arose in many western cities during the medieval period and which, in his view, in part accounted for the success of the urban challenge to feudalism in the west.[16]

This analysis could easily be elaborated, but to no important present purpose. It is sufficient to note that even within a given social stratum, even on a regional level, unity in responding to challenges did not exist and the likelihood of achieving it was remote.

Compounding this difficulty was the diversity of interest among major groups, including the important split between the aristocratic and middle-class interests. Co-operative effort by such groups would have been difficult to achieve, certainly in the absence of a formidable threat from the left and quite probably even in the face of one. This dimension of the problem is most profitably investigated from the standpoint of the social bases and policies of the nationalist movement, which, as everyone knows, was socially heterogeneous. What was the nature of the Congress coalition? How was it held together? What directions did its policies take? In suggesting answers to these questions, it will be possible not only to define better certain inter-group conflicts but also to suggest certain implications for the development of a cohesive, conservative opposition party in India.

The Congress, at least after the advent of Gandhi, had its centre of gravity among the middle peasant groups, with ample support from India's frustrated industrialists and much leadership from the urban intelligentsia. It is clear that there were many differences in the goals of these diverse components of the Congress coalition, yet they were held together. The latter fact is partly explained, of course, by common opposition to alien rule, which served as the broadest possible rallying point not only for these groups but for others as well. But it would be a mistake to underestimate the role of leadership and of ideology here. It was one of Gandhi's critical contributions that he emphasized the notion of 'trusteeship' and class harmony, tapping, in this respect and others, certain very traditional currents of thought in India, while providing no direct threat whatever to industrial interests.[17] Without Gandhi or someone like him, and without Gandhism or something akin to it, it would have been much more difficult to keep these disparate elements together, even with the anti-imperialist rallying point. Apprehension over the rise of socialist elements also played a part, which dovetailed neatly with Gandhi's contribution, as will be discussed subsequently.

Limited though the aspirations of the middle classes in the

Congress were, particularly with respect to the most depressed elements in Indian society, they proved sufficient to alienate the upper strata in many areas. Broadly speaking, the conflict between the middle class and the aristocracy was the most pronounced. The latter not only remained aloof from the nationalist movement but often actively opposed it; and particularly from the 1930s onward the aristocrats viewed the Congress with increasing hostility and alarm, turning more to the British to defend their interests. It is clear that the British played a key role in Indian political development here, in the sense that the anti-colonial struggle drove a wedge between the indigenous aristocracy and the industrial-commercial classes, precluding the emergence, at least in the short run, of a fascist-style alliance between them. It is significant, too, that while there was a growing concern over the rise of socialist elements, the threat from the left was not so acutely felt that the gap between these classes was bridged. Suggestive of the problem here—and it has proved to be an enduring one—is the fact that the aristocracy was inclined to look upon the Congress as a whole with a good deal of anxiety, while large groups of non-aristocratic conservative Congressmen were themselves becoming increasingly worried about the upsurge of socialism, both inside the party and out.[18]

Congress alienation of the aristocracy—as in what is now Rajasthan, where the States' Peoples' Conference drew upon a wide array of non-aristocratic groups—was the most visible social split, but others deserve attention. In the same state of Rajasthan, after independence, the lower caste Jats moved increasingly into positions of strength in the Congress (which built upon the States' Peoples' Conference), and this led to the decline and disaffection of some formerly prominent Brahmin leaders and other higher status groups. To cite a different but also important case, the Madras Congress was originally dominated by Brahmins, but in the face of strong anti-Brahmin movements in that state, the social basis of the party was broadened and newer sources of strength and leadership emerged. At present, Brahmins are conspicuous by their absence from high positions in the Madras Congress, and even some of the middle-caste, anti-Brahmin groups have been alienated as a result of an even further broadening of the social base of the party. In these and other cases, however, the ascendant elements were middle and lower middle caste groups for the most part, and their solicitude for those who remain below them is certainly suspect.[19] The hard core of the gradually democratizing Congress coalition was, in sum, non-aristocratic, middle class and moderately reformist, generally not desiring complete liquidation of superior classes and generally not desiring radical efforts to enhance the position of the lowest classes, particularly the untouchables. Thus, Rajagopalachari ('Rajaji', founder-leader of Swatantra), as premier of Madras from 1937 to 1939, used available legislation to control anti-princely state activity within the province; he sponsored land reform legislation which was designed to give greater security of tenure and somewhat greater income to tenants, but which left the existing landlords firmly in control; he insisted on substituting a permissive bill, based on the principle of 'local option', to permit temple entry by untouchables, in place of a bill which would have made it mandatory.[20] During his second term as political head of Madras, in the early 1950s, Rajaji, under the threat of communist gains in the state, carried forward some of this land legislation, in particular; but otherwise he remained generally moderate in his policies. Rajaji's non-Brahmin challengers and successors were more reform-minded than he, but even they fell short of radical programmes. Numerous other examples could be cited, but these will suffice in the present connection.

The relative moderation of the broad Congress coalition, even under Nehru's leadership, is evident from the fact that for one reason or another none of the elements whom he had belaboured were driven completely to the wall. The princes and landlords suffered serious setbacks, to be sure, but there were, in each case, some not inconsiderable consolations. On the probably sound assumption that 'the capacity for mischief and trouble on the part of the rulers if the settlement had not been reached on a negotiated basis was far greater than could be imagined at this stage', Sardar Patel insisted that in approaching the native rulers 'a spirit of give and take' prevail. He further 'expressed the hope that the Indian States would bear in mind that the alternative to co-operation in the general interest was anarchy and chaos which would overwhelm great and small in common ruin...'.[21] As a consequence, the princes received a wide array of *quid pro quos* in return for their accession to the Indian Union. Foremost among these was the annual, tax-free, 'privy purse', but in addition the princes were granted the right to retain all personal property and wealth, 'succession according to law and custom', exemption from customs and certain other duties, continued 'gun salutes' on certain occasions, privileged positions at certain state functions, special licence plates, permission to fly their old flags, among other perquisites, all of which were constitutionally guaranteed and non-justiciable. Furthermore, some of the pre-eminent rulers were named as *Rajpramukhs*, ambassadors, special advisers on government commissions, and the like, thus easing the impact of integration somewhat further in some important cases.[22] Patel justified these arrangements in the following terms:

> The minimum which we could offer to them as a *quid pro quo* for parting with their ruling powers was to guarantee to them privy purses and certain privileges on a reasonable and defined basis...Need we cavil at the small—I purposely use the word small—price we have paid for the bloodless revolution which has affected the destinies of millions of our people.[23]

Given the fact that many princes were phenomenally wealthy 'in the modern as well as in the feudal sense',[24] through investment in industry, integration was not the catastrophe it might have been, even though in almost every case a cut-back in the level of living was necessary.[25] And it is by no means insignificant for this study that Patel has been charged with expediting the integration of the states on this basis, in order to forestall more radical solutions to the problem.[26]

In the case of the landed aristocrats, comparable considerations apply. Prior to the introduction of abolition legislation it was observed that the intermediaries, 'for fear of the impending abolition...are directing their attention increasingly to non-agricultural secondaries'.[27] In almost every case, abolition legislation provided for compensation, and even Nehru argued that simple expropriation, 'though equitably perhaps justifiable, may lead to many cases of hardship' and, by implication, social discontent, and was to be avoided for this reason.[28] In some cases, rehabilitation grants were also provided and many acts permitted landlords to evict tenants in order to acquire land for personal cultivation.[29] Particularly in the case of the wealthier *zamindars* and *jagirdars* who had industrial investments, abolition legislation did not mean disaster, although as in the case of the princes cut-backs were well-nigh inevitable. It is an exaggeration to say that in

Rajasthan, for example, the legislation 'might as well have been drafted by the Jagirdars' Association',[30] but one can scarcely consider the broad approach to have been a particularly radical one either.

The position of the peasantry remained quite secure throughout this period. Taxation was generally less heavy and tenure more secure under the Congress than under the British and the landed intermediaries. Moreover, many government programmes—organization of co-operatives, extension of rural credit, improved transport, electrification, irrigation, and the like—were advantageous to these rural classes, although many fell far short of government expectations at least. Land ceiling legislation applied to very few, and those who were likely to be affected had ample time to divest themselves of 'surplus' lands to relatives and friends, thus escaping inclusion under the laws in many cases. In some instances the ceilings were made applicable only to future holdings, allowing the existing rural élite to escape completely. The famed 'Nagpur Resolution' (1959) on 'joint co-operative farming' was considered to mean 'collectivization' by very few, and Nehru insisted that no coercion would ever be used to bring it about. Thus, government economic policies did not provide a clear and present danger to the landed peasantry; and the diverse measures intended to improve the position of the untouchables and to democratize the village generally were heavily 'filtered' by dominant, upper castes, leaving in many instances only a relatively inoffensive residue. In some cases, projected reforms simply remained totally unimplemented.[31]

Business communities were also quite secure, even though there were loud complaints about the pattern of taxation and the range of government controls. Nationalization remained very much a 'red herring', as the Federation of British Industries noted in a report on investment opportunities in India; and many state-sponsored industries meshed well with private industry, assuring the latter of many necessary materials, power, and the like, at no private risk. In the area of economic infra-structure the government aided private enterprise considerably. Furthermore, even where theoretically excluded from certain sectors, private industrialists often found the government quite flexible; and where the government proved to be rigid, many industrialists successfully resorted to diversification, as they responded to standard capitalist impulses. Moreover, under the government system of licensing and issuing permits, some industrialists were established in privileged positions, although others might have been disaffected as a result. All in all, this was obviously not the best of all imaginable worlds from the standpoint of private enterprise, but it was not inordinately oppressive.[32]

The willingness of the Congress to be conciliatory in order to stabilize a shaky government testifies further to its generally moderate approach. In Rajasthan after 1952 and in Orissa after 1957, aristocratic elements were brought into the ministry, in the former case by outright absorption of opposition members into the Congress, in the latter through a coalition with a princely led party. Comparable accommodating tendencies have been widely evident in the realm of policy as well.

The failure of the Congress to mount a potent, radical challenge thus helps to account for the absence of a potent, coherent opposition to the ruling party, even though, as noted, there is no assurance that in the face of such a challenge the situation would be substantially different. However, Congress restraint by itself is insufficient to account for the condition of the opposition: the hegemony of the Congress also plays a major role.[33]

Briefly put, not only was the Congress relatively moderate in its policies, but where it did seriously offend certain segments of the population—and it surely did so—there was little prospect that anti-Congress activity would be worth the effort. Had there been a long-established opposition party to which the disaffected could repair, the situation would doubtless have been different. But under the prevailing circumstances, opposition was difficult and might only elicit more drastic treatment from the ruling party. Congress restraint and Congress hegemony are, however, linked: had Congress been radical to the point of complete dispossession of the aristocracy, for example, its hegemony might not have been much of a deterrent to desperate men. As it was, it was the fact that many adversely affected groups had still more that they could lose which accounts for much of the significance of Congress hegemony.

The princes, for example, were dependent on the Congress for the continuation of the annual privy purse, which, although constitutionally guaranteed, could be reduced or eliminated because of the ease with which the constitution is amended (given Congress' overwhelming legislative majority). An early effort (1951) by the Maharajas of Jodhpur and Baroda, in consort with some landed aristocrats, to form a 'Rulers' Union' and 'to work up an agitation amongst the rulers as well as the *jagirdars* and *zamindars* against the merger of the States' had little chance to gain momentum, because for this and other reasons the government deprived the Maharaja of Baroda of his title and his purse.[34] Periodically, as princes display an inclination to enter more widely into anti-Congress politics, they are reminded by representatives of the ruling party that the privy purse is not sacrosanct.[35] The fact that so few princes have chosen to fight the Congress is thus 'a posthumous tribute to Sardar Patel's shrewdness in...making them economically dependent on their foes...', and one prince put it quite succinctly: 'The rulers are letting themselves be hanged by these financial strings...We ought to stand on our dignity like men and tell the Congress "take away your bribes. Let us fight you at the polling booths like Indians."'[36] Exactly the same considerations apply to the *jagirdars* and *zamindars* who receive payments in instalments and mostly in long-term bonds, thus tying them to the régime as well.[37]

In so far as other groups were disaffected, their situation was not in principle different, although perhaps the Congress could not have moved quite so easily against them as it could against the aristocrats. Businessmen would have to deal with the Congress *raj*, and risky ventures into political opposition could lead to reprisals: threats of nationalization, loss of permits and licences already granted, denial of those applied for, and so on, were among the available weapons with which the Congress could not only induce the captains of industry to remain docile but also to help fill the Congress coffers, as they had done in the past. In short, as the party in power, with little indication that in the short run it would lose power, the Congress could convince potential opposition forces of the futility, if not the danger, of taking up the cudgels against it. It should occasion little surprise that many disgruntled elements chose to sit quietly on the sidelines or else to bore from within the Congress itself, rather than to go into the political wilderness. Couple this with the social obstacles to the mobilization of these elements, and the creation of a cohesive opposition was rendered even more difficult.[38] Add to all of this such critical, if somewhat more pedestrian problems as finance, and you have some very formidable barriers to the creation of such an opposition. Finally, given the hegemony of the Congress and Nehru's personal commitment to socialist doctrine, it is easy to understand why explicitly conservative positions had not been advanced, even by those who had the inclination to do so. Much conservative sentiment, both inside and outside of the Congress, remained unarticulated, introducing an important element of latency into Indian politics as regards the conservative interests in the country.

It should also be clear that in any reasonably open political context the hegemony of one party cannot be expected to last forever, and it is important, therefore, to recognize suppressed or latent elements which may become more influential as the domination by one party (or one individual) recedes. In the Indian case, after the first two general elections it should have been abundantly clear that there were such latent or suppressed elements, and that at least some of these were in a position to influence politics in a conservative direction. To indicate what the precise direction(s) might be, some estimate, however sketchy, of the doctrinal commitments of these groups must be set forth.

DOCTRINAL STRANDS

There can be little doubt that India's native aristocracy was in large measure a self-consciously proud, if not arrogant group, which explicitly referred to and defended its extraordinarily privileged position in Indian society. The princes' self-esteem is abundantly evident from the assertion that the Chamber of Princes (1921) 'was instituted...as the result of the desire of the rulers of the Indian States...to come together and to deliberate on matters relating to the Empire, and the States as a whole'.[39] Similarly, a spokesman for the *zamindars* argued that 'the landlord class, to which I have the honour to belong, have the largest and most important interests at stake in British India, and they should be adequately preserved and safeguarded'.[40] Throughout the constitutional deliberations of the 1920s and 1930s, they insisted that 'we cannot allow the rights and privileges of our class to be ignored or encroached upon'; that they must always be given constitutional protection 'commensurate with our interests'; and that they must 'preserve the inherited rights of their class, and secure legitimate guarantees in the new scheme of things...'.[41]

In confronting the British, the aristocrats quite understandably emphasized their 'ungrudging support and sincere assistance' and reminded the *raj* of their record of 'unalloyed loyalty to the Crown'.[42] The landlords frankly conceded that 'if we are to exist as a class', then 'it is our duty to strengthen the hands of the [British] Government'.[43] Many a British official frankly admitted the Crown's debts to the aristocracy and regarded the final disposition of the native states in particular as illegal, immoral and a despicable sell-out.[44]

While this style of argument commended itself widely to the British, it was not designed to appeal to the articulate, non-aristocratic elements in Indian public life, notably those who comprised the Congress. For the latter, a host of additional arguments was set forth, many of which suggested an awareness of the need to swim with the tide to some extent. One defender of the native rulers thus insisted that 'the natural instinct of mankind' is self-preservation, 'and no one should grudge it to the great Princely order'; and another insisted that 'we wish to preserve the individual and historical identity of our States which our forefathers carved out for themselves and handed down to us'.[45] But even this was too baldly put to stand alone, and other buttressing arguments were advanced. One ruler stressed 'the traditions of kingship and...the instincts and responsibilities of hereditary rule ingrained in our being', while others referred to the princes as 'custodians of ancient dynastic traditions' which 'they have the greatest duty of preserving...'.[46] The *zamindars*, although formally deprived of their autonomy, echoed the same sentiments by emphasizing that theirs was a class which could 'claim lineage from ancient houses, who have held lands for ages past...in recognition of military services...or for some other potent reason'.[47]

Such self-interested and fully conservative arguments could hardly suffice by themselves and the rulers were by no means oblivious of this fact. In addition to a variant of 'divine right' and 'tradition' from the aristocrats' own standpoint, there were other reasons for their preservation: the people, it was asserted, 'look upon their Rulers as a precious legacy of India's glorious past' and it became 'an essential element of patriotism that nothing should be done to damage the Indian States, though attack on individual rulers may sometimes be justified'.[48] While admitting that they were conservative 'to a certain extent by tradition and instinct', the aristocrats were insistent that they were 'conservators...of a great tradition, of an ancient civilization and of a proud culture' which was superior to the 'dynamic, machine-made civilization of the West' which was to some extent being imported into India by the British and westernized Indians.[49] The emphasis on the role of the princely states in the indigenous tradition and on Indian culture as superior to that of the west held out some hope for a more favourable response from the more conservative, non-aristocratic Congressmen, many of whom were sympathetic to the latter argument, at least.

Also indicative of their determination to exploit prevailing problems and sentiments, the aristocrats claimed that they were above the communalism of the newer class of politicians,[50] that they treated the people in their states as 'children' rather than as 'subjects', that by contrast with the complex, bureaucratic coldness of British India, 'there is much to relieve the monotony of life' for states' peoples, that there was widely 'a real feudal identity between chief and people', and that 'the demand for self-government [of the princely states] has had no greater argument for its support than the general success of the rule of the princes and the happiness of the people living under their care'.[51] The rulers of the smaller states took special pains to point out that in their domains all official business, and the dispensing of justice in particular, got done 'without endless formalities and dilatory proceedings' because, unlike the British *raj* and the great native rulers, the smaller prince 'is accessible to all and ready to redress grievances and to bestow the blessings of personal rule'; 'The special characteristic of the small State is the personal and direct relation of the Ruler with his people, and no one acquainted with them will deny the esteem in which a ruler is held by his people and the veneration that the people have for his decision and judgments.'[52] Here we find an effort to relate princely rule to popular well-being and we find a critique of western political institutions. The latter, at least, did not fall on entirely deaf ears among non-aristocratic groups.

Given such feelings, it is little wonder that most articulate aristocrats balked at any strong suggestion of the advent of parliamentary, democratic government on an all-India basis, especially under the auspices of the Congress. As one British supporter of the princes put it, 'democracy, as known in British India, they do not find alluring' in part because it represented rule by the lower classes, 'an inversion of the traditions of three thousand years'.[53] Another referred to the Congress as 'subversive elements and bile producers'[54] which justified the conclusion that 'in such conditions, one can hardly expect the Indian Princes to sit in their Durbars with folded hands, while the lawyers, school-masters, money-lenders and industrialists decide the fate of India'.[55]

The aristocrats themselves were no less vitriolic than the British who stood by them. One leading *zamindar* referred to the Congress as a 'new class' of 'demi-gods and career politicians' who exploit the ignorant masses 'for strengthening their own class rule'; and he insisted that the Congress 'is an upstart body and has not built up the traditions of authority and command through time with a corresponding attitude of obedience among the masses'.[56] Many reiterated their 'prolonged hostility to Congress ideas', scorned 'the talk of democracies and all such things', rejected the prospects of a Congress régime as one 'run by tradesmen who were not born to rule'.[57] The intensity of feeling which possessed some is nowhere better seen than in the assertion that 'when a eunuch is able to serve a woman, then this government will be able to rule with authority, and not before'.[58]

In light of such sentiments, it is also not surprising that many rulers, before the integration of the states, were quite outspoken in their insistence that 'we and our people will never submit to being governed by British India, over many parts of which our States in former times held sway', and most emphatic was the statement that 'we fought and sacrificed our blood to win power and we mean to hold it. If Congress wants to rob us, if the British should let us down, we will fight'.[59] In the event, these brave words were not matched by brave deeds, but two points remain clear. First, these words represent the authentic voice of aristocratic conservatism, defending the rule of *kshatryas* according to tradition and the precepts of *dharma*, although efforts were made to go beyond such defences, in order to appeal to non-aristocratic conservatives. It is abundantly clear, however, that the aristocracy did not look with favour upon the middle classes (whether westernized or not), let alone the 'masses'. Secondly, and related to this, is the fact that there is much smoldering resentment against the Congress régime, which the ruling party has by no means been able to obliterate. The aristocrat who said, in 1963, 'I do not believe in democracy, but in autocracy—benevolent, of course', can for the moment stand as a reminder that the old princely order still has its defenders.[60]

Not all of the aristocrats were vehement about the Congress, at least in public. Before independence, many were disposed to assure the nationalist leadership that they were not reactionaries who wanted to effect a total princely restoration or steadfast conservatives who refused to alter their own polities or to associate with the leadership of British India. These insisted only that they were Burkean conservatives who acknowledged the need for change but felt that it must be gradual.[61] This difference in emphasis was in fact underscored by the British, who recognized a representative of the 'conservative' princes, as opposed to the Burkeans, at the Round Table Conferences. In more recent years, the Maharaja of Bikaner, one of the politically active ex-rulers, has claimed to be a socialist and has insisted that no successful political party 'can be established if it is based entirely on the leadership of former rulers...'.[62] To this writer's knowledge, only the late, somewhat aberrant, Maharaja of Bastar has openly suggested, in recent years, the restoration of the Chamber of Princes or a comparable forum for former rulers.[63] Most, in the realm of external behaviour at least, have made their peace with the new order, if only as a matter of necessity and if only temporarily.

Still, resentment is quite widespread and has affected far more people than the aristocrats themselves. Events in almost every former state, but especially the larger ones, underscore one statement made about Mewar (Udaipur): '...nine tenths of the retainers have been turned away...Visitors were few, even the Jagirdars only putting in a perfunctory appearance; many of them had commuted with a cash payment the duty of attending upon their Ruler, which had once seemed a privilege.'[64] This parallels in most essentials the observation made over a century earlier, when the annexation of states by the British was generating considerable uneasiness, to culminate in the rebellion of 1857: '...when a great state falls, its nobility and its supporters must to some extent suffer with it: a dominant sect and party...cannot return to the ordinary level of society and the common occupations of life, without feeling some discontent and some enmity...'.[65] Those who would understand current Indian politics would do well to appreciate the contemporary relevance of this judgment. It would be a mistake to assume that India's aristocracy is fully reconciled to the new dispensation, and the sentiments discussed above still animate many. And as will be seen subsequently, the residual appeal of India's aristocrats is still great. They must, therefore, be considered potentially powerful actors in a conservative direction.

In some ways, the upper castes at the village level advanced positions comparable to those of the aristocrats.[66] As one scholar has observed, the decline of the Brahmins and *kshatryas* 'is not a happy thought' for these classes, and 'the prospect of...degeneration' which would bring the *sudras* and untouchables into greater prominence was 'an appalling prospect'.[67] Numerous village studies fully document this point, and in so far as the untouchable is to have any place at all, it will be through 'knowing his place' and hoping for the best.[68] Upper castes complain that lower castes 'are now swollen headed. They do not want to serve us, and we cannot depend on them.'[69] Efforts by some government servants to work directly with the lower castes at the village level have generated 'coldness and even hostility from groups on the higher levels of the social hierarchy' who ask themselves 'whether the government was out to destroy the social system of the Hindus'.[70] One effort by prominent private citizens and government officials to gain temple entry for untouchables elicited the response: 'The government is mixing the maize with the millet. We are helpless.' But not all felt helpless: upon turning the group back a local notable is reported to have said, 'you can tell Mr Nehru from me to go to hell. The whole town will back us.'[71] A wide range of coercive techniques has been employed by higher castes to keep the lower orders 'in their place', and this in its own way is an important manifestation of conservatism, albeit of a less politically organized sort.

Even middle-caste Hindus who might be vehemently opposed to Brahminical or aristocratic pre-eminence come down heavily on the lowest classes. Thus, the anti-Brahmin Justice party had this to say about temple entry for certain *harijan* groups:

> For many centuries these people most of whom until recently were Animists, were content to worship at their own shrines, and to try to force themselves into Hindu temples is not...to make themselves popular. Nor can we think that any grave wrong is done by their continued exclusion...They would be better occupied in improving their own conditions than in violent attempts to assert rights which no one heard of till a few years ago.[72]

Suggesting that some in government service share such sentiments is the pathetic statement from an official publication on the condition of *harijans*:

> Alcoholic liquor and other intoxicating drugs and drinks are, indeed, the Public Enemy Number One of the backward classes. Indulgence in these eats into their meagre resources and deprives them and their families of their essential requirements. It saps their vitality and undermines their physique and minds...much is being done to educate the *harijans* to reform their extravagant habits and customs.[73]

So, too, many middle peasants and substantial tenants have been quite willing to see the end of large-scale landlordism, without being in any way solicitous of those who are subordinated to them; and they frequently condemn efforts to give land to the landless as contrary to *dharma* or else as unproductive, i.e. land is given to people who are held to be incompetent to cultivate it properly. In these and other ways, caste Hindus demonstrate their sense of superiority either explicitly or implicitly to the depressed castes; and they demonstrate as well their refusal to confront the fundamental problems of rural India. Still, it is important to note that non-conservative vocabulary is often used (i.e. efficient cultivation) to deny the claims of depressed groups. Furthermore, it is also important to note that the exponents of these views are not necessarily sympathetic to aristocratic or Brahmin world-views: many anti-*kshatrya* and anti-Brahmin groups have challenged the position of these superior classes, while steadfastly denying the claims of those who remain below them.[74]

More difficult to come to grips with than such straightforward manifestations of conservatism is a doctrine whose practical consequences are profoundly conservative, even though its exponents profess to want certain major changes in Indian life. This doctrine has as its core an image of an idealized village community, sometimes alleged to have existed in ancient India. It has as its principal roots (1) the view that village India is the real India; (2) the reaction against imperialist arrogance and against the corrosive effects of British rule on traditional, village India, pitting the real India against the west; and (3) linked to this, the virtually universal reaction to the dislocations of the early stages of industrialization, including Indian variants on Luddite and utopian socialist themes.[75] The association of Gandhi's name, rightly or wrongly, with this strand of thought accounts in large measure for its potent emotional appeal.

Different exponents of this doctrine naturally give it different twists and embellishments, but some major perspectives are almost universally shared. Of central importance is the view that the Indian village is, or was at one time, almost an idyllic, self-reliant, harmonious, spiritual little republic. The caste system, one of the most uniformly condemned aspects of Indian life, was, according to this view, originally a plausible approach to the requirement of a division of social function and did not contain the rigidities commonly associated with it in recent times. Nor did it relegate a significant segment of the population to the position of untouchables. The 'good life' was approximated under this system, and even if the presently existing villages fall far short of this picture, it is only within the village context, somehow purified, that the 'good life' can now be attained by Indians.

The anti-western and anti-industrial themes are related to this one and are also almost uniformly articulated. The introduction of machine-made goods, both foreign and domestic; the introduction of western legal procedures, western education, western political processes, and the like, is widely portrayed as the cause of the present distress. There is a general rejection of individualism, in favour of social co-operation and concern for larger social groupings, Specifically, there is a rejection of the competition associated with *laissez faire* economics, of the win-or-lose struggle associated with western legal processes, and of its alleged parallel in western, 'adversary' style party politics. The individual is to subordinate his passions and needs to those of the extended family, the caste, and the village as a whole; and an important corollary of this basic view is the requirement that the rich, the wise and the well-born must use their advantages for the common good—the so-called doctrine of trusteeship. Because co-operation and harmony are major *desiderata*, conflict and coercion in any form are not permissible; and here the notions of 'class war' and even of legislation through majority rule are to be rejected. In so far as privileged classes use coercive techniques which are to be eliminated, education in the doctrine of trusteeship must provide the corrective. It is generally argued that the ideal can be approximated only in smaller communities unsullied by significant concern for material things; hence, urbanization and industrialization along western lines must be resisted. Indian spirituality must be maintained in the face of western materialism.[76]

The contention that such perspectives have conservative implications (in addition to certain explicitly conservative views) is based on the following considerations. First of all, for many exponents of these ideas, the principal dangers to the idealized village system lie not in the village itself, e.g. in the caste hierarchy, in the gross inequalities which prevail locally, or in the degradation of the untouchables, but in the forces outside the village which are undermining it, e.g. industrialization, party politics, and the rest. Hence, in many cases there is relatively little attention devoted to the actual distribution of power in the Indian village and to the manner in which those who have power use it. Secondly, when the rural power pattern is realistically examined and changes are deemed necessary, the latter are to be achieved through education in trusteeship, as already noted.[77] Other conceivable techniques are incompatible with the demand for harmony and co-operation and non-violence. Thirdly, the pattern of constraints within the joint family and caste are often totally neglected (as are the constraints within the village as a whole), and these social groupings are looked upon as instruments of social welfare and/or of moral discipline.[78] Fourthly, while there is some attention given to the desperate plight of the lowest classes, there is less than passionate concern for their unhappy material condition because a concern for material affairs tends to erode concern for spiritual matters. Thus Rajaji has supported Gandhi in the view that 'civilization consists not in the multiplication of wants but in the deliberate and voluntary restriction of wants', and he also supported the view that 'high thinking is inconsistent with a complicated material life, based on high speed imposed on us by mammon worship'.[79] Hence, the cynic could conclude, India's poorest people are really better off, or at least they have a head start in the race for the good life!

From some vantage points, it is really immaterial whether one calls the exponents of such views conservatives, reactionaries, 'messiahs of backwardness', utopian socialists, 'spiritualized Luddites', or something else more or less flattering.[80] In some respects, it also matters little whether one assumes that they genuinely desire the changes which they profess to want or whether one insists that they are frauds. The important point is that policies consistent with the model of the idealized village would serve as almost a total bar to any major transformation of the Indian village. In other words, the doctrine supports the *status quo* in fact, if not in theory. Particularly for the lowest strata of the population there is little hope for significant improvement, materially or otherwise. It is abundantly clear from the historical and current state of the Indian village that there is no salvation for the lowest strata within that framework, in all probability even with the advent of competitive politics and the impingement of external forces, but certainly not without them. And the entire history of mankind should be proof that privileged classes do not become trustees to any significant degree without substantial pressure from below or from competing élites who speak for the lower classes. If, as commonly argued, the capacity of the lowest classes to act successfully on their own behalf requires a secure economic base, then the defence of a rural economy and the scorn for material concerns is especially supportive of the *status quo*. Under existing and foreseeable Indian conditions (tremendous overpopulation relative to available arable land, etc.), the village itself simply cannot provide the economic underpinnings needed to sustain a movement for the betterment of the lowest classes.[81] Even efforts from supra-village quarters to improve the conditions of the 'poorest he' often founder as a result of the vulnerability of the lowest classes to coercion in one form or another on the part of the village élite.[82]

If the commitment to co-operation, trusteeship, and the like precludes any major changes in the village in the interests of lower class advance, the anti-urban, anti-industrial commitments clearly run counter to the interests of the urban industrial class. It is easy to see, therefore, why the exponents of the idealized village did not endear themselves to untouchable leaders, such as Ambedkar, or to India's captains of industry. But it is also easy to understand why the former were much more concerned than the latter. To the untouchable, a defence of the village was a defence of his prison. To the industrialist, a defence of the village was more a nuisance than a threat, although, as we shall see, it has given the captains of industry cause for some serious complaints.

Also important is the fact that in its defence of the traditions (real or imagined) of the east against the incursions of the west, this strand of thought overlaps with some parts of the aristocratic argument sketched above—although it is evident that the village model is essentially unencumbered by any concern for aristocratic institutions and values. Similarly important is the fact that this doctrine to some extent fuses anti-imperialism and anti-reformism, generating some of the analytical difficulties already noted. The fact that this doctrine does defend India against the west and that it can be sanctified by the invocation of Gandhi's name makes it an almost uniquely attractive refuge for all manner of knaves, scoundrels, reactionaries, etc., as well as genuine conservatives, in addition to those who earnestly desire substantial changes along 'Gandhian' lines. This is particularly important because of the difficulty of articulating explicitly conservative positions in India, especially in the Nehru era. Even in the hands of those who genuinely want change, this doctrine is conservative in its practical consequences; and, of course, it is quite explicitly conservative in some respects. Those who use it as a more respectable façade for a commitment to the *status quo* only re-enforce its conservative impact. In examining the nature, problems, and prospects of Indian conservatism, we must give much weight to the fact that this doctrine, which represents 'disguised' conservatism, is available and persuasive to many Indians; and it will be considered in further detail as it is advanced by one of its more articulate exponents, Rajaji.

Many of those who were adversely affected by and/or deeply resented the penetration of western ideas, whether via the British or via westernized Indians, did not in response take refuge in heavy-handed Hindu orthodoxy or in the *de facto* conservatism of the defenders of the idealized village. By contrast with these strands of thought, others espoused views which are more properly called right radical rather than conservative or reactionary and chose to emphasize a renascent, revitalized Hinduism as the basis for their commitment.

If one pieces together the assorted evidence, a strongly suggestive ideal-type may be sketched. The social bases for militant Hinduism are diverse, but prominent at one time or another have been various dislocated or dispossessed segments of the population: refugees from Pakistan, former princely state retainers, and many lower middle-class elements, such as lesser Rajput landholders, smaller businessmen and shopkeepers, traders, and the like.[83] Much of the leadership and intellectual inspiration for this component of the

Indian right has come from Maharashtra and from a singularly prominent community, the Chitpavan Brahmins of the Poona area, a militant and very 'political' caste associated with the Maratha confederacy. In the background stand many of the great figures of the Hindu renaissance—Dayanand Saraswati, Vivekananda, Aurobindo, Tilak, Lajpat Rai, Bepin Chandra Pal, V. D. Savarkar, among many others.

As in the preceding case, no simple characterization will apply uniformly to all of these leading figures and component groups, but in the present context, the individual variants are less important than the general thrust. And this thrust is clear enough. What is wanted is a unified, disciplined, militant and militarized Hindu community, bound together as far as possible in a full-fledged *gemeinschaft* by ties of blood, culture, language, religion, and the like, and capable of taking a leading place among the nations of the world as a consequence. In most formal statements, traditional caste distinctions are laid aside and even the untouchables are to be admitted to the fold of respectable Hindus, if only to keep alien religions (Islam, Buddhism, Christianity) from making inroads into Hinduism (thus 'denationalizing' Hindustan's people), and to prevent the exploitation of caste differences to the detriment of national solidarity and strength. India's historic political fragmentation and the instability of her macro-political institutions are seen as sources of great weakness. Therefore, instead of defending the congeries of princely states and instead of defending the idealized village (with supra-village institutions having minimal functions), the preferred polity is a highly centralized and if necessary a highly authoritarian state. The determination that India must not only become immune to internal discord and disintegrative forces, but must also be able to prevent further foreign conquests, leads in turn to an emphasis on military strength and its inevitable concomitant, modern industry—in sharp contrast with the emphasis of the 'Gandhians' on the village economy and asceticism. Tilak's insistence that 'one common religion becomes a great means to create mutual affinity and sympathy among people' and Savarkar's slogan, 'Hinduize all politics and militarize Hindudom', satisfactorily suggest the preoccupations of the militant Hindus.[84]

It is essential to stress that the militant Hindu ideal represents a considerable departure from traditional Indian norms and institutions, while conceding at the same time that many followers of

Tilak *et al.* were steadfastly orthodox and while conceding that the effort to 'return to the Vedas' represents an effort to relate this ideal to an earlier Indian tradition. The anti-traditional dimensions become somewhat clearer when we realize that many orthodox Hindus 'joined the Sanatan Dharma Sabha, which had been created in 1885 as a defence of orthodox Hinduism against the criticisms of the Arya Samaj', one of the early vehicles for a renascent, purified Hinduism.[85] That this ideal has strongly communal and proto-fascist tendencies is undeniable; that it makes no concessions either to secularism or to a solid sense of diversity and pluralism is also undeniable. But that at least on paper it represents a departure of no small proportions from the other streams of thought must also be conceded. While there is far from complete congruence between social group and doctrinal position there is sufficient overlap in some regions so that ideological and social splits are mutually re-enforcing, to the detriment of a broad, rightist coalition. In addition, because militant Hinduism is based on specifically Hindu appeals, and because the desired linguistic unity is to be achieved through the use of Hindi as a national language, non-Hindu and non-Hindi-speaking rightists will be largely alienated, rendering even more difficult the creation of a cohesive rightist force. The discussion of the Jan Sangh and of right-wing unity efforts, below, will elaborate all of these major points, as will the discussion of K. M. Munshi, of the Swatantra 'inner circle'.

In light of the diverse inquiries into the origins of capitalism in the west, it is particularly important to try to delineate the doctrinal position of the Indian bourgeoisie. To what extent did this class in India play a role comparable to its counterparts in the west? To what extent, in short, has it been anti-traditional and liberal? To what extent was the colonial setting responsible for departures from the pattern of one or another western nation? To what extent was anti-traditionalism suppressed, for example, in the interests of anti-imperialism, and to what extent was it suppressed as well in the interests of anti-socialism? To what extent can the contemporary Indian bourgeoisie be spoken of as a conservative or rightist force? Only sketchy answers to these questions are possible here, but even these will provide important materials for an understanding of contemporary Indian conservatism.

To put the matter in a nutshell, the Indian urban classes, both in ancient and more recent times, have fought against the constraints imposed by traditional Hindu institutions and by the political chaos which characterized the princely polities; but at no time has this fight resulted in a more or less complete, sustained victory for the urban classes. In recent times, when the urban classes took on more of an industrial and professional (rather than commercial) quality, there was still no broad-based commitment to a doctrine which was directed principally and explicitly against indigenous traditionalism.

Some historical points are pertinent here. It is well known, for example, that India's urban classes, in ancient times, gave considerable support to anti-Brahminical, protestant religions, notably Buddhism and Jainism, in an effort to escape the inferior position to which they were assigned by Brahminical teachings. Yet this did not result in a permanent breakthrough: Buddhism, though it left its imprint on subsequent religious development in India, has all but disappeared from the land of its birth; and Jainism, which survives, has only a tiny, if important following, which for the most part considers itself a reformed sect of Hinduism.[86] India's business communities were mostly re-embedded in the Hindu social order, in an inferior position, upon the Hindu 'restoration'.

A second major historical example concerns the distress of urban commercial groups under Akbar and other Mogul emperors. At some junctures, the Mogul imperial service itself undertook some manufacturing and commerce, and Akbar and some of his Mogul successors claimed and often availed themselves of the right to inherit the property of all subjects, including that of wealthy businessmen, who were tempting prey. These and other circumstances were obviously unsatisfactory from the standpoint of a stable, flourishing private commerce and manufacture; but about the best that could be done by the Marwaris, for example, was to repair to the relatively barren wastes of Rajasthan, in order to escape Mogul depredations. There was no breakthrough here either.[87]

Weber, in his studies of Indian religion and society and of urban development in the west, has, of course, stressed the absence of equivalents of the protestant ethic, in attempting to explain the weakness of India's urban classes in traditional society. This interpretation has, however, been widely and in some cases persuasively disputed. But Weber has also emphasized the social fragmentation of the Indian population, in explaining why India's burghers did not establish urban brotherhoods comparable to those which led the fight against feudalism in the west. The latter argument certainly deserves close attention, in view of the enduring social barriers to the creation of a business class in India, by contrast with the collection of communities and castes.[88]

Also important is the fact that many leading business groups supported the British in the rebellion of 1857. This indicates that the *Pax Britannica*, whatever its limitations, represented an advance over the political chaos, the depredations, the confiscatory policies, the customs and transit duties, and the like, which adversely affected Indian business prior to the stabilization of British rule. Implicit here is a rejection of the imperial-princely political order of pre-British days, but it says little specifically about the broader questions of liberalism associated with the rise of urban classes in the west. That Indian business later turned against the British because the latter seemed to impose great constraints on the former (but in the interests of British business, more than of traditional India), is also important in another connection to be discussed shortly. For the moment, however, it is sufficient to note that Indian business has historically shown certain anti-traditional tendencies but that these were never translated into a self-sustaining movement which overcame the constraints of traditional India.

In a detailed study, the preceding remarks would have to be qualified in a number of important respects. Certainly many Indian business elements managed to accumulate great fortunes, even in the darker days of political instability and chaos, or of autocratic abuse. Also, there were important variations in the pattern of inter-class relationships, depending on time and region. Lamb has argued, for example, that during certain eras, Indian businessmen seem to have been held in high esteem and seemed also to thrive; and Harrison, among others, has noted that in Gujarat, where businessmen are largely local, they have generally been held in higher esteem than in other areas, where leading businessmen were outsiders to the region.[89] (This in itself suggests some of the obstacles to the creation of a national business class.) So, too, the tiny Parsi community proved to be extremely adaptive, and many of their number Anglicized widely and rapidly. In and around Bombay, they served as an important nucleus of social mobility, outside of the Hindu social structure.

What has been lacking in recent times is a direct assault on traditional society. Even the Parsis were in no position to do much on this score, because they were so few in number (100,000), very much localized, and of alien origin. In fact, the rapid westernization of many Parsis and their close association with the British exposed them to some sharp criticism from more traditional and militant Hindu groups, although relations were, generally, good. There was certainly some anxiety among Parsis, lest a Hindu renaissance deprive them of their strong position in commerce and industry, while with the gradual democratization of politics, their fortunes in this area declined.[90]

By contrast with the westernizing Parsis, the Marwaris, even in Calcutta, remained 'an orthodox community...hardly touched by the social and intellectual reform movements launched by Bengali intellectuals',[91] although they did apparently support the British during the 1857 rebellion. If they were not in the forefront of reform movements, the Marwaris have more recently been in the forefront of anti-parochial political movements, as the most nearly national business community.[92] So also the Marwaris supported the States' Peoples' movement in what is now Rajasthan, and their southern counterparts (the Chettiars *et al.*) supported the Justice Party, indicating that there was resentment against the Rajput aristocracy on the one hand and against the Brahmin élite on the other.[93] But such opposition to an élite caste was not generalized into a broadly liberal movement against the rigidities of the Hindu social structure. Even so, sharp conflicts between Brahmin and aristocratic elements on the one hand and business interests on the other are discernible, as one would imagine from the *kshatrya* condemnation of the Congress, e.g. as run by tradesmen who were not born to rule.

During the twentieth century, business attacks were directed primarily against the British, not against traditional India. Emphasizing the privileged position of British interests and lack of support for Indian interests, Indian business leadership, within the context of the *Pax Britannica*, demanded much state assistance. Feeling increasingly frustrated by the British, they turned increasingly to the Congress as a vehicle for their demands. Because the aristocratic elements were alined with the British in delaying independence, the business interests criticized the aristocrats, often very sharply, but primarily on narrow, political grounds.[94]

This is another aspect of the business-aristocratic split, and in this limited sense can business support for the Congress be viewed as something of a surrogate for a stand against the old order. The need to maintain Congress cohesion seems to have precluded any broad-based attack on traditional India, and, in any event, it is far from clear that any but the Parsis, as a group, were particularly willing or anxious to see a massive erosion of traditional India. We can only speculate about this point, but it seems plausible that to have been anti-traditional might have been interpreted as being anti-Indian in the colonial situation, thus weakening business attacks against the *ancien régime*.

The attitudes of Indian business require further clarification, because of some rather superficial judgments made about business' apparently weak commitment to an industrial, free enterprise ideology. Some interpret business support for Gandhi as an endorsement of his economic preferences, while others stress a 'socialist' strain in Indian business thinking, which is sometimes related to the principle of trusteeship.[95] But either way, businessmen would seem ill-suited to perform a broadly liberalizing role.

It is probably true that Gandhi's involvement in such matters as a ban on cow-slaughter appealed to the more orthodox Hindu and Jain businessmen; and it is perhaps true that Gandhi's 'saintly' qualities struck a responsive chord. Both may help to explain business support for the Gandhian Congress, but this is far from proof that Gandhi's economic views were being endorsed. In fact, there is ample evidence to the contrary, including some from those very people who were most generous in their financial support for Gandhi's activities. For example, G. D. Birla, a leading Marwari businessman and a principal contributor to Congress coffers, observed that Gandhi 'believed in small-scale industries' while he (Birla) 'believed in the industrialization of the country through large-scale industries'. Many businessmen, among others, objected to aspects of Gandhi's constructive programme for rural uplift and to the requirement that Congressmen must spin some cloth by hand, wear homespun, and so on, which Gandhi emphasized. Moreover, in the post-independence period many businessmen (particularly in textiles) vehemently object to efforts to sustain the cottage textile industry through restrictions on machine output, excise levies, and the like. This is the point of most direct contact between Gandhian and urban-industrial values, and on the basis of the evidence available, it is not possible to conclude that business groups have embraced Gandhism, although they may feel obliged to pay lip service to it because of the appeal of Gandhian thought.[96] In terms of technology, then, Indian business is not particularly antiquarian in outlook, however conservative some may be religiously and socially. The idealized village model finds little favour among businessmen, at least in its critical economic aspects.

Whatever value one may want to attach to religious and saintly matters in explaining business support for Gandhi, it is obvious that there were other reasons; and these relate, in part, to the alleged socialist tendencies of Indian business. For one thing, given the generally bad image of Indian businessmen, Gandhi's emphasis on trusteeship could only be advantageous, because it helped to deflect certain kinds of criticism of the business élite. Nehru, for example, was quite abusive in the 1930s and was on record as saying that 'our captains of industry are quite amazingly backward in their ideas; they are not even up-to-date capitalists...', which ties in, of course, with some of the Weberian arguments about Indian business. In addition, many anti-industrial peasant leaders, such as N. G. Ranga (now the Swatantra President), were attacking Gandhi for being so solicitous of the interests of Indian businessmen.[97] In this light, Weiner's conclusion that the radical elements in the 1930s 'did not alarm the business community' simply will not bear scrutiny; and once again we have the unimpeachable testimony of businessmen themselves. At the Round Table Conferences, Birla warned the British that Gandhi, 'who has proved himself in many respects a greater Conservative than many of you', might not be able to check the rise of radicalism; and he urged Britain to yield to moderate demands before it was too late. In a letter to Sir Samuel Hoare, Birla was even more explicit, in arguing that Gandhi 'alone is responsible for keeping the left wing in India in check'.[98] Indian businessmen perhaps did not visualize the hammer-and-sickle flying over parliament house, but they certainly were apprehensive about the socialist tendencies in the Congress—in many cases even before the formation of the Congress Socialist Party (CSP) in 1934. The crisis of confidence, including a massive 'strike of capital', immediately after independence reflected the same apprehension.[99]

Other suggested indices of businessmen's socialist tendencies must also be viewed with caution. The much-heralded 'Bombay

Plan' did set forth a programme for Indian development in which the government was assigned a place. But it is clear, on the one hand, that it was partly inspired by a desire to outflank incipient planning efforts of the Congress itself, and, on the other, that it involved, from the standpoint of private enterprise, little more than maximum state assistance with minimum state control.[100] Similarly, the fact that the business communities have not rejected the underlying principles of the five-year plans is due partly to the benefits which accrue to private enterprise as a result of government planning and partly to the difficulties involved in running counter to the prevailing socialist rhetoric. Under the circumstances it is little wonder that private enterprise argues more over the details of the plans rather than the whole concept of planning, and it is little wonder that even the most steadfastly free enterprise group—the Forum of Free Enterprise (FFE)—explicitly renounces unbridled *laissez faire* and admits that at present the government must play a role in economic development.[101] But all of this is very far from proving that Indian businessmen have 'sold out' or are excessively timid. A careful reading of the statements of business chambers, of individual firms and of individual industrialists will indicate that the sum total of specific grievances constitutes a quite strong attack on the existing approach of the government and a request to revert, in effect, to the principles of the Bombay Plan.

In the best of all possible worlds, business would certainly like to have maximum state support with minimum state controls. Under Nehru, at least, this was not feasible, and the positions taken by Indian businessmen reflect the need to come to terms with the 'socialist pattern' as advanced by Nehru. In this connection, Weiner's conclusion about Indian private enterprise is worth noting: 'Most probably it could survive without it [representative government], and may take no steps to save it; but on the other hand, Indian business is not likely—in the foreseeable future—to take steps to destroy the institutions of representative government. That is of no small importance.'[102] This is admittedly a consolation, and it is of importance. But we must also ask other questions. To what extent will Indian business press for economic modernization, as, for example, in the opposition to subsidized cottage industries? The limited evidence suggests that this fight will, in some sectors, be carried on with vigour, even though it runs counter to much Gandhian rhetoric.[103] To what extent will business subordinate its own interests to broader social purposes, assuming that what is good for Indian private enterprise is not *ipso facto* good for India? Here the record is mixed, and much business behaviour described by Brecher, for example, leads to unfavourable conclusions.[104] To what extent would business aline with rural interests to suppress organized labour? There is limited evidence to suggest that business would go a long way in this direction.[105] To what extent would business aline with reactionary and/or conservative interests *within the framework of parliamentary institutions*, if the Indian left showed signs of increasing strength? This is one of the central issues of the Swatantra coalition, and we shall see here that the record is mixed but that there is perhaps more grist for the pessimist's mill than for the optimist's. These are also critical questions to ask about Indian business, and Weiner's conclusion about business and parliamentary democracy says little if anything about them. In approaching these and related questions, the historic alliance, in the Congress, between business and the peasantry is important, as is the gap which was created by the colonial setting between business and the aristocracy. To the extent that business fails to challenge the old order, to the extent that its fears of socialism drive it into alliances with the aristocracy or landed interests, to this extent business might be considered as a component of the conservative camp. The record thus far suggests a Janus-like stance between traditional India and socialist elements but one in which business has been unable or unwilling (or perhaps has found it unnecessary) to mount a potent attack on the former and thus play a broadly liberalizing role in Indian society. In part, this is due to the slowness with which business is overcoming the community and caste barriers to effective class action. All of this, too, 'is of no small importance'.

If we take an essentially western view of what is modern or developed, it is clear from the foregoing that the social groups and/or doctrinal strands just discussed have different potentialities for development, and it is well to spell these out, however briefly. At the same time it is necessary to bear in mind that within each group or doctrinal strand there are important variations, which make neat categorization difficult.

Of the doctrinal strands, the full-blown idealized village model seems clearly to admit the least progress, however much change its adherents may desire. It is quite explicitly anti-industrial, although some modest, local industries may be countenanced. In the political realm, it holds out little hope for a substantial alteration in the rural power structure and it is quite explicitly opposed to heavy reliance on national political institutions, working counter to the development of a modern nation-state. In the social realm, too, it holds out little hope for substantial alteration in relationships among broad social groups, and many of its proponents explicitly announce that little change is needed.

In some of these respects, the aristocratic strand of thought is more compatible with modernization. The feeling of social superiority certainly remains and there are some barriers to effective participation in contemporary party politics. But many aristocrats are fully committed to and involved in modern industry, even though few will be found in the lead of pro-industrial spokesmen. Somewhat fewer, it would appear, are committed to becoming Tory democrats. But if—and this is a big 'if'—more leading aristocrats were to broaden their perspectives beyond residual bitterness against the Congress and were to participate more in the industrial economy and the modern polity, a rather sanguine assessment of their potential role in Indian life would be possible. A combination of Tory democracy and a commitment to industrialization would go a long way to making the aristocrats agents of important changes, or, if not that, at least capable of adjusting to and accepting certain important changes, well beyond those tolerable to the Gandhians. At least in the realm of technology and in the development of a modern nation-state, the aristocrats could play a useful role, if they can be reconciled to and be persuaded to participate more widely in the modern economy and polity.

The strand of militant Hinduism is, as described here, explicitly committed to economic modernization, to social change, and to the creation of a modern nation-state. Its emphasis on Hinduism and on religio-cultural matters may disturb those who feel that pragmatism, secularism, and national citizenship are essential aspects of modernization; and communal tensions are a serious danger inherent in this approach. Yet an industrialized nation-state with altered class lines is called for, even if it is not secular and constitutional-democratic; and, unlike the Gandhians, the militant Hindus are willing to countenance almost any means to achieve their ends. There are, of course, differences among the militant Hindus, as between those whose principal concern is with the religio-cultural realm and those who are mainly concerned about an industrialized, centralized state; but in most major respects this strand of thought is not antithetical to and could well facilitate modernization in many areas of Indian life. In the discussion of right-wing parties which follows, further evidence about modernization in connection with these different strands of thought will be presented.

CHAPTER 3

DIMENSIONS OF INDIAN RIGHT-WING POLITICS: POLITICAL PARTIES

The diverse groups and doctrinal positions which have just been discussed were not effectively mobilized into a cohesive force during the years 1947–59. Many important groups and individuals simply remained on the political sidelines, whether through resignation, fear of reprisals, or, as in the case of the aristocrats, through an inability to transcend the ethos of the *ancien régime*, with its hereditary basis for political power.[1] Many leading individuals contested as independents rather than through an organized political group, and this again was particularly true of the aristocracy and other local notables who could capitalize on residual, traditional loyalties and on the 'organizational' aspects of the extended family and caste. Some, indeed, took great pride in the fact that they did not have to participate in organized party politics to ensure success. This is evident from the assertion of a former *dewan* (Prime Minister) of the Rajput state of Bikaner: 'We came in without any programme, without any party, and defeated these Congressmen', and from Bailey's report that 'one ex-raja told me "I promised them nothing. I had no arguments. I just asked them to vote for me. I suppose there were a few party workers, but I had nothing to do with them."'[2] Local and state-wide parties, often extensions of caste groups and/or *ad hoc* groups established for such purposes as fighting land reform legislation, represented another channel of political activity, further along the path toward more organized party politics.[3] Finally, more ambitious political groups, with all-India pretensions if not all-India impact, served as vehicles for one or more of these elements, but of all Indian parties, only the Congress was truly national in scope. In many areas, a number of rightist candidates contested against one another, further weakening the impact of already fragmented forces. The supposed compulsions of the single-member, plurality-vote constituency did little to generate a discernible trend toward a two-party system, even on the state level.[4] Given the overwhelming supremacy of the Congress in the days before independence and given the fact that it was virtually the only broadly based, well-organized political force in pre-independence India, it is no wonder that a comparable opposition political force did not emerge full-blown with the advent of the general elections. And, as we have seen, there were very substantial obstacles to the emergence of such a force, on the right, which was in part unmobilized and very much fragmented. As long as these conditions remained, the emergence of an effective right-wing opposition was precluded. None the less, if the support given to all of the disparate rightist forces—independents, local parties, and all-India parties—be considered in the aggregate, it was by no means as negligible as most students of Indian affairs have suggested.

A few preliminary observations will set the stage for an understanding of the parties to be considered here: the Hindu Mahasabha, the Jan Sangh, the Ram Rajya Parishad (RRP), the Ganatantra Parishad, and the Janata Party. First, only the Ganatantra Parishad had had even a share of power prior to 1959, and this occurred during a several-month-long coalition with the Congress in Orissa. Hence, it is not possible to judge these parties in terms of actual performance in office, even at the state level.[5] Secondly, the Ganatantra Parishad and the Janata Party were wholly local in inspiration, leadership, and orientation; and while the others had all-India pretensions, they were largely confined to the great Hindi-speaking heartland of north central India. Collectively, then, they were for all practical purposes confined to India north of the Vindhyas. Thirdly, only the Hindu Mahasabha had been established prior to independence but was still poorly organized; and only the Jan Sangh, via the para-military, 'cultural' group, the Rashtriya Swayamsevak Sangh (RSS, which was also formed prior to independence), showed signs of a more modern, disciplined organization. Generally speaking, party structures were rudimentary and were based heavily on residual support for traditional leaders.[6] Thus, in speaking of these parties as our examples of the rightist opposition, it is important to remember that they were generally of recent origin, poorly organized, and geographically circumscribed, both individually and collectively.

The Janata Party, on which the least information is available, was organized in 1950 by Raja Kamakhya Narain Singh of Ramgarh, a fiery and fiercely proud Rajput *zamindar*-businessman,[7] in order 'to demonstrate that the sponsor [K. B. Sahay] of the *zamindari* abolition measure [in Bihar] has no support in his own district'.[8] In fact, as one report observed, Ramgarh's feud with Sahay 'has gone to the point of political fanaticism'.[9] Growing out of efforts to invalidate abolition legislation in the courts, Janata had its principal stronghold in the Hazaribagh plateau region of Bihar, with its heavily tribal population. An energetic organizer, the Raja has not only been supported by those who fell within the former Ramgarh *raj*, but he has extended Janata's influence beyond these boundaries, into adjacent, still largely tribal areas. Having given away personal forest rights and much land of unknown quality to the *bhoodan* (land-gift) movement of Vinoba Bhave, he is earnestly trying to develop the image of a Tory democrat, but with a marked *führer-prinzip* embodied therein. At the same time, his ample modern business interests have freed him of any great dependence on the land for his continued personal comfort and they also suggest that he is personally forward-looking in the economic sphere. The key elements in his party's formal programme have been 'land to the tiller', reduced land revenues, and a redrawing of state boundaries to restore to Bihar certain areas now in West Bengal. Suggestive of the Raja's political style, the Janata members of the legislative assembly (MLAs) resigned *en bloc* over the boundary issue and threatened *satyagraha*. Less often emphasized—although suggested by the Raja's own *bhoodan* contributions and his fight against *zamindari* abolition—is the fact that land reform is to come about through voluntary abandonment of holdings, i.e. never. Finally, it is important to note that some of the *zamindars* who joined with the Raja in fighting abolition legislation in the courts declined to join him in his subsequent political activity.[10]

A good deal more has been said about the Ganatantra Parishad, even if most of it has been based on 'logical' extrapolations from the fact that it was founded by former rulers in highland Orissa. Thus, the most careful student of the Ganatantra Parishad to date has rightly observed: 'The Ganatantra Parishad seldom gets a good press. It is "reactionary" or "dominated by feudal interests and medieval traditions" or it is a party of "disgruntled princelings". Its rank and file are supposed to be illiterate tribals, hoodwinked by the Rajas, and incapable of realizing that they are in the twentieth century...'[11] However, while acknowledging the party's aristocratic origins and the debt which it owes to these origins for its considerable success, and while acknowledging as well that it contains some 'spectacularly atavistic rulers', this same observer rejects the stereotype of the Parishad. In this view he has received support from seemingly improbable sources—the former socialist leader, Asok Mehta, and from an official election analysis by a prominent Congressman, Sadiq Ali.[12]

The Ganatantra Parishad took shape shortly prior to the 1951–2 elections under the leadership of the Maharajas of Kalahandi and Patna. While drawing on other royal families as well, the party's leadership came to include some middle-class professionals who had no connection whatever with the aristocracy. Despite efforts to broaden its base of support by organizing modestly in the coastal regions of Orissa, the party has had its greatest success in the heavily tribal, former princely areas of highland Orissa and in small adjacent districts of Bihar, which contain Oriya-speaking peoples.

There are many signs that the Ganatantra Parishad is not motivated by a desire to restore the good old days of princely rule, although as expected the leaders defend their privy purses and other perquisites whenever they come under attack. In addition to the emergence of some middle-class, professional leadership,[13] one could point to the fact that both Kalahandi and Patna 'had introduced administrations of the modern variety in their respective states' and had established the rudiments of legislative assemblies.[14] As an adopted heir, Patna in particular seemed to take his ruling responsibilities quite seriously indeed.[15] While they speak of the weakness of a non-personal administration, which strikes our ears as decidedly 'feudal', the leaders of the Parishad are correct to the extent that the administrative framework of the Government of Orissa has not been effectively established in the highland regions, leaving something of a vacuum.

Beyond this, the Parishad has spent much of its parliamentary time speaking well for the people of highland Orissa, demanding resettlement assistance for those displaced by the waters behind the Hirakud Dam, demanding an end to the government's *kendu* leaf monopoly, and demanding, in general, greater government efforts to develop the Orissa highlands, among the most backward parts of India. In addition, the party has placed a good deal of emphasis on the Oriya-speaking peoples in present-day Bihar, whose territories the party wants attached to Orissa state, and on 'Orissa for the Oriyas'.

Still further, the Parishad's programme has included a defence of large-scale and even nationalized industries, and recommended nationalization of those 'which have been established mostly at the cost of the government and yet are in private hands'; it has recommended nationalization of industries 'in which competition between the State and individual enterprises will not be conducive to public benefit'; and it recommended nationalization of mines 'which shall be worked in the future'.[16] The party has also advocated the substitution of a progressive agricultural income tax for existing land revenues, a ceiling on agricultural incomes, a national minimum wage, some protection for cottage industries, and co-management and profit-sharing by management and labour in the industrial sector.[17] The leadership of the Parishad subscribes to the view that it would be futile to organize political parties solely on the basis of former aristocrats and for a restoration of their historic position, and they insist that theirs is a Burkean conservative, centrist party, as suggested by its slogan, 'neither right, nor left, but a middle path'.

It is for these reasons that Morris-Jones could quite safely refer to the Parishad as 'a party of mixed princely and popular character', and it helps to explain why Sadiq Ali could call it 'a respectable party with all appearances of a respectable programme and with some leaders who command some respect'.[18] It is for the same reasons that Bailey has such a high assessment of the party and that Mehta could say that 'the most interesting party combining traditional loyalties with resilient outlook is the Ganatantra Parishad'.[19] In light of the available evidence and these estimates, it simply will not do to label the party 'feudal' or 'reactionary' and let it go at that. The Parishad seems clearly to have been the best example of Tory democracy which has arisen in India, and in light of the approach of some aristocrats this is no mean accomplishment.[20]

The Hindu Mahasabha, Jan Sangh, and RRP, in their communal aspect and in their concern for cultural matters such as religion, language and education, are best understood in terms of 'the history of the Hindu reaction to the Western impact'.[21] However, the broad similarities in this respect are not as important, for the present analysis, as the differences among them. Generally speaking, the RRP is far and away the most steadfastly conservative, if not reactionary, in terms of the orthodox, hierarchical, village-based model sketched above, while the Mahasabha and the Sangh represent the more militant, reformist Hindu elements. All three parties stress the 'despiritualization' or 'denationalization' of Indians (more specifically of Hindus) through contact with the Muslim and European conquerors and westernized Indians, but the Mahasabha and the Sangh also emphasize the need to overcome the rigidities and the less attractive excrescences of recent Hinduism, as the RRP does not. The Mahasabha and RRP, as receding forces in Indian political life, will receive little attention here, while the more viable Jan Sangh will be examined in some detail.

The Mahasabha grew out of the formation of the first Hindu *sabha* in 1907, founded to counter the demands of the Muslim League, and throughout its existence the party has kept up its attacks on the League and its demand for Pakistan, on Pakistan itself after 1947, and on any Indians, including Gandhi and Nehru, who seemed excessively 'soft on Muslims'. Among those most vehemently castigated was veteran Congressman Rajaji, whose early recommendation that the Congress accept in principle the demand for Pakistan elicited some venomous attacks.[22]

Specifically restricted to Hindus, the Mahasabha has not only condemned allegedly pro-Muslim or pro-Pakistan positions, but it has also condemned the failure to support energetically the Hindu cause through education, support for religious institutions and efforts at reconversion of one-time Hindus, including former untouchables. Beyond this, the Mahasabha, in its official programme, has followed the major contours of militant Hinduism, as already outlined. Doubtless, not all Mahasabhites adhered to the reformist positions set forth by Savarkar and other leaders, but on the level of formal doctrinal pronouncements the commitment is clear enough. In the post-independence period, the Mahasabha suffered because Gandhi's assassins had been associated with it and with the RSS and because of Nehru's vehement condemnation of communal parties. On the whole, its electoral impact has been almost negligible, it lost ground from 1951–2 to 1957, and many of its former adherents have repaired to the banner of the Jan Sangh. Where it has had some modest success, it drew on refugees from Pakistan and on urbanites in the interior areas of

India, particularly in former princely states, where the impact of the west and of various post-1947 reforms has been relatively light but by no means absent.[23]

By contrast with the more militant, chauvinistic and formally reformist posture of the Mahasabha, the RRP, founded in 1948 by one Swami Karapatri, is certainly the most orthodox of all the rightist parties which have achieved any renown. The party manifesto waxes eloquent about the halcyon days of Lord Rama, about a largely rural economy based on the traditional *jajmani* system and on barter, about traditional systems of medicine such as *ayurveda*, about prohibition of alcoholic drink and of cow slaughter, and about comparable items, most of which are drawn from the catalogue of the 'messiahs of backwardness'. About as progressive a position as one can find in this handbook for Indian reactionaries and obscurantists is the recommendation that high positions in sanitation departments be given to untouchables, because this is in keeping with their traditional calling as sweepers and scavengers!

The RRP did manage to gain some support in India's most backward areas, such as Rajasthan and Madhya Pradesh, where it capitalized on the residual appeal of some local notables, mainly aristocrats, who accepted the party label. Virtually the only small consolation is the fact that many RRP standard-bearers did not believe in the absurdities of its programme (just as many Mahasabhites did not believe in reformism). This does not do much to rescue the RRP from its obscurantism, but it does remind us that the RRP—and the other parties—cannot be judged entirely at face value. It is not represented solely by those who wish to march backward to the days before the Muslim and British conquests and the industrial and scientific revolutions.[24]

Far more important in terms of its electoral record and organization is the Jan Sangh, founded in 1951 by Shyama Prasad Mookerjee, a former leader of the Mahasabha, and by members of the RSS, which 'had been informally connected with the Mahasabha for some time'.[25] Mookerjee, the prime mover in creating this new party, was a somewhat chastened militant Hindu—no 'wild-eyed fanatic' as one writer has put it. He insisted on open membership for the party, by contrast with the Mahasabha, and he seemed personally to have been 'a constitutionalist and a parliamentarian'.[26]

It is important to stress, moreover, that Mookerjee, prior to the formation of the Sangh was urged to, and did, join the Congress Cabinet in order to strengthen the right wing of the party, symbolized by Sardar Patel. Only after holding a Cabinet post for some time did he resign in protest over the government's policy toward Pakistan and join with some RSS associates to form the Sangh.

It is also important to stress that Mookerjee was adamant in insisting that the new party have open membership, i.e. that Muslims be admitted. This represents a step forward in the direction of secularism and national citizenship and in this sense it represents an important advance over the explicit communalism of the Hindu Mahasabha. But neither this, nor the occasional non-Hindu candidates put up, nor the prohibition against holding office simultaneously in the Sangh and the RSS has been able to remove the stigma of communalism from the Sangh. Ties with the RSS are very close; the Sangh's English-language weekly, *The Organiser*, regularly abuses Muslims for their allegedly anti-national proclivities; and Tinker, a reasonably sympathetic observer, summarily disposes of the Sangh's Muslims as 'Uncle Toms'.[27] For these and other reasons, one is justified in considering the Sangh a militant *Hindu* party.

The Sangh, like the Mahasabha, places great emphasis on national unity and strength, opposing all disintegrative tendencies at home and insisting on military, and hence industrial strength in the international community. Support for Hinduism as a cohesive force, support for Hindi as a common language for all Indians, and kindred measures bulk large in the Sangh programme. Thus, the secessionist agitation of the Dravida Munnetra Kazagham (DMK) in Madras and the demand for a separate Punjabi-speaking state by the Akali Sikhs (the Punjabi *suba* demand) are anathema, as are disturbances in the tribal regions of the Indo-Burman frontier. Illustrative of the party's perspectives is the assertion that

> India is one and an indivisible whole...This conviction is a cardinal principle of the Jana Sangh...The federal character of the constitution is exotic and does not symbolize unified nationhood. There should be a unitary centre with...decentralization...The Jana Sangh stands for modernizing and augmenting the defence potential of the country. 'Militarize the Nation' and 'Modernize the Military' should be our motto.[28]

Similarly, it was considered deplorable that 'after 14 years of freedom our boys and girls continue to be fashioned into Macaulay's mould' rather than in a way consonant with the genius of India herself.[29] Obviously a united, militarized nation, animated by specifically Indian symbols, is the central concern.

Economic issues have generally been understated in the Jan Sangh programme, but over the years there has been increasing attention to this subject, in part reflecting the party's desire to present a well-rounded alternative to the ruling party. On the whole, the party's approach has been an eclectic one: it has recommended a mixture of large-, medium- and small-scale enterprises, and a mixture of public and private enterprise, with the public sector controlling the 'commanding heights' of the economy. By contrast with the so-called Gandhians, however, the Sangh in 1962 declared itself in favour of 'a time limit within which the [*khadi*] industry will be required to become self-sufficient', because 'in spite of heavy subventions it has not yet become economic'.[30] Quite naturally there is an emphasis on self-sufficiency, on 'made in India', and on the Indianization of foreign-dominated firms.

The party's position on private property, especially on large-scale corporate holdings, remains somewhat ambiguous. It professes to favour a mixed economy in which key industries will be nationalized, a view which might be inspired by a number of factors. It might reflect a genuine commitment to the principle or the practicality of state-owned key industries. This would seem plausible in terms of the desire for national unity, because it would permit a greater disciplining of the national economy. It might reflect the impact of socialist rhetoric, which is well-nigh inescapable in India, to which the lip-service (at least) which almost every party pays to 'socialism' attests. Or it might reflect the predominantly lower middle-class base of support for the party, which would be more solicitous of smaller property holders as opposed to the corporate giants.[31] The last view gains credence from the Sangh's stand on some agricultural questions, particularly its willingness to attack large landholders while defending the more modest cultivators. While the issue is by no means clear, and while Sangh leaders are by no means committed to one single position here, it would appear that on balance large-scale property in industry and land receives no principled endorsement and that the Sangh would not be averse to attacking it. In short, there is at least a strand of *petit bourgeois* 'national-socialism' evident here.

Finally, the Jan Sangh, like the Mahasabha, is constantly preoccupied with foreign policy, particularly relations with Pakistan.[32] However, in recent years the Peoples' Republic of China has bulked larger in Sangh thinking. The ultimate reunification of the subcontinent is a professed goal, as it is for the Mahasabha, but here, too, there is a difference in emphasis which deserves note: for the Sangh, the goal is 'Akhand *Bharat*', while for the Mahasabha it is 'Akhand *Hindustan*'. The Sangh's views on relations with China indicate that the party cannot be accused of timidity: 'Jana Sangh is confident that our armed forces are quite competent to turn the Chinese out. The Government apprehension of a world war, if there happens to be an armed conflict in Ladakh, is nothing but an aberration of a weak mind.'[33] The Chinese invasion also propelled the Sangh into a leading position among those who favour the development of an Indian nuclear arsenal. On a more modest level, the goal of absorption of all French and Portuguese enclaves in India was always a major tenet of the party, which also concerns itself widely with all Indians overseas, especially those in Africa, Ceylon and Burma.

To sum up, the Jan Sangh is the principal political vehicle for the militant Hindu or right radical element in Indian politics. Many of its leaders are, indeed, no 'wild-eyed fanatics' and hope to temper the overall belligerence of the party. However, its emphasis on a centralized, militarized and now nuclear state, its rather aggressive foreign policy statements, and its close ties with the RSS, for the moment preclude a shedding of the 'proto-fascist' brush with which the party has generally been tarred. With respect to the development of a cohesive, right-wing opposition, the emphasis on discipline and militancy has alienated many of the aristocratic elements, who appreciate neither quality, and its communal tendencies have alienated more. In general, the Sangh's 'Hindu-Hindi' emphasis severely impairs its aggregative capacity.[34]

In the 1951–2 and 1957 elections, the overall performance of these five parties was decidedly poor, especially in voting for the *Lok Sabha*, the lower house of the Indian national Parliament.[35] This was not substantially offset by improvement in the position of the Jan Sangh, by the strong showing of the Ganatantra Parishad in Orissa, and by the combined rightist groups in Rajasthan, primarily RRP and independents. If all of the diverse rightist elements be considered together, they amassed upwards of 25 per cent of the popular vote for and seats in the *Lok Sabha*—by no means a sign of eclipse. It was abundantly clear, however, that to do battle with the Congress, more co-ordinated action was an absolute minimum. An awareness of this obvious fact impelled some leaders to seek greater unity, at all levels.

At the parliamentary level the most notable effort was undertaken by Mookerjee shortly after the elections of 1951–2. In order to co-ordinate the work of the 'democratic' opposition and to build toward the fifty-man group required for official recognition as the opposition party, Mookerjee approached virtually every non-communist, non-socialist, and non-Muslim opposition group in the *Lok Sabha*, in order to establish a legislative 'front'. The result was the formation of the strictly parliamentary 'National Democratic Party', which included members of the Sangh, Mahasabha, RRP, Ganatantra Parishad, Akali Dal (a party comprised primarily of conservative Sikhs, confined to the Punjab), Commonweal and Tamilnad Toilers' parties (both lower middle caste Madras parties), and some independents.[36]

Mookerjee's death in 1953 removed the leader of this unity effort and the group collapsed within one year, but to put the burden of the collapse entirely on the death of Mookerjee is quite unwarranted. Internal strains became evident very quickly, as Dr A. Krishnaswamy, 'one of Tamilnad's wealthy Mudaliars' (a principal trading-financial caste) resigned from the group because of the emphasis on Hindi as the national language, favoured by the Sangh-Mahasabha axis.[37] Similarly the alinement of the Akalis with this group was a very shaky marriage of convenience, because the demand for a separate Punjabi-speaking state was totally unacceptable to the Sangh-Mahasabha forces, and this was *the* issue for the Akalis. Without underestimating the creative role of leadership in such a context, it is evident that there were very substantial cleavages which even a man of Mookerjee's admitted abilities could have overcome only with the greatest difficulty.

Differences separating the Sangh, Mahasabha and RRP also existed, and these are well illustrated by the extra-parliamentary merger talks. The latter did not include any south Indian elements, who by no stretch of the imagination would have rallied to the standard of a group dominated by pro-Hindi forces. Nor did they include the Akali Dal, for reasons already given. The talks did, however, include the Sangh, Mahasabha and RRP, and, at one stage, the Ganatantra Parishad, which, according to one source, had the 'full sympathies' of the Sangh in Orissa.[38] What became clear is that each wanted merger essentially on its own terms.

Difficulties in Kashmir provided a strong impulse for these parties to co-operate, and it was in this context that the merger talks were undertaken. N. C. Chatterjee, speaking for the Mahasabha, further insisted that in his party at least there was rank-and-file sentiment for merger. But Swami Karapatri (RRP) underscored his party's determination to sustain the village order by refusing to yield significantly on matters of religion and social policy, in the face of the right radical, reformist demands of the Mahasabha and, more importantly, of the Sangh. Also, Savarkar and other Mahasabhites underscored their party's firm communal commitment by rejecting the Sangh's insistence on admission of Muslims and other non-Hindus. Chatterjee, who favoured a united 'Hindu' party devoid of Muslims, seemed genuinely willing to contemplate the demise of the Mahasabha, but other Mahasabha leaders, such as Deshpande, wanted only a 'united front' and electoral alliances, not an outright merger.

Further complicating the process was the persistent aggressiveness of the Jan Sangh, even after Mookerjee's death when Chatterjee insisted on sustaining the talks. The Sangh, considering itself a young, dynamic party, termed the Mahasabha a 'communal body' and censured it because it 'welcomed princes, zamindars and vested interests in its midst'.[39] The latter charge was energetically denied by Deshpande and others, but this is not the important point. What is crucial is the Sangh's effort to project itself as a non-communal party of the common man and to disclaim any connection with leading aristocratic or capitalist elements. The Sangh charge, in short, suggests something about the social composition and 'style' of the party, to which we referred above. In any event, amidst repeated charges by the Sangh that the Mahasabha was reactionary and dead politically, and demands that merger be on Sangh terms in all important respects and with full acceptance of Sangh discipline, the negotiations broke down—

even though to the end, Chatterjee seemed anxious to find some common ground with the Sangh.[40]

It is Weiner's contention that there was very little genuine feeling that unity was desirable, apart from leaders such as Mookerjee and Chatterjee. There were, of course, some programmatic differences and the dispute over membership provisions, but Weiner chooses to understate these in favour of a social-psychological explanation for failure of the talks: that because Indian social structure has traditionally been based on small, compact groups, many Indians who are loosened from their traditional moorings turn toward small, compact political groups as a substitute. This, he suggests, helps to explain the reluctance of much of the membership of the several parties to submerge its identity in a broad, more disciplined party, as would have been the case in a Sangh-dominated 'Hindu' party.

However insightful this hypothesis may seem, it must be approached with caution. First of all, it is too much 'inward-looking' in the sense that it disregards the environmental factors which play a part in party realinements. The Congress, after all, was a national party comprised of highly disparate groups which *were* willing to submerge their local identities at least partially. A consideration of the factors which enabled the Congress to overcome parochialism would be pertinent for an understanding of the right-wing unity efforts and would force us to look beyond the 'inner psyches' of the individual parties.

Moreover, there would seem to be a simpler explanation for the failure of merger talks even if we do not look beyond the discussants themselves. There are, after all, many local politicians with essentially local ambitions and constituencies who simply could not survive in a larger arena. Such people would for reasons of prestige and individual self-interest, if not for personal power, oppose amalgamation of smaller groups into one large one. They could hope to dominate the former, not the latter. It is important to have some feeling for these different explanations for the failure of right-wing unity efforts, because they have a bearing on the Swatantra Party. Be that as it may, the obvious fact is for the present the important one: even though a serious effort toward unity was made, the right wing remained highly fragmented, even in the face of electoral reverses and a seemingly unpromising future.[41]

Thus, although negotiations continued until 1956, no mergers and no significant 'united front' activity came to pass, even among the Sangh, Mahasabha and RRP. By and large, the Ganatantra Parishad remained aloof, as did the Janata Party, the Akali Dal, and other local groups, particularly south Indian conservative interests. Leaders of many of these groups did, however, profess to desire the creation of a significant, all-India opposition party, if the proper leadership, programme and financing could be secured.[42]

Paralleling the efforts—and reflecting the difficulties—at the national level were efforts and difficulties at the state level. In Rajasthan, which will suffice for an example here, the RRP, Jan Sangh and some independents constituted themselves as a united front in the assembly, only to fall apart after a short time. The proximate cause seems to have been the 'Pant Award', a judgment on smaller *jagirdari* holdings which was deemed to affect adversely the *Bhoomias*, or lesser Rajputs, for whom the Sangh claimed to speak, and for whom the big *jagirdars*, primarily independents and RRP-men, displayed little concern. Still, they *were* united for a time and they doubtless would have held together somewhat better had the leader of the front, the Maharaja of Jodhpur, not died shortly after the elections of 1951–2. As in the case of Mookerjee, one should not expect miracles from a leader, but leadership remains one of the critical problems in all merger and united front activity.[43]

On a more modest scale, there were also successes and failures, as the right-wing parties groped toward a more coherent effort against the Congress. There were, for example, many local 'non-aggression' pacts, through which parties agreed to defer to one another on a reciprocal basis, to avoid multi-cornered fights which would include more than one rightist candidate. But quite common also were some very fierce battles among the rightist parties, which only serve to underscore the point that much remained to be done if the Congress were to be challenged effectively.[44]

To speak of challenging the Congress is, however, misleading to the extent that the ruling party itself contained many elements indistinguishable from those just discussed. For a long time, for example, dual membership in the Congress and the Mahasabha was permitted, and when this was no longer possible, many Mahasabhites-cum-Congressmen remained with the Congress. We have seen that, for a time, Mookerjee was in a Congress ministry, where it was hoped he would strengthen the right-wing elements. More importantly, throughout the history of the Congress, defections have occurred primarily on the left flank, suggesting the weight of a well-entrenched right wing in the nationalist movement. Both prior to and after independence the impact of the right wing on personnel and policy decisions has been evident, and this point has been sufficiently well documented in many standard sources. Brecher is particularly effective on this point, and there is a useful case study of the Hindu Code bills which bears on the same issue. Here it will suffice to cite Tinker's account of one battle between secularist reformers and some right-wing elements in the Congress:

> Nehru, Krishna Menon, and other spokesmen of the 'secular' school of politics have so frequently argued that the Hindu communal parties have failed to gain a footing, that the argument has been widely accepted. Yet, over the central features of Nehru's secular programme, the Hindu Code Bill, the communalists have to a large extent had their own way. The Hindu Code Bill was first introduced by Nehru in 1950 as a comprehensive measure to reform the whole structure of Hindu marriage, divorce, inheritance rights and adoption custom. The bill met with widespread opposition, in and out of Parliament. In October 1951, President Prasad threatened to use his power of veto, unless the measure was withdrawn. The bill was delayed, and its provisions whittled away. At last in 1955, a major part of the code was placed on the statute books as the Hindu Marriages Law. The ranks of the Congress parliamentary party contained few prepared to support the measure, and many who spoke against it: but when the vote was taken, the party whip was obeyed. As a demonstration of the secular spirit, all this was not very impressive.[45]

Comparable cases could be cited from the areas of economic policy, land reform, *harijan* 'uplift', and the like, to indicate the impact of the right-wing elements who are often obscured behind the socialist façade of the Congress. It is quite remarkable that after so commenting on the Hindu Code Bill, Tinker could go on to argue that the right wing was weak in India, supporting his argument by reference to non-Congress opposition parties.[46] The 'sad' performance of right-wing parties to which he referred, and the 'almost total eclipse of our so-called rightist parties' to which another writer pointed, become less surprising if one appreciates the very substantial strength of certain right-wing groups in the

Congress itself, coupled with the other factors examined above. The extremes of militant Hinduism, of aristocratic conservatism, and of reaction were doubtless not particularly potent, but non-aristocratic conservatism, including the 'disguised' conservatism of the idealized village, certainly was strong. Put in admittedly exaggerated form, we may ask those who emphasize the weakness of the Indian right, 'how many conservative parties does India need?' The contemporary Congress is quite enough to satisfy a good many conservatives, and some of those whom it did not satisfy still remained in the party, paying lip service to socialism and boring from within, because of Nehru's commitment to socialist positions and because of the apparent futility of fighting him openly.

None the less, there was no opposition party which seemed likely to fulfil the function of an open, explicitly conservative force, to speak for those who were offended and who could not be content with silence or with boring from within. The Jan Sangh impressed some observers as moving in this direction, i.e. of 'responsible conservatism', but on balance it had a less sanguine image which seemed to preclude effective aggregation of some key elements, notably conservatives (as opposed to right radicals), and the non-Hindu, non-Hindi speaking groups.[47] It is clear also that urban business interests were poorly represented by the available opposition parties, and even the Jan Sangh, with its right radical style, gave many big businessmen a few anxious moments.

Although the right side of the political spectrum was by no means unpopulated, and although the record of the years 1947–59 could scarcely be encouraging to any new entrant into the political fray, the Swatantra Party entered the arena in mid-1959, as the self-appointed non-leftist alternative to the Congress. Its arrival might have been expected only to fragment further the opposition forces. As Humayun Kabir put the matter, Swatantra was 'at a disadvantage because of its late appearance. As the latest comer in the field, it has to establish its claim against all existing parties.'[48] Admitting this, it was still by no means foreordained that Swatantra would only further complicate matters. Both the context and the nature of Swatantra itself held some promise.

With respect to the context, it might have been tempting to assert that India's social diversity, various legacies of the colonial situation, and the rise of the Congress would combine to prevent a more 'rational' alinement of political forces in India. This argument has considerable merit and it has been freely employed in the preceding pages. But it must also be recognized that many powerful and effective political groupings, among which one must count the Congress itself, have been comprised of very heterogeneous materials; and it must also be acknowledged that basic realinements of political forces have occurred in many countries where they might have seemed improbable. If Gandhi could create a Congress in which widely disparate elements existed cheek-by-jowl for the purpose of ousting the British, could not another leader also build a broad coalition, given a certain objective situation and perceptions about it? Could not a serious famine in the present context precipitate a political emergency and new political alinements? Could not an international crisis do much to restructure political life in India? Could not a strong, frontal attack on a wide range of long-standing customs and beliefs and institutions work in the same direction? To ask these questions is not to answer them, but neither does a catalogue of historic political fragmentation by itself preclude future political cohesion.

With respect to the Swatantra Party itself, as a potential vehicle for a more formidable conservative effort, there were some grounds for modest optimism. It came into being as a result of a series of policies of the Congress, culminating in the 'Nagpur Resolution' on 'joint co-operative farming', and the party self-consciously set out to exploit the alleged menace of collectivization of agriculture, while at the same time relating this specific issue to a broader pattern of 'statism' which it felt prevailed. It had a number of very distinguished leaders, including some from the south of India, where the major right-wing parties received negligible support. Its leaders, moreover, included some veteran Congressmen of great stature, who were thus more likely to appeal to right-wing Congressmen than were the other opposition parties. Furthermore, Swatantra was not, on the surface at least, committed either to militant Hinduism or to reaction, which gave it a more 'respectable' image in these respects than the Jan Sangh and the RRP. Most important, perhaps, was Swatantra's explicit determination to set forth a minimum programme on the basis of which it would hope to create a cohesive, non-communist alternative to the Congress. These and other factors seemed to augur well for Swatantra, although everyone knew that its task would not be easy.

The stage may be set for the following analysis by indicating briefly, by way of anticipation, some general but basic points. In the elections of 1962, the Swatantra Party established itself as a significant, if highly controversial political force. Founded only in mid-1959, it must be credited with a strong showing by contemporary Indian standards for the performance of opposition parties. Polling about 8 per cent of the popular vote, it secured the third largest contingent in the *Lok Sabha* and the second largest total of state assembly seats. It secured the position of principal opposition party in the states of Bihar, Gujarat, Rajasthan, and Orissa; and after the split in the Communist Party of India (CPI) in 1965, it became the principal opposition in the *Lok Sabha* as well.

From the outset, the nature and role of the party have been hotly disputed subjects. It has been described as a party of 'conservative rich peasants in the South, a few finance capitalists in the West, some Bihar and U.P. feudal atavisms, and communalist chiefs in the North'.[49] It was condemned by the CPI as one of the 'forces of dark, right reaction'[50] and by Nehru as belonging to 'the middle ages of lords, castles and zamindars' and as becoming 'more and more Fascist in outlook'.[51] One American scholar labelled it 'a communal conservative party',[52] while a British observer concluded that 'the victory of this party could be an unmitigated disaster for India...'.[53]

By contrast, its supporters see it as 'a progressive liberal party'[54] which will 'slow down the Congress steamroller' by providing a non-communist, non-socialist, secular and constitutionalist alternative to the ruling party.[55] The reaction of the Indian press was, at the outset, guardedly optimistic along these lines,[56] while the American magazine *Life* almost surpassed Swatantra Party literature itself when it contended that 'the Swatantra program could really get that huge country moving in a direction favorable to free institutions. The free world can wish this little party a big future.'[57]

It is tempting to conclude that these divergent estimates derive from different perspectives on key Indian problems, as polarized by the heat of political battle. This is to some extent true. In addition, however, the cleavage in critical opinion reflects the fact that Swatantra is in some fundamental ways an enigma, one important aspect of which is the diversity of social forces within

Swatantra and the balance of power among them. By probing in detail the nature of this enigma and this special aspect of it, we shall not only understand this intrinsically important political party, but through it we shall also gain insights into the problems and prospects of political conservatism (and of the right more generally) in India.

CHAPTER 4

THE BIRTH OF A PARTY

The formal decision to establish the Swatantra Party was made public in Madras on 4 June 1959. Only in the narrowest sense, however, does this tell us anything about its birth. The date of conception is uncertain, although the period of gestation is known to have been long. Paternity is difficult to specify. And the new party was on the verge of entering the political world earlier, in Bangalore, if not elsewhere. The date, 4 June 1959, is significant primarily because it post-dates the Nagpur Resolution, and Madras is important primarily because it suggests a south Indian origin.

Commenting on the birth of Swatantra, one writer has argued that 'in one sense this was not the emergence of a new political force, but only the regrouping of the conservative elements in Indian society which were making themselves felt in the working of other parties earlier'.[1] Although there is more than a grain of truth in this contention, it is necessary to go beyond it, for the following reasons: as it stands, the statement is both incomplete and inadequate because it fails to indicate that some previously latent elements were mobilized and because it fails to specify precisely what forces were regrouped and on what basis. Swatantra to be sure represented a confluence of many diverse social forces and personalities, animated at the doctrinal level by one general and one specific problem ('statism' and the Nagpur Resolution respectively), and dominated by one towering figure, Rajaji. But as the preceding analysis has suggested, it is essential to understand the nature of the forces involved and the basis on which they came together, including the impact of the objective situation and subjective perceptions of it, the nature and role of leadership, the doctrinal stance, relations with other parties, and so on, if we are to understand properly the nature and significance of Swatantra.

Of the more formally organized social forces which helped to generate the Swatantra Party, two stand out, although neither stands in the front rank of organized interest groups in India: the Forum of Free Enterprise (FFE) and the All-India Agriculturalists' Federation (AIAF), founded in 1956 and 1958, respectively. Concerning them, three general points are in order. First, each took a decisive stand against government controls, taxation, and general economic policy, in the area of industry and agriculture respectively. Secondly, Swatantra leaders are quite willing to acknowledge their debts to both, as Rajaji did at one juncture: 'I shall be failing in my duty if I do not say how grateful we are to the Agricultural Federation of India for the inspiration they gave us for the formation of this Party and to the Forum of Free Enterprise that helped us so greatly in the preliminary work.'[2] Thirdly, because it grossly underestimates the original and enduring contribution of the FFE, Rajaji's statement reflects the determination of the leadership to identify the party with the agricultural rather than the industrial sector. For the moment, however, it is important simply to stress the party's debt to the most aggressively 'free enterprise' segments of the business and agricultural communities.

The FFE was founded by a group of businessmen in Bombay, notably the late A. D. Shroff of Tatas and Murarji Vaidya of the Indian Rayon Corporation and the All-India Manufacturers' Association. They were brought together in this venture by a prominent one-time Tata official, M. R. Masani, a veteran anti-communist (and more recently anti-socialist) ideologian and severe critic of the Nehru government.[3] Ultimately expanding to include centres in many cities in addition to its home office in Bombay, the Forum, by and large, was scrupulously careful not to carry on a vendetta against Nehru or the Congress, and it never identified itself with any political party, for obvious reasons.[4] Thus, the Forum explicitly claimed that it was 'a non-political and non-partisan organization' which would 'disseminate authoritative information to educate public opinion...[and] bring to public notice the achievements of Free Enterprise in this country and the manner in which it can make its contribution to the economic development of India in order to raise the standard of living'.[5] It contended that 'today the case for Free Enterprise is going by default', and to the end of 'educating the educated' about the relationship which it felt existed between free enterprise and economic development *and* politics, it organized meetings of various types and distributed literature, the latter often of a second-hand sort.[6]

In addition to arguing that the organization was non-partisan, the FFE also took pains to insist that it did not stand for *laissez faire.* According to one leader, 'we consider that "Laissez Faire" or Nineteenth Century Capitalism has no place in contemporary Indian life' and that these systems 'are as dead as the dodo and can make no contribution to the industrial, social and economic advancement we seek'.[7] None the less, the leaders and spokesmen of the FFE did seek to expand the sphere in which private enterprise would be secure and they also sought to articulate in reasonably coherent fashion the accumulated grievances of the business communities. In particular, they hammered at the theme that a largely free enterprise economy was necessary both for rapid economic growth and for the maintenance of political democracy. They warned, sometimes guardedly, sometimes vigorously and stridently, that wide government controls, heavy taxation, and a large public sector not only destroyed economic initiative but led ultimately down the familiar road of Friedrich Hayek.[8]

Thus, the Forum—its non-partisan protestations notwithstanding—necessarily took on an anti-Congress image, because if there was a danger of statism in India, it could have emanated only from the Congress or some segment of it. Moreover, some of those who were associated with the activities of the Forum either adverted to or explicitly discussed the need for the formation of a new, anti-statist opposition party, although on every occasion the FFE entered a familiar disclaimer, viz. that the views expressed were not necessarily those of the FFE.

One of the foremost of those who stressed the need for a new party was Masani, whose advocacy well ante-dated the Nagpur Resolution. At one stage he referred to the 'dangerous polarization' of Indian political life, between the Congress, not yet viewed as a menace, and the CPI.[9] He deplored the fact that 'consistent ideological opposition to communism has hitherto been negligible'.[10] Moreover, he questioned the judgment of Rajaji, one of India's most determined anti-communists, that as of the mid-1950s the CPI was losing ground. By contrast, Masani insisted that there was a threat of paralysis of the will in confronting communism and he argued that 'only purposeful democratic leadership that arouses the country to the internal and external dangers with which it is faced can immunize India from this threat'.[11] At this juncture, Masani pointed to the anti-communist role of the Indian Committee for Cultural Freedom (1951), with which he was closely associated, and to the Democratic Research Service in Bombay, which was 'somewhat more polemical' in its anti-communism and with which Masani has also been involved.[12]

Through such channels Masani attempted to build up anti-communist sentiment in the country, and at least as early as his election campaign of 1957, he stressed the need to forge a non-communist alternative to the Congress. As was suggested in his book on the communists in India, Masani at this time defended the declared need for an opposition of this type *not* because the Congress itself was being communized but because people who objected to the Congress had nowhere else to go, in his view, but to the CPI. According to Ramgarh, sometime Janata Party leader and Swatantra stalwart, Masani had broached the idea of a more coherent, non-communist opposition to him at an 'all-parties' conference shortly after the 1957 elections, in which Masani was returned to the *Lok Sabha* from a district adjacent to Ramgarh's own stronghold.[13] In the early months of 1959, however, the tempo of Masani's efforts increased and, concomitantly, he insisted that the Nehru government itself was heading toward communism. Thus, Masani termed the Nagpur Resolution an 'insidious attempt to bring in Collective Farming of the Communist pattern by the back door', a view which was echoed throughout India by those who now lead the Swatantra Party.[14] As a consequence, he came to insist more forcibly that a 'middle of the road' party be founded.[15] In the early 1950s Masani had praised Rajaji, 'to whom, above all, credit goes for having protected southern India from Communist rule after the last [1951–2] General Elections', and it was perhaps only natural that Masani look again to this most respected of Indian elder statesmen for leadership of an anti-communist movement.[16]

Among those who responded favourably to the efforts of the FFE and of Masani was Rajaji. But pressure from Masani in 1957 and 1958 found Rajaji unrelenting on the question of his own personal involvement in an anti-Congress movement. Vaidya, a founder-leader of the FFE, went to Madras in 1958, met Rajaji, and was asked what the Forum proposed to do when and if it succeeded in 'educating the educated' to the menace of statism and to the virtues of free enterprise. Vaidya insisted that he and his colleagues were writing as businessmen and economists and that authentic political leaders would have to come forth to challenge statism politically and to channel the efforts of the Forum's supporters in that direction. Here, as in his dealings with Masani and others, Rajaji insisted that he was too old (over eighty), too long a Congressman, and too close to Nehru personally to consider a re-entry into politics on an active, organized basis.[17]

Against this backdrop, the Nagpur Resolution came as something of a god-send to spokesmen for and supporters of the FFE who were anxious to develop an anti-Congress, anti-communist party. Having been labelled as apostles of 'reactionary' *laissez faire* capitalism (a charge which was vehemently denied), the leaders of the FFE could exploit the more ominous implications of 'joint co-operative farming', and could identify themselves with free enterprise in agriculture, thus linking themselves with men of property in the countryside.

In the early months of 1959 the Forum sponsored many meetings in which the Nagpur Resolution was the main topic. Other groups were doing the same on a reasonably wide scale, and Rajaji became more and more involved with these in the south, particularly in Bangalore. Anti-Congress efforts were gaining some momentum, and on 29 May 1959, the FFE sponsored a meeting in Bangalore with Rajaji in the chair and Masani as first speaker, and although it was a Forum-sponsored meeting, it was concerned almost exclusively with the Nagpur Resolution. Masani, who termed the atmosphere 'electric', launched into a vehement denunciation of the Congress, after which Rajaji spoke even more vehemently, complaining that Masani had been too restrained. Rajaji, Masani, and others decided at Bangalore to form a new party, continuing a process which had started long before, but in part because the Bangalore meeting was Forum-sponsored, it was decided to postpone the public announcement about the new party until a later date.[18] That date proved to be 4 June 1959, for which the AIAF had scheduled a meeting in Madras and to which most of the participants in the FFE-sponsored Bangalore meeting were going. Thus the birth of Swatantra was announced at an AIAF meeting, but the role of the Foum and its adherents was so obvious that 'some people say the party is, in fact, the Forum's political arm'.[19] Yet it is important to note that there was much reluctance to have Swatantra too closely and too openly identified with the FFE, both because of dangers to business interests and to the party.[20]

The AIAF, founded in Bangalore in 1958, was, from all available indications, a group of very modest dimensions and impact. However, it numbered among its leaders N. G. Ranga, a veteran peasant leader, and its President in mid-1959 was Sardar Bahadur Lal Singh (now deceased), an agricultural economist and sometime adviser to the national Planning Commission—a fact which did not escape attention when Swatantra was founded at a meeting sponsored by the AIAF.[21] The group was very heavily south Indian in leadership and membership, and while it claims to be a 'peasant' organization and while upon occasion it may speak convincingly for cultivators generally, it is dominated by *kulaks* and by other larger landholders.[22]

The activities of the AIAF paralleled in many respects those of the FFE. The Federation organized meetings, distributed literature, and, in a few, isolated cases, local units ostensibly set up candidates for public office.[23] Further paralleling the FFE's efforts, the AIAF severely criticized the government's agricultural policy. The AIAF stood four-square behind the more prosperous landholder, by taking exception to *some* government tenancy legislation, by insisting that the goal of individual peasant proprietorship was not only utopian but unnecessary, by adamantly opposing land ceiling legislation, and, finally, by denouncing 'joint cooperative farming' in Masani-like fashion. All of these moves were held to destroy initiative and productivity among those most capable of increasing India's agricultural production, i.e. those presently in possession of larger holdings and those who had historically been tillers of the soil.[24] At a number of junctures, again primarily in Bangalore, Rajaji had met with AIAF leaders and other kindred spirits to discuss the Nagpur Resolution and possible counter-moves; and there is little doubt that Rajaji personally had greater sympathy for the AIAF than he did for the FFE. It was for this reason, as well as for the more practical one already mentioned, that the announcement of Swatantra's entry into the lists was deferred until the AIAF meeting in Madras.

The determination of the founders of Swatantra to identify the party with the rural sector is widely evident and played an important part in the selection of former *kisan sabha* leader Ranga as party President. Thus, even Masani, through whose initiative, in large part, the FFE took shape and whose own identification is with modern, urban interests, has emphasized that 'it is not an accident that the move for the establishment of the Swatantra Party should have taken place at a meeting convened...by the All-India Agriculturalists' Federation and that Professor Ranga should be nominated as its leader. This is as it should be. India is, and will remain, for many generations to come, a peasant country.'[25] Without any intention to impugn the sincerity of Rajaji and Masani, it is none the less clear that the role of the AIAF has been emphasized and that of the FFE understated for practical reasons. Assertions such as Masani's—necessary because business sponsorship would have been a liability—cannot deflect attention from Swatantra's debt to the FFE. Meanwhile, the AIAF, because of its stand on a wide range of land reforms, has been accused of defending 'feudal landlordism'.[26] It is not easy to estimate accurately the relative importance of the Forum and the Federation among business and agricultural groups respectively, or in terms of their role in the Swatantra Party. It is fairly clear, however, that neither group stands in the front rank of interest groups in India, and it is beyond dispute that most of the leaders of the two organizations are either members of or very sympathetic to the Swatantra Party.[27] Swatantra's roots in the most aggressively free-enterprise sectors of the business community and of the rural propertied class are thus abundantly evident. But while it is important to point out that this background militates strongly against an image of a 'common man's' party, it is equally important to stress three other facts. First, both the FFE and AIAF were animated more by economic than by religio-cultural issues, and their economic arguments were pitched in decidedly modern terms, i.e. efficiency and productivity. The contrast between their commitments and those of the Gandhians, the aristocratic conservatives, and various cultural groups and more religiously oriented parties is obvious and important. Secondly, the emphasis of both was on freedom from state controls, not on freedom from the constraints of traditional Indian society, even though the FFE included many Parsis and other modern businessmen and even though the AIAF leaders were in many cases opposed to the great landed aristocrats of pre-independence days. As Swatantra leaders would subsequently make very explicit, the greatest threat to freedom lay on the left, not on the right. Thirdly, it is necessary to emphasize, because of later developments, that at this juncture in its history, Swatantra did not draw to any significant extent upon the great aristocratic classes of north India; and, as we have already suggested and as we shall see further, most of Swatantra's founding fathers were, at least in the past, hostile to the aristocracy.

If the success of the new party had depended on the potency of the Forum and the Federation alone, it would doubtless never have been formed, or, if formed, it would have failed miserably. As we have seen, however, there were diverse currents of discontent which could be tapped, and those who eventually brought Swatantra into the world were well aware of this fact. And even some aristocrats figured into these calculations. The Raja of Ramgarh had expressed interest in a new national opposition party at a seminar in Bombay, shortly before Swatantra was founded.[28] The Maharaja of Kalahandi, a leader of the Ganatantra Parishad, had approached Rajaji, as Vaidya had done, well before the Nagpur session of the Congress in 1959, to discuss the possibility of forming a new party.[29] Jankinandan Singh, uncle of the then Maharajadhiraj of Darbhanga (formerly premier *zamindar* in Bihar and leader of the Maithil Brahmin community) and a member of the Bihar Legislative Council, asked Rajaji in 1957 to rally all dissident Congress groups, such as Jankinandan Singh's own Jan Congress.[30] Many others of lesser political stature, including some (like H. N. Kanoongo, an Orissa lawyer) who had not previously been involved in politics, had also turned to Rajaji prior to 1959, as the man most likely to provide the requisite leadership for the type of opposition party which so many people had contemplated.[31]

In addition to the discontent of relatively long standing, there was the storm of protest elicited by the Nagpur Resolution. A number of distinguished individuals and local groups responded with great alarm, conjuring up the image of Soviet-style collectives or Chinese communes. Even before the actual passage of the Nagpur Resolution, a *kisan* convention, which reportedly included many AIAF leaders and about one hundred Congress MPs, was held in Delhi, to protest against the proposed resolution. Late in January 1959 a Punjab *kisan* convention was called to protest against the Nagpur Resolution, and Ranga, then Secretary of the Congress parliamentary party, the late Sardar Udham Singh Nagoke, former Akali leader and then a Congress MP, General K. M. Cariappa, retired Chief of Staff of the Indian army, and the Maharaja of Patiala shared the platform.[32] The Gujarat Khedut Sangh, with which Ranga was associated and which brought him into close touch with some prominent local leaders, was, according to one report, the first organized group to enter its protest against 'joint co-operative farming'.[33] For months, Ranga, Masani, and others spoke against the Nagpur proposals in various parts of India, often at the behest of prominent local leaders and groups.[34]

There were, in addition, some veteran Congressmen who joined with Ranga, Masani, Nagoke, *et al.*, in what took on many qualities of an anti-Congress crusade. K. M. Munshi, a most distinguished Bombay Congressman of very long standing, 'made a scathing criticism of the idea of co-operative farming' in an address to the Delhi Historical Society, and S. K. D. Paliwal, an almost equally distinguished Congressman from UP, sought to work up a storm of local protest.[35] Nagoke and Paliwal were, moreover, attempting to organize at least state-wide groups which might better channel the opposition to the Nagpur Resolution.[36] Elsewhere, there were groups of dissident Congressmen, such as the Indian National Democratic Congress in Madras and the Democratic Party in Andhra, who had split themselves off from the parent organization, although not necessarily for doctrinal reasons; and these were potential recruits. In fact, the Democratic Party, some of whose leaders had been with Ranga in the old Krishikar Lok Paksh, had asked Rajaji to preside over its inaugural convention.[37] In short, anti-Congress sentiment was widespread, and those (like Ramgarh) who had been in opposition for a long time were joined by those for whom the Nagpur Resolution was the last straw—or who at least felt that it provided an opportunity for previously suppressed opposition to come into the open. These opposition groups were obviously fragmented and most of the obstacles previously mentioned worked to keep them apart. But the would-be founders of a national opposition to the Congress had much material on which to draw, and Ranga among others had had a chance to 'feel out' potential recruits in his widespread travels to publicize the alleged menace of the Nagpur proposals. If distinguished leadership were available, if there were a key issue on which to capitalize, and if there were at least a fair prospect of decent financial support, there was reason to think that some of the barriers to a cohesive opposition might be overcome.

Those who had looked to Rajaji to assume the leadership of an opposition party not only knew that he was one of the most distinguished of all Indian statesmen-politicians, but they were also encouraged by many of his post-retirement pronouncements about the Indian political scene, particularly about the need to combat 'statism'.[38] Typical of his assessment of the political situation in the mid-1950s was his short essay, 'Our Democracy', in which he argued that

> every change must necessarily produce dislocation, disturbances and distress...the pain involved...must be taken into account in any orderly advance. A Party on the Right, as it is called, gives expression to these distresses and disturbances, which are not less real or important than the need for change and progress.[39]

He further insisted that 'since...the Congress Party has swung to the left, what is wanted is not an ultra or outer-Left [viz. the CPI or the Praja Socialist Party, PSP], but a strong and articulate Right'.[40] He also added a remark which is crucial in terms of the argument about rightist elements in the Congress itself, viz. that this opposition must 'operate not privately and behind the closed doors of the party meeting, but openly and periodically through the electorate'.[41]

While thus tempting anti-Congress forces of conservative temper to seek him out, Rajaji at the same time continued to enphasize his old age, long service in the Congress, and personal attachment to Nehru as the factors which precluded his assumption of leadership of these forces. The Nagpur Resolution was, according to Rajaji himself, the proverbial last straw.[42] Having lived four-score-plus years, with the end in sight, he felt that he must make one last, if desperate effort, to deflect the Congress from the path which it was following. He was, as one foreign observer put it, a man with 'a deep moral sense...prepared to go down fighting in a last crusade'.[43]

When he was finally prevailed upon to come out of retirement, Rajaji provided a fillip to many of the disparate rightist forces and he provided the much-sought distinguished leadership almost single-handed. Kabir overstates the case only slightly when he argues that 'the only rallying point of the Swatantra Party is the personality of Rajagopalachari', but there can be no doubt that Rajaji 'is the stellar attraction' and 'commands wide attention' whenever he speaks and acts.[44] Rajaji is thought of 'as a member of Gandhi's generation, the liberators, because he was involved in the movement from the very start', and 'as Gandhi's old friend and lieutenant he has a very special status'.[45] Not without his severe critics, Rajaji has also been termed 'the most astute intellectual among the elite of Indian nationalists',[46] and Nehru wrote of him in 1940 that his 'brilliant intellect, selfless character, and penetrating powers of analysis have been a tremendous asset to our cause'.[47] Although Nehru was not so generous in later years, this judgment will stand as a suggestion, at least, of the sort of person who became the founder-leader of the Swatantra Party.[48] That Rajaji had been approached by so many people from all corners of India testifies further to the esteem in which he was held and to the importance which these appellants attached to leadership of great stature, in their efforts to constitute a broad opposition party.

The Nagpur Resolution specifically, and 'statism' generally, provided the key issues which had potential mass appeal, if only the peasantry could be convinced that these constituted a 'clear and present danger' to their interests. It was argued above that one factor in right-wing disunity was the relative moderation of the Congress Party, and the resultant feeling that however bad things were, they could still get worse, and would get worse if the Congress were opposed. Swatantra's task—and hope—was to convince the populace that action was necessary *then*, before it was too late. It is also very important to observe, in this regard, that if the threat of communism could be satisfactorily communicated, it was a potential solvent for the disparate elements and doctrines which had previously comprised the disorganized Indian right, and it could also hope to appeal to liberal, middle-class groups. It could, in short, serve as a rallying point akin to the anti-British focus of the nationalist movement, i.e. one which could mobilize disparate groups with different positive goals but with a common negative goal. This, at least, was a potentiality which was seen to be inherent in the Nagpur Resolution.

Not to be underestimated in all calculations concerning the birth of Swatantra was the presence of Masani and the extensive, if formally unofficial support of the FFE—and the connection of both with the Tata empire, one of the premier industrial-financial complexes in India. Although no one expected the keys to vast industrial treasuries to be handed over, some support from Tatas could easily have been envisaged: Masani had very close ties, and Shroff, a founder-leader of the FFE, had for a long time been prominent in the organization. The All-India Manufacturers' Association, for a time headed by Vaidya and a supporter of the

FFE, was also a possible source of financial support, through its constituent units.

Combined, these factors—Rajaji's leadership, exploitable issues, and the possibility of funds—provided the basis for very cautious optimism, which one more traditionally minded Indian tried to reinforce by gratuitously providing a very favourable horoscope for the new party.[49] The prospects were far from bright—everyone knew that—but to many, particularly those getting on in years, it seemed a matter of 'now or never' and the decision to proceed was taken.

For the most part, there were no illusions concerning the problems confronting the new party. This was again particularly true among the older men, many of whom linked their own limited days with the fate of India and who took up the challenge more with an attitude of resignation in a 'last-gasp' effort than with confidence in a successful outcome. Rajaji reflected this, for while he was convinced that the need for a cohesive opposition was clear, he was far less sanguine when it came to the prospects of creating one:

> Although there is today abundant material for a powerful opposition, hypnotic fear and the pressure of individual interests operate to prevent the gathering together of the forces...Unless the conservatives realize their duty, throw off their dejection, overcome their fears and unite to build a worthy opposition, parliamentary democracy in India has a dismal future.[50]

Masani, upon whom time weighs less heavily, echoed the same sentiments in less despairing terms:

> The Swatantra Party can succeed in giving effective opposition to the State Capitalist policies of the present government and in providing the country with an alternative government only if it can mobilize a broad based coalition [of peasantry and professional men, especially]. The middle classes of the cities and towns must join hands with the peasants in the villages in defence of their rights and property. If they do not hang together, they will assuredly hang separately.[51]

It is pertinent to point out not only that these observations were entirely correct, but also that Rajaji, here and elsewhere, explicitly referred to the need for a conservative or rightist party, and that Masani, here and elsewhere, explicitly referred to the propertied, middle-class basis which he envisaged for the Swatantra Party. Was such a party likely to be progressive and a defender of the interests of the non-propertied common man? That, and a good deal more, remained to be seen.

There were doubts, too, concerning the leadership. Rajaji, for all his undeniable stature and intellect, was not a mesmerizing public figure by any means, and Palmer's claim that he was 'the only living Indian who has the kind of appeal to the Indian masses—combining personal magnetism with a messianic quality—that Gandhi had'[52] is unsupportable. More apt is the view that he 'always seemed unable to sense, still less anticipate, the sentiment and mood of the people...[and] was never able to capture the imagination of the Indian masses'.[53] Here was a figure, then, who was more respected than loved, a man who would get a respectful hearing but would arouse few passions. Even with these limitations, however, Rajaji provided Swatantra with a figurehead, at least, who was undeniably superior to those whom the other rightist parties could offer.

Beyond the problem of Rajaji personally was that of the 'founding fathers' as a whole. Among the founders were such people as Jinraj Hegde of the AIAF, a landowner and advocate of the Mysore High Court, and the late V. P. Menon, the venerable and desperately ailing assistant to Patel in the integration of the princely states—and these two men were nominated as the 'Joint Secretaries' of the party at the Madras meeting. All told, the slate of officers nominated did not inspire abundant confidence or enthusiasm among many prospective supporters, or, indeed, among some of the founders themselves. Notwithstanding the presence of some prominent, anti-collectivist Gujaratis and a scattering of people from other northern states, the thirty-odd men who assembled in Madras were heavily drawn from the south of the Vindhyas, and certain early, if tentative decisions reflected this. The headquarters of the party were to be in Bangalore, and the President (Ranga), the Joint Secretaries (Menon and Hegde), and the Treasurer (B. V. Narayana Reddy), were all from the south as, of course, was Rajaji himself.[54]

One prominent party man explicitly charged that this group was too much 'a southern Brahmin clique'; and another referred to it as a group of 'old fogies' who were 'out of touch with politics'.[55] Masani was prevented from reaching the Madras meeting for its opening session and arrived to find a slate of officers and a general atmosphere very far from his liking. It was no surprise, then, that Masani was anxious to 'politicize' the leadership and to give it wider geographical scope. It was also no surprise that, within a short time, Masani himself became General-Secretary, that party headquarters were moved to Bombay, and that the 'preparatory convention' of the party was scheduled first for Ahmedabad and then moved to Bombay. (This also suggests the importance of the FFE's role in the party.) That even Rajaji and Ranga were themselves concerned is suggested by the serious effort that was made to have Jayaprakash Narayan (who had attended the Madras meeting at Rajaji's invitation) assume the leadership of the party.[56] Masani himself stated publicly that this effort to recruit Narayan was made—but failed.[57] It remained to be seen whether the 'founding fathers' would prove sufficiently attractive in the political marketplace to contribute substantially to the party's organizational and electoral efforts.

There was also considerable anxiety concerning finances, because, with ample justice, many feared that big business would not dare to offend the Congress by making substantial contributions to Swatantra. This problem and the association of Swatantra with the FFE led most party leaders to comment on the financial prospects. Thus, Masani took pains to explain his view, and there can be no doubt that he was very serious in making the following statement:

> It has been suggested that the Swatantra Party is depending on large funds from Big Business. Not only our opponents but many of our supporters are under that wrong impression...At a meeting in Bangalore on May 29, with Rajaji in the chair and even before this Party was formed, I had said that it would be futile for us to wait for Big Business to make up its mind to give us support...The reason for this state of affairs is not far to seek. It lies in a controlled economy...At this point, may I be permitted, without hurting the susceptibilities of my business friends, to say that the lack of imagination and vision, the supine attitude to government and the pathetic desire to clutch at any straw that may come their way in the shape of soft words thrown at them occasionally by government spokesmen, displayed by certain sections of Business are not qualities that are calculated to help them fill the important role they have in the country's economic life.[58]

As we shall see below, not only was Masani serious, but with respect to the response of Indian big business, he was also entirely correct.

Little concern was expressed at this stage about the ability of the party to mobilize mass support on the basis of the anti-statist programme which the founding fathers envisaged, but the problems were clear enough. To communicate this message as the common bond among the more conservative opponents of the Congress would clearly have required a substantial re-orientation of Indian political thinking. Among other things, it would have required a subordination of religious, linguistic, and caste differences, and a transcendance of many historic animosities, in the interests of a common stance concerning political economy. There were no illusions concerning the ease with which this could be accomplished. The opportunity and the difficulty here were both suggested by Masani, who wrote that 'the Nagpur resolution is both a challenge and an opportunity. *If properly explained*, it brings to the landed peasants in the villages, who constitute 53·7 per cent of our greater population, and to the middle classes in the city an awareness of their common interests and their common peril.'[59] Furthermore, the successful communication of this message did not depend on Swatantra alone. It depended as much, if not more, on the 'co-operation' of the Congress, in the sense that a broadening and deepening of controls, heavier taxation, and the like, would be necessary to help Swatantra establish the credibility of its claims about statism. Yet the Congress record has consistently been more moderate and more conciliatory than would have seemed necessary for Swatantra's good. Thus, on the Nagpur Resolution in particular, Nehru was very insistent that coercion would never be used to impose 'joint co-operative farming', and Shastri made some very conciliatory remarks about the fate of private enterprise, which had been sharply castigated in a report of the All-Indian Congress Committee (AICC) Planning Seminar at Ootacamund some months before.[60] A number of journalists and political figures aptly pointed out that in the months after the creation of Swatantra, the Congress, both in word and deed, sought to pacify some of the key groups to whom the new party had to pitch its appeal. Finally, as suggested by the fact that the FFE quite explicitly aimed its appeal at the educated classes, Masani-style arguments about political economy were not likely to find much resonance among the masses, without ample help from the Congress.

Thus, the prevailing conditions posed some very critical

problems in terms of Swatantra's ability to 'make a go of it', with respect to leadership, finances, and doctrine. At best, very cautious optimism was possible. But prospects were not hopeless, and many would in any event have persisted on the grounds that it was 'now or never'.

The weeks between the Madras meeting and the 'preparatory convention' held in Bombay, 1 and 2 August, were hectic ones for some of the leaders.[61] There was the by no means trivial discussion of the name of the new party (the selection of which will be discussed subsequently), but more important was the effort to line up potential recruits; and Ranga himself cited Paliwal's Gram Raj Party (UP), the Janata Party (Bihar), Nagoke's Dehati Janata Party (Punjab), the Democratic Party (Andhra), the Krishikar Lok Paksh (Gujarat) and the Peasants and Workers Party (Bombay) as existing or incipient groups which were possibly vulnerable to a merger appeal.[62] Ranga and many other Swatantra recruits travelled widely to agitate against the Nagpur proposals and to gauge more effectively the potential support for the party, both from existing groups and from the unorganized.

This in turn raised a question about the basic structure of the new party. Would it seek to establish its own identity and its own programme throughout India, as Masani favoured (a 'unitary' party), or would Swatantra exist only at the level of the national Parliament, as a 'holding company', allowing local parties already in existence to maintain their own local interests and their own electoral symbols, as Paliwal and others favoured (a 'federal' party)?[63] The important and persistently vexing issue of party structure and centre-state relations was thus broached at the outset.

Finally, there were pre-visions of other important developments which would play a major part in the life of the party. There were savage attacks on the fledgling party by Nehru and other leading Congressmen (as well as by the CPI, of course), which put Swatantra very quickly on the defensive in many respects. In particular, the charge that it was a 'rich man's party', a 'projection' of the FFE, and otherwise associated with 'reactionary' and 'selfish' vested interests, gave the party a negative image in many quarters, an image against which it has had continually to struggle.[64] In addition, there was a very early suggestion of a Swatantra-Jan

Sangh merger, which raised the general question of the new party's relations with the more important, existing opposition groups.[65] Just having been born, Swatantra was obliged to learn to stand on its feet and to defend itself in a hostile environment. All of the problems notwithstanding, by the time of the preparatory convention, some leaders of existing parties had already decided to cast their lot with Swatantra and many locally influential people from all parts of India had evinced more than passing interes tin the new party. A party had been born; but it was at Bombay that it suggested a capacity to survive.[66]

CHAPTER 5

THE SWATANTRA 'INNER CIRCLE'

INTRODUCTION

During the years covered by this study of Swatantra (1959–66), the 'inner circle' of the party's national élite has consisted of Rajaji, Ranga, Munshi, and Masani, with Sir Homy P. Mody as a much less visible and less active colleague. Around these men a variety of personalities and purposes have clustered, ebbing and flowing, and they would seem to constitute the 'experienced and responsible politicians' whose emergence as the nucleus of a conservative party was predicted much earlier. By any reasonable standards, the careers of these five men are exceptionally distinguished.

Rajaji, the founder-leader, was one of the towering figures of the Nationalist movement, Premier and Chief Minister of Madras, Home Minister in the central government, Governor of West Bengal, and the only Indian Governor-General of India. Ranga, the President, was educated at Oxford, has been an economics professor, and was a stalwart in the Andhra Congress, a founder of the *kisan sabha* movement, a leader of many agriculturalists' organizations, and a frequent delegate to international conferences concerning agriculture. Munshi, the senior Vice-President, was also a veteran Congressman who was Home Minister of Bombay, Agriculture Minister in the central government, Governor of UP, and a principal architect of India's constitution; and he is well known also for his distinguished legal, literary, and educational-cultural work. Masani, the General-Secretary, was educated in Bombay and London (London School of Economics), was called to the bar at Lincoln's Inn, has been a lawyer, economist and management consultant. He was also a veteran Congressman, a founder of the Congress Socialist Party (CSP), Mayor of Bombay, Ambassador to Brazil, and Chairman of the UN Subcommittee for Prevention of Discrimination and Protection of Minorities. Mody, party Treasurer, is one of India's pre-eminent businessmen-financiers, was a member of the Viceroy's Council (1931–43), a representative of Indian business at the Round Table Conferences, and Governor of UP. This truncated list of the accomplishments of the inner circle suffices to show why the party's leadership 'was too distinguished or too popular to be ignored', and it does no violence to their stature to insist that they were and are far more 'distinguished' than 'popular'.[1]

Beyond this it would seem difficult to generalize about the inner circle, save to say that they are all 'comparatively older men' who are united in their opposition to communism and to what they regard as the increasingly 'statist' policies of the Congress, especially under Nehru.[2] Certain differences among them are obvious from even a superficial familiarity with the men and their backgrounds. Masani and Mody are Parsis, the other three are Hindus. Of the three Hindus, two (Rajaji and Munshi) are Brahmins, while Ranga is a 'clean' *sudra* (a Kamma). Masani and Mody are very highly westernized and very much oriented toward the modern business-industrial world, while the others are, in varying ways, more in tune with non-industrial India. To complicate matters even further, Ranga and Masani were radical relative to the main thrust of the Congress in the 1930s, while the others were, in varying ways, relatively conservative. The diversity is so apparent that it has elicited the oft-heard, derisive comment that the party is a 'melange' or a 'medley' of fundamentally uncongenial bedfellows—which is particularly strange when coming from a Congressman.[3] But the question remains: what forces are represented and on what basis have they come together? Surely there were disparate elements involved in the rebellion of 1857, just as there were disparate elements in the nationalist movement, but it makes a great deal of difference to specify just who was represented and on what basis. By the same token, we must ask if the key Swatantra leaders simply represent old interests in unmodified form, jostling uncomfortably cheek-by-jowl, or do they in combination, if not individually, represent a new direction in Indian political life? Put another way, is Swatantra simply the Jan Sangh or the RRP or some other force in disguise, or all of them lumped together, or something new?

From this standpoint, we can in fact say a good bit more than the assertion that Swatantra's leadership is a medley of older men united in their opposition to communism, although this is in itself important. We can say that within the inner circle there are representatives of at least three major strands of thought: the idealized village, militant Hinduism, and modern industrial capitalism. But

6-2

we can say still more. Historically, none of the Swatantra inner circle has displayed any appreciable affinity for aristocratic conservatism, and while the other three strands of thought are represented, the leadership, collectively, has a centre of gravity which lies outside of the pale of the 'messiahs of backwardness' and of the militant Hindus. The Swatantra inner circle is, in this very broad sense, more moderate than one had previously found in most parties of the right. Whether this moderation, as we shall define it further, conforms to India's needs, and whether the conditions are at all favourable to such an approach, are different questions for which answers will also be suggested in due course.

THE INNER CIRCLE AND THE ARISTOCRATS

Apart from the obvious fact that none of the key national leaders was himself a member of the 'feudal' élites, it is also true that none had any particular commitment to the historical position of these classes and the views they expressed. This was in part due to the nature of pre-independence politics, i.e. the association of the princes and the landlords with the British and their combined resistance to the aspirations of even moderate nationalists. But it flowed also from an awareness that it would be sheer folly to retain the princely states and unthinkable to retain the landed aristocracy.

The animosity of Masani and Ranga toward these classes flowed from their leftist posture in the 1930s, i.e. their affiliation with the CSP and the *kisan sabha* movement, respectively. The CSP, of which Masani was a founder-leader (1934), was not homogeneous in its 'socialist' outlook, and Masani was a representative of the social democratic or Fabian strand of thought.[4] Yet the group as a whole and Masani personally were extremely hostile to the aristocratic classes. The CSP programme of 1934 urged 'elimination of Princes and Landlords and all other classes of exploiters, without compensation', and Masani, in 1938, deplored the fact that in recent Congress declarations 'the people of the Indian States, who form a fourth of the nation, are told to fight on their own and to expect no direct aid from the people of British India'.[5] Even after he turned his back on socialism and embraced a variant of 'Gandhism', Masani, a highly anglicized Parsi from a wealthy urban family, remained hostile to the basic perspectives of the

Hindu traditionalists, whether aristocratic or non-aristocratic.[6] By and large, it is fair to say that 'no figure in Indian political life could be more unambiguously modernist than ...Minoo Masani'.[7]

Ranga, as a *sudra* by caste background and as one of India's pre-eminent peasant leaders, was similarly extremely hostile toward the aristocracy, as well as toward the Brahmin priesthood, whose world-view relegated his caste to a position slightly above perdition. In addition—and here he differed sharply from Masani—he was fundamentally anti-industrial in outlook. Both then and now, Ranga is first and foremost a peasant 'populist', and his conception of what is good for an independent peasantry has been the pole-star in his ideological life. Both the anti-aristocratic and the anti-industrial themes are present in his assertion that 'influenced so powerfully as I had been by the inspiring Russian achievements and Leninist destruction of the monopoly of power held by the traditional, feudal, princely, commercial and industrial classes, and even the priestly and intellectual orders of society', he found it inevitable that he seek to lead India's peasant masses against these same forces.[8] Similarly, he frequently spoke at length of the need 'to set right the present inequalities of wealth and income, and consequent achievement of social and cultural opportunities as between the agricultural and non-agricultural peoples, as between the toilers as a whole and the capitalist-cum-feudal-cum-priestly orders and to save the State from the exploiting classes...'.[9] Throughout the 1920s and 1930s he was critical of Gandhi and other leading Congressmen for their seeming tenderness toward the landlord class, and he claimed, for example, that the 'agitation led by the Mahatma in Champaran did not lead up to any fight against the main causes for the terrible poverty and sufferings of Champaran peasants...It does strike us rather significant that both he (Gandhi) and Rajen Prasad should have remained scrupulously silent upon the ravages of the *zamindari* system...'[10] Emphasizing always the needs and 'revolutionary' aspirations of the world's peasants, Ranga, displaying 'an element of the proselytizing missionary in his restless political crusading',[11] articulated a 'peasant socialist' theory which boiled down 'in concrete terms to a defense of peasant proprietorship as opposed to land nationalization'—and, it is important to add, to 'feudal' landlordism.[12] Whatever the precise quality of his 'socialism' may be, there can be no doubt about his historical antipathy to India's aristocratic and priestly classes and to the world-view which they advanced to justify their superior positions.[13]

Munshi and Rajaji were far from implacably hostile to the princely order,[14] yet both favoured Patel's approach to the princely states. Munshi, from his rather militant, nationalist perspective, was happy to call Patel the 'Bismarck of India',[15] while the more restrained Rajaji announced that 'history has taken a course which we cannot alter now...we need a new form of government ...we have to integrate India into one'.[16] He added that while the rulers might serve a useful, if largely symbolic and ornamental function as governors of states, for example, this 'does not mean you should have 560 Princes to confuse matters'.[17] Finally, Rajaji urged the princes, many of whom had viciously condemned the Congress, to contribute to the success of the new government, for 'if the Princes love the people, they should love the Ministers whom the people have elected...'.[18]

The same broad considerations apply as well to the great landed intermediaries, the *zamindars* and *jagirdars*. Masani and Ranga, during the 1920s and beyond, adhered to the view that these were exploiting classes which had to be eliminated. Rajaji and Munshi were again less hostile, but they, like so many non-radical Congressmen, found the position of the intermediaries indefensible, because of the extreme misery of the tiller of the soil and the social instability which this could carry in its wake. Even so conservative a person as Sampurnanand (now—1966—Governor of Rajasthan) could not confront the situation in rural India with anything but horror:

> The whole picture is heart-rending...Everywhere it was the same monstrous tale of heavy rents, illegal demands, arrears, ejectments, debts of *mahajans*, sale of belongings and trees, semi-starvation, and semi-nudity, beatings and tortures by *zamindars* and their employees to compel payments of legal and illegal demands, and bleak outlook for the future...The Kisan passes his life in an atmosphere of perennial terrorization.[19]

Rajaji and Munshi both realized that an improvement in the position of the tenant was mandatory, for humane reasons and to forestall more radical solutions to the problem; and Rajaji supported the famous 'Karachi Resolution' on abolition of the *zamindari* system. Furthermore, when Premier of Madras (1937–9) he proposed some fairly drastic (by prevailing standards) land reform legislation, even though it never approached expropriation of landlords; and when he returned as Chief Minister after the first general elections, he saw to the passage of legislation which provided greater security of tenure and a larger share of produce for tenants.[20]

With respect to both the princes and the landed aristocrats, Mody was generally restrained. None the less, as a leading spokesman for Indian business, Mody also came to be critical of the aristocracy, which, by and large, served to retard constitutional and economic progress of the type he desired.[21] Showing no particular animus beyond this, Mody still shared with Masani the outlook of a highly westernized Parsi, fundamentally at odds with the traditional, aristocratic world-view; and he would have to be classified as a non-aristocratic moderate in this context. Whatever the present attitude in the inner circle may be toward the princes and landlords, it should be clear that historically Swatantra's leaders favoured *as a minimum* Patel's approach to these classes.[22]

RAJAJI AND INDIAN CONSERVATISM

If the Swatantra inner circle neither individually nor collectively was inclined to defend aristocratic conservatism, the same cannot be said for the other strands of thought outlined above. In particular, Rajaji's views are crucial here, not only because he is Swatantra's stellar attraction, but also because he is a determined exponent of a refined, 'high culture' version of the idealized village model. Inasmuch as this strand of thought is one of the most appealing in recent Indian intellectual history, because of its association with 'Gandhism', its exposition by Rajaji requires the closest attention.[23]

Rajaji's general approach is suggested by Sheean's observation that the Swatantra founder-leader shows a 'yearning for a homespun and disarmed society, a sort of Gandhian abstraction', but we need not and cannot rest content with such an imprecise characterization.[24] Rajaji himself has provided ample documentation for such a conclusion about his views, by endorsing Gandhi's belief that 'civilization consists not in multiplication of wants but in the deliberate and voluntary restriction of wants'. And similarly he has endorsed the contention that 'high thinking is inconsistent with a complicated material life, based on high speed imposed on us by mammon worship'.[25] This commitment need not, however, involve a defence of the traditional, village-based order, although it is quite compatible with it. To understand the full range of Rajaji's thought, it is necessary to go beyond this basic posture.

A second basic point, which might seem at first glance to conflict with the first, is reflected in Rajaji's assertion that he, like Gandhi (in his view), believes that 'machinery has its place, it has come to stay'.[26] So too he insists that he, like Gandhi, is 'an enemy of the machine when the machine became the master and man became its slave'.[27] While thus trying to separate himself from those who oppose machinery as such, it is also clear that 'slavery' is considered to be inherent to some extent in all large-scale enterprise in heavily urban-industrial settings. The latter feeling pulls Rajaji back toward the village and more modest technology.

Equally important to understand is Rajaji's approach to the manner in which, and the scale on which, machinery should be introduced, and, more generally, to the way in which economic change should be undertaken. Briefly, he insists that economic change minimize the 'dehumanizing' aspects of modern industry, that it minimize dislocations attendant upon its introduction, and that it keep technology as close to 'human scale' as possible. This is clear from cases which Rajaji himself has raised to illustrate his views. What, he once asked, if the only son of a village potter decided to seek alternative employment (not necessarily in modern industry) outside the village? The local producer would no longer be there to meet traditional needs in the traditional, predictable manner; the villagers would, he said, be unable to afford machine-made substitutes; and, as a consequence, the level of living of the common man in the village would actually decline as a result of economic change.[28] Obviously, insistence that all such dislocations be minimized implies a rather strict adherence to the hereditary, caste-based division of labour, with its hierarchical implications. Rajaji thus defends the *ancien régime* indirectly, on grounds other than strictly traditional ones.

The second case illustrates equally critical dimensions of Rajaji's conservatism and shows the vehemence with which he can respond to the 'improper' introduction of modern technology. Speaking of the position of the handloom weavers during a particularly acute 'time of troubles', Rajaji asserted that they 'have fought bravely against foreign mill manufacture and next, against Indian mill manufacture', and he insisted that 'we cannot allow the capitalist mill industry to create unemployment on a monstrous scale...No sacrifice is too heavy, no measures are too harsh, if we find that by such measures we can avert the disaster that is slowly but surely advancing towards us.'[29] In this case, unlike the first, the obvious implication is that the villager could more easily afford machine-made goods, but that the economic change must be resisted because of the involuntary and sudden displacement of a certain class of producers, without alternative employment. Thus, whether the producer deserts his post voluntarily and causes dislocations in the village through non-availability of goods or services, or whether he is involuntarily displaced, causing dislocations of a different type, is really immaterial: all dislocations should be minimized. It is immediately obvious that only the most gradual economic change is compatible with such an approach, which justifies the charge that there are very formidable elements or 'disguised conservatism' embedded in Rajaji's views. It becomes somewhat less hidden when we note that Rajaji has explicitly endorsed the 'trade-school' function of caste in the absence of alternative facilities and that his educational plans for Madras included training in one's hereditary caste occupation, as an important component.[30]

Ranga, from his perspective as a peasant populist, shares this anti-industrial and to a lesser extent the gradualist bias, as is clear from his condemnation of the Congress, because

> they wish to draw millions of our artisans into the embraces of the small factories tied up however loosely to the growing large-scale money economy as is evident by their plans to replace the whole of the handloom weavers...by the introduction...of power looms through the sugar-coated weavers' power loom co-operatives. They also want to replace crores of small shopkeepers and their family economy of trading by introducing state-controlled, regulated or owned grain shops...[31]

In this case, we are moving toward the conclusion that no matter how gradual or how close to 'human scale' technological change may be, it is undesirable, and Rajaji is by no means unsympathetic to the idea.[32] There are some differences, to be sure, because Rajaji adopts a more philosophical approach to this issue, by contrast with Ranga who is something of a fanatical populist. A key point, however, is that such positions lay the basis for conflict with those who are more urban-industrial in orientation, both inside and outside the party.

While Ranga by and large rests content with this, Rajaji goes well beyond it, and a further examination of his views leads toward the heart of his conservatism and into an area where he and Munshi join hands. The key point is this: overarching all other views and preoccupations is one which transcends dislocations and types of technology and levels of living. This is brought out in Rajaji's assertion that

> planned economy and cooperative life in place of the competitive and selfish motive [associated with *laissez faire* capitalism], is modern economy. This cannot be effectively achieved if it depends on mere authority, however powerful. We must have a generally accepted culture which works as a law from within, to assist the law imposed from without. Unless we have the help of culture, mere material planning culminates in fraud and corruption.[33]

Embellishing this same theme, Rajaji asserted that

> properly designed and *placed on a spiritual basis*, a regulated economy need not be inconsistent with individual satisfaction and individual zeal. The restraints and habits of mind that are required to be developed for altruistic action must flow from faith and inner conviction.[34]

If 'culture' restrained people, virtually any type of technology and any level of living would seem to be acceptable—even though this seems to contradict the view that 'high thinking is inconsistent with complicated material life...'. If 'culture' prevailed, due respect would be shown by all economic actors for the interests of others: the village potter would not desert his job, the capitalist would not be a robber-baron and would not exploit his workers, economic planners would not pursue policies which generate severe dislocations, nor, in a more general sense, would 'social engineers' attempt to reconstruct the lives of the people. This is the 'responsible individualism' which Rajaji understands by the notion of 'trusteeship', and in this version, Rajaji's doctrine falls on responsive ears in India.[35] But it is clear that too many people, and especially the incumbent government, are not disciplined by culture and by spiritual principles. Here, Rajaji is in complete agreement with Munshi, who once wrote of the 'complete identity' which existed between the Gandhian leaders and the masses, as opposed to the westernized leadership which 'has not learnt to reflect the mind of the masses. It does not know the idiom of their life. It is too deeply engrossed in leading, directing and organizing them from a higher pedestal.'[36] Both Rajaji and Munshi agree that only through a restoration of 'culture' and 'spirituality' can India progress and be true to her own destiny, and both place a great deal of emphasis on trusteeship in this connection.[37]

If we now ask how 'culture' and 'spirituality' can be secured, we get close to bed-rock. In part, as we have already seen, it depends (more for Rajaji than for Munshi), on very modest material commitments and interests, although Rajaji is not free from apparent contradictions on this point. But, apart from this, it depends on other circumstances as well. Defining 'culture' as 'essentially the prevailing pattern of joyous restraint accepted by the people',[38] Rajaji links it to the maintenance of *dharma*, or moral duty, which is 'an organic growth which it is our duty to respect and which we should not treat as mere Indian superstition or eccentricity'.[39] This, in turn, depends on the maintenance of religious values in a *high culture* sense, as Rajaji conceives them, as he made explicit in his contention that 'if there is any honesty in India today, any hospitality, any chastity, any philanthropy, any tenderness to dumb creatures, any aversion to evil, any love to do good, it is due to whatever remains of the old culture'.[40] And, to put it briefly, he said that 'if our four-hundred millions strike out religion from their lives, India will be wiped out'.[41]

To maintain *dharma* and 'joyous restraint' it is necessary, according to Rajaji, to sustain those institutions which have inculcated them over the centuries in India, and here we do arrive at bed-rock. For on this score, Rajaji asserts that the joint family is an 'institution which gives a distinctive feature to life in India', and that it is the *jati* which is 'the most important element in the organization of our society'.[42] Over the years, Rajaji has bemoaned the fact that these were weakened by 'the cult of individuality' which came to India through 'the impact of the West'.[43] Noting that these institutions had been weakened but not totally undermined 'by the impact of Western individualism and *perverted movements of social reform*', Rajaji has expressed the hope that 'perhaps we may yet see the light and revise our opinions and revive and strengthen these so-called reactionary virtues of helping people around us and acquiring merit in the eyes of the Gods and saving the welfare state a lot of trouble'.[44] Thus, rather than being viewed as coercive *vis-à-vis* the individual and parochial *vis-à-vis* society as a whole, the great pillars of Indian society (joint family, *jati*, and village) are seen as beneficent institutions which serve a number of critical social purposes. They develop the sense of 'culture', force attention to larger social groupings than does western individualism, and they are, moreover, structures of 'decentralized socialism', which have long insulated the Indian (or at least the Hindu) against the ravages of his natural and man-made environments.[45]

It is here that the Congress has committed its greatest sin:

> The loosening of the religious impulse is the worst of the dis-services rendered by the Congress to the nation. We must organize a new force and movement to replace the greed and the class hatred of Congress materialism with a renovated spiritual outlook emphasizing the restraints of good conduct as of greater importance than the triumphs of organized covetousness. Every effort should be made to foster and maintain spiritual values and preserve what is good in our national culture and tradition and avoid dominance of a purely material philosophy of life which thinks only in terms of the standard of life without any reference to its content or quality.[46]

The need, then, is for a strong party which will first check the Congress and then re-emphasize the values and institutions which are quintessentially Indian. Should such a reversal be effected, viz. from the government's 'atheistic' policy to one which is 'secular' but supports all religions equally,[47] benefits would be evident in all areas of Indian life. The quality of government would be enhanced, because religion would serve as a 'force counteracting the baser pulls of politics'; the 'modern economy' would develop properly; and even the 'poorest he' in India would derive great benefits, because the all-pervading sense of spirituality has meant that 'beggars are honoured in spite of their obviously unsatisfactory way of life' and 'the poor man commands not only respect but a religious status by reason of his poverty'.[48] And if this can be said of the beggar and the pauper, can the rest of the society be so bad?

Taken together, the emphasis on restriction of wants, on minimizing dislocations, on the need to sustain 'culture' through the family and the *jati*, and the like, would go far toward maintaining the *status quo* in India. In this sense, Rajaji is fundamentally a conservative, which he himself freely admits, without invoking traditionalist dogmas of the type found in RRP pronouncements, and Rajaji draws close to the 'messiahs of backwardness' in some respects.[49] It may be a consolation that Rajaji eschews traditional justifications for supporting many traditional institutions, practices and values, but it is, to this author, a small one.

But even more than this remains to be said, and some of the pertinent points have already been touched upon. As we have seen, Rajaji favoured the integration of the princely states and limited action against the interests of the landlord class. During his term as Premier of Madras he favoured a permissive bill, on the principle of local option, to permit temple entry by *harijans*. He helped to pass a bill to prohibit the exclusion of *harijans* from all facilities built with or maintained by state funds. He has spoken in favour of, although he would never dream of compelling, inter-caste marriage, and he permitted it in the case of his own children. He has told the practitioners of traditional forms of medicine that 'vested interests should never be allowed to mar the progress of science'. He reprimanded Indian businessmen for preferring in some ways the 'placid pool' of the British *raj* to the 'swift river' of independence politics, He is, moreover, well aware that many Congress reforms are irrevocable and that many processes of change have been set in motion which can be moderated but not arrested. In particular, he has come recently to insist that it is too late to go back to a village economy and he has emphasized instead the decentralization of more modern industry. And it is worth recalling that he defended his call for a 'party on the right' by saying that dislocations, etc., 'are not less real or important than the need for change and progress', which not only makes clear his conservatism but also indicates that he considers himself very much a Burkean in this respect.[50] Some of these matters may be largely symbolic gestures of little practical significance, viz. temple entry through 'local option', but there are some people for whom even these symbolic departures from the *status quo* are anathema, and it is well to remember that Rajaji is not among them. On other points, the departures from orthodoxy and tradition are significant and they serve to pull Rajaji back from the RRP and its spiritual kinfolk.

Furthermore, from his high culture perspective, Rajaji is fully confident that Hinduism is compatible with very substantial progress. He insists that 'the fathers of Hindu religious thought approached their subject in a scientific spirit. They treated religion as a whole as a search for truth and not as a matter of dogma.'[51] Vedantic thought, which he has termed 'the root of Indian culture', is 'fully consistent with the awe-inspiring and beautiful universe as it is unfolded by science', while 'the way of life preached in the Gita is fully consistent with progressive views of citizenship'.[52] Thus, provided Hinduism is properly understood, it is no bar to 'modernization'. But there is a problem here which obliges us to approach Rajaji's formulations with some caution. In addition to the refined Hinduism of the Brahmin intellectual and of the high culture, there is also the popular Hinduism of the masses, which is more bound up with dogma, social orthodoxy, and, especially, the full panoply of considerations related to the hereditary caste system. To emphasize its flexibility may liberate the intellectual, but this will escape the common man, whose connection with Hinduism is scarcely liberating. Put another way, in his analysis Rajaji uses the term *dharma* in a rather abstract fashion, but more relevant in popular Hinduism is the more 'earthly' notion of *varnashramadharma*, or the moral duty of a man in terms of his social status (*varna*) and his stage of life (*ashrama*). The former usage may be flexible, the latter is not, and in this sense, too, there is an element of 'disguised conservatism' which intrudes into Rajaji's approach.

Rajaji himself is by no means oblivious to these criticisms. He quoted Nehru's view that much that was deplorable in India flowed from the 'old culture' and he quoted Nehru's contention that 'I do not see how by means of that traditional system you can ever get rid of the problem of poverty'.[53] He has also admitted that 'the tyranny of the community may by some be considered worse than that imposed by any form of state control'.[54] It is clear, however, where Rajaji's sympathies lie.

There are still some critical, concluding points to be made about Rajaji. First, in his more recent statements, Rajaji has emphasized the need to increase industrial output, when applying the doctrine of trusteeship to the modern sector. Thus, he has backed away somewhat from a general emphasis on voluntary restriction of wants. Secondly, as we have already seen, he has proved to be enough of a realist to acknowledge that it is impossible to go back to the village and that it is impossible to prevent the spread of modern industry. Thus, he has come to stress the decentralization of modern industry, favouring smaller-scale projects and favouring the distribution of all industry, large or small, over as wide an area as possible, to minimize dislocations and to avoid a mad rush to overcrowded and otherwise undesirable urban areas.[55] Thirdly, the struggle against 'statism', Rajaji's present preoccupation, has allowed him to supplement his more traditional formulations with more liberal ones, because 'statism' is worse than either and menaces both. Thus, while generally stressing self-restraint and insisting that it is necessary to curb 'the free play of individual ambitions',[56] he can also argue, in the present context, that 'the individual is the only reality. The State is a non-living entity. The Leviathan has no soul. If the individual is wiped out we reduce the nation to a soul-less existence.'[57] This, however, still allows the individual and his soul to be defined by the family and the *jati*, and hence it is more important to stress his view that 'to let every person act creatively *as he chooses*, looks no doubt reactionary and chaotic; notwithstanding this, it is the best means of making people work'.[58] Although his primary emphasis has long been anti-individualistic and conservative, Rajaji here advances arguments which are more classical liberal in flavour. He has, in short, supplemented his conservatism with a modicum of liberal individualism. Even individualism, it appears, does not look so bad when juxtaposed to the spectre of statism which haunts Rajaji.[59] In these important respects, Rajaji has been groping toward a more resilient position which combines his older Burkean conservatism with a more recent infusion of liberalism. It is probably too much to say that Rajaji is 'an ingenious and perfect combination' of traditional and modern conservatism,[60] but it is clear that he does not feel able to turn his back on the twentieth century. To put the matter somewhat differently, if Rajaji were made dictator of India, he would doubtless act along strongly (non-aristocratic) conservative lines, but in the present, competitive political context he has become more flexible in outlook and less close to a full-blown conservative position.

MUNSHI AND MILITANT NATIONALISM

Munshi, while a close personal friend and associate of Rajaji and while sharing his determination to sustain the spirit of Indian (more specifically Hindu) culture, displays a markedly more militant approach to public affairs. Both historically and currently, Munshi has been acutely sensitive to problems of national unity and cohesion, which have had a decisive impact on his views of religion, language, caste, political organization, and the like.

A useful starting-point, because it illustrates differences between Munshi and Rajaji, is the matter of partition and the more general problem of religious and other minorities in the subcontinent. Here we see that Munshi withdrew from the Congress during the Second World War so that he might carry on the fight against the Pakistan demand, which Rajaji, almost alone among top Congress leaders at this stage, wanted to accept in principle so that a wartime 'national' government could perhaps be formed. In a kindred vein, Munshi emphasized his concern for national unity and strength after it became clear that Pakistan would become a reality, by stating to the Constituent Assembly:

> I feel, thank God, that we have got out of this bag at last. We have no sections and no groups to go into, no elaborate procedure as was envisaged, no double-majority, no more provinces with residuary powers, no opting out, no revision after ten years, and no longer only four categories of powers for the Centre. We feel free to form a federation of our own choice...We have now a homogeneous country.[61]

Munshi was determined to establish a very strong central government in India, and to this end he reminded the members of the Constituent Assembly that India's most 'glorious days' were those spent under 'a strong central authority' and 'the most tragic days were when the central authority...was dismembered by the provinces trying to resist it'.[62] Virtually every one of Munshi's key positions is embedded in these remarks.

Munshi to this day remains fearful of religious divisions in India, admitting in effect that he was premature in his view that India had become a homogeneous country upon the creation of Pakistan. Thus, he found it necessary to support a suggested ban on religious parties as electoral participants, while at the same time arguing that a complete ban on all religiously based groups would be unconstitutional:

> Religious appeals evoke the most intimate of responses. Such appeals if issued by religious parties would mean that Hindus, Muslims, Christians, and Sikhs would be pitted against one another in the elections on the basis of their religious attitudes and interests. A stage would have been

set for a religious conflict during the elections which would be transferred into the arena of legislatures. Ultimately, it would strengthen disruptive tendencies, dividing the nation into warring religious interests. We have enough danger in linguism without having to create another equally dangerous front.[63]

That a suppression of religious appeals would leave most of the trump cards in the hands of the overwhelming Hindu majority is one of the least of Munshi's worries, because he has always been far less concerned about Hindu chauvinism and communalism than about other forms of parochialism.[64] It is an awareness of this which makes Muslims, Sikhs, and other minorities very suspicious (to say the least) of Munshi, as he has made clear his hostility to them when they engage in what he regards as anti-national behaviour.[65]

The contrast between Munshi and Rajaji on this point is very sharp. Concerning the same proposed ban on communal parties, Rajaji said that the ban would be 'a foolish and unconstitutional enterprise...attacks on minorities by the majority are not only unconstitutional but mean', and he asserted that 'any grouping for protecting the interests threatened or under oppression is not communalism, but is an exercise of the right of association and must be deemed lawful'.[66] Once again, Rajaji sees virtues in family, caste, religious and other groupings, while Munshi is inclined to see only, or primarily, their vices as parochial forces.

In all areas, according to Munshi, the Congress is responsible for having injected into the younger generation 'the venom of provincialism and communalism', which, in his view, accounts for the fact that 'it is very difficult to find an Indian in India'.[67] On language more specifically, he has said that linguistic states were deplorable, because 'this aggressive group sentiment has tended to give undue prominence to one's regional languages against the paramount importance of a national medium without which national consciousness would wither away', and he has insisted that education and all public business should be kept 'from lapsing into regional media'.[68] Yet to foster linguistic unity, Munshi does not favour a rapid and perhaps forcible imposition of Hindi, as does the Jan Sangh, among other groups. In fact, Munshi was one of the authors of the fifteen-year compromise formula, whereby English would be retained from 1950 to 1965, until Hindi could be satisfactorily developed. Even now, however, Munshi is wary of the imposition of Hindi. To counter linguistic parochialism, Munshi has favoured a zonal rather than a linguistic division of India, to which Rajaji has also subscribed, and he has favoured retention of English both for official and educational purposes, with a major university in each zone to shift eventually from English to Hindi.[69] Be this as it may, Munshi has not only condemned religious and linguistic parochialism, but he has also come down hard on such would-be secessionist groups as the DMK in Madras, favouring a ban on secessionist propaganda, as most of his colleagues did not.[70]

Resembling the militant Hindu position again is Munshi's concern for unity and strength among Hindus, for example, overcoming caste parochialism. He was, for example, quite insistent that the constitution specifically allow the government to legislate in the area of social reform and to guarantee temple entry to untouchables;[71] and from his earliest days, he had some harsh words for the socially orthodox and those who cited scriptural authority in defence of the caste system. In this spirit, he abused the *sanatanist*

> whose notions of Hinduism are so wonderful that he will not and cannot be reconciled to the opening of the temples to Harijans. He believes that his Hinduism is an arrogant creed which bases its existence on the superiority of one caste over the other. His faith is in social inequality. He believes in hereditary social injustice... Sir, it is a very unfortunate mentality, though I am very glad to say that it is restricted to a very few... The social structure of Hindu India is entirely different from the spirit of Hinduism and we do hope that Hinduism will be purged of its greatest disgrace of which we really feel ashamed... We would be untrue to the Nation and the whole spirit of Hinduism if we allowed such notions of social inequality to be prepetuated in times like this.[72]

The claim that the 'spirit of Hinduism' is entirely different from the social structure of Hindu India is a familiar one among would-be reformers of Hindu society; and those who advance this view endeavour to stress a few key principles which all Hindus may embrace, and to stress the flexibility of Hinduism, as Rajaji has done.

In his effort to capture the 'spirit of Hinduism', Munshi has availed himself of both traditional and novel means. When he was Minister for Food and Agriculture, Munshi 'declared that respect for the cow was a unifying sentiment for Hindus and that there was "no higher Dharma" than her protection'.[73] But far more important than such isolated, if recurrent pronouncements of a topical sort is Munshi's role as founder-president of Bharatiya Vidya Bhavan, an organization devoted to the study and renaissance of Indian (not specifically Hindu) culture.[74] The element of renaissance is well illustrated by the organization's statement of principles:

> The ultimate aim of Bharatiya Shiksha [education] is to teach the younger generation to appreciate and live up to the permanent values of Bharatiya Vidya [knowledge] which flowing from the supreme act of creative life-energy as represented by Shri Ramachandra, Shri Krishna, Vyasa, Buddha, and Mahavira have expressed themselves in modern times in the life of Shri Ramakrishna Paramahamsa, Swami Dayanand Saraswati, and Swami Vivekananda, Shri Aurobindo and Mahatma Gandhi.[75]

It is important to emphasize that the stress is on the spirit of India, not on any particular institutional arrangements or specific customs. This is evident from the fact that the principal bearers of Hinduism in modern times who are cited are all associated with very substantial efforts at reformation and renaissance, not with maintenance of the *status quo*. But the statement of principles leaves no doubt about this:

> Bharatiya Shiksha while equipping the student with every kind of scientific and technical training must teach the student not to sacrifice an ancient form or attitude to an unreasoning passion for change; nor to retain a form or attitude which in the light of modern times can be replaced by another form or attitude which is a truer and more effective expression of the spirit of Bharatiya Vidya; and to capture the spirit afresh for each generation to present it to the world.[76]

Suffice to say, Bharatiya Vidya Bhavan and the principles for which it professes to stand remain as one of the principal institutional channels—itself an innovation in this field—for the expression of the 'spirit' of Hinduism and of India. This, coupled with Munshi's other efforts, doubtless justifies Harrison's contention that Munshi is 'the most sophisticated ideologian of Hindu revivalism',[77] and it helps to account for his popularity in Jan Sangh circles.[78]

Tempering Munshi's militancy and centralist proclivities is not so much a Gandhian influence (with which he has felt recurrently uncomfortable) as his western-oriented legal training and his outlook on political institutions more generally. Munshi declined to support the Gandhi-led Congress during the 1920s, because, in his words, 'Gandhi captured it and changed its creed and method', to an emphasis on the attainment of 'Swaraj by peaceful and legitimate means' rather than the earlier 'attainment of Dominion Status by Constitutional means'.[79] In short, Munshi gives as his own reason for leaving the Congress at this early stage in his career the abandonment of more strictly constitutionalist procedures and more limited goals. The same tendency is suggested by his association with the Swarajist forces, the group which wanted the Congress to enter the legislatures and function therein as best it could.

Munshi was also alienated from many of the so-called Gandhians in the realm of political organization. In keeping with his determination to secure a strong political system for India, he felt obliged to insist on the retention of the British political model as the base upon which India should build, with modifications drawn from the American experience in particular.[80] This brought him into sharp conflict with those who deplored the proposed retention of an alien pattern of government and who wanted to revert to something more 'Indian', specifically more 'Gandhian'. In Tinker's view, for example, there were two broad schools of thought in the Constituent Assembly: first, 'the Liberals and the Moderates, former administrators and jurists', who 'welcomed the constitution as a worthy instrument of government'; and, secondly, 'a much larger element' which 'deplored the whole constitution as a betrayal of Gandhian ideals and of the ancient spirit of India'.[81] Sampurnanand, a leading Gandhian conservative from UP, insisted that 'the attempt at centralization of all power is hardly veiled... this is bad', and he added that 'our constitution is a miserable failure. The spirit of Indian culture has not breathed on it: the Gandhism by which we swear so vehemently at home and abroad does not inspire it. It is just a piece of legislation like, say, the Motor Vehicles Act.'[82] Others argued that 'if you look into this Constitution it would be difficult to find anything Indian'; that what was wanted was 'the music of the Veena or Sitar, but here we have the music of an English band'; and that the constitution represented 'a slavish imitation—nay much more—a slavish surrender to the West'.[83] K. Hanumanthaya, a leading Mysore Congressman, insisted on great attention to grass-roots institutions as the foundation of the new constitution, and he was seconded here by two of Munshi's Swatantra colleagues, Ranga and Masani. The latter, seeking to fuse some of his earlier socialist sentiments with Gandhism, spoke of Gandhi's conception of *panchayat raj*, not because of its traditional aspect but because of its potential for 'grass roots democracy'; and Ranga insisted upon a 'co-operative commonwealth, as Bapu was good enough to call it', based similarly on grass-roots institutions.[84]

Munshi, as we have seen, also talked of the 'spirit' of India and of the need to sustain it, but he did not accept the view that this meant retention of a decentralized, village-based political system. It could be plausibly argued that no indigenous political model seemed likely to assure the unity and strength which Munshi desired; and it could also be argued that in Munshi's view, a strong state was necessary to protect the 'spirit' of India against future subjugation and erosion. Both are doubtless true, but it is also true that many of the 'messiahs of backwardness' failed to respond to either point and made a fetish out of the village, and it is not a matter of splitting hairs to point up such differences, because they illustrate important, divergent styles of thinking which must be understood for a proper appreciation of Indian political development and of Swatantra's role in it. On this point, too, Rajaji has turned his back on the village and has accepted stronger, national political institutions, at least as a matter of practical necessity.

Munshi's defence of the strong, highly centralized political system would seem entirely compatible with the views of the militant nationalists, such as those in the Jan Sangh. Here, however, there are also certain differences, at least *vis-à-vis* the prototypical Jan Sanghi. For one thing, Munshi did not favour as highly centralized a state as did many of the militant nationalists, but recommended instead a federal scheme along zonal lines. In addition, as we have already seen, he rejected the pro-Hindi fanaticism of many militants by advocating the compromise language formula.

More important yet, there has always been a very strong emphasis on legalism in his approach to politics and a great respect for constitutional niceties, neither of which bulks very large in the concerns of the RRP, the Mahasabha, or the Sangh. Munshi is aware of this legalist strain and he has quite emphatically defended it by arguing that 'the rule of the tribe of lawyers is any day better than the rule of the tribe of tyrants'.[85] Munshi tempered his own centralist bias with an emphasis on judicial review and on 'due process', which were borrowed explicitly from American constitutional experience, and he defended this in part by citing the overwhelming strength of the Congress as a principal reason for establishing a strong and independent judiciary and for demanding scrupulous attention to civil liberties.[86] Munshi's anxiety on this point well ante-dated the surge of the 'socialist pattern' of society and even ante-dated the passing of the great 'iron man', Patel. Still, it is possible to argue that Munshi could see the handwriting on the wall and favoured steps to check political power as it might be used by Nehru and the secular socialists. This clearly seems to have been the case in Munshi's more recent defence of the autonomous powers of the President of the Republic and his efforts to prevent the offices of law minister and attorney-general—an independent legal adviser to the President—from being fused.[87] This concern for constitutional issues, for whatever reason, is still of the utmost importance, because not every opponent of socialism has responded in this fashion. Munshi steadfastly talks in legalistic, constitutionalist terms, which is to be much admired in a country which is seeking to establish a constitutional democracy and the 'rule of law'.

The legalistic, constitutionalist strain is quite widespread in the Swatantra élite as a whole (and not only in the inner circle), and two party undertakings with which Munshi was intimately involved illustrate this. First, there was the 'Public Advice Committee', established by the party in December 1959, to consider 'matters relating to public policy, Fundamental Rights, corruption and favouritism of Ministers and officials, and interference by members of the ruling Party in administrative and judicial matters'.[88] Munshi was chairman of this short-lived body, whose premature demise was in part caused by difficulties with the legal profession over the question of tendering free legal advice; but the main point has nothing to do with its demise or with the fact that the body was obviously intended to embarrass the government. The main point is that Swatantra, and Munshi, sought to challenge the government *in this particular fashion*, by holding up constitutional and legal standards as the basis for judgment.

The second Swatantra body with which Munshi was connected was a Swatantra-sponsored committee of inquiry into alleged Congress repression of the Akali Sikh agitation in the Punjab. Munshi was chairman of this body, too, and was joined here by

N. C. Chatterjee (former President of the Hindu Mahasabha, and a Senior Advocate of the Supreme Court of India), Sardar Kartar Singh Campbellpuri (retired High Court judge, former PEPSU state), and C. B. Agarwalla (retired judge, Allahabad High Court, and Senior Advocate of the Supreme Court of India). Their report reveals both Munshi the militant nationalist and Munshi the legalist-constitutionalist: there was ample, careful criticism of both the agitation and the government's handling of it, but Munshi was severely criticized by many Sikhs, in whose view he went beyond the terms of the commission to attack the Punjabi *suba* demand.[89] It seems fair to conclude that while Munshi does display some unbecoming hostility toward certain minority interests, or at least a lack of sympathy for their position, he tends very markedly to stress constitutional remedies here, as part of a broader legalistic strain in his thought. If such an emphasis helps to establish constitutional morality more securely in India, it is to this extent an important 'plus' mark on Munshi's ledger, and on that of the party.[90]

MASANI AND LIBERAL CAPITALISM

Because of Masani's central role in the formulation and propagation of Swatantra's formal doctrine (see chapter 8) and in the realm of party organization, we shall defer detailed consideration of his views until a later point, and then it will be from a different angle. However, in addition to radical views in the 1930s, a few points should be noted here, which will suffice to point up some of the differences between his outlook and those of Rajaji and Munshi. First, Masani, with Rajaji, opposed the proposed ban on communal parties, but he declined to take Rajaji's approach. Masani, for his part, expressed his dislike for communalism and for other forms of parochialism and sectarianism; but he insisted that a ban would be akin to treating the symptoms and not the disease itself.[91] Most specifically, education (in the broadest sense) to develop a sense of secular, national citizenship was, for Masani, the appropriate course of action. Secondly, in a view also at variance with Rajaji, Masani has referred to the joint family system as 'a remnant of the primitive tribal community' which 'had its advantages but often led to family discord and encouraged idleness and dependence even among the able bodied'.[92] There is no concern here for the moral discipline which the joint family (or the *jati*) is presumed to foster; and, if anything, there is a clear implication that the effects of the system are pernicious in terms of moral development. Implicit here is an individualistic system, in which everyone is permitted, encouraged, and perhaps even obliged to 'sink or swim' on his own merits. That he is, furthermore, opposed to artificial maintenance of cottage industries, Masani has made quite explicit;[93] and his reference to the concept of limited liability as a 'sacred principle' and to the joint stock company as 'an institution invented by the genius of man to increase industrial production' further mark him as a spokesman for modern industry —and more specifically for private enterprise.[94] His urban, Parsi, highly anglicized background, and his association with modern capitalism combine to define him as, perhaps, India's leading apostle of a chastened classical liberalism (and he is, in fact, a patron of the Liberal International). On balance, it is fair to say, with Morris-Jones, that no person prominent in Indian public life today is more unambiguously modernist than Masani.[95]

THE INNER CIRCLE: A BALANCE SHEET

From the preceding discussions, it is obvious that Rajaji reaches out toward those who defend the idealized village, that Munshi reaches out toward the militant nationalists, and that Masani reaches out toward the more secular, urban, industrial elements. It is also clear, if somewhat less so, that Rajaji pulls back a good deal from the prototypical spokesman for the Gandhians and the RRP, and that Munshi stays a bit shy of the Jan Sangh. It is also important to note that neither was in fact drawn into the Jan Sangh or any other pre-Swatantra opposition party, although ideologically there was some overlap with one or more of these. Munshi has been offered the presidency of the Sangh but has never accepted it; Rajaji has addressed Sangh conventions, has written for *The Organiser*, and was in many ways sympathetic to the Sangh's cause—but neither, to repeat, turned to this party as the principal vehicle for opposition to the Congress.

More generally, the three Hindus in the inner circle do not present a united front. None, certainly, is a defender of aristocratic conservatism or of the explicit, hierarchical conservatism of the traditional village. As a trio, they cannot be classified as militant nationalists, because Rajaji and Ranga balance Munshi here.

Together, they come closer to the 'messiahs of backwardness' with their emphasis on spirituality and the village, but Ranga is quite wary of the hierarchical aspect of the village (at least *vis-à-vis* those who are above his caste) and Munshi is more concerned with national institutions, national economy, and national strength flowing from these, than is Rajaji or Ranga. Of the three, however, Munshi finds the least resonance in the party as a whole, leaving the Rajaji–Ranga emphasis on the village as more important in this respect.

It is against this backdrop that the significance of Masani and Mody can be partly understood. As Parsis, they serve to balance excessive Hinduism. As secularists, they help to tone down excessive emphasis on religious matters in general. As westernized urbanites bound up with modern industry, they are less village-oriented and more 'materialistic' than their colleagues. So, too, they find less that is attractive in caste as a social welfare institution and in spirituality as a substitute for material progress. This contrast is in some respects too sharply drawn, as we shall see subsequently. But for the time being we may say that as highly westernized and cosmopolitan men, whose 'native' tongue is English, whose dress is invariably western, whose style of life is decidedly upper-class modern, whose tastes in food and drink deviate from the orthodox Hindu norm by the widest margins, whose image of the new India draws heavily on the west, and who would perforce be disturbed by efforts in either a militant Hindu or village-based direction, Masani and Mody help to place the centre of gravity of the inner circle in the more moderate part of the political spectrum.[96] We shall say more in a later chapter about these modern perspectives in the party and about the tensions related thereto. For the time, the most important conclusion is that neither individually nor collectively could an observer confuse the Swatantra inner circle with that of an aristocratically based party or with those of the RRP, the Mahasabha, or the Jan Sangh. In this respect, Swatantra, through its inner circle, does represent something new; but to define more precisely just what it is and how well it might survive, further issues must be raised.

One matter which is of obvious importance in gaining a still clearer picture of the inner circle and its capacity to build a viable party on an essentially moderate basis is the political appeal and political power of these leaders, individually and collectively. On this point, we have already seen that there was some doubt about the inner circle even among the most highly placed Swatantrites, and that by-and-large they were more respected than popular. Beyond this, however, we must recognize that as the Congress evolved, all of the Swatantra inner circle came to be pushed to the fringes of Congress power, albeit in different ways and for different reasons. For convenience, we shall term this situation one of 'power marginality'.

In the case of Sir Homy Mody, the matter is entirely straightforward. He was never a Congressman and was, for the most part, apolitical. In fact, he served on the Viceroy's Council from 1931 to 1943 and from this vantage point he did battle with a number of leading Congressmen—some of them now his colleagues, in Swatantra. In addition, he served as Governor of UP after independence. About the most that could be said for Mody and the political 'mainstream' is that he resigned from the Viceroy's Council in 1943, in protest against the treatment of Gandhi, and that in 1957 he stood for Parliament but was defeated.

Masani, although very much involved in politics, could not sink substantial roots in Indian political life, in part because he was an extraordinarily anglicized Parsi. His seat in the Constituent Assembly was provided by Patel and in 1957 he was returned to Parliament from a tribal district in Bihar, whence his return was facilitated by the Jharkand Party leader, Jaipal Singh. There is, moreover, the apolitical dimension to his career, i.e. that of ambassador to Brazil and representative to the UN.[97]

Rajaji, Munshi, and Ranga, as 'political' Hindus, were much more in the mainstream of nationalist activity, but each experienced more than a little discomfort. Rajaji, as 'the only South Indian leader to achieve nation-wide prominence as a Congress leader',[98] always felt a bit remote from the seat of national power for that very reason, and the rise of non-Brahmin power in Madras eventually undermined his local position as well. In addition, he seemed quite anxious to remain in office in 1939, but bent to the Congress order to terminate his ministry; he resigned from the Congress itself, in order to protest against the 'Quit India' resolution of 1942, which he regarded as suicidal in the face of a possible Japanese invasion; and he, too, moved into apolitical positions, including, first and foremost, that of Governor-General of India.

Munshi, as we have seen, declined to remain in the Congress when Gandhi 'captured' it in 1920, though he did rejoin in the 1930s. Moreover, after rejoining the Congress, he endeavoured to revive the Swaraj Party as a constitutionalist wing of the nationalist movement, and in the 1940s he withdrew once again from the Congress, this time to oppose the Pakistan demand.[99] Throughout this long period, he also devoted much time to his legal, literary and educational pursuits; and after holding for a time the thankless portfolio of agriculture after independence, he, too, moved to an apolitical position—as Governor of UP.[100]

Ranga's rather unstable political career is in part traceable to the fact that he was a Kamma in the Reddy-dominated Andhra Congress, but for whatever reason, he was recurrently at the fringe of the Andhra power structure. He did achieve the position of President of the Andhra Pradesh Congress, but after narrowly losing a bid for re-election, in 1951, Ranga and many of his followers defected to form the Krishikar Lok Paksh, which contested the 1951–2 elections with some success.[101] Communist successes in Andhra in 1951–2 led the Congress 'high command' to seek a *rapprochement* with Ranga, and largely on the condition that Ranga be permitted to name the candidates for a number of predominantly Kamma districts, a Congress-KLP united front was formed, and Ranga was virtually back within the fold. Perhaps not very surprisingly, Ranga did not gain a position on the APCC executive at this time, although his co-operation was rewarded at a different level, when he was named Secretary of the Congress Parliamentary party. It was from this position that he resigned after the passage of the Nagpur Resolution.[102]

Not too much should be made of these facts, but it is fair to say that for a variety of reasons all of those in the Swatantra inner circle became 'power-marginal' as they personally and the Congress developed over the years. This is suggested by the executive positions which they have held. It is this fact which has given rise to the frequently heard but largely irrelevant wail that they are 'frustrated power-seekers' and nothing more.[103] It is far more important here to observe that they have all had difficulty in sinking and/or sustaining roots in Indian political party life and to try to understand what this in turn suggests about the future of the party. Could such people be expected to mobilize a mass following to oppose the Congress? Masani was concerned about the presence of Menon and Hegde as 'joint secretaries' for this reason and he was determined to 'politicize' the inner circle of the party. But there is reason to believe that even the new inner circle lacks a good deal that might be required to build a new party.[104]

In concluding this discussion of the Swatantra inner circle, especially in light of its apparent 'power marginality' and present lack of mass appeal, it is pertinent to point out that at the 'preparatory convention' in Bombay, portraits of Gandhi, Patel, and Tilak were chosen to adorn the platform on which Swatantra's leaders appeared. It is possible to explain this quite simply. Everyone must pay homage to Gandhi; there is genuine regard for Patel among Swatantrites, who appreciate his tough, law-and-order, anti-socialist approach; and it was the time of the birthday of Tilak, whose famous 'Swaraj is my birthright' commends itself almost universally in India. Furthermore, all three were local giants—Gandhi and Patel from Gujarat, Tilak from Maharashtra. Perhaps the simplest explanation is the best, but one of the organizers of the convention acknowledged that the choice of Tilak was, in his words, 'Machiavellian', because of the popular image his name would evoke.[105] Was Swatantra, by this choice, trying to link itself more to the mainstream of Hindu nationalism than its own élite is able to do? Was Swatantra attempting to modify its own image as a party led by old, frustrated, often apolitical people? The admission about Tilak suggests that this might have been the case, and one might want to speculate about what this means with respect to the leaders' own self-image. At least for the adventuresome investigator, it would seem possible to get some clues about Swatantra not only from the distinguished living but also from some knowledge of the revered dead.

CHAPTER 6

THE SWATANTRA COALITION: GROWTH AND SCOPE

The Swatantra inner circle confronted a host of pressing problems, as it prepared for the 1962 general elections, a short $2\frac{1}{2}$ years distant. Organization, finance, dissemination of propaganda, popularization of the electoral symbol, and adjustments with other parties were formidable tasks, particularly in view of the party's stated aim of building an effective, national opposition to the Congress.

The first task, of course, was to rally the potential faithful, and here Swatantra had a number of alternatives. It could attempt to build its own cadres and mass membership from 'scratch'. It could attempt to capitalize on available 'vote banks', i.e. locally dominant caste groups and local notables. It could attempt to absorb existing parties and to pry loose some elements from the Congress, using whatever formal and informal organizations these might provide. Once it had achieved some support, it could seek to take maximum advantage of its own strength by restricting its efforts on the one hand and by seeking to avoid undesirable multi-cornered contests on the other. Not surprisingly, Swatantra operated on all these fronts.

In seeking to build an effective opposition to the Congress, Swatantra had to decide whose support would be welcomed. Would any and all anti-Congress elements be greeted with open arms, or would Swatantra be discriminating in admitting people into its fold? The answer here depended in part on the leaders' sense of urgency in checking the Congress and on their ability to mobilize large numbers of people on the basis of their own party programme. A feeling of intense urgency, coupled with an inability to propagate effectively Swatantra doctrine, would encourage an 'open-door' policy. The reverse conditions would be more favourable to a process of selective admission.

In this chapter, we shall trace the growth of Swatantra, particularly during the period 1959–62, by indicating the existing parties which merged with it, caste groups which gave it support, and other groups and individuals who rallied to the party banner. Their doctrinal commitments will also be discussed. In the following chapter, the *interaction* of the major components of the Swatantra coalition will be considered.

MERGERS AND CASTE SUPPORT

Given the available, localized discontent, it was only natural that Swatantra leaders should try to absorb many existing opposition forces, as a short cut to electoral strength and as a means of rationalizing the opposition to the Congress. Swatantra doctrine encouraged the hesitant, parochial forces by giving them virtual *carte blanche* on all issues not defined by the party as 'fundamental' to the anti-statist programme.[1] Rajaji's presence, the prospect of Bombay money, and a possibility of some national prominence represented further inducements, doubtless more significant.

At the outset there was, however, a good deal of doubt that the parochialism of many of the existing opposition parties could be overcome. One leading Indian journalist argued that a potent challenge to the Congress was unlikely, in part because 'where there are local parties, like the Jharkand Party of Bihar, or the Ganatantra Parishad of Orissa, they attach to their local status far more importance than their national loyalties and are desperately anxious to maintain a rigid local position which prevents their emerging into a national party which may conceivably need to compromise for Coalition at the Centre'. He added, in anticipation of the 1962 elections, that 'because of the failure of the middle parties—the Praja Socialist, Swatantra, and Jana Sangh, and other local parties, the Jharkand, the Ganatantra Parishad, Ram Rajya Parishad, the Tamilnad Democratic Party and so on—to merge, the Congress Party's ascendancy should not be in question'.[2] Indeed, Congress ascendancy in 1962 was not in question, and here da Costa was quite right. But Swatantra did make an almost herculean effort in the direction of a united opposition and achieved considerable success. It is also fair to say that most of the blame for the fragmentation which did persist cannot be laid at its door.

The first merger, according to official sources, was that of the the Indian National Democratic Congress (INDC) of Madras,[3] whose General-Secretary, S. S. Mariswamy, announced at the preparatory convention:

I am the General-Secretary of that Indian Democratic Party which was formed two years ago on the eve of the elections to fight mainly against Congress candidates. We contested 46 seats and we managed to capture 23 seats. Our party is now functioning in the local legislature as the major official opposition party. When the news came that Rajaji had started this party, all the members of the party unanimously agreed to join hands with the newly formed Swatantra Party.[4]

In spite of this seemingly decisive statement, some INDC leaders obviously did not consider themselves to be Swatantrites and there was even some question about the actual extent of merger.[5] None the less, the principal leaders of the Madras unit have for the most part been former INDC men—e.g. H. Venkatakrishna Reddiar, the first state President; Saw Ganesan, the incumbent President; and Mariswamy, the incumbent General-Secretary—although Reddiar, among others, withdrew from Swatantra in the early stages.[6] Thus, the leading opposition group in Madras, as of 1959, cast its lot with Swatantra.

The centre of gravity of the INDC lay among upper middle castes, such as Chettiars, Mudaliars, and Naidus, whose position in the Congress had waned with the broadening of the party's social base under Kamaraj. Coupled with Rajaji's appeal for Brahmins,[7] whose political fortunes had dropped precipitously as a result of lower caste pressure both inside and outside the Congress, the presence of the INDC gave Swatantra in Madras a decidedly upper-caste complexion—or, in the words of one hostile source, Swatantra was 'the forum only of conservative Brahmins and profit-minded baniyas'.[8] However, many of the INDC men had only shortly before been in the forefront of the effort to oust Rajaji as the head of the Madras Congress; and this will not be the only instance of former political enemies finding a common home in the Swatantra Party.

This upper caste image in Madras was in some districts offset partially by the later entry of S. S. Ramaswamy Padayachi, a leader of the Tamilnad Toilers' Party, who announced his group's desire to join Swatantra 'for the purpose of achieving further prominence and thereby serving our community better'.[9] The community in question was the Vanniyars, a group of lower but upwardly mobile castes of agriculturalists, who, as a result of their inability to penetrate the Congress when Rajaji was still at its helm (and even for a time after), developed two political parties, the Tamilnad Toilers' and Commonweal. The local successes of these two parties led ultimately to their absorption in the Congress and to the inclusion of Padayachi and other Vanniyars in the state ministry or other high posts. However, Padayachi and other Vanniyar leaders still felt that they had been insufficiently accommodated and withdrew from the Congress, although only a segment of them turned to Swatantra, thus joining hands with two erstwhile adversaries, Rajaji and the INDC.[10]

Wavering for a time on the brink of merger was the Forward Bloc of Madras, based on the highly communal Thevar group which was reasonably strong, and in some places dominant, in a few districts in the southern part of the state. No merger occurred, although there was close co-operation between the Forward Bloc and Swatantra in some districts; and the late Forward Bloc leader, U. M. Thevar, did associate himself with the Swatantra group in the *Lok Sabha*.[11] All told, Swatantra seemed to have made a good start in the home state of its founder-leader.

Another existing party which merged with Swatantra at the outset was the Janata Party of Bihar, at that time the third largest party in the state. The Janata leader, the Raja of Ramgarh, was, as we have seen, a prominent *zamindar*-businessman and a Rajput, though not of the highest status. An energetic and skilful political organizer, the Raja had for a long time entertained higher political ambitions than the leadership of a small local party and he was always looking for new ways to carry on his vendetta against the architect of Bihar's *zamindari* abolition act, K. B. Sahay.[12] Unable at the time to pursue either goal effectively through the Congress (which he was by no means averse to joining on the proper terms) or through Janata, the Raja saw an opportunity in the Swatantra Party. Thus, as a participant at the preparatory convention, Ramgarh announced:

> I represent the Janata Party at this convention. We have in the Assembly today 23 members...and in Parliament we have four members... When I received the invitation, we were all very happy in Bihar, that the day has now come for a unified opposition, not only in one state but throughout the country. I have been sent here as an observer, and the views that have been expressed...have really inspired me. I can assure you that the Janata Party of Bihar will decide to co-operate wholeheartedly with you and we shall be able to give you a Swatantra Party Government in the State of Bihar.[13]

The Raja's promise of a Swatantra government in Bihar in 1962 was far-fetched, although he certainly pursued that goal with uncommon zeal verging on ruthlessness. This apart, the Janata merger had the immediate effect of giving Swatantra a small contingent in the *Lok Sabha* (and in the Bihar assembly), to stand behind Masani, Ranga, and a few other MPs who had joined them.[14] In addition, it brought into Swatantra one of the most energetic political organizers in Bihar, if not in all of India, in the person of Ramgarh, who was almost immediately co-opted to a position as national Vice-President, with Munshi.

Also merging from Bihar, at a later date, was the Jan Congress, a group of dissident Congressmen with a tiny legislative contingent, led by Jankinandan Singh, who was a member of the Bihar Legislative Council (MLC). The latter was the uncle of the late Maharajadhiraj of Darbhanga, who was the leader of the Maithil Brahmin community and formerly the premier *zamindar* in Bihar. Together with Ramgarh's entry, this further reinforced the landed, aristocratic complexion of Swatantra in Bihar and further bolstered Swatantra's hopes in the state,[15] although of the two groups Janata was by far the more important.

Encouraging on the face of it, too, were the decisions of two veteran Congressmen, Paliwal and Nagoke, to join Swatantra in UP and the Punjab, respectively, and to bring with them modest, semi-organized groups of supporters. Paliwal, who left the Congress in 1951, had for fifteen years been either President or General-Secretary of the UP Congress, had sat in the Central Legislative Council prior to independence and in the state Cabinet afterwards. He was, then, a man who had been a local power. Nagoke, who left the Congress only after the Nagpur Resolution, was one of the most senior Congressmen in the Punjab and was, moreover, a former leader of the Akali Sikhs, a very potent minority in that (now bifurcated) state. As a veteran leader who had served very long terms in jail prior to independence, Nagoke was widely esteemed.

Paliwal, in his own self-description, cited his long association with and admiration for Rajaji and Ranga and his long-standing opposition to Nehru and the latter's brand of socialism. Stressing his 'cent-percent Gandhism', Paliwal pointed with pride and delight to the fact that in the mid-1940s he was labelled by the CPI as one of the 'three evil Ps'—Patel and S. K. Patil being the other two—among the prominent Congressmen of the day.[16]

As a result of familiar factional battles, involving the inevitable charges of corruption and favouritism against some highly placed colleagues, Paliwal came to be isolated from the UP Congress leadership; and neither Nehru nor Pandit Pant seemed responsive to his charge that a leading Cabinet member in UP had stolen 'many *lakhs*' of rupees. In addition, Paliwal's marriage to a Muslim lady brought forth a stream of abuse from some of his colleagues, contributing to the widening breach. After first leaving the state Cabinet and then the party itself, Paliwal sat in the assembly and led a group of independents (variously estimated at between twenty and thirty-five) in the UP assembly—the so-called 'Independent Progressive Legislature Party'—and he was in the process of organizing an extra-parliamentary party, the Gram Raj (Village Rule) Party, whose principal tenets were rule by rural people and opposition to co-operative farming. A very staunch anti-socialist, anti-communalist, and anti-aristocrat, Paliwal decided to cast his lot, too, with Swatantra, which, in his view, represented a combination of Gandhism and modern capitalism, with (it must be noted) too much of the latter for his liking.[17] Thus, the IPLP and the Gram Raj Party were also merged with Swatantra,[18] and soon, thereafter, Paliwal was also co-opted to serve as Vice-President, with Munshi and Ramgarh.

Nagoke, highly respected but not a political power in 1959, explained that his connection with the Congress was not broken 'in any light-hearted manner'; but the Nagpur Resolution was, in his view, a menace which had to be opposed by leaving the Congress: 'We consider ourselves morally bound to announce our disapproval of this policy by resigning from the Congress, before the country is actually driven to economic disaster.'[19] To structure his anti-collectivist protest, Nagoke formed the Dehati Janata Party (Rural Peoples' Party), which, at the outset, was intended to be solely a vehicle to oppose the Nagpur Resolution, without, however, contesting elections itself or giving support to any one political party.[20] This non-partisan approach was quickly discarded, however, in part due to pressure from Ranga.

The Dehati Janata Party received some support from members of the Sikh ruling family of Patiala, which gave it a boost in that area. It was described by one source as 'landlord-led and anti-collectivist but fairly influential',[21] and by another as a 'natural extension into politics of the forces of tradition in the village—the big *zamindar*, his associates in commerce and such of his tenants as were tied to him by personal or caste loyalties'.[22] Thus, in the Punjab, too, Swatantra gained some support and once again it was landed and conservative (although the term *zamindar* in the Punjab does not have the same connotations as it would in Bihar, for example). Two Sikhs, Nagoke (until his death in January 1966) and Basant Singh, served as state President and General-Secretary, respectively; but it is significant that both had abandoned open association with the Akali Dal in favour of less communal, economics-oriented channels of protest. For a short time, until his death, Nagoke also served as a Vice-President of the national party.[23]

The most significant merger was that of the Ganatantra Parishad, which 'unanimously decided to merge with the Swatantra Party' in mid-November 1961.[24] The actual merger did not take place, however, until after the 1962 general elections, but the Swatantra Party contributed to the Parishad's campaign treasury and considered the latter's candidates as its own.

From the time Swatantra was born, efforts were made to bring the Parishad into the fold; and, as we have seen, the Maharaja of Kalahandi was among those who had approached Rajaji prior to 1959, concerning the possibility of forming a broader opposition party.[25] Ramgarh, among others, negotiated on behalf of Swatantra, but the early efforts proved unavailing; and any intimation that there would be a merger was usually met with prompt and emphatic denials by Parishad leaders. For a time, in fact, it was strongly suggested that the Parishad would merge with the Congress (which would virtually have obliterated the opposition in Orissa).[26]

Until 1961, there was an obvious and understandable reason for the failure of merger talks and for the posture adopted by the Parishad: the Parishad was in a coalition ministry with the Congress in Orissa and thus had a share of power in the state. Both Parishad and Swatantra leaders felt that from this vantage point the Parishad could do more to stabilize its position in the highlands and perhaps to extend its influence to the coastal regions (where it was virtually impotent) than it could by leaving the coalition and joining Swatantra. It is not surprising, then, that the Parishad leaders wanted to assure the Congress in the strongest possible language that no merger with Swatantra was contemplated. Swatantra, for its part, confined its organization in Orissa to the coastal region; and even when Kalahandi said that rumours of a merger were 'baseless', Swatantra happily refrained from challenging the Parishad in any fashion.[27]

The situation changed drastically when the coalition ministry was terminated in 1961, as a result of Patnaik's determination to have the Congress dissociate itself from 'feudal' elements and establish itself more securely as an independent force in the state. This put the Parishad out of office and forced it to confront mid-term elections, for the state assembly only. It was at this juncture that serious negotiations were renewed, bringing Swatantra and the Parishad more openly and more closely together.

In this setting a variety of rumours was circulated. One was that the Parishad 'may seek the help of the Swatantra Party' in the mid-term elections, in return for Parishad support for four Swatantra *Lok Sabha* candidates in the 1962 general elections.[28] What is clear is that the Swatantra unit in Orissa wanted to contest the mid-term elections on a wide basis, leaving the highlands to the Parishad; but the Swatantra central office refused to countenance this and authorized only one Swatantrite to contest.[29] Efforts to reach an accord were unsuccessful at this stage, even though the Parishad felt at a disadvantage *vis-à-vis* the Congress, particularly in a mid-term election, where the ruling party could concentrate all of its efforts on this one state.[30]

The results of the mid-term elections gave further impetus to Parishad leaders to seek closer co-operation with Swatantra. Although the Parishad lost many seats by very narrow margins, and although the party's leaders knew that the Congress would not be able to concentrate its forces as fully in general elections, they still did not feel at all confident about the future. What troubled the Parishad the most was Patnaik, who was seemingly intransigent concerning future coalitions (unnecessary after the mid-term elections, in any event), who was personally wealthy, and who, in the words of one Parishad leader, controlled 'the keys to a vast treasury'.[31] The future thus looked less bright than the past, not only for the Parishad but also for some of the Congress 'old guard' in Orissa; and it was at this juncture, as we shall see below, that Rajaji referred to the possible entry into Swatantra of the displaced Chief Minister of Orissa, Harekrushna Mahtab.

The renewed Swatantra-Parishad talks 'were satisfactory' at all stages, and the decision to merge was announced at the Parishad convention, which found the principles of the Swatantra Party 'remarkably similar to the ideals of the Ganatantra Parishad'.[32] The main reason given for the decision was the need for a united opposition at the centre, to 'arrest the growing menace of the Congress Party'.[33] It is pertinent to point out, however, both in light of the Parishad statement and in light of da Costa's remarks about parochialism, that many of the Parishad leaders had some reservations about the merger. One expressed concern because Swatantra, in his view, had a less progressive image than did the Parishad, and he was particularly distressed by the 'free enterprise' image which Swatantra had acquired. On both ideological and practical gounds, this man thought that a bit more 'socialism' would help. Still, he said that 'a small party cannot tell a big party what to do...We were not happy with parts of the programme but could do nothing.'[34] Many felt that they would not be able to emphasize local issues as much as they had done in the past; and, for example, Parishad leaders pressed Swatantra, unsuccessfully, to make an explicit commitment in favour of redrawing state boundaries so that all Oriya-speaking peoples would be under Orissa jurisdiction.[35] None the less, most seemed to agree with Kalahandi, who said that in the final analysis 'Swatantra means independent, and we are all pretty much independent' with respect to local issues.[36] Thus, the second strongest party in Orissa and a reasonably serious contender for power in that state sought refuge under the 'all-India umbrella which Rajaji supplied', hoping, in part, that more ample funds would be available to battle the Patnaik-led Orissa Congress.[37]

Elsewhere, mergers, or alinement almost indistinguishable from merger, also helped to provide support, but of much more modest dimensions, prior to the 1962 elections. Raja Anand Chand of Bilaspur, a sitting MP (*Rajya Sabha*) and a relative of the Raja of Ramgarh, joined Swatantra and brought with him the Himachal Pradesh Sanyutka Morcha, an anti-Congress front which controlled a bloc of seats in the Himachal Pradesh territorial council.[38] Ranga attracted remnants of the KLP, a party dominated by Kemma landed interests in the Andhra delta; and the Andhra Democratic Party (a mélange of ex-Congressmen, ex-Justiceites, ex-KLPers, etc.) split upon the formation of Swatantra, with some joining the new party. Although by 1959 there was no Justice

Party, a number of landed ex-Justiceites from Andhra did join the party; and among them was Swatantra's first state President, B. Ramachandra Reddy, once a CBE, who had been in the Justice Party from 1923 to 1952, head of the Madras Legislative Council from 1930 to 1937, and a prime mover in the AIAF.[39]

The KLP and Ranga personally had some supporters in Rajasthan and Gujarat, and some of these also joined Swatantra. In the Bharatpur area of Rajasthan, the old KLP had some influence among Jat peasants and had some support from the former ruling family of the Jat state of Bharatpur. In Gujarat, there were some small local parties and dissident groups, including the Saurashtra *khedut sangh*, which drew primarily on landed peasants; and among these Gujarat elements were some locally influential Patidars, whose caste brethren dominate the Gujarat Congress.[40] From other corners came assorted factions, fractions, splinter groups, and the like; but in no case was the strength of any one of these groups sufficient to assure Swatantra of even a good, localized electoral showing.

Through the Ganatantra Parishad, Janata, etc., Swatantra inherited existing political organizations, although in some cases the term 'organization' is decidedly generous.[41] The past electoral performance of these groups (and, in particular, the residual influence of the aristocracy) also augured well for the new party. Given the short time in which Swatantra could go to the electorate on its own terms and through a new, independently created organization, such support was indispensable, if the party were to make a good showing in the 1962 elections and thereby to encourage others to join.

Of great importance, too, in this effort was the support given to Swatantra by certain caste associations, some of which did not have an explicit political party 'front'. Here, however, distinctions are far from neat and sharp. The Vanniyars of Madras created two parties to serve as their political vehicles, and it is often said that the Janata Party was nothing more than a vehicle for Ramgarh's caste and business interests. But the *kshatrya mahasabha* in Rajasthan relied heavily on the RRP, although the RRP was not created by the *mahasabha* or for that purpose. In other cases, the connection between a caste group and a specific party is even more tenuous.

The most conspicuous and the most important of the caste groups which turned to Swatantra were the Rajput and, more generally, *kshatrya* associations in northern India. At one point or another the following groups all allegedly urged support for the Swatantra Party: the *kshatrya mahasabha* and *bhooswami sangh* in Madhya Pradesh; the Rajput Brotherhood of Pathankot and the Zamindara League in the Punjab; and the Kutch Rajput Sabha, the Saurashtra Girasdars' Association, and the *kshatrya mahasabha* in Gujarat.[42] And at the all-India *kshatrya mahasabha* conference in May 1960, the presiding officer, the Maharawal of Dungarpur (Rajasthan), encouraged support for the Swatantra Party, which he himself had joined; and the conference as a whole reportedly endorsed his plea.[43] Most of these groups were heavily dominated by, if not comprised exclusively of landed Rajputs, and collectively they reinforced the aristocratic, upper-caste, landed component of Swatantra in the northern states. Here, however, Gujarat requires special note, because, in addition to Rajputs of high status who dominated their areas (as in Kutch), there were many lesser Rajputs, often impoverished tenants from Patidar-dominated areas in the central part of the state. Moreover, the Rajput leadership of the *kshatrya mahasabha*, especially Narendrasingh Mahida, had welcomed into the organization a large number of non-Rajputs and accorded them *kshatrya* status. The latter included many ritually and economically lower status elements, whose entry—often opposed by the 'big' Rajputs—broadened the social base of the *kshatrya mahasabha* and, therefore, of Swatantra, by bringing into the party lower caste elements on an essentially non-derivative basis. In some cases, the 'little' Rajputs and those whom they embraced as fellow *kshatryas* strongly favoured precisely those land reforms which were opposed by the 'big' Rajputs, in Gujarat and elsewhere.[44]

In some ways, the case of the Gujarat *kshatrya mahasabha* parallels that of the Vanniyars. There was much pressure for Congress tickets, beneficial programmes, etc., and there was for a time a very close association between Mahida (and the *mahasabha* generally) and the Congress. However, the Gujarat Congress did not satisfactorily accommodate the *kshatryas*, whose numerical strength was steadily increasing through recruitment. Frustrated by the Congress in 1957 and after, they turned eventually to Swatantra, where they found much greater opportunity, on the whole, to move into leading positions, to secure tickets, etc.[45] In addition, they found in Swatantra a political vehicle which had been selected by other Rajputs in other states; and this 'outside' factor, overlooked by those who have analysed the Gujarat *kshatryas*, also played a part in drawing the Gujarat group into the new party.[46]

By and large, Swatantra did not benefit from substantial bloc support in the southern states, and neither the *Swatantra Newsletter* nor *Link*, both of which for different reasons dutifully record such support, contains more than fleeting references to such a phenomenon. The southern units of the party, particularly in Andhra and Mysore, have been built around smaller nuclei of landed interests, some of whom had been associated with local parties and/or the AIAF, and some of whom were able to 'deliver' part of the lower caste vote in their areas.[47] Disorganized Brahmin groups also gave some support. In Andhra, however, a highly respected *harijan* leader and a disciple of Ranga's, G. Latchanna (now state President), chose to follow Ranga into Swatantra rather than to remain in the Congress, where he was quite welcome. Latchanna's following among certain *harijan* groups introduces a low caste element into the Andhra unit, although it is generally conceded that the party's strength in Andhra, such as it is, derives primarily from the aforementioned landed interests.[48] It is well to remember, however, that not all of Swatantra's support is upper caste and that not all of its lower caste support comes to it on a derivative basis, i.e. through local notables.

SWATANTRA AND THE ARISTOCRATS

Further along the continuum ranging from organized parties to the 'common man' were many eminent individuals who had some local appeal, at least. For present purposes, these may be categorized as follows: (1) aristocrats; (2) non-aristocratic 'old warriors' from the Congress; (3) non-aristocratic, non-Congress old warriors; and (4) a broad and somewhat amorphous group of former administrators. We shall consider each of these in turn but will start with the aristocrats for two reasons. First, because of the prominence of aristocrats among the leaders of certain merged parties and of the major caste groups which turned to Swatantra, consideration of the aristocrats here follows logically from what has preceded. Secondly, because traditional loyalties still persisted over wide areas, the aristocrats—and notably the major ex-rulers—

were important 'vote banks', indeed in many cases exceeding the capacity of some of the organized parties to help Swatantra.

As the experiences in 1951–2 and 1957 showed, the aristocrats had abundant support in their areas, although relatively few were active *and* prominent politically, Moreover, because of caste and family ties, a successful appeal to one ruler could set off something of a limited 'chain reaction'. With this large group of vote banks available, it is not surprising that Swatantra looked hopefully to the aristocracy, to secure candidates or at least open support, while for the same reason, the Congress sought to keep the aristocrats neutral, at least. The struggle was prolonged, tense, and often bitter. The pitched battle was fought in Rajasthan over the great houses of Jaipur, Jodhpur, Udaipur, Bikaner, and one or two others, but there were more than minor skirmishes in parts of Bihar (especially over Darbhanga), in Gujarat (especially in Kutch and Saurashtra), in the Punjab (particularly over Patiala), and in parts of UP, Madhya Pradesh, and Maharashtra.

With few exceptions—Ramgarh, the late Raja Raghavendra Pratap Singh of Mankapur (UP), and a handful of others—the list of participants at the preparatory convention reveals few aristocratic names, and those who did attend were certainly not among the most eminent ex-rulers and ex-landlords.[49] Even the states which were the bastions of the aristocracy before independence were represented very largely by commoners, and there is no evidence to indicate that the actual participants were in any way agents for aristocratic interests.

Very shortly after its inception, however, the aristocrats started to evince greater interest in Swatantra, and vice versa, and it was not long before a fairly steady trickle from this quarter flowed into the party. To anticipate one of the main points, however, the outcome was disappointing from the Swatantra standpoint. Relatively few aristocrats entered the party, and those who did were primarily of lesser status or were relatives of leading families. Few leading ex-rulers chose to aline themselves, at least openly, with the party.

Of the early entrants from this group, Ramgarh, by virtue of his position in the Janata Party, was by far the most important. The Raja of Mankapur, a smaller *zamindar* and a Congressman from 1930 to 1955, had served in the UP assembly continuously since 1937 and brought much political skill and experience as well as great local influence, into the party.[50] Raja Bhalindra Singh and Raja Maheshindra Singh, the younger brother and uncle of the ex-ruler of Patiala, respectively, attended the preparatory convention and quickly joined the party, which buoyed Swatantra's hopes around Patiala. Raja Kalyan Singh of Bhinai, a Rajput *jagirdar* who had previously been associated with both the RRP and Jan Sangh in Rajasthan, and Maharajkumar Hukam Singh of Jaisalmer, also in Rajasthan, both attended the convention and also joined the party at an early date.

In Rajasthan, Bhinai and the Maharajkumar of Jaisalmer took the lead, with the former as 'convenor' of the state unit, but joining and superseding them very quickly were Maharawal Laxman Singh of Dungarpur, Maharawal Chandra Vir Singh of Banswara, and Raja Man Singh of Bharatpur, the brother of the ex-ruler of this Jat state. The major Rajput houses remained aloof, however.[51] In UP, Mankapur was immediately joined by Raja Mahendra Ripudaman Singh of Bhadawar and later by Raja Ram Singh of Gangwal, helping to give Swatantra some pockets of strength in the northern part of that state.[52] From Madhya Pradesh came Rajkumar Udaisingh of Kaluhera and a Brahmin landholder named N. C. Zamindar, who over-optimistically asserted that the party had great appeal in some of the state's 'feudal constituencies'.[53] Some of these were certainly influential on a local level and some were reasonably seasoned politicians. This was to Swatantra's good, but for several months the roster of aristocrats did not include any of the leading families, save perhaps the well-known house of Patiala. But even Patiala was not represented by the ex-ruler himself.

In this light, the prize 'catch' and a principal catalyst in the entire struggle for the aristocracy was the beautiful Maharani Gayatri Devi of Jaipur, whose entry into the party was dutifully announced in January 1961 by the *jagirdar* Man Singh (Mahar), formerly with the RRP. With the Maharani came two of the Maharajkumars of Jaipur (Jai Singh and Prithviraj) and a number of leading Rajput *jagirdars*, some of them with more than a little trepidation.[54] Even this development should not be overestimated. The Maharani is not herself from Rajasthan, and hence does not have the same appeal for Rajasthan aristocrats that a native would have. In addition, she does not speak Hindi (or the local variant thereof) fluently and this helps to mark her further as an outsider. Finally, the Maharaja of Jaipur steadfastly proclaimed that he could best serve 'his' people by remaining 'above politics', as an independent.[55] Yet a major royal house had associated itself with Swatantra, and few would believe that the Maharaja did not endorse his wife's activities. Furthermore, after some Congress tirades against the Jaipur family during the election campaign, the Maharaja himself took a more active part in supporting anti-Congress candidates, although he continued to remain an independent.

The impact of the Maharani's entry cannot be stressed too strongly, even considering the *caveats* just mentioned. Her political debut came on the heels of the Jaipur 'durbar' in honour of Queen Elizabeth II, for which former rulers and landed aristocrats come from far and wide to participate in a massive display of pomp and pageantry. Many saw in this event demonstrable proof that the old aristocracy was still strongly attached to its old ways and they speculated that it presaged a resurgence of the great royal families.[56] This would have been less upsetting to the Congress leaders, both state and national, were it not for the realization that the aristocrats still had great appeal and were it not for the painful awareness that in the 1952 elections, the Maharaja of Jodhpur led an anti-Congress, aristocratic front (principally RRP, Jan Sangh, and independents) which nearly swept the Congress from office.[57] The Maharani's entry, then, conjured up the image of another aristocratic assault on the Congress, and there were few who were confident that the Congress in Rajasthan could withstand such an assault. As one source aptly put it after the Maharani's decision was announced, 'the feudal snowball threatens to be turning into an avalanche'.[58]

All of this scarcely took the Congress by surprise, and there was evidence of considerable anxiety in Congress circles, in Rajasthan and elsewhere. Discussions were held by Congress MPs, by the AICC, and other bodies, to consider a possible ban on princely participation in politics or else possible adjustments in the privy purses. Open and private threats concerning the purses abounded, although in Orissa, where the Congress assemblymen were considering an end to all privy purses, Morarji Desai insisted that such talk should stop and that all historic assurances to the princes be honoured.[59] According to the Maharani of Jaipur, she had been asked to contest a *Lok Sabha* seat in 1957 on a Congress ticket, to help fend off anti-Congress activity by the Rajput aristocracy; and, in addition, Rajasthan Chief Minister Sukhadia had worked hard for many months to dissuade the aristocracy, including the Maharani, from opposing the Congress.[60] Among the more serious moves to stem a possible anti-Congress Rajput tide was the inclusion in Sukhadia's Cabinet of Maharaja Harishchandra of Jhalawar, a Rajput and the only one in the ministry.[61] The seriousness with which the Congress took the Maharani's subsequent decision to contest a *Lok Sabha* seat is suggested by the fact that for a time her scheduled Congress opponent was Damodarlal Vyas, the Revenue Minister in the state Cabinet and one of the strongest candidates upon whom the Rajasthan Congress could call.[62]

Thus, even in 1960 the battle for the aristocracy was going on, but after the Maharani's entry it took on new intensity. On the Swatantra side it was hoped that the association of the house of Jaipur with the party would win over other major families, and the latter were pursued with renewed vigour. In fact, Dungarpur, Swatantra state President, pursued some rulers so assiduously that other forms of 'organizing' the party were virtually neglected.[63]

Throughout this battle, in Rajasthan and elsewhere, ties of family and caste played an important part. Ramgarh and Bilaspur were related, as we have seen; Dungarpur was Bikaner's father-in-law; the Maharaja of Devgadh-Baria (a major recruit in eastern Gujarat) was the son-in-law of the Maharaja of Jaipur; and so on.[64] In addition to the attempted exploitation of these connections, Udaisingh of Kaluhera sent a written appeal to most of the leading aristocrats in Madhya Pradesh urging them to join the party;[65] Dungarpur joined Bhailalbhai Patel in efforts to mobilize the aristocracy in Gujarat; Dungarpur and others used *kshatrya mahasabha* and Rajput *sabha* platforms to encourage support for Swatantra; and V. P. Menon became as much of a roving ambassador to the princes as his poor health would allow.

The long and tedious story—of pulling and hauling, of entry and defection, of the almost countless claims and denials of entry—need not detain us here, beyond a few important cases and a few general points. In Bihar, Maharajadhiraj Kameshwar Singh of Darbhanga was eagerly sought by Swatantra, and, as an independent candidate for the *Rajya Sabha*, he had been assured by Ramgarh of the support of the Swatantra (*née* Janata) MLAs in that state. Some of Darbhanga's friends and relatives, like Jankinandan Singh of the Jan Congress/Swatantra and Munshi, pressed him to join the party, while others urged him just as strongly to remain independent or to join the Congress. Swatantra itself was proceeding with somewhat less than unilinear purpose, for the Swatantra state Treasurer—wealthy businessman Parmanand Kejriwal—was also a candidate for the *Rajya Sabha*, even though Darbhanga had been promised Swatantra's support. Kejriwal was finally prevailed upon to withdraw, but Darbhanga still vacillated and did not join Swatantra, deterred in part by the presence of Ramgarh at the helm of the state unit; but he remained a much sought-after figure until his death.[66]

The story was much the same elsewhere. Of the leading pre-independence rulers, Hyderabad, Kashmir, and Mysore were beyond reach, although some very influential former members of the Mysore maharaja's service were prominent Swatantrites.[67] Kolhapur, a well-known state in Maharashtra, and Gwalior, where M. A. Sreenivasan (a leading Mysore Swatantrite) had been Prime Minister and about which Menon had said more than a few kind words, were courted but remained aloof.[68] The Maharaja of Bastar (Madhya Pradesh), a somewhat 'erratic' man whose legal adviser, Rameshwar Agnibhoj (an untouchable) was a Swatantra leader in the state, played no active political role;[69] and Kaluhera's appeal to the Madhya Pradesh aristocracy yielded very few recruits. Leaders of Swatantra in Gujarat felt that the best policy to pursue regarding the Maharaja of Baroda was to leave him alone as a Congress candidate, lest he be forced to become an active campaigner to Swatantra's disadvantage, although one of the Maharaja's brothers did join Swatantra at a later date.[70]

In Rajasthan, the greatest stronghold of the Rajput aristocracy, the Maharaja of Jaipur refused to declare openly for Swatantra, even though others would have joined if he did; and in the 1962 elections he also supported some Jan Sangh candidates. The Maharaja of Bikaner, whose entry into Swatantra was often predicted and claimed, resisted the blandishments of Dungarpur and remained an independent—and was rewarded by the Congress, which refrained from setting up a candidate to oppose him.[71] There were similar reports that the mother of the late Jodhpur Maharaja would contest as a Swatantrite and that she would campaign with Gayatri Devi and the two Maharanis of Banswara, to rally the women-folk, aristocratic and otherwise. She was strongly urged 'to complete the work left half done' by her late son; but this, too, proved unavailing, as she contented herself with an endorsement of a long list of opposition candidates, neither contesting herself nor campaigning on behalf of Swatantra.[72] Udaipur and Kotah wanted nothing to do with Swatantra politics, and the Maharajkumar of Jaisalmer returned to the Congress.[73] Strenuous efforts in Gujarat netted only a scattering of aristocrats prior to the 1962 elections, although in Masani's victory in the Rajkot by-election in 1963, somewhat greater support from this quarter was evident, as members of the royal families of Rajkot, Jasdan, and Wankaner aided Masani's campaign effort.[74] Subsequently, there has been even more open support from Gujarat aristocrats.

Swatantra was thus unable to recruit the major princes, and it often had to be content with relatives of ex-rulers. Even worse, it also had to battle some of these same ex-rulers, who supported the Congress candidates against their own Swatantra relatives. Thus, Raja Man Singh's brother, the former ruler, supported the Congress and toured widely with the Congress candidate for a *Lok Sabha* seat.[75] Raja Bhalindra Singh's brother, the former ruler of Patiala, refused to give him open support, which contributed to the Raja's decision to withdraw from a scheduled *Lok Sabha* contest, in which his successor was strongly opposed by the Maharani of Patiala, who openly supported the Congress and abused Swatantra.[76] In Gujarat, the Maharajkumar of Kutch received no open support from his oldest brother, the former ruler. This is not to say that within Swatantra itself the aristocracy is not potent. It means only that Swatantra was able to recruit a relatively small segment of the aristocracy, and those who did join were by no means the most useful in electoral terms.

All told, the outcome was a disappointment for most Swatantra leaders, for substantial aristocratic support was desperately needed if the party were to make a really strong showing in the short run. Admitting that some aristocrats were convinced Congressmen and that others had no heart or talent for politics, most Swatantra leaders agreed with the Rajput *jagirdar* who said, 'in their heart of hearts, all of the princes are with us, because they know we will protect their vested interests, but they are afraid to join'.[77] But if Swatantra is, as Sukhadia said, the 'natural home' for the princes and other aristocrats, the Congress has been notably reluctant to let them repair to it *en masse*, forever holding the privy purses and compensation payments, as well as more positive inducements over their heads.[78] It is ironical that one of Swatantra's principal liaison men with the princes was Menon and that many Swatantra leaders fondly remember Patel as a bulwark against socialism, because to the policy engineered by Patel and Menon can be attributed most of Swatantra's difficulties in recruiting the former princes. Still, the problem goes beyond the threat of punishment. The Maharajas of Jaipur and Patiala were offered and accepted ambassadorships; and it is difficult to conclude that partisan political considerations were not involved here. Particularly in the case of the Jaipur family, even a diminution of political activity could well be disastrous for Swatantra in Rajasthan.[79]

In the tense battle for princely support, there was a moment of comic relief when the ex-ruler of Bastar, after being deprived of his title and privileges, announced that 'Minoo Masani, the Swatantra Party leader, will be co-founder of the proposed chamber [of princes] with me'. Masani, in denying this claim, stated that 'there can be no place in such a move for us commoners'—which did not prevent Ranga and other Swatantra leaders from criticizing the government for its alleged heavy-handed treatment of Bastar.[80]

The influx of the aristocrats, through party mergers and individual entry, has certainly been the most important development following the consolidation of the inner circle of the party.[81] India's ex-princes and landed nobles either dominate or are very important in the Swatantra units in Bihar, Orissa, Rajasthan, UP, the Punjab, and, to a lesser extent, Gujarat; and in higher circles, first Ramgarh and then Gayatri Devi have served as Vice-Presidents of the party. The Maharani's remark, 'I am not a politician and God forbid I should ever become one',[82] suggests that she is something more of a symbol than was Ramgarh; but her presence among the top national office-bearers must come as a happy reminder to aristocrats that even in Swatantra traditional rank seems to have its privileges. But more important than party offices held is the fact that Swatantra's legislative strength is very heavily dependent on the residual appeal of the aristocrats.

The entry of the aristocrats, who in Swatantra are very heavily Rajput, introduced into the leadership cadres the element of aristocratic conservatism and the often overweaning pride of this *kshatrya* group; and this was true even of the 'little' Rajputs long separated from dominant positions. One of the latter, fiercely proud of his *kshatrya* background, insisted that the government of the country be returned to the 'martial races', especially the Rajputs.

These alone, he said, could protect the country against aggression and maintain effective rule domestically; and to emphasize his point he noted with obvious disgust and equally obvious conviction that the commander-in-chief of the Indian armed forces (President Radhakrishnan) could not even ride a horse or fire a rifle.[83] A 'big' Rajput from the same state casually remarked: 'I do not believe in democracy, but in autocracy—benevolent, of course.'[84] In addition the same man wrote that 'it is my firm opinion that the only persons who can take over power from the Congress Party immediately and run the affairs of the country successfully are the princes of India. They are not only capable of ruling the country well, but they have the affection and backing of the people. They are being well-received and trusted even in British India.'[85] Similarly, a Rajput leader from Rajasthan, who described himself as 'conservative socially, conservative economically, and conservative politically', echoed the words of almost every Swatantra aristocrat when he said, 'the people now realize that they were not so badly off when we ruled them'.[86] It was Ramgarh who referred to the Congress as a 'new class' of 'demi-gods and career politicians' who exploit the ignorant masses 'for strengthening their own class rule' and who termed it 'an upstart body' which 'has not built up the traditions of authority and command through time with a corresponding attitude of obedience among the masses'.[87] A fitting last touch to this monument to aristocratic arrogance was the passionate statement of the same Raja: 'If I am to function as the Instrument of the people's Will, then I must not be fettered from above or within...If I am not allowed to work out our destiny, then this is the time someone else is put in charge of Bihar affairs and I am absolved of historic responsibilities.'[88] These by no means exhaust the available supply of such statements by Swatantra aristocrats, but they will serve as evidence that aristocratic sentiment of the type described earlier is far from dead.

One should remember, however, that even some of the more vituperative aristocrats, like Ramgarh, are committed to modern industry and are willing to participate in the existing political system, as least as long as there is no plausible alternative. Moreover, we must also remember that the ex-rulers of Patna and Kalahandi took the Ganatantra Parishad along a generally moderate path and both proved to be resilient in outlook and Tory democrat in their approach. Kalahandi, in addition to being an effective spokesman for the hill people of Orissa in the *Lok Sabha*, acquitted himself well in other respects. No friend of the CPI by any means, Kalahandi could still say, upon the termination of the Communist ministry in Kerala: 'I simply shudder to think that an Assembly could be dissolved and a Ministry dismissed, even though it enjoyed the confidence of the House.'[89] Such examples are not sufficient proof of the acceptance of the new order, because some of the most arrogant and reactionary aristocrats have acquitted themselves tolerably well in legislative chambers, and many will try to score against the Congress, even if it means defending the CPI. But taking his public record as a whole, Kalahandi fares quite well. If anything, at the state level, Patna fares even better. Similar differences between 'old-style' and 'new-style' aristocrats have been noted elsewhere, as, for example, by the Rudolphs in their comparison between Dungarpur and Gayatri Devi in Rajasthan.[90] However, it is worth stressing another point made by the Rudolphs: that in some cases, the very act of participation in the democratic process has helped to make this process more respectable among strongly conservative segments of the aristocracy.[91]

SWATANTRA AND THE 'OLD WARRIORS'

The 'old warriors'—by which we mean veteran politicians with some standing—could be useful to Swatantra as vote banks also, if they retained some support on a caste or factional basis. This was, of course, particularly true of Congress old warriors, because of their association with the nationalist movement and/or with the party which had had overwhelming control of India's political life since independence.

As ex-Congressmen themselves, some of the leading Swatantrites understandably hoped that former colleagues would join them in their new political venture. As interview and questionnaire data bear out, the ex-Congress Swatantra leaders were convinced that the vast majority of old Congressmen were ideologically at one with them,[92] and they were particularly anxious to recruit certain of the old warriors of the generation of Rajaji, Munshi, *et al.*; and it was in large part because of Munshi's presumed appeal to such groups in north India that so much pressure was put upon him to join the party.[93] On the other hand, the Swatantra leaders knew that they had to be wary of carreerists and opportunists, who might seek (temporary) refuge in Swatantra because they had been denied a Congress ticket, etc., and who would be likely to rejoin the Congress under more favourable circumstances.

At the outset, Rajaji seemed to draw no distinction among Congressmen. All, in his view, had been corrupted by the lure of power and pelf. As he put it on one occasion: 'I do not want to attract Congress members into this—God forbid. Let them be in the Congress and let them carry on, and maybe, they will improve also by competition.'[94] At least on the verbal level, Rajaji was content simply to encourage Congressmen to do some soul-searching and to rethink their positions.

None the less, many of those who quickly joined Swatantra were Congressmen and of the careerist type; and in almost every area there was a scattering of such poeple who tried to move into leading party positions. Many early organizational problems in Madras, Rajasthan, and Delhi, for example, are traceable to this influx, which generally resulted in the self-declared leadership of these ex-Congressmen and in conflict between them and long-standing anti-Congress elements which had also been attracted to Swatantra.

Little was done by Swatantra leaders to keep such opportunist elements out of the party, but by the same token they were not always given full tether to do as they pleased. Some departed voluntarily after failing to make much headway, after being superseded by other entrants into the party, or after realizing that the Swatantra treasury was not a bottomless pit which could satisfy all of their desires. Others (including some INDC leaders) were pressured into leaving. One member of the Swatantra inner circle tells the story of a party meeting at which Rajaji heard an ex-Congress Swatantrite promise a Swatantra ministry in his state in the near future. Rajaji's mumbled reply, according to this source, was a terse 'God save us from that'.[95] This neatly captures the essential flavour of the issue: Swatantra was not about to turn recruits away from the door, but many leaders were far from ecstatic about some of the early entrants into the party.[96]

Some Congressmen were, however, *persona grata*, viz. the old warriors who stood shoulder-to-shoulder with Rajaji during the nationalist struggle. Paliwal was, of course, such an old warrior, but he had left the Congress in 1951; and Rajaji was anxious to recruit those who still remained, such as Mahtab in Orissa,

Hanumanthaya in Mysore, Jai Narain Vyas (now deceased) in Rajasthan, among many more. Thus, after Mahtab's fortunes declined in Orissa (after the termination of the Congress-Parishad ministry), Rajaji commented on a press report that Mahtab would join Swatantra by saying:

Not only Dr Mahatab but all the old warriors of the Congress who do not approve of and are not happy with the permit-quota-license raj that goes by the name of socialism, are to join hands with me...I know that some senior politicians hope to improve the Congress from within, but I am trying to make them see that this is no longer possible and that they will thereby become instruments for the continuance of the present Congress policy.[97]

An élite comprised of such people would have been much more congenial to Rajaji and much more homogeneous than the one which actually developed. But Mahtab did not join, nor did most of the others whom Rajaji had in mind, even though many of them repeatedly made public pronouncements of which any Swatantrite might have been proud.[98]

Failure was not total, however. In addition to old warriors already mentioned in other connections, Swatantra was able to attract a few Congressmen whose names would mean something, locally, if not nationally. Dahyabhai Patel, son of the Sardar, once mayor of Bombay and President of the Bombay Congress, and a man who described himself as 'fairly orthodox', 'non-westernized', and a supporter of modern private enterprise, was among these, and his has been a dominant voice in the Swatantra *Rajya Sabha* contingent, of which he is the leader.[99] Harihar Das, son of a former Congress Chief Minister, joined the party in Orissa and sought to organize it in the coastal regions; and Maganlal Joshi, a veteran member of the States' Peoples' organization in Jamnagar (Gujarat) and then the Congress, speaker of the Saurashtra assembly, an *arya samajist* and retired advocate, joined Swatantra at its inception, because of 'its Gandhian outlook'.[100]

A major entrant into Swatantra was Bhailalbhai Patel ('Bhaikaka'), a highly respected Gujarati who escapes easy classification here. An engineer by profession, with a distinguished career behind and ahead of him, Bhaikaka responded to Sardar Patel's call to engage in Gandhian 'constructive work' and abandoned his career in 1942. Since that time, his abundant energies have been occupied on many fronts, but mostly in education and 'rural uplift'. However, rather than idealizing village India and insisting on maintaining (or restoring) its pristine purity, Bhaikaka has instead worked for a different solution: to bring modern techniques, modern education, and modern amenities to rural India, i.e. the direction in which Rajaji is now tending. A major, modern, residential college in a rural setting and a wide range of modern, highly efficient small-scale industries are among the accomplishments which have earned him the respect and admiration of the people of central Gujarat, and elsewhere. He is, then, no technological primitivist, no obscurantist, but a man who wants swift attention to the desperate problems of rural India; and his entry into politics, at the age of sixty-plus (via the *Lok Paksh*, in 1952), flowed largely from his desire to redirect what seemed to him a lethargic, inept, and urban-oriented government, along these lines. Although he is not, strictly speaking, a Congress old warrior (as this term is used here) and although he had no political following in the strictest sense, his appeal and his energy have played a major part in building Swatantra in Gujarat, where he is state President.[101]

Among the non-Congress 'old warriors' there were also some very distinguished men. One of the most outstanding of these was Chatterjee, the former President of the Hindu Mahasabha, whose role in right-wing unity talks has already been cited. Despite his connection with the Mahasabha, Chatterjee has been described by a most unlikely source of favourable comment as 'only a causal politician' but a 'brilliant lawyer' and one of the 'ablest opposition members' in the 1952–7 *Lok Sabha*. A man whose 'objectivity' was acknowledged even by the CPI, Chatterjee was regularly courted by the CPI as well as by the Jan Sangh, because, as a minimum, everyone respected his legal acumen and parliamentary skill and diligence.[102] Upon his entry into Swatantra he was designated as President of the West Bengal unit.

Less well known than Chatterjee but also highly regarded was Professor M. Ruthnaswamy, one of the 'founding fathers' of Swatantra. A veteran politican, Ruthnaswamy had combined a career as professor of political science, Vice-Chancellor of Annamalai University (Madras), and extensive work as one of India's most prominent lay Catholics, with his involvement in the Justice Party in the old Madras presidency. After the effective demise of this party, Ruthnaswamy remained aloof from organized politics until Swatantra was established, although for four years he published a paper called *The Democrat*, which, he said, expressed Swatantra-type principles. Ruthnaswamy contemplated starting an opposition party as early as 1951 but did not consider himself sufficiently notable or wealthy to take the lead personally.[103] With Dahyabhai Patel, he has been one of Swatantra's ablest spokesmen in the *Rajya Sabha*, and after the resignation of Paliwal, Ruthnaswamy was named as a Vice-President of the party. As a Catholic and one who had a long-interrupted political career, Ruthnaswamy was a less significant recruit than Chatterjee, although he was certainly respected locally and among Indian Catholics generally.

Still another prominent non-Congressman who joined Swatantra at the outset was J. Mohammed Imam from Mysore. Imam was a member of the Mysore legislature in princely state days since 1930 and was a member of the Muslim League until 1947. He joined J. B. Kripalani's Kisan Mazdoor Praja Party (KMPP) but was alienated when this Party joined with other socialist groups to form the Praja Socialist Party (PSP). After independence he was the leader of the opposition in the Mysore assembly from 1952 to 1957 and sat in the *Lok Sabha* from 1957 to 1962, joining Swatantra in 1959. A very staunch secularist and anti-communist, Imam felt very strongly the need to consolidate the opposition forces in India and, more generally, to reduce the number of parties overall, with the ultimate objective of establishing an approximation of a two-party system in the country.[104] One could cite other recruits of comparable stature, but these three—Chatterjee, Ruthnaswamy, and Imam—will suggest the potency of Swatantra's appeal. And it is not to be overlooked that these three men were of three different religions and from three different political parties, yet all were willing to cast their lot with Swatantra.

On another front, Swatantra leaders turned for a time to some leading independents in the *Lok Sabha*, first to bolster the small contingent of converts in the 1957–62 *Lok Sabha* and then to provide some possible leadership in the absence of Masani and Ranga, who were defeated in the 1962 general elections. The most prominently mentioned in this category were Prakash Vir Shastri (UP) and M. S. Aney (Maharashtra). The former, a leading independent, a very vocal and competent MP, an *arya samajist* and a leading exponent of Hindi as the national language, would certainly have been a significant addition to the Swatantra *Lok Sabha* group. Aney, a former Congressman and Governor of Bihar, has been a spokesman for the *sanatanist* elements, the most orthodox segment of Hindu society, and he has stressed the need for a simple, spiritual life, for Hindi as the national language, and for a renaissance of Sanskrit as an indispensable aspect of India's regeneration.[105] Shastri would have reinforced somewhat the more militant strand in Swatantra, Aney would have pulled more strongly toward the conservatism of the RRP, and both in this sense would have run counter to the broadly moderate character of the Swatantra inner circle. The fact that efforts were made to recruit them suggests that some leaders were not overly concerned about this point, but, in any event, Swatantra did not have to confront the issue: neither Shastri nor Aney nor any other independent of stature in the *Lok Sabha* joined the party, although according to certain Swatantra records, Aney had actually committed himself, but subsequently reneged.[106]

SWATANTRA AND THE ADMINISTRATIVE-PROFESSIONAL GROUP

In addition to the groups and individuals just discussed, a number of distinguished professionals and former administrators also joined the Swatantra Party. Their utility as vote banks was obviously quite limited, but it was not in every case non-existent. Their importance, however, lay primarily in other areas.

The presence of V. P. Menon among the founding fathers provides a useful starting-point. Menon entered government service in 1914 and in 1942 (the year of the 'quit India' movement) he rose to the position of constitutional adviser to the Viceroy—a most prestigious post, indeed. After serving as Patel's principal lieutenant in the integration of the princely states, he became for a short time acting governor of Orissa, before withdrawing from active public life. He was, thus, another older, distinguished man, without any roots whatever in mass politics; and in this sense he reinforced some of the tendencies we have already noted in the Swatantra inner circle. After his quickly aborted role as Joint Secretary of Swatantra, Menon held no major party office, but he was involved in high-level national deliberations and in Mysore state affairs. In addition, he played a major role in liaison work among India's ex-rulers. For much of this period, however, Menon was extremely ill and virtually immobilized; and in January 1966 he died.

Menon, however, also serves as a symbol of the attraction which Swatantra has had for the older generation of civil servants, judges, educators, etc. For many of them, the entry into Swatantra represented the first venture into partisan politics; and the fact that they, in a sense, waited for Swatantra for their political baptism must not be overlooked.

Here, too, even a partial list indicates the stature of some of these recruits and their role in party affairs. One of Swatantra's principal spokesmen on economic affairs and general administration, and a Vice-President of the Mysore unit, is J. M. Lobo Prabhu, a Christian and former ICS officer of the highest rank; and Lobo Prabhu noted with satisfaction that when he served under Rajaji, the latter did not 'meddle' in the administration as does the more recent group of politicians.[107] Also prominent in the Mysore unit are K. H. Srinivasan, former director of agriculture in Mysore state, and M. A. Sreenivasan, civil servant in a number of princely states, Prime Minister of Gwalior state, director of the state-owned Kolar gold fields (after independence), and a businessman with wide-ranging and formidable interests. With Menon and Jinraj Hegde (AIAF, lawyer), Lobo Prabhu, Srinivasan, and Sreenivasan combined to give the Mysore unit leadership an almost awesome aura of administrative experience and professionalism, to an extent not duplicated by Swatantra in any other state.[108]

Elsewhere, other individuals of comparable background gave Swatantra much help; and even where they did not hold party office, they played a role in the party's propaganda efforts, or as candidates, etc. As we have already noted, B. L. Singh, who headed the AIAF at the time Swatantra was founded, was a professional agricultural economist and an adviser to the national Planning Commission. In addition, T. Krishnamma, a retired sessions judge, has served as General-Secretary of the Andhra unit; Col. H. R. Pasricha, a former army doctor and now a practising surgeon in Delhi, once was President of the Swatantra unit in that city; V. Narahari Rao, a retired Comptroller and Auditor General of India, contributed frequently to *Swarajya*; Narayan Dandekar, another former ICS officer and now a businessman and a partner in a firm of chartered accountants, has headed the party in Bombay and Maharashtra and is now national Joint Secretary and a most articulate MP; R. V. Murthy of the *Eastern Economist* has served as Joint Secretary of the Bombay city unit; and Lt. Gen. Thakur Nathu Singh of Gumanpura, a retired Sandhurst-trained Rajput general, has been sporadically active in the Rajasthan unit.[109] More recently (1966) two exceedingly prominent ex-ICS men joined Swatantra in Gujarat and were designated to stand as *Lok Sabha* candidates in the 1967 general elections. One was C. C. Desai, who at one stage was the Indian high commissioner in Pakistan. The other was H. M. Patel, who had held the highest administrative posts in the finance and defence ministries and who, after his premature retirement in the wake of the Mundhra scandal, served as chairman of the Gujarat electricity board and was associated with Bhailalbhai Patel in his various activities.[110] This does not exhaust the list, and it excludes in particular a number of prominent businessmen who have joined the party, and others, like Professor B. R. Shenoy, probably India's leading free enterprise economist, who have given aid at key junctures, though they are not officially party members.[111] In almost every state in which it has sought to organize (and in some where it has made only a very feeble effort) Swatantra has managed to attract at least a small group of such distinguished professional men.

The former civil servants and some of the other British-trained professionals brought a uniform outlook into the party only in a very general sense. The tie that binds is a marked feeling that since independence the 'politicians' have let the country down, that there has been a too rapid expansion of political—as opposed to 'expert', 'impartial', or 'enlightened'—decision-making, that there has been a too rapid democratization of political life generally and that there has been excessive political interference in all spheres.[112] This has led, in their view, to sordid political manoeuvrings, corruption, a disregard for law and order, and appalling decline in administrative efficiency and *esprit de corps*, and a precipitous deterioration of educational standards—all quite apart from the government's 'socialist' tendencies.[113] This group displays, in short, an élitist and administrative approach to public affairs, a more 'Platonic' view, if you will; and it displays great distress at what appear to be inevitable concomitants of the shift from the 'detached' and 'expert' rule of administrators and of the educated in general to mass politics and the ascendancy of the politicians. In so far as politicians are mentioned with any approval, they are of the tougher, law-and-order type, including Patel, Rajaji, and Munshi.[114] In Rajaji's case, at least, the admiration was reciprocated: in the mid-1950s, he was calling for a 'professional authority' of senior civil servants to oversee public affairs, in order that 'the administrative services should be saved from the pressures of state politics', which in his view were verging on anarchy.[115]

An important aspect of this administrative mentality is grave suspicion about universal suffrage, at least under present Indian conditions. Few advertise this publicly, of course, although some have indeed done so. Many more admit it in private. One of the prominent Swatantra professionals from Mysore insisted that 'the voting right should be conceded only to those who have a minimum educational qualification', and he added that simple literacy was insufficient.[116] Another Mysore professional stated flatly, 'if this is democracy, we would have been better off under the British and the princes'.[117] Lobo Prabhu has commented that 'it is one of the consequences of democracy that enthusiasts are preferred to experts in the administration', and Phiroze Shroff, a frequent contributor to *Swarajya*, has insisted that 'in our country...the overwhelming mass of the people are not equipped to exercise the franchise'.[118] He added, as other Swatantrites have, that 'adult franchise, which is supposed to be a boon for the people, actually works to their great disadvantage', largely because they are 'deceived and misguided by professional agitators' and are themselves too stupid to realize the cause of their misery.[119]

This view is, of course, shared by many non-administrators in Swatantra. Ramgarh's views on the subject have already been noted, and like him, Dungarpur accused the Congress of seducing 'his' people by making unfulfillable promises which he would not make, because he was 'above misleading them'.[120] A. D. Shroff betrayed the same sentiments when he commented in derogatory fashion that Nehru and the Congress had been put in office by an illiterate electorate; and Nehru, among others, was not long in spelling out the more ominous implications of such views.[121] Even Rajaji himself recurrently refers to the extreme 'gullibility' of the people, although he is very careful to disclaim all anti-democratic implications of such remarks.[122]

A 'thinking man's' bias runs through all of these remarks, linking many of the disparate groups which comprise Swatantra. It should be clear, but must be underscored, that in general this view goes beyond the charge that the masses cannot govern themselves. Most of these remarks indicate that the people are not even capable of supporting a sound élite in office, and they indicate, too, that the argument about the people knowing 'where the shoe pinches' is probably not apt either.[123]

Vestiges and undercurrents of a more strictly conservative outlook intrude into the broad administrative-professional position. Suspicion about universal suffrage may flow from experiences under the British, but it may also flow from, or be reinforced by upper caste fears about lower caste assertiveness. Pertinent here is Menon's contention that *hereditary* village officers in Mysore should be retained, because 'the efficiency of the hereditary cadre can never be equalled by men recruited on miserable salaries from other families'.[124] Similarly, the Mysore unit of the Swatantra Party, heavily influenced by Menon, Lobo Prabhu, Hegde, M. A. Sreenivasan, and other administrative-professional men, opposed the transferral of local government functions from hereditary officers to those elected under the system of *panchayati raj*.[125] This was in part due to the fear that the Congress would control these elective bodies and reinforce its 'statist' tendencies, but it is clear from Menon's contention that other factors were involved here as well. In analogous fashion, Sreenivasan has used the plea of 'efficiency' to censure the government for its efforts to bring depressed classes into government service, through reservation of positions.[126]

Beyond this, Menon took a very explicitly conservative stand. He expressed his own personal aversion to and suspicion of 'mass' politics, and said, on one occasion, that 'rightly understood, the Swatantra Party is a conservative Party, but there is nothing to be ashamed of in wise conservatism'. He insisted that conservatism was not synonymous with reaction, that given the 'fact of incessant, bewildering change' there was a need for a conservative counterweight, because 'men must have stability; they must have something to cling to...Only those who think that nothing in the national past was good can wholly oppose conservatism.'[127] On this basis, he defended the inherent scepticism of the conservative, especially with respect to what he termed the two major sources of change, 'technology and social theories'. On this, he and Rajaji obviously had a good deal in common.

As in the case of Rajaji's defence of the 'old culture' on non-traditional grounds, views such as Menon's and Sreenivasan's raise important questions in terms of political development. As was true in Rajaji's case, the use of a newer vocabulary, i.e. 'efficiency' for Menon and Sreenivasan, represents an advance over an explicit defence of the old caste hierarchy and of the inherent superiority of the Brahmins and/or *kshatryas*. Eventually, the arguments about efficiency might be used against some of those who now expound them, but in the shorter run they reinforce the *status quo*. In short, as in Rajaji's case, though the defence is not explicitly traditional, is not the practical outcome much the same, i.e. a substantial reinforcement of the old order?

The anti-democratic bias is not particularly edifying or encouraging, and it certainly does not help the prospects for democracy, if one repeatedly hears that the masses and the politicians who emerge from them are incapable of managing public affairs properly. But the inveterate optimists, at least, could point out that this is a less serious matter than might seem at first glance. Most of the administrative-professional élitists are reluctant politicians at best, many are only part-time politicians, and few, if any, have any roots in mass politics. If they are not dedicated democrats, neither are they dedicated counter-revolutionaries. They certainly display no enthusiasm for the more frenzied militant Hindus and, to a lesser degree, they are not enamoured of aristocratic pretensions either. As Weiner said of the businessmen, they are not likely to seek the overthrow of the democratic régime, although many would not be inordinately sorry if others did.[128] In this sense, the unreconciled aristocrats are more to be feared.

As long as the political structure remains substantially secure, the administrative-professional viewpoint may, on balance, be viewed in a more optimistic fashion. The presence of this group in Swatantra suggests a willingness to work within the contemporary political framework, even though they dislike some of its basic contours. Even if their use of 'efficiency' as a criterion contains elements of 'disguised conservatism', it does reinforce a more modern political vocabulary. They are often conservative not through the weight of indigenous Indian traditions or through a desire to revert to some nobler Indian past. Rather, they are influenced as much, if not more, by more recent—although perhaps not less outmoded—political attitudes: those of the early Congress 'Moderates' on the one hand and of the administrative state 'above politics' on the other. If they do bring to bear the administrative, judicial, educational, and other standards of the British *raj*, their presence in Swatantra would seem to reinforce the moderate centre of gravity in the party and to give added substance to the party's emphasis on constitutional propriety and administrative efficiency and integrity. Frequently heard assertions that Swatantra has proved attractive to Parsis, Christians, and Anglo-Indians would seem further to underscore the arguments about secularism, moderation, and a respect for the British *raj*: like the administrative-professional groups, these elements received some preferential consideration from the British and all suffered, at least pyschologically, upon the termination of the *raj*.[129] We may borrow the words which Rajaji applied to businessmen and say that many such people preferred the 'placid pool' of the British days to the 'swift river' of post-independence politics.[130] The same, needless to say, is true of the aristocrats as well.

SWATANTRA'S MORE 'MODERN' MEN

Swatantra has also managed to attract some elements whose roots are less deeply embedded in India's past. This more modern component would include many of the businessmen, but it would also include some of the administrators and professionals as well. Most prominent, of course, is the Bombay contingent, including Masani, Mody, Shroff, Vaidya, Dharamsey Khatau, among others who are primarily associated with business and finance; and Dandekar, Murthy, and others who are associated with other professions. A small but powerful group of predominantly Patidar businessmen from Baroda, headed by Nanu Amin, has for a long time been with Swatantra; and recently (1966) they have been joined by Vadilal Mehta, a prominent Ahmedabad industrialist, who was a close associate of Morarji Desai and former Treasurer of the Gujarat Congress. There has been other scattered support from this quarter—R. P. Patodia and S. P. Agarwal (Calcutta), K. Sundaram (Coimbatore), S. S. Koder (Cochin), R. G. Gupta (Kanpur), for example—and since the 1962 elections a few more businessmen have openly identified themselves with Swatantra—as, for example, Chiranjit Rai, who was designated as a Swatantra

Lok Sabha candidate from Rajasthan. Thus far, however, the names of Birla, Bajaj, Sarabhai, *et al.* have been conspicuous by their absence from the roster of Swatantra supporters.

These men are modern primarily in the sense that they are either engaged in or are supporters of technologically advanced, large-scale industry; but many are also secular and liberal (in the classical sense) in outlook as well, and here they derive support from Lobo Prabhu, Pasricha, Ruthnaswamy, among others already mentioned.[131]

One very crude index of the modernity of this group, in comparison with most of the aristocratic and non-aristocratic conservatives in Swatantra, was established by questionnaire data, which showed that almost all of the business and professional men approved of, without significant qualification, the so-called Hindu Code measures; while among the other groups, opposition not only ran high but explanations for opposition were studded with references to the *vedas*, *shastraic* principles, the 'genius of Hindu society', etc.[132] In the economic sector, artificial maintenance of cottage industries is stoutly opposed, putting this group at odds with the 'Gandhians'.

The spirit of this group can be captured easily by examining Lobo Prabhu's weekly, *Insight* or by considering his recommendations for help to the backward classes in his *New Thinking*.[133] In both, statism and the *ancien régime* come in for sharp criticism. Here, however, we shall let Ruthnaswamy and Pasricha speak for the group, remembering that in all important respects, Masani, Lobo Prahbu, *et al.* are with them.

Consider, for example, Ruthnaswamy's estimate of the accomplishments of free India:

> Nothing has been done to make the people want more, and better things—in the matter of food, clothing, housing, nor to turn their minds and their lives to new ideas of freedom, equality, justice, progress, patriotism—to detach them from their addiction to caste and community and family loyalties at the expense of larger interests of country and State. That is why so much of recent social legislation—the Child Marriage Restraint Act, the Anti-Dowry Act, the Inter-Caste Marriage Act, the Women's Property Act—is a dead letter.[134]

Here is a list of desiderata which jar uncomfortably with Rajaji's basic positions: materialism as opposed to restricted levels of living, concern for national citizenship as opposed to attachment to parochial loyalties as an important aspect of social life, a movement toward reform along liberal, individualistic lines, as opposed to an aversion to 'perverted' movements of social reform, and the like. Ruthnaswamy is very much oriented toward western liberalism in values and institutions, while Rajaji is only marginally so, although as we have seen he has moved in this direction of late.

Pasricha was even more outspoken in challenging most of Rajaji's basic perspectives, although as in Ruthnaswamy's case this was far from a battle between equals. Pasricha was a quite reluctant politician; his voice was never loud in party circles, and, with his departure from the presidency of the Delhi unit, it is very largely stilled. But Masani was quite favourably disposed toward him and considered Pasricha the type of educated professional whom he hoped would come into the party in larger numbers.

According to Pasricha's almost complete indictment of things Indian, the 'national mind' is 'largely feudal' with 'caste and group considerations immensely strong'. He further asserts that most Indians, in the face of any criticism of Indian culture, 'react violently and passionately and the pattern is the same though the shades may vary...The stock-in-trade...is composed mostly of two items: transcendant spiritual philosophy and antiquity of the nation.' Noting that the 'claim of antiquity is unassailable', Pasricha denies that it has any connection 'with greatness' in a nation, which is 'determined not so much by age and antiquity as by its achievements in the sphere of human activity'. Here he bemoans the 'complete stagnation and retrogression' of India's 'meagrely educated and under-developed' society; insists that 'Western liberal education opened and broadened the mental horizons', and that this, coupled with the common bond of the English language (against which 'a number of cranks have raised their voice in a loud wail') amounts to an 'enormous debt of gratitude we owe' to the English people and their culture. In his attack on all segments of Indian society, Pasricha censures the isolation of the enlightened Indian from the bulk of the population, his aversion of social reform work, and his 'willing readiness' to 'submit to superstitious rituals at the time of marriage or deaths or any of the numerous other ceremonies that afflict an Indian'.[135] It makes little difference in the present context whether these views are sound or not, and it makes little difference that Pasricha reflects the widespread destructiveness of many an Indian intellectual, taking almost fiendish delight in abusing his own country. What is important is that these views have been expressed and co-exist in a party whose founder-leader is Rajaji, and whose cadres are heavily manned by the aristocratic and non-aristocratic conservatives.

THE GROWTH OF SWATANTRA: SUMMARY

From 1959 to 1962 (and beyond), the Swatantra leadership made a determined bid to build a party which would be an effective, nation-wide opposition to the Congress. In the process, it confronted a wide array of social forces, which were organized and self-assertive in varying degrees. It absorbed many parties, received support from many caste groups, drew upon more modern associations such as the FFE and AIAF, as well as upon segments of the aristocracy and upon many distinguished individuals. The initiative was not in every case taken by Swatantra, but eventually many diverse interests came within the purview of the party. On the surface of it, this would seem to have constituted an impressive start, at least.

Even without knowing anything about the interaction of the major components of the coalition or about the internal balance of power, some specific points deserve to be stressed. The geographical spread, with all its limitations,[136] is noteworthy, because the party did embrace significant elements from both north and south India. If, on the whole, Swatantra's élites were upper caste and generally conservative, there were some lower caste elements on a non-derivative basis in some states, and a few untouchables have held high party offices.[137] If, on the whole, the élites were predominantly Hindu, non-Hindus were very prominently represented both at the national and state levels, which suggests a non-denominational, if not a more strictly secular orientation.[138] Finally, despite the old adage about politics making strange bedfellows, we should note that the coalition included many elements who were, in the not-too-distant past, political enemies; and it included both aristocratic and industrial elements, which is of major importance.

Electorally, the start could also be considered impressive, in light of the 1962 data.[139] To be sure, the party was for all practical purposes non-existent in Assam, Bengal, Madhya Pradesh, Maharashtra, and Kerala—and it remains so as of this writing. In Madras, the mergers and Rajaji's personal appeal produced very meagre results; in Mysore the poll performance was weak, although Swatantra stood a strong second in many constituencies; and in the Punjab, where the emphasis was on the Sikh elements, the poll performance was weaker yet. However, in Andhra, the diverse elements which entered Swatantra gave it some small pockets of support; and in northern UP it had some strength as well. In Bihar, Rajasthan, Gujarat, and Orissa, it emerged as the principal opposition group; and it ultimately achieved this position in the *Lok Sabha* as well. This was no mean achievement.

The electoral data for 1962 merit a few more detailed observations. Eight per cent of the popular vote and contingents of the size secured certainly fell far short of Swatantra's professed goal of providing a strong opposition to the ruling party. Yet by prevailing Indian standards, the Swatantra electoral achievement was still notable; and if one considers the four states in which it was the major opposition group, the picture brightens, as the party stood roughly 1:2 to 1:3 to the Congress in terms of the popular vote, of which it secured roughly 20–25 per cent.[140]

Of decisive importance, however, is the fact that in terms of electoral support and legislative strength, the critical element in the coalition was the aristocracy in the northern states. In the 1962 general elections, only one Swatantrite was elected from south of the Vindhyas to serve in the *Lok Sabha*; and almost all of Swatantra's MPs (*Lok Sabha*) were from aristocratic areas, and were either aristocrats themselves or hand-picked followers thereof. Three of the four Swatantra MPs from UP were themselves aristocrats and the fourth, Dandekar, was elected from Mankapur's district, Gonda. Rajasthan sent the Maharani and one of the Maharajkumars of Jaipur, as well as a scheduled caste man from the Maharani's jurisdiction;[141] Swatantra's three MPs from Gujarat included the Maharajkumar of Kutch and a scheduled tribe man from an area influenced by the Maharaja of Devgadh-Baria; and the Orissa contingent came wholly as a result of aristocratic influence through the Ganatantra Parishad. Bihar must be singled out, however, because it not only sent the largest group—seven—but the members included Ramgarh's mother, wife, brother, sister-in-law, and business manager! The same general pattern is evident at the state assembly level as well. Thus, not only was the influx of aristocrats notable in terms of party leadership positions, but it was also striking in electoral terms as well. Of Swatantra's apparent strongholds, only Gujarat seemed to escape this total dependence on aristocrats, through a more heterogeneous combination of big and little *kshatryas* and some non-*kshatrya* landed and business interests, led by Bhailalbhai Patel.

We have noted in passing some of the negative aspects of Swatantra's effort, as of 1962—it was virtually non-existent in many states, and it fell far short of its own aim of providing a potent opposition to the Congress. Others, of course, could be cited: its failure to absorb the so-called all-India rightist parties; its failure to absorb many like-minded local parties; its inability to pry loose the Congress 'right'; its inability to recruit the major aristocratic families, industrialists, or business groups; and its extreme weakness in India's advanced cities. More important for the moment, however, is the fact that prior to the 1962 elections, Swatantra was not able to keep all of its recruits in the fold. There were minor defections among former INDC leaders and some of Ranga's followers;[142] some ex-Congressmen in Rajasthan, Delhi, and elsewhere, rejoined the ruling party; some aristocrats, including the Maharajkumar of Jaisalmer, defected; and Chatterjee left the party in 1961, on the eve of the elections, about which more will be said subsequently. Some Ganatantra Parishad leaders responded to the 1961 merger decision by entering the Congress or by retiring to the political sidelines; but here, at least, the key figures (Kalahandi and Patna) remained with Swatantra.[143]

In this respect, the period from 1962 to 1967 was more serious from the Swatantra standpoint. Paliwal, who contributed little in 1962 but who was still a major figure in the party, departed in 1963; Ramgarh and Bilaspur departed in 1964; and Padayachi and Mahida departed in 1965, upon most of which we shall dwell later on. Death also took its toll as B. L. Singh, Shroff, Mankapur, Menon, and Nagoke, among others, passed away. These developments have meant, most importantly, that Bihar, a major source of support, has been totally lost for the moment; that the important Gujarat *kshatrya mahasabha* front may split; and that the limited support in UP has been weakened. In terms of Swatantra's own organization and resources, Gujarat alone offered cause for optimism, as increased aristocratic, business, and ex-ICS support seemed to balance Mahida's defection.

From this vantage point, it could be said that Swatantra not only achieved a modest coalition, but also an unstable one. However, to have expected Swatantra, in such a short time, to build a coalition nearly equal in strength to the Congress would have been most naïve; and one must never forget the difficulties which the Congress itself had in creating and maintaining its coalition, with the advantage of the anti-imperialist rallying point. On balance, Swatantra in 1962 should have been judged quite successful, in quantitative terms.

But a quantitative approach will not suffice here, for we must also know what kind of coalition has been created, not only in terms of viability but also in terms of orientation and performance. Some of the qualitative aspects of the coalition have already been touched upon, e.g. the social bases, the strong element of conservative élitism, the appearance of secularism. However, we must consider in more detail how the different components fit together, where the stresses and strains are, and where the balance of power lies, before we can come to any major conclusions concerning Swatantra's performance in qualitative terms.

CHAPTER 7

THE SWATANTRA COALITION: THE BALANCE OF POWER

The Swatantra inner circle is itself a heterogeneous group. With the entry of the parties, groups, and individuals discussed above, some of the existing perspectives in the inner circle were reinforced, while some new ones were introduced. Men like Paliwal were akin to Rajaji and Ranga, and they strengthened an already strong element in the party. Chatterjee temporarily supplemented Munshi's more militant viewpoint, but this continued to remain a very minor theme in Swatantra. Some business recruits augmented the strength of Masani and Mody, but direct business participation is less important than its role in party finance. The administrative-professional elements introduced some new perspectives into Swatantra, although in some cases these turned toward Rajaji's conservatism, in others toward Masani's liberalism. The aristocrats unquestionably added the major new dimension to the Swatantra élites. Thus, social and doctrinal diversity is present; and, for that matter, there is evidence of considerable conflict among the components of Swatantra prior to the creation of Swatantra. What, if any, are the problems flowing from this diversity and from this prior conflict? What, in particular, are the relationships among the aristocrats, the non-aristocratic conservatives, and the more modern (and sometimes liberal) elements in the party, and what is the balance of power among them? These are the questions which must now be answered.

There is probably a tendency to be excessively rationalistic in trying to explain how and why such diverse forces managed to come together under the Swatantra banner. Motives and goals were certainly diverse, and even on some fundamental policy issues, such as land reform, there is far from universal agreement in the party. Indeed, there is far from universal agreement on the minimal doctrinal points to which the party members are supposed to assent.[1] To say that all Swatantra leaders, at least, are opposed to communism as they construe it, is doubtless true; and to say that they are also opposed to Congress socialism as they construe it is probably true, too. At least, most have rejected the more concrete manifestations of 'statism' which they have encountered. On the other hand, there is good reason to suspect that not all Swatantra leaders would be averse to the 'right' type of statism—a strong, law-and-order, private-property-oriented régime which, shall we say, 'curbed' democratic 'excesses'.

There is also a general condemnation of the Congress for allowing (or even encouraging) the political life of the country to decay; but even here we must be cautious. Many of those who are presently in Swatantra would have been very happy to remain in or to join the Congress, if only the ruling party had allowed the political process to decay in *their* favour.

There is certainly a broad current of conservative élitism in Swatantra, in which aristocrats, some non-aristocratic conservatives, and some professionals share. There is, moreover, some resonance for this view among the more liberal business and administrative groups, in a manner reminiscent of much nineteenth-century European liberal thought. But even here, there are ample differences within the party élite, as we shall see shortly. None of this should be very surprising, but it is worth repeating, so that no unwarranted conclusions are drawn about what holds Swatantra together. Virtually all that may be said with confidence on this score is that Swatantra embraced many groups, of generally conservative inclination, which were for various reasons at least temporarily anti-Congress.

Whatever the ties that bind may be, there are, in addition, many serious conflicts in the party, due to the social and doctrinal diversity of its component groups and due to the manner in which the party grew. An exhaustive account of these would not only be tedious, but in terms of the main focus of this study it would serve no useful purpose. Here, the following problems will be examined, in the following order: (1) religious diversity and the question of secularism; (2) status and caste considerations, particularly the relationship between aristocrats and commoners; (3) more strictly organizational problems related thereto; and (4) the use of the party's financial resources and other devices, by Masani, to strengthen the position of the modern elements as against the conservatives and to establish the power of the natonal party as against the states, which is a closely related problem.[2] The conflicts between the aristocrats and the non-aristocrats (both conservative and liberal) and between the conservatives (both aristocratic and non-aristocratic) and the liberals are obviously more important in terms of social change and will, therefore, be emphasized here.

RELIGIOUS DIVERSITY AND SECULARISM

The Swatantra Party, as already noted, has managed to attract people from all religious groups in India, and almost all are represented in either national or state élites. This is, by itself, *prima facie* evidence of the party's capacity to contain religious diversity. It suggests an emphasis on matters other than religion, if not a strictly secular orientation.

There are, however, many people at the higher levels of the party for whom religion is not a matter of indifference or of narrowly private expression, as it is for many of the liberals. Thus, two sets of relationships deserve attention, viz. the relations between men of different religions who take their religion seriously, and those between people who take their faith seriously and those who do not.

Rajaji, although devoted to the Hindu tradition, cannot be faulted here, as he has abundantly demonstrated his tolerance of men of all faiths, regardless of how devout they may be.[3] Most of the problems relate, rather, to Munshi's more militant Hindu approach; and among the true believers, the Sikhs are the most disturbed. One Swatantra Sikh, for example, asserted that 'Munshi hates us...and considers us a menace', while another insisted that 'even in the Jan Sangh he would be considered an extremist'.[4] Even disregarding Munshi, however, Hindu-Sikh relations in Swatantra have been far from good, especially in the Punjab, of course. Having relied primarily on the Sikhs in that state, Swatantra leaders were obliged to demarcate spheres of influence, in effect, ostensibly along linguistic lines but with an unmistakable religious dimension.[5] This is, however, the only reasonably serious instance of religious tensions within the party.

Those who are inclined to be more secular in their approach to public affairs have also taken exception to some of Munshi's concerns. Masani, Mody, and Paliwal have at one time or another bemoaned the inclusion of certain Hindu ceremonies at Swatantra meetings, with Munshi allegedly being the villain of the piece.[6] But have the more secular elements been successful, in fact, in going beyond mutual respect among true believers to the point where religion—anyone's religion—is reduced substantially in importance?

Here the situation is quite complex. To be sure, the Hindus in Swatantra have had to display some restraint in order to retain the support of non-Hindus in the coalition, and this is not to be lightly dismissed. However, this is not a one-way street. The religious minorities in the party must certainly be discreet in confronting Hindu religiosity; and by and large the minorities and the liberal elements (which sometimes overlap) have displayed becoming 'tolerance' of conservative, if not militant Hindu opinion. For example, Masani often insisted that the late President Rajendra Prasad had every right to advance his rather conservative views, which is fair enough; but Masani shows little zeal to argue strongly against them, which is not the mark of an aggressive, anti-traditional liberal.[7] Further, a number of non-Hindu Swatantrites declined to express an opinion on the Hindu Code legislation, on the grounds that as non-Hindus they were not concerned.[8] Moreover, the utility of religion as a brake on the alleged surge of communism further serves to diminish the conflict implicit here. Masani himself looked upon India's religions as a bulwark against communism, presumably useful for this purpose, if for no other; although he also deplored the fact that most religiously based parties did not seem to acknowledge the seriousness of the communist threat.[9] Thus, many secularists have blunted their critique, in much the same way as many early Congress leaders sought to suppress the issue of social reform, in the interests of solidarity against the British.

Swatantra is incontestably more secular than the Hindu Mahasabha, RRP and the Jan Sangh, many of whose leaders explicitly eschew secular politics.[10] Although not without its religious tensions, Swatantra has satisfactorily accommodated men of all religions within its ranks. This is to the good. But as in earlier periods of Indian history, there is a question which must be raised: to what extent can the Indian population be effectively mobilized without invoking strongly religious appeals? This question, for which an answer will be suggested in the discussion of Swatantra's *formal* ideology, is of central importance in connection with secularism within the party and the role of the Swatantra liberals.

STATUS AND CASTE ISSUES

Conflicts within Swatantra in the area of status and caste are evident at a number of levels, too, and have an important bearing on the nature and role of the party. For example, the relative standing of various aristocrats has been a major issue in a number of states, indicating that Swatantra has not been entirely successful in overcoming this aspect of aristocratic parochialism. In Bihar, Ramgarh's commanding position deterred higher status Rajputs, as well as the Brahmin Darbhanga ruler, from joining the party.[11] In Gujarat and Rajasthan, there is evidence of strained relations between the 'big' and 'little' Rajputs; and in the former case there is some difficulty with the *nouveaux kshatryas* as well.[12] In Rajasthan, considerations of status and seniority among Rajput ruling families have led to the almost automatic ascendancy of the most prominent Rajputs, to the dismay of others who may be younger and/or of lower status, but who joined Swatantra earlier and were quickly demoted or found the path of advancement blocked. During the courtship of Bikaner, a central issue was the re-organization of the state party leadership, in view of his status; and one highly placed Rajasthan Swatantrite said at one point that Bikaner would probably join if he were made leader of the state party, but that this was impossible as long as the Jaipur family was involved.[13]

All of this is, however, like a minor family squabble compared to relations between Raja Man Singh of Bharatpur, a Jat, and the Rajputs generally; but this spills over into the area of inter-caste animosities as well. Raja Man Singh, one of the earlier aristocratic entrants into Swatantra in Rajasthan, evidently coveted the position of state General-Secretary. However, upon Dungarpur's ascendancy in the state, Man Singh was advised that this post was beneath his status as a member of a ruling family and that he should be made a Vice-President, with special responsibilities in the field of organization—a decision which Man Singh evidently interpreted as being inspired by anti-Jat prejudices. Suffice to say, Raja Man Singh was also dismayed (to put it mildly) when a Rajput who had likened Jats to 'two legged animals' was appointed to an important party position and when some Rajputs (when 'in their cups' as one of them put it) at party meetings have made vicious or derogatory remarks about Jats, in his presence. Man Singh would also doubtless be gratified to know that one of his closer Rajput associates in the party explained his (Man Singh's) discomfort by saying that 'he, like all Jats, has communist tendencies'.[14] It is little wonder that Man Singh has often threatened to resign from the party's governing bodies, if not from the party completely, and, short of this, that he has asked that the Bharatpur area be removed completely from the jurisdiction of the state party.[15]

Thus far, there has been little animosity evident among aristocrats across state lines (although it is interesting to speculate what might happen if some Maratha ruling families joined Swatantra). However, it is clear that the Rajasthan Rajputs consider themselves the superiors of others who have joined Swatantra; and there were some complaints from Rajasthan when Ramgarh was named a national Vice-President—a difficulty now presumably overcome, with Gayatri Devi's ascent to that office.[16] In short, many of the historic animosities among aristocrats themselves remain to trouble Swatantra; and very often matters pertaining to aristocratic status supersede all considerations of ability, party loyalty, doctrinal commitment, and so forth.

The inter-caste problem is, not surprisingly, evident in many states. It is discernible in the unhappiness of some lower caste southerners at what they regard as the excessive 'Brahminism' of some local party units; and this, according to one report, played a role in Padayachi's departure from the party.[17] It is certainly the crucial element in Gujarat, where Patidars and *kshatryas* are often at odds (in Congress as well as Swatantra). This was underscored by the report that the intransigence of some Patidars led to the exclusion of *kshatryas* as candidates in certain districts, to the detriment of the Swatantra poll performance in 1962; and there is evidence, too, that Mahida's defection from Swatantra was in part based on difficulties with some Patidar leaders.[18] (It is interesting to speculate, too, that inter-caste problems may arise between the large number of scheduled caste and tribe MPs and MLAs in the Swatantra ranks and the higher caste leadership.) However, the intercaste conflict is in many cases tied to the aristocrat–anti-aristocrat cleavage, which is one of the most serious to confront the Swatantra Party.

At the state level, relations between aristocrats and commoners have naturally varied according to local conditions. In Gujarat, the aristocrats are important to Swatantra but they do not dominate the state party unit and they have, in general, worked co-operatively with the commoners. However, in the period between 1962 and 1967, more aristocrats have come into the Gujarat unit, and if electoral support in non-aristocratic areas should diminish (or remain fairly stable) while support in aristocratic areas should increase, it would not be surprising to see a change in group relationships in Gujarat.[19] In Orissa, the aristocrats are clearly the dominant element, but they have opened the doors of the Ganatantra Parishad/Swatantra to commoners, some of whom have held high positions in the state unit. There is no marked conflict here, and Morris-Jones' assessment of the Parishad as a 'party of mixed princely and popular character' is well founded.[20] Even so, one Swatantra commoner in Orissa stressed the importance of 'enabling some persons who actually come from amongst the mass to hold some prominent offices', and his was not a lone voice.[21] The problem is (or was) serious but somewhat suppressed in Rajasthan and Bihar, brutal and open in UP.

In Rajasthan, the state unit is so completely dominated by the Rajputs that the conflict has not been particularly visible. However, the Rajput-Jat problem was not only present at the aristocratic level, but more generally as well. Aware of the fact that Swatantra in Rajasthan has an anti-Jat image, Dungarpur, the state President, has taken special pains to assure Jats that they were welcome in the party and that 'unusual' concessions would be made to them, to prove the *bona fides* of the Rajput leadership.[22] Furthermore, Swatantra files contain ample evidence to show that many interested commoners were deterred from entering the party, because of the hegemony of the Rajputs, and that the Swatantra central office is sensitive to this problem. Masani has occasionally sought to persuade the state unit to enlist support from and to open party offices and meetings more widely to Jats and other non-Rajputs.[23] Much the same situation prevailed in Bihar, where Ramgarh and his close associates monopolized high party positions, *de facto* if not *de jure*, to such an extent that loud and frequent complaints were heard about lack of representativeness in the composition of the state executive bodies and about the reluctance of commoners to join the party. In Bihar, however, the Jan Congress/Swatantra elements—scarcely commoners themselves—had some influence and often invited central office intervention in state affairs, thus opening the latter to central office scrutiny.[24] There was, for a short time, an analogous situation in Rajasthan, when some ex-Congress elements and the Rajputs were vying for supremacy; but, with the ascendancy of the Rajputs, Raja Man Singh was virtually alone in pressing for central office attention.

In UP the battle was not only visible, but, figuratively speaking, bloody and was fought largely on home ground. It was in the main a contest between Paliwal (and some of his followers) and the aristocrats. On a very modest level was the complaint of one disputant who said, in reference to the aristocrats, 'Swatantra Party needs more democratic ways'.[25] But at one juncture the language became extraordinarily abusive, earning a reprimand to the 'commoners' from the central office.

The basis for the reprimand requires little elaboration. Paliwal complained in a periodical that 'these feudalists, because of their craze for power and their undemocratic and uncommon ideas and activities, have created a doubt in the minds of the common man and the active workers in particular' about the nature of the party, which they are making 'a seat or jagir for their relatives and caste brothers'. Paliwal concluded his attack by speculating that this 'may prove fatal to the party in the long run'.[26] In the same spirit, but more colourful, was the article by D. D. Dubey, who announced that 'in this party the blood-suckers out-number the people who are really ready to shed their blood'. Lack of middle-class support and workers was, he continued, 'due to the Rajas and other feudal lords. Nobody is prepared to work with them because they are out-dated and ill-famed. They have more or less become the backbone of the Swatantra Party. It is high time that the great thinker, Rajaji, finds out a way to get rid of them from the backbone of the party.' Failure to do so, Dubey concluded, would mean 'suicide, after a brief stage show' by the feudalists.[27] The central office had repeatedly attempted, unsuccessfully, to effect a compromise, by assigning spheres of influence to Paliwal and Mankapur; but neither was happy with these efforts. Finally, Paliwal resigned from the party in the fall of 1963, expressing doubts about its 'Gandhian' quality and objecting to the nature of the UP executive, i.e. the ascendancy of the 'feudalists'.[28] This sort of struggle has had its subdued parallels in many areas, but nowhere did the localized aristocrat-anti-aristocrat battle assume the vehemence that obtained in UP.

It should be clear, however, that absence of conflict is by no means a sign of a satisfactory state of affairs. It may only mean that one group so overwhelmingly dominates a state unit that others are deterred from joining, thus avoiding a conflict situation. But what happens if the dominant group in a state is an aristocratic one? Do the commoners, in other party units or at the centre, assert their positions?

As General-Secretary of the national party, Masani has had to worry about such questions for organizational reasons, but he also worries about them for ideological reasons, as there is good reason to doubt the aristocrats' commitment to Swatantra doctrine and their ability (or willingness) to speak forcefully for the interests of the private industrial sector. The fact that aristocratic dominance in so many northern areas has deterred professional and business interests from coming into the party is a related problem.

The entry of the aristocrats has also received attention, because it was widely heralded by opponents of Swatantra as a sure sign of the party's submission to reactionary interests. Even some sympathetic sources entered *caveats*, for fear that the party's image and appeal would suffer. Swatantra leaders have been so sensitive about this point that they have repeatedly taken pains to indicate that there are more aristocrats in the Congress than in Swatantra. This, alas, is not the important point: the fact is that in Swatantra, these elements completely dominate some state units, as they do not in the Congress; and, as we have noted, first Ramgarh and then Gayatri Devi have served as Vice-Presidents of the national party. What, then, has been Swatantra's policy—if it had one at all—toward the aristocrats?

Least persuasive of the views proffered was Rajaji's statement that entry into Swatantra would purify unreconstructed aristocrats (among others) much as a dip in the Ganges would help to expiate sins.[29] More pertinent is a reminder that when he was Governor-General, Rajaji did seek to reconcile the princes to the new régime and that Menon was second to none in his efforts along these lines. Sardar Patel's policy was, to repeat, the minimum favoured by the Swatantra founding fathers.

For a more elaborate statement of the Swatantra approach generally, we may quote Ruthnaswamy's words at some length:

> There is one community, especially, which has recently 'swum into the ken' of the Swatantra Party and to whom a special appeal is due. That is the community of the princely order...deprived of the opportunities of political work which they had enjoyed and used for centuries. Now in

the era of freedom and independence new opportunities for service have opened to them. From rulers in India they have become citizens of India. And as citizens they have a right to take part in the political life of the country.[30]

The last point is not as trivial as it might sound, because some people have, in fact, challenged this right, either on technical grounds (as recipients of certain types of compensation from the government) or on straightforward political grounds (as representatives of reactionary interests).

Ruthnaswamy had more important things to say, however. He insisted that the princes *should* be politically active, because 'members of this order have the education, leisure, and the independence which come from the possession of property, the experience of administration which will enable them to give disinterested service to the country'[31]—this being a variation on the trusteeship theme. Moreover, he was emphatic that modern political life was organized and based on parties, and that, as a consequence, politically active princes should not contest as independents, but as party men.[32]

But why Swatantra, and what must the princes do to be good Swatantrites? On the first point, Ruthnaswamy said:

Of all the parties in India claiming the allegiance of the princely order, the Swatantra Party is the one that ought to appeal to them the most. It will conserve all the rights and liberties guaranteed to them in the Covenants they concluded with the Government of India... The principles of the Swatantra Party must be agreeable to them for it will conserve the traditions spiritual and secular to which as an order they are attached... It offers them opportunities for the service of leadership.[33]

On the second point he said:

all they have to do is to step down from the high places in which they have lived and moved so far. They must cultivate 'the common touch' of democracy, rub shoulders with and act with the common people... They will have to work hard to secure the knowledge... to become wise and competent leaders of the people. They have only to follow the example of the English aristocracy...[34]

Ideally, then, the princes should be well-rounded, dedicated 'Tory democrats', who are reconciled to the new order.

Ruthnaswamy did not himself explore the extent of this reconciliation, which would have been a most revealing exercise, indeed.

However, another of Swatantra's more modern men, Murthy, argued that Menon had made much progress in the direction of reconciling the princes not only to the new régime but to association with political parties. Similarly, Vaidya has also argued that Swatantra has educated the princes in what he called 'the economic dimension of conservatism'.[35] That is, in his view, Swatantra had induced some princes to go beyond a bitter, diffuse, and largely socio-political anti-Congress posture and to become more rounded and more constructively critical in their opposition to the ruling party. Masani's efforts in this direction are unceasing and considerable; and, as we have seen, there were grounds for both optimism and pessimism, in surveying the attitudes of Swatantra's aristocrats.

Whether India would be better off with princes on the political sidelines is a question we shall not attempt to answer; but if the princes are going to participate in politics against the Congress, it is probably better if they do so through existing political institutions and organized parties, thus helping to establish these on a sounder footing and to serve the modern nation-state and the processes which make it function effectively on a competitive, constitutional basis. And it is also better if the princes who participate in this fashion do so with well-rounded, constructive programmes. Here, Swatantra's self-interest may also work for the public good, if the party's efforts in political education are successful. But that is a very big 'if', indeed.

Some Swatantra leaders, as well as the present author, remain unconvinced by the arguments about or prospects of princely 'conversion' on a wide scale. Most, for example, were quick to agree with the Gujarat businessman who labelled Ramgarh 'the Machiavelli of Bihar...a man no better than a communist...the end justifies the means'.[36] Other aristocrats were similarly censured. But while many leaders felt this way, none supported Paliwal's recommendation that princes should be admitted to the party but should not hold any high party offices, i.e. he would try to force them to be the commoners (of sorts) desired by Ruthnaswamy.[37] In fact, Ramgarh received much support from party leaders in Madras, in Bombay city, and in other 'non-feudal' areas.[38] Conflicts with Ramgarh and others were generally suppressed as much as possible and where they did erupt, they were, as a rule, very much localized. The explanation and the implications seem clear enough: with very few exceptions, only those for whom the ascendancy of the aristocrats makes a tangible difference in terms of power have done battle with the aristocrats. For most, the aristocrats are regarded as necessary vote banks in the accretion of Swatantra strength. This view was, however, reinforced by the feeling that efforts by the *national* party to tame Ramgarh and other aristocrats would set an unhappy precedent for action against other state units, aristocratic or not.[39]

The decisive issue has been the maximization of anti-Congress support, and, for this reason, even many of Swatantra's more liberal elements felt that 'petty' differences had to be suppressed and some doubtful elements in the party had to be tolerated. Rajaji made this quite explicit in discussing the Ramgarh affair, which ended with the dissolution of the Bihar unit and the expulsion of the Raja by the national executive, in the fall of 1964:

> Quite a few friends from all parts of India have been writing to me deploring the dissolution of the Swatantra Party unit in Bihar. Our biggest legislative party was there and naturally all persons interested in the Swatantra Party's progress are shocked and grieved. We tried to get on with Sri Kamakhya Narain Singh and his group all these years in spite of many complaints from other friends in the party in Bihar. Acharya Ranga, Sri K. M. Munshi and I supported him over every complaint and kept his authority in tact [*sic*], because we thought we should not weaken his hands or his group.

After then recounting some of the more recent developments, Rajaji concluded.

> This is the story of Bihar. I wish to assure friends that it is with the greatest reluctance, and under a compelling sense of duty, that we resolved to face the difficulties of beginning on a clean slate in Bihar on democratic lines. We have sometimes to reconcile ourselves to losing what looks like strength, when that strength is illusory and is accompanied by dissension and total failure of work.[40]

What Rajaji did not say is that the party would probably have been humouring Ramgarh to this day had Ramgarh not taken it upon himself to seek admission to the Congress, during the course of the crisis in Swatantra's dealings with the Bihar unit. He also did not bother to note that some other Swatantra aristocrats are little better than Ramgarh, when it comes to functioning on 'democratic lines'.

As Rajaji's statement indicates, Masani was not among those who supported Ramgarh over every complaint; and, indeed, it was in large part due to Masani's handling of Ramgarh that the crisis came about.[41] Certainly Masani kept much pressure on Ramgarh, as he did on Dungarpur and other aristocrats as well. The cynics could easily say that this was due to Masani's personal irritation at not getting a safe seat from Ramgarh or from some other aristocrat and they could point to the fact that Masani was quite prepared to censure Paliwal and Dube for their anti-aristocratic tirades. But this would miss a main point, even if it contained a germ of truth: Masani has a vastly different conception of party organization and discipline than do most of his colleagues, and he is absolutely determined to assert the position of the more modern elements in the party. To both of these ends, Masani has applied pressure, even where the matter of a safe seat did not arise and even where aristocrats were not involved. Here is where the social composition and the broad organizational structure of Swatantra overlap; and for this reason, we must restate some of the modern perspectives and digress to consider some more general organizational matters, before concluding with an examination of Masani's major efforts in this direction.

Briefly restated, the issue is this. The more modern, urban, and sometimes more liberal elements in Swatantra differ sharply in outlook from the other major components in the coalition, whether aristocratic or not. This may be underscored, for example, by noting that Paliwal, although anti-aristocratic, complained that in the Swatantra mixture of Gandhism and modern capitalism there was too much of the latter for his taste. And the fact that many aristocrats are involved in modern industry has done little to blur the lines of demarcation here: even those who are themselves important industrialists have not been good spokesmen for private enterprise (cf. Vaidya's argument) in the *Lok Sabha* or in the state assemblies. For this reason, Masani and those who are most closely alined with him have sought to avoid complete inundation by the aristocrats and by the conservatives more generally; and as a minimum they are determined to see that more effective spokesmen for modern private enterprise sit in the *Lok Sabha*.[42] Even though they frequently stress the points that all Swatantrites allegedly hold in common,[43] and even though they have been obliged to avoid pressing certain positions and have compromised others widely, they have by no means abandoned the field completely. In their efforts, they have used two levers. One is their heavy involvement in formal party doctrine. The second, more critical lever, used with greater zeal in recent years, is the real or potential access to funds in the modern industrial sector, which Masani and a few others have. After considering some of the organizational problems related to the balance of social forces within Swatantra, we shall see that it is very much through the power of the rupee that Masani *et al.* have tried to assert their position.

SOCIAL BASES AND PARTY ORGANIZATION

Swatantra's organizational problems are intimately related to the way in which the party grew (i.e. the absorption of many existing groups) and to the attitudes of those who came into the party (i.e. the parochial outlook of some, the aristocratic aversion to party discipline). It is certainly incontestable that in the areas of its greatest electoral strength, Swatantra is heavily dependent upon the aristocrats; but elsewhere, local notables—both aristocratic and non-aristocratic—play a major role. Paliwal may have accused Mankapur and others of trying to make the state unit of the party a *jagir* for themselves and their caste brethren, but Paliwal and others like him were no less anxious to establish their own control over particular areas. One theme running through discussions with Swatantra leaders was the importance of the notion, 'there but for the grace of God go I', as it pertained to efforts to regularize and to discipline the functioning of the party.

While Masani, in particular, was anxious to establish a well-disciplined, bureaucratically organized party, which would function on the basis of clearly defined procedures, many important, short-run considerations militated against this. For one thing, there was an almost universal use of co-option, on a strictly *ad hoc* basis, for a prolonged period. Thus, as a local notable entered the party, or as an existing party was absorbed, the leading individuals were nominated by the national leadership to hold state leadership positions, as 'convenors' or as formal office-bearers; and many were immediately co-opted as well to serve in national offices or on the party's General Council and the Central Organizing Committee (COC).[44] Particularly in view of the way the party grew, this was a reasonable approach in the early stages of party development.

However, continued use of co-option did not augur well for the emergence of a stable organization based on orderly procedures; and by the time party elections were held, many people who had been co-opted to prominent positions were very well entrenched, indeed.[45]

The frequent demarcation of spheres of influence within a state unit, through action by the national leaders, further indicates the impact on organization of the way in which the party grew and, in turn, created further obstacles to the establishment of the type of party desired by Masani. In those cases where divergent interests came into the same state unit, there was wide recourse to this technique of 'solving' apparently insoluble problems. Thus, Paliwal and Mankapur were assigned different spheres of influence in UP, and the same was true for Ramgarh and Jankinandan Singh in Bihar. The problems in Rajasthan, between Raja Man Singh and the Rajputs as well as among Rajputs themselves, led to the creation of a zonal division of the state, with Gayatri Devi and Man Singh as two of those who were assigned areas over which they would have more or less complete control. As we have already seen, Man Singh has repeatedly pressed to have Bharatpur district declared completely 'off limits' to the state leadership, with which he gets on so poorly.[46] Power struggles, as well as death, have settled some of the underlying problems; but where they have not been so settled, the sphere of influence principle has been difficult to overcome, even with regular party election procedures.

Swatantra's problems here must be differentiated from those which exist in any highly pluralistic society and in federal systems which are not merely formal, wherein essentially local interests and parochial feelings will take shape in local political groupings which resist national party discipline. For one thing, in many pluralistic-federal settings, there is more than a rudimentary party organization which provides a framework within which local notables function and which can survive even after a major defection. In addition, in countries where the electorate is politicized and mobilized, there is often a marked identification with a political party, as opposed to loyalty to an individual leader. Swatantra, at least for the moment, has a weak bureaucratic structure within which its notables function, and there is, not surprisingly, little identification with the party as such. This is particularly important because of Swatantra's dependence on aristocrats, because many of the latter retain the old 'style' and inject 'feudal' values into the party, i.e. they tend to resist regularization of party control, either from above or from below, and they still cherish territorial control on the basis of highly personalized loyalties. (It is significant that within the southern units of the party the sphere of influence principle has not been invoked, suggesting that the conditions which have given rise to its use are tied to the presence of aristocrats, and to their relations with one another and with commoners.) What this means, however, is that a few key defections can virtually obliterate entire state units—just as the RRP in Rajasthan was virtually destroyed in many areas, when some of its key standard bearers switched to Swatantra. Much depends, of course, on who the local leaders are and on how fully they control the local scene; but by and large it can be said that a very small group of people has the power of life-or-death over the short-run future of Swatantra, precisely in those areas where its electoral strength has been greatest.[47] In this sense, Swatantra seems to be little more than an umbrella under which a number of disparate elements have taken refuge; and, to pursue the analogy a bit further, it would seem quite likely that if it either stopped raining or if someone came along with a better umbrella, Rajaji and his colleagues could well find themselves deserted. This is one of the major reasons for Masani's concern.

Other, albeit related effects of an organization based heavily on local notables are discernible in many states and in both parliamentary and extra-parliamentary affairs. Of Swatantra's strongholds, Gujarat has consistently given the least trouble, because the principal aristocratic figure at the state level—Devgadh-Baria—has proved to be a reasonably co-operative party man, amenable to some control from above, at least. Still, Devgadh-Baria's other interests and commitments have kept him from devoting the necessary time to his role as General-Secretary of the state unit; and this, among other reasons, was responsible for the major organizational role entrusted to H. M. Patel, upon his entry into Swatantra in 1966.[48] Orissa has given little trouble here, although grass-roots organizational work continues to be decidedly limited; and with Paliwal's resignation and Mankapur's death, the problems in UP have not flared up. Rajasthan and Bihar merit attention in detail.

In Rajasthan, as already noted, leadership in the Swatantra

Party is very much a matter of seniority in the Rajput hierarchy. Dungarpur was almost automatically raised to the positions of state President and leader of the opposition in the state assembly. With him in these positions, Swatantra has not only been able to survive in the state but also to do tolerably well. Furthermore, in his legislative performance, Dungarpur introduces a measure of dignity and restraint, by happy contrast with the disruptive tactics preferred by some Indian legislators.

The negative aspects of Dungarpur's positions are also evident, however. His rise alienated some earlier entrants into the party. His preference for associating with other leading Rajput aristocrats and for attempting to organize the party on this basis has not only alienated lesser Rajputs and non-Rajputs, but it has also meant that other aspects of building up the party have been neglected, much to Masani's displeasure. This, in turn, led to an effort by Masani to appoint a special organizer who would tour the state, to do the job that neither Dungarpur nor the General-Secretary, Devi Singh (Mandawa), seemed willing to do.[49] As part of his general approach, Dungarpur doggedly refused to clean out 'dead wood' from state cadres, and he was reluctant even to eliminate from leadership rosters the names of some individuals who were, ostensibly, no longer connected with the party, because to do so would have obliged him to take action against fellow Rajput aristocrats.[50]

Another episode which illustrates Dungarpur's negative impact on party affairs was the election of members to a committee in the assembly, where Swatantra's strength would have justified three committee men. At one of the relatively infrequent formal party meetings—itself an index of Dungarpur's style—three names were agreed upon, but someone reportedly prevailed upon Dungarpur to depart from the agreed list and to name him as a party candidate for committee assignment. This greatly upset Raja Man Singh as well as some younger Rajputs in the assembly party, but in part through Man Singh's efforts, all four men were ultimately elected to sit on the committee in question.[51] More generally demoralizing, both inside and outside the assembly, is Dungarpur's well-known view that he has 'had his innings' and that he does not aspire to become state chief minister.[52] Yet it has proved impossible thus far for younger, more energetic, and in many ways more able leaders to come to the fore while Dungarpur is at the helm of the party. Even by relatively modest standards, Dungarpur is an ineffectual leader and the Swatantra unit in Rajasthan is a travesty, rising from its doldrums only when a handful of aristocrats decide something must be done. Opposition to Dungapur is by no means confined only to non-Rajputs, but little can be done to replace him or to regularize party procedures while he remains.

The entry of the Maharani had comparable effects, although she has been more willing than Dungarpur to adapt to the modern political style. Her swift rise, too, led to resentment among many long-standing Swatantrites and many were upset that a celebration was held in her honour when she joined the party. Others sneered at the sum (Rs. 5,000) which she allegedly contributed to the party upon her entry and with which she 'bought' the party, according to these critics. Most important in the present connection was her impact on the organization of the party. As the great Swatantra luminary in Rajasthan, she was aware of her critical role, but as a political novice, she was uncertain as to the best way of establishing her position and of protecting her interests. Thus, she is reported as insisting that as a *quid pro quo* for joining the party, the state General-Secretary must be a man whom she knew and trusted implicitly. The post was bestowed almost by fiat on a Rajput *jagirdar* (the aforementioned Devi Singh), again much to the consternation of many other Swatantrites. At a later juncture, when Masani secured Dungarpur's agreement to have an 'organizing secretary' appointed, the man selected was Ayuwan Singh, one of the Maharani's personal assistants. Neither Devi Singh nor Ayuwan Singh have particularly happy reputations but this seemed to be no deterrent: loyalty to the Maharani outweighed all else. No wonder that many Swatantrites in Rajasthan and elsewhere are disturbed at the course of events.[53]

The moral of this is clear. Dungarpur, although a weak leader, is almost unchallengeable within the state, as is the Maharani. Organizational efforts have been pathetic, and no one in the state leadership seems willing or able to establish a stable, bureaucratic organization or to spread the Swatantra message. What passes for an organization is heavily dependent on the wishes and whims of the leading Rajputs. Meetings are held at their pleasure, party officers are appointed or replaced almost at their pleasure. Given this pattern of events, it is reasonably clear that should the Maharani leave the party, or remain in it but lose interest, many of the *jagirdars* who responded to her call would probably fall by the wayside, leaving Swatantra little, if any better off in Rajasthan than it was before the Maharani's entry into the party.

This situation, and the Rajput-Jat problem would seem to constitute an open invitation for intervention by the central office, and Masani has intervened on many occasions. He has sought to establish a *modus vivendi* between Rajput and Jat but has largely failed in the face of Rajput recalcitrance; he has sought to have Dungarpur take up his role with greater zeal and to refrain from announcing that he had 'had his innings' again with little successs; he has sought to place the functioning of the assembly group and of the state unit as a whole on a more regularized basis, but again with little success. As we shall see in more detail subsequently, Masani also applied considerable pressure to have Dungarpur forget his dislike for Congressmen and to seek to establish cordial relations with Sampurnanand, Governor of Rajasthan and a leading conservative Congressman. Even in the matter of appointing an 'organizing secretary', about which he felt very strongly, Masani yielded to local feelings and agreed to Ayuwan Singh, one of the last men in the state unit who could secure the confidence of Jats. In sum, Masani has thus far relied primarily on persuasion and even this has elicited resentment and charges of 'meddling' among state leaders, although not openly from Dungarpur or Gayatri Devi. Masani would dearly love to establish the Rajasthan unit on a sounder footing, but thus far he has sought to do so within the broad framework imposed by the dominant Rajput interests and related patterns of deference. Any efforts beyond this would require steps inimical to the interests of Dungarpur and the Maharani, and neither Masani nor other national leaders have been willing to take this risk (cf. Ramgarh). It is little wonder that many Swatantra leaders look with envy upon the RSS-Jan Sangh cadres, which are more stable, more disciplined, and more likely to function on a sustained basis than the highly personalized and more traditional associations upon which Swatantra has to rely in many states.[54]

The impulse to intervene in state affairs and the dangers related thereto are best illustrated by the situation in Bihar. As we have seen, Ramgarh was one of the earliest entrants into the party and he was certainly one of its very best organizers, which could not be said for Dungarpur or Gayatri Devi. Although some Swatantra leaders have argued that the Ramgarh-Janata Party forces represented a minority in the state unit, the electoral results indicate that

Swatantra successes were virtually co-extensive with Ramgarh's sphere of influence in the state unit. A tempestuous and headstrong man, Ramgarh, again unlike Dungarpur and Gayatri Devi, made abundantly clear his determination to be free of all unnecessary encumbrances on his personal position—and in his view all were unnecessary. Given his undeniable organizational abilities, and his desire for complete autonomy, Ramgarh (by no means feeling he had 'had his innings') was perhaps an obvious choice for a *laissez faire* approach on the part of the central party. But as in the Rajasthan case, where the problem with Man Singh and the Jats obliged the central office to take cognizance of the state situation, there was a serious internal rift in Bihar. This, again coupled with Masani's determination to establish a modicum of party discipline, set the stage for a bitter and decisive battle.

The seeds of conflict were sown early in the history of Swatantra in Bihar and lay in the differences between the Ramgarh/Janata and the Jankinandan Singh/Jan Congress elements. Very quickly, however, the conflict went beyond the state boundaries. Masani's position as General-Secretary obliged him to take cognizance of difficulties in Bihar, and his own interest in securing a safe constituency, possibly in Bihar, reinforced his official concern. Munshi's friendship with the Darbhanga family added another dimension to the problem. The conflict was by no means unexpected, and with two such strong personalities as Masani and Ramgarh involved, it had the potential to become a very bitter one, indeed.

On Ramgarh's part, there were a number of provocations—whether intentional or unintentional we cannot say—of the centre and of Masani in particular. Ramgarh was generally not very responsive to requests for information about the state unit of the party, and, for example, certain information about party nominees for public office was not forwarded to the central office as requested. Similarly, the list of names for election to the *Rajya Sabha* was not, in Masani's view, properly cleared with the Parliamentary Sub-Committee of the COC. Also irritating to Masani was Ramgarh's successful appeal to the Election Commission that he be permitted to retain the 'bicycle' symbol of the Janata Party for the 1962 elections. This was an indication that Ramgarh considered the Bihar unit virtually co-terminous with Janata, which was not far off the mark, and, in terms of communicating with the electorate,

Ramgarh's request made much sense. For Masani, however, this was a sign that Ramgarh was not disposed to be a good party man, and a plausible interpretation was that Ramgarh was anxious to protect his political future—which did not necessarily include Swatantra—by retaining the Janata symbol.[55]

Throughout 1961 there were serious problems in Bihar, and the central office attempted to resolve some of them by ordering a reorganization of the state executive, to make it more representative of different interests in the state, and by the aforementioned technique of delimiting spheres of influence, both of which Ramgarh doggedly tried to subvert. The situation became so bad that not only were Jankinandan Singh and his group given the right to designate the candidates for certain districts and to disburse certain funds, without reference to Ramgarh, but Ramgarh was also requested to stay out of those districts for a specified length of time. This caused tremendous resentment among the Ramgarh forces, who felt quite rightly that they constituted the hard core of the state unit, that Ramgarh was the most effective organizer in the state, and that as President of the state unit, he ought not to be deprived of the right to screen candidates and to travel at will on behalf of the party. There is some evidence to show that Ramgarh-designated 'independents' stood against Jankinandan Singh's official party nominees, in a move calculated to subvert the latter's position and to show that Ramgarh was the only man to be reckoned with in the Bihar unit. After the elections, in which Ramgarh fared less well than he had hoped, these accumulated grievances came to the surface, in a bold move by Ramgarh to establish himself as 'king' of Swatantra in Bihar and to weaken the position of Munshi and Masani, particularly the latter.[56]

The principal vehicle for Ramgarh's attack on the central office was an appeal from the Bihar unit of the party, submitted to the General Council of Swatantra while Ramgarh, who was in ill-health, was in Europe. There was no doubt, however, that it accurately represented Ramgarh's personal sentiments, for it was a lengthy catalogue of alleged efforts on the part of the central office to meddle in Bihar affairs and to subvert Ramgarh's personal position, with the result that Swatantra in Bihar fell far short of expectations electorally and was in a state of demoralization and disarray. According to the appeal, if only Masani, *et al.*, would have refrained from meddling and allowed Ramgarh to have complete, unrestricted control of the Bihar unit, Swatantra would have been much better off—and there were many people outside of Bihar who fully agreed with this view. The reason for Masani's intervention, according to the appeal, was his difficulty in securing a safe seat.

The matter came to a head early in 1963, when the appeal was considered by the General Council, which had also been advised of Masani's threat to resign if the appeal were sustained. Each side had deputed certain people to line up supporters prior to the meeting, which ended with at least a nominal victory for Masani.[57] Ramgarh, almost obsequiously contrite for having been associated with an appeal which was somehow (!) misconstrued as an attack on the party's leaders, was prevailed upon to withdraw it, and this action was followed by an explicit vote of confidence in Munshi and Masani. All of this fully satisfied none of the principals, but Ramgarh, who had been forced to eat a modest amount of crow, was far less pleased than Masani. But even many of the more modern interests in the Party felt that Ramgarh was too valuable to offend and felt that Masani himself had gone too far in provoking the Raja.

In the aftermath of the elections and the bitterness flowing from the outcome of the appeal to the General Council, Ramgarh, still in control of his bicycle symbol, came to consider a restoration of the Janata Party, which had disappeared in name only. In addition to long-standing grievances, there was a more recent one. During the 1961 election campaign, a very substantial loan was secured by the Raja from the Central Bank of India (the 'Tata bank', of which Mody was chairman of the board) to purchase jeeps for the state unit of the party. After the election, Ramgarh failed to commence repaying the loan, claiming that the party as a whole, not he personally or the state unit, was responsible for this debt. The Central Bank then brought suit against Ramgarh who tried in vain to have the court declare the Swatantra Party as the responsible party. This incident, which suggests the manner in when the men who control funds can seek to bring pressure to bear on local leaders, was regarded by Ramgarh as an obvious, malicious move, inspired by Masani, to 'break' him.[58]

Relations between Ramgarh and the Swatantra leaders were, thus, very poor and the situation in the Bihar unit was just as poor and deteriorating. As indices of this, the party's first candidate

(Parmanand Kejriwal, a businessman) for the *Rajya Sabha* was not elected, because Swatantra MLAs withheld votes from him, while the second candidate (the Raja of Bilaspur) was elected; and a similar incident occurred in an election for the state Legislative Council, which is also indirectly elected. Moreover, twelve Swatantra MLAs, opposed to Ramgarh, defected from the party and applied for membership in the Congress. At this juncture, Ramgarh succeeded in passing a resolution to expel Jankinandan Singh from the party, and at the same time he belaboured his old political adversary, Chief Minister K. B. Sahay, for 'attempting to kill democracy in the State', by weaning away members of opposition parties. This, Ramgarh said, was in direct violation of the National Integration Committee's directive concerning political parties, and he warned that 'naziism, fascism and some other form of dictatorship will emerge if the Opposition parties are wiped out one by one'.[59]

The central office of the party demanded a full account of the disintegration and 'demoralization' of the Bihar unit, but this was not forthcoming. As a result, the national executive, through Munshi, dissolved the state unit, another in a long series of actions taken against the state unit by the centre.[60] Coupled with the other difficulties with the central office, this action pushed Ramgarh even further toward defection. Driven to despair by his difficulties with Masani and still nursing a long-standing grudge against Sahay, who was then the Chief Minister of Bihar, Ramgarh came to feel that the time was ripe to seek entry into the Congress and to throw his weight behind Sahay's opponents, the so-called non-ministerial wing of the party. This seemed more likely to lead to power, pelf and privilege than did continued participation in Swatantra; and at the same time it gave Ramgarh hope that he could even the score with Sahay. Finally, Ramgarh applied for entry into the Congress, and he obviously spoke as well for the overwhelming number of Swatantra MPs and MLAs in Bihar.[61]

The national executive discussed these developments and considered an appeal from Ramgarh against the decision to dissolve the state unit. Confronted with the fact that Ramgarh had already asked to be admitted to the Congress, the national executive rejected the appeal and expelled Ramgarh and one other state leader from the party. The national executive insisted, however, that all other state office-holders, MPs, MLAs, etc., were, in its own eyes, still members in good standing in the party, even though most of the MLAs had affixed their signatures to the request for Congress membership.[62]

The expulsion may seem to have been quite academic, given Ramgarh's negotiations with the Congress. It was, however, at least marginally important and still required a modicum of courage, just as the fairly steady pressure maintained by Masani on Ramgarh required some courage. Whatever inspired Masani to bring such pressure to bear, it was clear from the outset that it was going to antagonize Ramgarh. This meant that Masani, at least, was not so desperate to maximize the anti-Congress effort that complete *laissez faire* would be observed in state units. Similarly, the expulsion of Ramgarh from the party meant that it would be more difficult to re-establish him in Swatantra, if the Congress turned a deaf ear, as had been the case until 1966. The party's declaration that all other Bihar party men were considered members in good standing, even though many had joined Ramgarh in applying for Congress membership, flowed in part from the desire to make it easier to reconstitute the Bihar unit, if Kamaraj turned the applications down; and Dahyabhai Patel was sent by the party to salvage as much as he could in Bihar, in co-operation with some 'loyalists'. Thus, for all practical purposes, ended the Ramgarh affair, as far as Swatantra was concerned; and here, as earlier, the party high command was praised by various journalists for refusing to allow Ramgarh to function unchecked.[63]

The Ramgarh affair points up many aspects of Swatantra's internal functioning, as well as of the context in which it functions. Masani's sense of party organization, his own personal political interests, his influence in the realm of finance, his impatience and quick temper, were all evident here. On Ramgarh's side there was an imperiousness and arrogance, and a determination to be an autocrat, which offended many, both inside and outside the state, and which revealed one aspect of the aristocratic ethos at its worst. From Rajaji we have the admission that he, Ranga and Munshi—and most other Swatantra leaders, for that matter—bent over backward to keep Ramgarh happy, in the interests of their anti-Congress crusade, subordinating their doubts and criticisms to this end. With respect to the Congress, we see that factionalism provided an opportunity for exploitation by outside interests and that political alinements in India are still extremely fluid.

What is most pertinent in the present context is that Ramgarh's departure has virtually destroyed Swatantra in Bihar, notwithstanding some brave words by the central office. With at least five MPs and most of the fifty Swatantra MLAs in his pocket, Ramgarh has amply demonstrated that Swatantra's largely derivative organization is very precarious. Commenting on a reported visit by Masani to reorganize the Bihar unit, Ramgarh overstated only slightly when he said, 'there is nothing left now in this state to be reorganized. Mr Masani will have to start from scratch.'[64] The same would be true if a few other key aristocrats were to leave the party in other states.

PARTY FINANCE

Party finance is of great importance for a variety of obvious reasons. Funds are necessary for the normal bureaucratic activities, for the inevitable transportation and propaganda involved in an electoral campaign, and for other basic requirements. Further, in the absence of dedicated volunteers, funds are necessary to secure paid workers to perform some of these tasks.

Beyond this, however, finances are critical. Assuming that a party is anxious to contest a sufficient number of seats to make an impact—usually enough seats so that it is mathematically possible for it to form a government if it wins all or most of them—the quantum of funds available determines in large measure the options which will be open to the party. If resources are no problem, then the party leaders (or those who control the funds) can seek to set up those candidates who are most congenial to them, who are ideologically sympathetic, reasonably hard workers, etc., or at least people who combine some of these qualities with local appeal. In the absence of ample funds, however, a high premium is put on self-financing candidates or on notable local figures who can win with a modest expenditure of funds. In this case, the central party organization becomes extremely dependent on such candidates and is not likely to establish substantial control over them.[65]

Shortage of funds also makes the party less attractive to possible recruits. In the case of Swatantra, this is especially true regarding some right-wing Congressmen who might well be sympathetic to the party but who might also require financial support and some modest prospect of getting elected, if they are to join. It is naïve to expect veteran politicians to commit their futures to a party—especially a new one—if a decent prospect for public office does not exist. In sum, this makes it difficult to rally the potential faithful and it induces many to bore from within the Congress rather than to go into opposition. This helps to account for the fact that Swatantra has drawn so heavily on elements who either never were in the Congress or who were 'power-marginal' within the Congress; and it also helps to account for the general tendency of opposition parties to put up a number of Congress 'rejects' as candidates.[66]

Thirdly, party discipline and party doctrine are likely victims of insufficiency of funds. It is not uncommon in India for a *Lok Sabha* candidate to spend Rs. 75,000 to Rs. 100,000 and even quite prosperous people do not look forward to that sort of expenditure with equanimity. Those who are willing to pay their own way on such a scale are not likely to submit to the discipline of a party which does little else but give encouragement and, perhaps, lend some modest prestige to a candidacy.

Notwithstanding the ties of some leading Swatantrites with Bombay and other business interests and its reputation as a rich man's party, Swatantra confronted all of these problems in acute form in 1962. As we have seen, Masani has been anxious to disabuse people of the idea that the Swatantra treasury is a bottomless pit from which all would-be candidates can be well supplied. Rajaji, with considerable justification, said that 'the very rich are in the grip of the ruling party'; and as Mody put the matter, most businessmen 'are busy cultivating the ruling party' and though belaboured, periodically they get their due.[67] G. D. Birla, one of India's pre-eminent businessmen, suggested as much when he told a business gathering 'that Swatantra politics were not good businessmen's politics', and a writer generally hostile to Swatantra grudgingly conceded that 'indications are that India's industrialists and capitalists do not want to burn their boats with that Party'.[68] Suffice to say, Swatantra's treasury at the national level was of modest proportions even though many of its policy recommendations were very congenial to India's capitalists.

Swatantra, for a time, sought to underscore the superior financial position of the Congress by recommending a ban on all corporate contributions to political parties; but there was no immediate prospect for such a ban. While reiterating the party's position that corporate gifts should be banned, Masani said that if they were to be permitted, 'we want a fair share of it', and Rajaji and Mody took the lead here.[69]

The nature of the Swatantra appeal is instructive in terms of the party's aims and its assessment of the prevailing climate of opinion in the business communities. Swatantra leaders sent letters to two key businessmen—J. R. D. Tata and Dharamsey Khatau—who were known to be sympathetic to the party, asking for funds for Swatantra. The request emphasized the need for a strong, constitutional alternative to the Congress, if parliamentary democracy were to flourish in India; and Swatantra was, of course, presented as that alternative. At the same time, the letter cited the role of the Congress in achieving independence and stability in the country and encouraged continued support to the Congress for that reason. In short, Swatantra leaders tried to provide businessmen with a rationale for giving to both Swatantra and the Congress, and that rationale was not couched solely in terms of explicit business self-interest.[70]

When, as expected, Tata and Khatau responded favourably to the appeal, Swatantra circulated copies of the Tata-Khatau replies, together with a further request for funds by Rajaji or Mody, to scores of other businessmen. The latter were thus provided with evidence that some leading industrialists were willing to support Swatantra and with a reason for doing the same, viz. to help develop an opposition party, which only 'incidentally' happened to be markedly more pro-private enterprise than other major parties.

The result of Swatantra's courtship of the business communities fell far below party hopes and needs, and only a few businessmen were openly identified with the party, but that was expected. More importantly, the party's hopes for a 'fair share' of corporate contributions were not fulfilled. Between 2 February 1960 and 1 March 1961, the central office received donations of a modest Rs. 250,000. The appeal for funds outlined above led to further contributions of Rs. 3,200,000 between 1 April 1961 and 1 July 1962, the latter date falling after the election period. There were some very substantial donations during this period, including: Rs. 400,000 from Tatas, Rs. 300,000 from Indian Iron and Steel, Rs. 200,000 from Associated Cement, and about Rs. 200,000 from the Martin Burn group of industries. There were a number of contributions ranging between Rs. 25,000 and Rs. 50,000, mainly from the Bombay-Baroda area. Finally, there were contributions of approximately

Rs. 1,000,000 from donors who asked to remain anonymous, lest their support for Swatantra hurt their relations with the Congress. Most of these firms, as well as most of the anonymous donors, gave more money to the Congress than to Swatantra, and most of India's leading businessmen gave only to the Congress. Symbolic of this was Bhailalbhai Patel's claim that a group of Ahmedabad textile men whom he approached (at the state level) ultimately gave Rs. 750,000 to the Congress but only Rs. 5,000 to Swatantra. As far as this author has been able to determine, Nehru's threat to reject any gifts from a firm that also gave to Swatantra remained an idle one.[71]

As the election approached, it became clear that the projected national campaign fund of slightly over Rs. 5,000,000 would not materialize. The central office repeatedly sent out the bad news that it would have to trim its aspirations and to renege on some promises.[72] All candidates for Parliament who were scheduled to receive financial aid from the central office were advised that instead of the Rs. 40,000–50,000 promised, the available funds permitted only Rs. 20,000 to be disbursed. They were also advised, however, that a last-minute appeal for funds would be made to increase this to Rs. 30,000 per candidate, and the evidence indicates that this was finally achieved.[73]

The precise figures are not of great importance, because it is evident that Swatantra was in difficult financial straits. Interviews and party files make it clear that relations with many state units and many key individuals were severely strained, as a result of the inability of the central office to meet its financial obligations.

What was even more distressing to Swatantra leaders was the expectation on the part of many wealthy aristocrats that they, too, get their 'fair share' of election funds from the national treasury, and the Maharani of Jaipur was among them. To illustrate this expectation in a different situation, we need only note the circumstances attendant upon the appointment of one of the Maharani's personal assistants as the special organizing secretary for Rajasthan. In the course of the discussions it was estimated that a minimum of Rs. 4,800 would be required to secure the services of the man whom they wanted. When asked by a representative of the central office if the Maharani would 'foot the entire bill', a state leader said that she would not, and would not contribute at all, unless the state party and the central office contributed as well.

When asked if the Maharani would pay half the amount, the state leader replied that equal shares alone would probably be acceptable, and it was decided that the Maharani, the state party, and the central office each contribute Rs. 1,600 per annum for the organizer's salary and expenses. That such a laborious discussion should take place over Rs. 4,800 suggests neither a generous aristocracy nor a well-filled central party treasury.[74] What this suggests further is that some local notables feel that they cannot only demand money but also refuse to submit to party discipline, because Swatantra needs them more than they might need Swatantra.

In light of such developments, it is little wonder that Masani emphasized 'two basic reasons' for the party's 'distressing experience' in the financial realm:

> The first is the supine and cowardly attitude of the larger part of Big Business in India, which, aside from a few honourable exceptions who practice enlightened free enterprise, continues to turn its back on a Party that stands for a way of life in which free enterprise can flourish, while lavishing its financial support on the ruling Party which is progressively engaged in destroying a free economy.
>
> All one can do is to deplore the fact that fear of reprisals from those in office under a highly controlled economy and the short-sightedness of those who wish to make a quick rupee through obtaining permits and licenses should thus combine with an inadequate awareness of the need to make sacrifices for a way of life in which one believes. The party must persist in its work in the strong conviction that, however unworthy the attitude of many of those in business may be, it has to work for the cause of a free society of which competitive free enterprise is an integral part.
>
> The second reason for the Party's financial plight is the failure of Party members to contribute adequately from their own pockets...and to collect small contributions from those in their respective towns and villages. Small contributions in the way of the poor man's mite spread over a large number of people can give just as much money and in a manner much more satisfying to all concerned than dependence on a small number of people with means.[75]

Swatantra may have had relatively wealthy leaders and it may have spoken on behalf of men of property in both rural and urban India. In these respects alone was it a 'rich man's party'. No one who has seen the party's financial records would conclude that it was generously supported by India's richest men.

In the months between the 1962 elections and Nehru's death, and particularly after the Chinese invasion and its aftermath, Swatantra's financial future seemed brighter, although aspirations could well have run higher as well. Reports from Baroda and Jaipur, for example, indicated greater sympathy and support for Swatantra from some locally prominent businessmen. Also important was the increasing support from Ahmedabad textile interests which had been very reticent prior to the 1962 elections.[76] This is particularly important, because it could help to tilt the balance in Gujarat more toward the modern, capitalist side (both urban and rural) than it is elsewhere.

This improved prospect flowed in part from Swatantra's respectable showing in 1962, coupled with a certain post-invasion boldness on the part of anti-Nehru and anti-leftist forces. Furthermore, those who had supported Swatantra seemed to have 'gotten away with it', although there have been arguments to the contrary. However, to capitalize on this, Swatantra could not rest on its past laurels. Its organization had to be stabilized and to be kept trim, if the party were to build upon the accumulated grievances of the population. Yet, in many areas, this was not done. Stagnation has set in in Rajasthan and in some other states, and the unit in Bihar has disintegrated. This is not the sort of situation which is likely to induce India's captains of industry to 'burn their boats' with Swatantra in 1967 any more than they were willing to in 1962. Furthermore, business support is contingent upon another matter in which Swatantra has been deficient: returning its ablest pro-private enterprise spokesmen to the *Lok Sabha*, and this in turn depends on the ability of the more modern wing of the party to assert itself in the face of the more conservative elements. In short, Swatantra must consolidate and strengthen its position and it must send more modern spokesmen to the *Lok Sabha* if it is to stand a chance of improving its financial position markedly. Furthermore, the behaviour of the Congress toward private enterprise also cannot be ignored in these calculations.[77] Few, if any Swatantra leaders have betrayed much optimism on any of these points.

The fact that business is supporting Swatantra to some modest extent does, however, give the party an edge over the Jan Sangh, whose volunteer cadres make fewer dollars go a good deal further. In this area, one can see a multi-sided battle: within Swatantra, between the conservatives and the more modern interests, and between the Jan Sangh's militant, more disciplined but poorer cadres and these Swatantra forces.

FINANCE, ORGANIZATION, AND CANDIDACIES

The broad relationship between finance, organization, and candidatures in Swatantra's short history owes much to (1) the limited funds, given the party's aspirations; (2) the Swatantra estimate of the Indian political situation; and (3) Masani's determination to create a reasonably disciplined and ideologically committed party. Under any circumstances, Masani would have been anxious to use the financial resources of the central treasury to discipline the party, by screening candidates before funds were allocated. However, this tendency was reinforced because of the shortage of funds; and Swatantra's view that the seat of really pernicious power was New Delhi, not the state capitals, gave an important twist to the national party's effort to affect candidacies.[78]

The approach decided upon by the Swatantra élite restricted central treasury funds to approximately one hundred screened *Lok Sabha* candidates and constituencies and left it to the approved nominees to decide how, if at all, to help the aspiring MLAs in their constituencies. This was consonant with the party's desire to 'go for the jugular'; it enabled the national leadership to cope with (at some peril, to be sure) the almost universal tendency for local leaders to exaggerate local strength, and to ignore the 'careerists' who wanted Swatantra tickets and who claimed they were sure of election, if only the party gave them ample funds; and it was a potential asset in the battle to overcome parochialism, in the interests of a national, anti-statist effort. Depending on how much leverage Masani could muster, this approach also could be favourable to the modernists in the party, who generally lacked substantial political roots of their own.

This decision was not an unmixed blessing, for a number of reasons. For example, happy though some of the leaders might have been with a small but dedicated cadre of MPs, it was evident to all concerned that for 'psychological' reasons, many more than one hundred MP candidates would have to be set up. In part, Swatantra hoped to meet the psychological problem by having a far larger number file nomination papers, with the understanding that many candidates would be withdrawn at the last minute, to relieve the central treasury of any financial obligations. This principle was to be applied at the state level, too, where it was felt that the party ought to nominate at least enough candidates so that, if all or most of them won, it would be possible to form a Swatantra ministry. In both cases, however, the desire to make a respectable showing over a wide area, combined with local pressures, led Swatantra to spread its limited resources too thin, which probably cost the party a few seats.[79]

This was not the only problem, however. By emphasizing parliamentary constituencies, the central office was asking a host of local aspirants to subordinate their own ambitions (mostly to sit in the assemblies) to the goal of securing more MPs; and even if the full complement of MLA candidates were to be set up in the approved constituencies, the funds were still earmarked for the MPs. Not very surprisingly, such self-sacrifice was not easy to secure, and many local leaders expressed their strong dislike for the approach favoured by the central office.[80] Also, by insisting that all supported MP candidates had to be given prior clearance by the parliamentary board, the national leadership (especially Masani) opened itself to the charge of meddling in state affairs. This led to much strain on relations between the national leadership and the state units.

Moreover, shortage of funds, coupled with the desire to set up a respectable number of candidates, put a heavy premium on self-financing candidacies, in order to free central party funds for 'needier' cases. As Duverger has pointed out, 'investiture' in such cases is relatively easy to secure;[81] and, as we have suggested, ideological commitment and party discipline are likely to be victims of heavy reliance on the local notables who are likely to be self-financing. Finally—and this is central to an understanding of Swatantra's financial-organizational problems as they relate to social bases—the reliance on local notables and self-financing candidacies *hurt* the party's efforts to secure financial support from big business. The Swatantra modernists in particular found themselves in a vicious circle involving finance, big business and the aristocrats, and a breaking of this circle is one of Masani's greatest personal concerns.

The situation in West Bengal illustrates the problem of finance, organization and candidacies in one form. A key figure in the nascent West Bengal Swatantra party was Chatterjee, a man who could be a valuable asset in the *Lok Sabha*; and Swatantra was as anxious as Chatterjee himself to win a seat. However, Chatterjee and the West Bengal unit wanted to contest a very large number of seats, which the central office, on the basis outlined above, refused to countenance. The organization in Bengal was rudimentary, local funds severely limited, and derivative support (through local notables) minimal, and the central office was unable to pour vast sums into any state, let alone such an unpromising one. The parliamentary board announced that it would authorize and support only one *Lok Sabha* candidate in Bengal, or, if Chatterjee were self-financing, it would authorize two (supporting only one financially, of course). The outcome of all this was the resignation of Chatterjee from the party and considerable strain in relations between the state unit and the central office.[82]

Chatterjee was apparently the only leading figure who defected as a consequence of these financial-electoral problems, but in many other ways the same issue intruded. Ruthnaswamy was repeatedly denied additional funds for his 1962 campaign; the party leaders in Madhya Pradesh—where the organization never really took shape, even on a derivative basis—were ostensibly not given any election funds at all, in spite of repeated requests; and comparable cases could be cited from most other states. It is understandable that people should turn to the central party and that they should be disturbed when their requests are turned down; but the Swatantra files indicate that his occurred on a very wide and in many ways damaging scale.[83]

Relations with the unit in Orissa provide one example of a general finance-related strain within the Swatantra Party. As noted, one element in the decision of the Ganatantra Parishad to merge was the desire to be placed on a sounder financial footing in order to fight the Patnaik-led Congress. However, some leaders of the Parishad/Swatantra have felt that the hoped-for financial benefits of merger have not materialized and may not be forthcoming, even though Swatantra did give a substantial sum for the Parishad *Lok Sabha* candidates in 1962. In the absence of ample financial support, it may well seem more attractive to some Orissa leaders to reconstitute the Parishad. This would enable them to concentrate on local issues and be free of the association with the 'rich man's party'. There is no immediate prospect of such a defection in Orissa, but once again the danger to Swatantra is magnified because of the dependence on Patna and Kalahandi for the party's position in Orissa. It goes without saying that neither organizationally nor financially could this be called a satisfactory situation for the Swatantra Party.

Another absolutely critical aspect of Swatantra's financial problems and its relations with big business and the aristocracy turned on the matter of candidacies. A number of leading industralists had expressed a willingness, and some a determination, to support Swatantra, on the condition that certain key individuals, like Masani, Dandekar, and Shroff were reasonably sure to sit in the *Lok Sabha*. Some industrialists specifically tied their prospective support to the candidacies of the more modern Swatantra leaders. However, such men find it difficult to locate even reasonably 'safe' constituencies without the benevolent assistance of local notables. Thus in 1957 Sir Homy Mody ran as an RRP-Independent from Rajasthan and R. V. Murthy, of the *Eastern Economist* and another more modern Swatantrite, ran as a Jan Sangh-Independent in the same state—both being defeated. Masani himself was returned from a tribal constituency from Bihar—about as far away as he could get physically and psychologically from the highly westernized Parsi family in which he grew up in Bombay.

Swatantra did, of course, contain within its ranks a number of people (i.e. the aristocrats) who could have helped to return these men, had they themselves been willing to forego their personal ambitions, or at least those of relatives. The national leadership sought such co-operation but generally found it wanting. Masani's case is the most pertinent because he was not only the party's General-Secretary but he was also the most able parliamentarian in the party's ranks.

At one or another juncture, Masani and those who were anxious to return him to Parliament considered two or three constituencies in Ramgarh's area, at least three in or around the former Jaipur state, among others in Gujarat and Himachal Pradesh, where aristocrats could have helped him. In most cases Masani expected there to be more enthusiasm for his candidacy than was actually evinced. In almost every instance he was deterred by doubts expressed by the local notables concerning his electoral appeal, and in some cases there were *quid pro quos* demanded, which he found distasteful. In Rajasthan, for example, Dausa (won by

Maharajkumar Prithviraj of Jaipur), Sikar and Pali were mentioned as possible seats for Masani; and Dungarpur, who thought Dausa the safest, estimated a plurality of between 5,000 to 10,000 votes for Masani. Dungarpur insisted, however, that as an outsider whose Hindi was poor, Masani would face an uphill fight, and the Maharaja of Jaipur agreed to give only two or three talks on Masani's behalf, instead of the more sustained campaigning for which Masani had hoped.[84]

Much the same situation obtained in Bihar, with the added problem of the poor relations between Masani and Ramgarh. It is generally conceded that Ramgarh offered the Giridih and other constituencies to Masani (who claimed that unacceptable *quid pro quos* were demanded) but that no final decision was taken in the matter through August 1961. Ramgarh did not submit a list of *Lok Sabha* candidates from the Hazaribagh area, but he assured Masani that every effort would be made to find a secure seat. However, it was noted by the Bihar leadership that 'there was vehement opposition from all sides to the proposal of giving a seat to Shri Masani on two main grounds'—fear that the change in nomenclature from Janata to Swatantra would confuse the electorate and that well-known local people could alone overcome this obstacle, and fear that an outsider simply would not have sufficient appeal to win the *Lok Sabha* seat and to carry the MLAs with him.[85] A letter containing the assessment was sent to Masani, to which he sent a reply urging Ramgarh not to trouble himself further. Rajaji was, however, most anxious to have Masani sit in the *Lok Sabha* and he kept a modest amount of pressure on Ramgarh. In late September, however, the internal dissensions in Bihar and growing suspicions about Masani on Ramgarh's part led Masani to write to Rajaji as follows: 'I feel far from happy about being beholden to the Raja Saheb for being put up from one of the two Hazaribagh constituencies...Personally I would rather not stand for Parliament at all if this is the atmosphere in which one has to function.'[86] Shortly thereafter relations became so strained that for a time, at least, the question of a safe seat from Bihar did not arise in any serious fashion.

Masani's election prospects seemed somewhat brighter when, after considering some constituencies in Rajasthan, he apparently came to an understanding with the Raja of Bilaspur (Himachal Pradesh), one of Ramgarh's relatives. However, according to

Masani, some last-minute subterfuge, related to the Bilaspur-Ramgarh tie, weakened his prospects there and he claims to have withdrawn his candidacy. None the less, in the official election returns Masani's name appears, although he did not campaign, and he is listed as a very poor second.[87]

Even this did not put an end to the matter. After the elections, efforts by Masani and his friends continued unabated. The suggestion was made in at least two cases where Swatantrites had won both a *Lok Sabha* and an assembly seat—the Maharajkumar of Kutch and Ramgarh's mother—that the *Lok Sabha* seat be resigned, to permit Masani to stand in a by-election. Here, the role of finance in connection with organization is once again evident, because at least in the Bihar case a prominent Bombay businessman agreed to finance the by-election if Masani were permitted to stand. Yet even with this sort of assurance, co-operation was not forthcoming, even though some Swatantra aristocrats were notably uninterested in spending much time in Parliament and/or were incapable of helping the party as much as Masani could have in that forum.[88]

Further details of these efforts need not detain us, save for the following points: relations between Masani and some state leaders were severely strained as a result of this activity; no one seemed to respond eagerly to his candidacy, while on Masani's part warnings about his position as an outsider and personal doubts made him reluctant to enter some constituencies in which he might have stood; and it was only in mid-1963 that Masani was elected to the *Lok Sabha* from Rajkot district in Gujarat. Here he was somewhat less of an outsider and his candidacy was supported not only by all of the top Swatantra leaders (including the Maharani of Jaipur, Dungarpur, the Maharajkumar of Kutch, the Maharaja of Devgadh-Baria, who solicited the Rajput vote), but by some local aristocrats (notably members of the families of Rajkot, Jasdan and Wankaner), the recently victorious J. B. Kripalani, and A. B. Vajpayee, a Jan Sangh leader and MP (*Rajya Sabha*), who deployed the local Sangh cadres to good effect.[89] In short, it was a long, hard battle to fight, in order that Swatantra's ablest parliamentarian could sit in the *Lok Sabha*, and the victory was by no means due to Swatantra strength alone.[90]

While Masani's case was the most important, it was by no means the only one. Dandekar, also a Bombay man, had also to find a suitable constituency; and he finally stood from Gonda, Mankapur's district in UP. In a very close election, he was declared loser on a recount, after winning on the original count; but he finally gained the seat after a judicial inquiry revealed improprieties on behalf of the Congress candidate. The point here, however, is that some local Swatantrites resented his candidacy and, in some cases, their weak efforts on Dandekar's behalf reflected this.[91] Moreover, with Mankapur's death and the new Raja's loyalty to the Congress, Gonda was not even seriously considered as a possible seat for Dandekar, who has once again had to embark on the great search. As of November 1966, Dandekar had still not found a seat, although there were reports (1) of an abortive approach to Devgadh-Baria to facilitate Dandekar's return from Panchmahals in Gujarat, and (2) of the possibility that he might stand from Jamnagar (also in Gujarat), where Swatantra expected much help from the newly recruited Thakur of Dhrol. There was, moreover, a report that Dandekar might well not contest in the general elections, but would stand in a by-election for a resigned seat, much as Masani tried to do in 1962. Thus Dandekar, one of Swatantra's very ablest spokesmen in the *Lok Sabha*, is in the same boat with Masani and some other modern Swatantrites.[92]

In analogous cases, Swatantra MLAs showed little enthusiasm to use their votes to return such men to the *Rajya Sabha*, although it is far from clear that Masani, at least, would have tolerated the indignity of entering Parliament via this route. In any event, Rajasthan MLAs voted for the Maharaja of Jaipur, nominally an independent, rather than for a declared Swatantrite of any stripe. This may seem only natural (Rajputs supporting a friendly Rajput) but necessary (as a reward for his help or perhaps to bring him into the party), but it did mean that a *Rajya Sabha* seat was lost to Swatantra and to its modern wing in particular.[93] And it should be recalled that Jaipur did not seem notably co-operative in the matter of supporting Masani's own candidacy from Rajasthan. Kindred factors were at work when Kejriwal, a businessman openly in Swatantra, was asked to withdraw from one *Rajya Sabha* race in favour of Darbhanga, also an independent; and in the death throes of the Bihar unit, Kejriwal, Swatantra's first candidate for the *Rajya Sabha*, was not elected, while Bilaspur, the second candidate was.[94]

Swatantra was thus caught in something of a vicious circle. The leaders felt that a strong showing had to be made in 1962, and the aristocrats provided the possibility of a short-cut to success. But this success was obviously purchased at a very high price, in terms of party organization, discipline, legislative performance, and so on. Moreover, because local notables displayed little enthusiasm for facilitating the return of more modern Swatantrites to the *Lok Sabha*, Swatantra's financial position suffered, because its candidates were not widely acceptable to many people who were anxious to contribute, if only the right candidates were put up. Thus, Swatantra's financial future depends in part on the nature of the organization—more specifically on the ability of the more modern wing to assert its position, at least in the matter of some key candidacies to the *Lok Sabha*—just as its organization obviously depends in part on its financial position. It was no accident, then, that two men in Swatantra's inner circle, when asked where the party was best organized in terms of its fundamental principles, cited Bombay City, Delhi, Gujarat, and Mysore, and omitted Rajasthan, Orissa, and Bihar. And it was no accident, either, that of the last three, Orissa was judged the most satisfactory.[95]

More important than this evidence of distress with the nature of the party in certain areas are certain post-1962 developments which are obviously designed to escape this multi-faceted impasse. First, the party declared its intention to become a 'cadre' rather than a 'mass' party, a decision which in part reflects the feeling that the Swatantra message could not be effectively communicated to the masses.[96] This meant that the party would try to recruit a smaller number of 'better' people, who alone would be dues-paying, card-carrying members and who alone could vote in party elections. Certain organizational and propagandizing tasks were also assigned to these people, at least in principle.[97] From the standpoint of the national party, however, the key point was that membership cards for such people were to be issued only by the central office, directly to the prospective worker (by registered post). The central office hoped that this technique would enable it (1) to minimize bogus membership; (2) to have on hand an up-to-date list of active workers; (3) to have some information (to be forwarded by the state unit with the application for membership) on them; and (4) to have more direct access to party workers, without relying on the state leadership as heavily.[98]

The second major step, foreshadowed in 1962, was the recommendation for electoral strategy. Once again, this involved the selection of a number of *Lok Sabha* seats upon which the national party would concentrate its resources, but there was to be an added effort. Constituencies and prospective candidates were to be designated well in advance of the elections; a three man group, including the prospective candidate, was to supervise the 'cultivation' of the constituency; and satisfactory reports of work and of disbursement of central office funds were required for continuation of financial support and for retention of the prospective candidate as the final candidate. This represented a partial retreat from an idea that had once been mooted, viz. that the central office itself designate and pay special organizers to cultivate constituencies; but, even so, the adopted method has the clear purpose of strengthening central party control over *Lok Sabha* candidacies, at least. A major aim of this is, of course, the developing of constituencies for Swatantra's modern men; and it is no secret that several businessmen assured Masani of support for this venture, with this specific purpose in mind.[99]

As of this writing (1966), the effects of this strategy are by no means clear. In some cases, constituencies have been cultivated without a prospective candidate being designated—either because no satisfactory candidate was at the moment available or because a potential candidate did not want to commit himself before the constituency was 'tested'. Elsewhere, central office aid has been terminated, owing to the prospective candidate's failure to submit the required reports and financial statements—action which goes beyond anything that was done in 1962. Finally, this strategy (and the effort to control membership more closely) has already been a source of irritation to many state and local leaders, while at the same time, it has not solved the problems of a man like Dandekar.[100] But Masani has none the less made it clear that he regards this approach as indispensable, if Swatantra is to be placed on a proper organizational and ideological footing.

A third significant post-1962 development, related to this one, concerns the prospective candidates. Here one can see a fairly strenuous effort to find seats for more of the administrative-professional-business elements in the party; and one can see as well a heightened feeling on the part of businessmen that they themselves should stand for the *Lok Sabha*, to assure the type of representation they desire. For example, Swatantra designated as *Lok Sabha* candidates in Gujarat the following group from the ranks of its more modern men: Masani; Dandekar; leading Bombay industrialists Viren Shah and Manu Amersey; Pashabhai Patel, a relative of Sardar Patel and a prominent Baroda industrialist who contested as an independent in the two previous general elections; Piloo Mody—Sir Homy's son, a Bombay architect; the aforementioned H. M. Patel and C. C. Desai, both ICS retired; U. N. Mahida, a retired chief engineer of Bombay State; and economics professor R. K. Amin. There was also considerable pressure brought to bear on Nanu Amin, a very prominent and highly respected Baroda industrialist, to stand for the *Lok Sabha*, but this was resisted. Throughout this effort, Vadilal Mehta, Ahmedabad industrial tycoon and former Treasurer of the Congress, played a major role for the Swatantra Party.[101]

Comparable developments can be seen in Rajasthan as well. Chiranjit Rai, another wealthy industrialist, was designated to stand from Dausa, a seat won by one of the Maharajkumars of Jaipur in 1962.[102] More important, however, was the decision finally taken by R. K. Birla to stand for the *Lok Sabha* from Jhunjhunu, where the Swatantra candidate in 1962 was a prominent Rajput *jagirdar* and for which constituency the same man had already received the party's blessings for 1967. It was not clear whether Birla would stand officially as a Swatantra candidate or as an independent using the Swatantra symbol; and there was always the possibility of a withdrawal under pressure. But Birla, as of November 1966, had reportedly assured the Swatantra Party that he would not stand as a Congressman, that he would be entirely self-financing, and that he would support, financially and otherwise, the Swatantra MLA candidates from his district. Whatever the outcome, even a tentative decision by a Birla to stand against the Congress is something of a landmark in Indian business politics; and the willingness of the local aristocrats to stand aside in two Jaipur-area constituencies is also notable. Needless to say, considerable pressure had been brought to bear by Congress leaders on G. D. Birla, patriarch of this industrial empire, to dissuade R. K. Birla from this venture or to persuade him to support Congress MLAs, the apparent *quid pro quo* being the absence of a Congress opponent in the *Lok Sabha* contest.[103]

Whatever the outcome of these specific contests may be, it is clear that business interests (both inside and outside of Swatantra) are not content to leave the field to aristocrats, Gandhians, *et al.* who have not proved to be sufficiently attentive to the needs of the private sector industrialists. Masani has also underscored his personal desire to build an effective, articulate, and less conservative *Lok Sabha* contingent by pressing for the inclusion of some major ex-ICS figures in the list of prospective candidates. Lest the significance of this be overstated, we must note that in most of the specific cases mentioned above, the prospective candidates were local men or had strong local ties, which still does not solve the problems of men like Masani and Dandekar. Still, the significance should not be missed, either. Through the power of the rupee and through strenuous personal efforts by Masani in the central office, the more modern elements in Swatantra are trying to make themselves felt, and to a modest extent they have succeeded. This may be more a victory for private enterprise than for liberalism; but in the intra-party battle between the conservatives and the non-conservatives, this is in itself an important development.[104]

CHAPTER 8

SWATANTRA DOCTRINE

After a detailed examination of the views of the Swatantra inner circle and of the elements which grouped around it, it may seem redundant to add a discussion of Swatantra's formal doctrine. However, a consideration of party doctrine will provide a clue, if nothing more, to the basis on which the coalition was brought together and to the framework within which the components were presumably to function. It will indicate which of the diverse perspectives present in the party has been emphasized for public purposes. That is, the formal doctrine represents what at least *some* doctrinal leaders would like party members to be, in terms of personal commitment and in terms of public image. And even if there be a substantial gap between formal doctrine and the views of individuals or groups within the party, the formal doctrine *may* exert a disciplinary influence, as public ideology often does. These are not irrelevant matters.

THE FUNDAMENTAL PRINCIPLES

Rajaji, in responding to Nehru's charge that it was impossible to know what Swatantra stood for because it contained diverse elements, once said that 'the straight and easy path to understand our party is to read what has been said in the twenty-one short articles of the party's foundation document. There is no ambiguity or prolixity in it.'[1] The heart of the party's doctrine is, to be sure, embodied in these few 'fundamental principles', and in elaborations of and additions to these. Unhappily, these would not suffice to define the nature and role of Swatantra, even if they were crystal-clear; and the truth is that the fundamental principles are by no means as unambiguous as Rajaji has asserted. Many of the conflicts and tensions revealed by a study of the social bases of the party emerge in the realm of doctrine as well. None the less, since attention must be paid to the official pronouncements of the party, the twenty-one points serve as the appropriate starting-place.

If one had to categorize them *en bloc* and briefly, the twenty-one points could be called predominantly classical liberal in tone, suggesting a moderate, non-traditional outlook. They reflect the general aversion of the national leaders to reactionary and to authoritarian nationalist views; and they reflect, as well, the influence of the modernists in the realm of doctrine. The Indian heritage, especially via Gandhi, is also present, but in an understated way; and socialist rhetoric, also virtually inescapable in contemporary India, also intrudes. In the latter case, too, however, it is important to stress the limited extent to which it does so.

The fundamental principles are important, moreover, not only for what they say and how they say it, but also for what they do not say. Much is excluded from their purview, and on all such issues, party members are permitted to advance any position not inconsistent with a fairly narrow reading of the twenty-one points. Significantly, foreign policy, linguistic policy, and religious and cultural issues *in detail*, receive little or no explicit attention within the framework of the fundamental principles. This reflects the conviction that the principal task is that of opposing Congress 'statism', and that those who can agree on this should not be divided by other issues deemed to be less significant. The extent to which this can be successfully accomplished is one of the most important problems in evaluating the position of the Swatantra Party.

The liberal aspects of the twenty-one points are abundantly evident. The first, for example, calls for equality for all, 'without distinction of religion, caste, occupation, or political affiliation'.[2] This is followed by a defence of 'individual initiative, enterprise and energy' in all areas, with emphasis on the economic sphere. The subsequent points are best described as rigorously anti-statist, with attacks on 'the policy of Statism', 'expropriation', 'the conferrment of more and more powers on the officials of the Government', 'collectivization and bureaucratic management of the rural economy', 'crippling taxation, abnormal deficit financing, and foreign loans which are beyond the capacity of the country to repay', and so forth. The party also condemns 'official directives' on education, 'political pressure...on officials', the 'wastefulness and inefficiency' inherent in state 'controls and official management' and 'the pervading sense of uncertainty that has been created by the present policies of the Government'. In calling for 'minimum interference by the State' in all spheres, with emphasis again on economic affairs, Swatantra's leaders urge the restoration of private initiative 'in land, ship and factory alike' and emphasize 'freedom of property', 'just compensation for any property compulsorily acquired', and 'strict adherence' to all basic constitutional rights. To this last end, there is a plea for 'the full play of the powers of judicial review given to the Courts by the Constitution'.[3] All of this is reminiscent of the 'night-watchman' state, and party men are not only fond of quoting Hayek but also have insisted (in the 1962 manifesto) that 'that government is best which governs least' and that 'the business of the State is not business but government'. This is entirely consistent with Rajaji's assertion that 'the Swatantra Party stands for the protection of the individual against the increasing trespasses of the State. It is an answer to the challenge of the so-called Socialism of the Indian Congress party.'[4] Masani, arguing from a different vantage point, none the less concurs in the basic judgment, viz. that 'under the cloak of a socialist pattern, the new Brahmins of New Delhi are trying to create a new class of sudras who will remain hewers of wood and drawers of water for the greater glory of what Djilas...has rightly described as the new class of State capitalists'.[5]

This basic conviction is translated into a variety of specific proposals on topical issues. Among those which the party has stressed, at one juncture or another, are: (1) the creation of an Ombudsman to hear grievances against and in general to police the bureaucracy; (2) the creation of a non-political board, along the lines of the Election Commission, to assign all permits and licences necessary under present government legislation; (3) an early termination of the state of emergency declared during the Chinese invasion, and, related to this, greater discrimination in the use of the preventive detention law; and (4) a voluntary departure from office by the Congress six months prior to a general election, so that the ruling party could not use the agencies of government to enhance its electoral prospects. The last of these was naïve, if not preposterous, but the others have received much more than passing attention of a serious nature. However, none of these issues is particularly likely to animate very many people: they are, by and large, issues for the intelligentsia, as is the general plea concerning the need for an opposition party to help establish viable constitutional-democratic procedures.

Getting closer to mass issues, the Swatantra Party also took exception to a number of measures adopted as a consequence of the

Chinese invasion. Included here were the rise in the level of taxation, a compulsory savings scheme, and the gold control order whereby it became illegal for anyone to have or to process gold of twenty-two carats, which had theretofore been the Indian norm. The last, in particular, was given a mass twist, through the argument that it was an attack not only on the large numbers of goldsmiths but on the customary practices of all Hindu women, who prized their twenty-two carat gold jewelry for the security it provided, if for no other reason. The party tried to gain maximum advantage, however, from the proposed seventeenth amendment to the constitution, by which, in its view, the meaning of the word 'estate'—theretofore applicable only to such tenures as *jagirdari* and *zamindari* holdings—would be expanded to include *ryotwari* tenures. In the Swatantra view, this violated the basic right of private property by removing questions of 'public purpose' and compensation from the purview of the courts, and, it was argued, was the stepping-stone to collectivization of agriculture. Granted, the threat was not palpably felt, but it was the party's hope that by tying this to land ceiling policy, tax policy, and the like, a pattern of action against free agriculture could be delineated. And this, at least, would make it a broad middle-class issue.[6]

The Gandhian element is not absent, but it provides only a thin veneer on this essentially liberal document. The fundamental principles call for a reaffirmation of 'the cardinal teachings of Gandhiji', but these are not spelled out in any elaborate way. The party also wants 'to foster and maintain spiritual values and preserve what is good in our culture and tradition', but this is also not spelled out. However, these formulations allow Gandhians and others of a more conservative stripe to 'read in' virtually anything they want, and this is precisely what Rajaji and others have done. Thus Rajaji, Munshi, and others may defend much of the Indian tradition, on the grounds that 'survival is a proof of fitness, not of worthlessness',[7] and one prominent Swatantrite in Andhra can condemn the Hindu Code legislation 'as it has not only tried to root out the Shastraic Principles and doctrines of Dharma (Religion) but important principles of health and medical science'.[8] On the other hand, Pasricha and Ruthnaswamy can belabour the very same things as not worthy of preservation.[9] This is but one aspect of the ambiguity of the twenty-one points, wherein almost diametrically opposed opinions can be held by members of the same party, each ostensibly being blessed by the obscure wording of the fundamental principles. This down-grading of social issues in favour of a politico-economic one is reminiscent of the Congress' own problem during the pre-independence days, when many leaders insisted that all social questions should be avoided in the interest of a maximum anti-imperialist effort. Swatantra is obviously attempting to do much the same thing. The Swatantra hope is clear; but it is also clear that the failure to define that which is quintessentially Gandhian or Indian—whether it be in terms of prohibition, ban on cow slaughter, ayurvedic medicine, cottage industries, village institutions generally—will irritate if not alienate many for whom anti-statism is not sufficient as a battle cry.

Virtually the only specific Gandhian item which is developed is 'the principle of trusteeship adumbrated by Gandhi' which reflects 'the sense of moral obligation, the pride, satisfaction, and fulfilment felt by individuals in serving others, which are inherent in our tradition'. In general, this concept implies an abandonment of coercion, including legislative 'coercion', as an instrument of policy and a reliance on voluntary use of advantages by the rich, the wise and the well-born in particular, for the good of society as a whole. Rajaji makes this explicit in his assertion that 'the new party does not believe that legislative compulsion, any more than violence...can contribute to true or lasting human happiness. We must depend on the moral sense of the people in order to equalize without destroying freedom.'[10]

It is important to understand that this particular item, while not without its appeal to dedicated Gandhians as well as to the more self-interested people whom it protects, was not only included largely at Rajaji's insistence but also that it played a larger part in the earlier drafts of the party's doctrinal statement, viz. a fourteen-point manifesto presented at the Madras meeting and an eighteen-point draft submitted for consideration at the Bombay (Preparatory) Convention.[11] The fact that it stood first among the original principles but was subsequently 'demoted', in favour of a more liberal statement about individual equality reflects, in part, the hand of Masani, among others, who soon became involved in doctrinal matters.[12] Here, too, is an indication that the fundamental principles are by no means as unambiguous as Rajaji might like; and here again is evidence of liberal assertiveness, now in the realm of doctrine.

The emphasis on 'decentralized distribution of industry' also has a Gandhian ring (and Rajaji and Ranga, among others would give it a Gandhian interpretation), but this is somewhat misleading. Swatantra's leading ideologians, especially Masani and his Bombay colleagues, have in mind the decentralization of larger-scale, modern enterprise, not the maintenance of primitive technology such as characterizes village India and as advanced by the extreme Gandhians. Thus, while Ranga has objected even to the smaller-scale introduction of power looms on a local level,[13] the party 'believes in a balanced development of capital-goods industries, organized consumer goods industries, and rural industries that afford supplementary employment in the small-scale processing of the products of agriculture'. There is no defence of small-scale, handicraft production because of any virtues it is presumed to foster; and the above principles presumably would not justify the creation of rural industries, with restrictions on urban output, simply to give supplementary income to villages.[14] Here is where Masani, Mody, Vaidya, and other businessmen come into conflict with Rajaji and Ranga, regardless of the 'clear' implications of the fundamental principles.[15]

One of the most critical aspects of Swatantra doctrine is that which defines the proper role of state intrusion into the economy and into social life more generally, and a number of introductory points are relevant here. First, the doctrine of trusteeship severely blunts the edge of legislative efforts to close the gap between India's wealthy and her poor, to effect social reforms, and the like. This is reinforced in the economic sense by the party's view that taxation is already 'crippling'. Secondly, Swatantra's *Lok Sabha* votes against the five-year plans and the condemnation of the Planning Commission suggest further a *laissez faire* approach;[16] and thirdly, many of Masani's statements about free enterprise only add grist to the mill of those who charge Swatantra with adherence to nineteenth-century economics.[17]

Few things elicit more derisive comment in contemporary India than support for *laissez-faire* capitalism, and the party's critics quickly sought to tar it with this brush by calling it a 'projection' of the FFE and a 'rich man's party'. In fact, this view seems to be quite widely held, both within and outside the party, and fragmentary evidence suggests that this image has hurt the party badly. One indication of this is the list of prospective candidates who asked the central office for permission to contest as independents, because of the bad party image, with the promise that they would join formally at a later date; and these requests came from virtually every state unit.[18]

One indication of the image which the party had acquired and the manner in which it jarred with the prevailing socialist rhetoric is the justification given by some Swatantrites upon their resignation from the party. A one-time convenor of the Kerala unit, K. C. Jacob, resigned with the statement that a party which 'bravely fights shy of all shades of socialist thought is an anachronism today'.[19] Similarly, Raja Hutheesing, for a time organizing secretary of the Bombay (city) unit, gave the following reason for his resignation: 'I have gone through the party platform most carefully and I am extremely disappointed. The programme, if ever put into practice, will subject the Indian people to economic chaos and ruthless exploitation...Must India go through the inhuman suffering of the industrial revolution in Europe?' Criticizing what he regarded as the party's attachment to *laissez faire*, he termed it 'an historical and ridiculous oddity' and claimed that 'selfish and evil forces have worked to mislead the party'.[20] It is really immaterial whether this was the actual cause for defection in these and comparable cases. The important thing is that such views were obviously expected to strike a responsive chord. It goes without saying that the same terms of abuse were used against Swatantra by virtually all other parties, including, in some instances, the right-wing opposition.

From the outset, Swatantra has been of two minds as it confronted this issue. On the one hand, the leadership was anxious to develop a sharply distinct alternative to the Congress, by contrast with the other major parties, all of which echoed in one form or another the 'socialist' rhetoric of the ruling party. Moreover, Masani was particularly anxious to develop a strong ideological challenge to Congress socialism. This suggested that the role of the state should be minimized, and to this end Rajaji urged the deletion from a draft of the 1962 manifesto many items which in his view too closely resembled Congress positions. And he did this in some cases not because he actually opposed the draft statement but because he wanted to present as sharp an alternative as possible.[21] On the other hand, the prevalence of socialist rhetoric and the recognition by even the most ardent champions of private enterprise that some state activity was indispensable, worked in the opposite direction.

In the fundamental principles themselves a role for the state is present, both explicitly and implicitly. For example, the state may establish 'heavy industries such as are necessary to supplement private enterprise' and may start 'new enterprises which are difficult for private enterprise'. While the state is to interfere minimally, this principle must be 'consistent with the obligation to punish anti-social acts, to protect the weaker elements of society, and to create the conditions in which individual initiative will thrive and be fruitful'. Specifically, there must be 'adequate safeguards for the protection of labour, and against unreasonable profits, prices and dividends where there is no competition and where competition does not secure the necessary corrective'. This, of course, is a tacit admission that trusteeship, by itself, is insufficient; but the divergence in emphasis and outlook (between those who stress trusteeship and those who stress legislative correctives) has in no significant way been resolved.[22] And once again, some of these specific items represent additions to the original party programme tentatively set forth at the Madras meeting.

If these principles and their implications be broadly conceived, the re-entry of the much-condemned statism would be justified. In the existing economic situation, there is relatively little competition of the type that would regulate profits, prices and dividends; and there is abundant scope for the state in the development of the economic infrastructure, at least. It is no secret, for example, that many leaders of Indian private enterprise favoured the entry of the government into the iron and steel industry, which private industry was not able to develop on the same scale and which provided much indispensable material for private enterprise. Moreover, if the weaker elements are to be protected and if they are to be given equal opportunity, regardless of caste, the state must intrude in a vigorous fashion into the social life of the country—in a way which would appal Rajaji, and probably most other Swatantrites. The abundant village studies demonstrate that a 'hands-off' policy will not suffice to rescue India's depressed millions from their misery, much of which is due to the self-conscious animosity of the dominant rural castes. As one source put it, however, 'the positive aspects of the obligations of the State have thus been given grudging recognition even by the

Swatantra Party and its differences with other political parties on this point would be one of degree rather than of principle'.[23] Swatantra, on its part, has come around to the view that a good deal must be done to protect and to strengthen the weak but that total control over the entire society and economy was not an acceptable means to this end. Once again, however, we are confronted with a good deal of ambiguity on the matter of where the lines will be drawn between legitimate and illegitimate intervention for these purposes.

In the economic sphere, Swatantra has steadfastly denied that it stands for *laissez faire* and that it opposes all planning; and it has moved more toward Congress views, suggesting once again the importance of taking a 'dialectical' approach to Swatantra's position in Indian political life. In response to the charge of *laissez faire*, many Swatantrites have echoed the words of Shroff, already quoted: 'It should be clear...that Free Enterprise...is not advocated today in terms of the outmoded doctrine of *laissez-faire*... The *laissez-faire* is as dead as dodo. It is a singular triumph of the dynamic urge of democratic ideals to have developed a new awareness of social justice and equality.'[24] In the same vein, party leaders deny that they are opposed to planning *per se*. Instead, they object to 'Soviet style' planning—'total' and heavy-industry-oriented—as now undertaken by the Planning Commission, which they hold is a non-constitutional body not properly accountable to Parliament.[25] At many junctures, Swatantra leaders insist that they would engage in planning, if called upon to form a government. As Ranga put it in his usually flamboyant language, '...we believe in plan. But our plan is a Gandhian plan, a plan that has for its foundation Dharma, a plan that is based on the initiative of our people, a plan that stands for self-employment and security of our people, a plan that believes in our people.'[26] Most other leaders agree, in less florid language, that the party would have to plan, but they insist that it would pay greater heed to smaller-scale projects which would yield tangible, short-run results; and the planning itself would be done by a Cabinet sub-committee.[27] But here, too, there are ambiguities. Obviously, if the word planning is to have any meaning, a government cannot respond to every possible public pressure; and it is just as obvious that no plan can content itself solely with miniscule projects that are cheap and have immediate impact. Thus, the Swatantra preference for the 'Gandhian' test, i.e. how will this particular project affect the life of the common man, does not get us very far. Even such 'display' projects as the Bhakra-Nangal Dam, which Swatantra leaders like to abuse, are of immense benefit to the common man, in terms of irrigation and power, if in no other way. Once again, Swatantra differs in degree, not in principle, save with respect to the 'total' planning which it attributes to the Congress.

To avoid further the anti-plan image, Swatantra leaders recurrently announce that they are trying to develop 'an alternative plan' and they have succeeded in convincing some observers that the party 'has travelled far since the days when planning was anathema to its founding fathers'.[28] Nothing much has yet seen the light of day, nor is anything of consequence likely to, but this does reflect Swatantra's concern with its public image, as a 'rich man's', *laissez faire*, capitalist party. The party's emphasis on a rural-oriented, 'people's plan' reflects the same concern.

Students of intellectual history should be intrigued by another phase of the Swatantra effort to come to grips with the problem of socialist rhetoric in India. For a variety of reasons, 'socialism' is a good word in India and, again for a variety of reasons, individualism and competition, as associated with *laissez faire*, are bad. The former is progressive, the latter retrograde or reactionary. Swatantra then not only confronts the problem of cutting through a variety of parochial issues to establish its anti-statist position; it also has an uphill fight to overcome the weight of socialist rhetoric. The burden of this effort has been assumed by Masani, and his arguments reflect his own cosmopolitan interests, his Marxist background, and his desire to relate the Indian experience to 'world-historical' issues. The main thrust of the Swatantra counter-attack against the charge that it is reactionary while socialists are progressive is simple. The argument is inverted: in world-historical terms, socialism as advanced by Nehru, the PSP, the CPI, *et al.*, is retrograde, while the controlled free enterprise of Swatantra is progressive, and is, in fact, more representative of the 'spirit' of socialism.

The argument is woven from a number of sometimes inconsistent strands. On one level, Swatantra leaders simply quote from Marx, Lenin, and other spokesmen for socialism to the effect that socialism was to come about only in advanced industrial countries and that collectivized agriculture was an impossibility in a primitive economy.[29] The plea is entered to let capitalism perform the world-historical task that Marx assigned to it. No matter that some contradictory interpretations of the socialist revolution could be cited and that many positions have been updated: Swatantra takes the old Menshevik line, in effect, and tells the socialists and the CPI to go back and read Marx and Lenin afresh.

Were Swatantra to stop here, it would be obliged to admit that socialism has a future, if not a present, in India. In attempting to cut closer to the heart of the socialist–communist position, Swatantra's dominant theme is that socialism was either *never* relevant or is *passé*. Party leaders insist that the USA, Canada, and West Germany, among other leading nations, achieved material prosperity under controlled capitalism. The Swatantra conclusion is that if this was the path of the richest nations in the world, it is the best way for India. This still does not account for welfare-statism in Great Britain, nor does it demonstrate that socialism has no future. Arguing the latter point, Masani contends that the 'débâcle of world socialism is spreading from country to country', and Rajaji terms the idea of class war 'obsolete in Britain... premature [*sic!*] and most dangerous in India'.[30]

Masani takes pains to enumerate the specifics of the 'débâcle'. He cites Tory victories and the ideological retreat of the Labour Party in Great Britain; the split in the Japanese socialist movement, with a social democratic offshoot repudiating more doctrinaire Marxism; defeats of or ideological retreats by Socialist parties in Austria (1958), the Netherlands (1959), Sweden (1960), and Ceylon (1960).[31] Very heavily stressed by Masani is the fact that the German Social Democrats, long regarded as the most dedicated standard-bearers of orthodox Marxism, have explicitly rejected doctrinaire socialism, in favour of a more moderate, 'pragmatic' approach. Swatantra leaders delight in juxtaposing excerpts from their manifesto and similarly worded counterparts in the German social-democratic programme, to show the virtual identity with the erstwhile socialist forces of the west.[32] Thus, Masani has argued that 'the whole world, including the peoples in the Iron Curtain countries, is moving away from the shibboleths of collectivism. The danger of India's being committed to outmoded dogmas which the rest of the world is discarding must be combatted.'[33]

Accepting the 'socialism' of the Tories in Great Britain, of the German Social Democrats, and so on, Swatantra leaders alternately called Nehru, a 'nineteenth-century socialist' as opposed to Swatantra's 'twentieth-century socialists', or else a 'reactionary state capitalist' and no real socialist at all![34] While this set of arguments can hardly be called a logical *tour de force*, it has permitted Swatantra leaders to argue that the socialists are outdated, not Swatantra. This illustrates an important dimension of intellectual history, viz. the compulsion to respond to the strong and proximate challenge of Marx and socialism and the need to accept, to some extent, the enemy's political vocabulary. This was noted in passing in connection with the Jan Sangh and the Hindu Mahasabha; and Swatantra is only joining the throng (at which it shakes a censuring finger most of the time) albeit in a different way than the other parties.[35]

If Swatantra has been obliged to make concessions to the rhetoric of socialism in the field of economic development, it has thus far declined to dwell in detail on the implications of bringing about equality for all. We see that Swatantra has emphasized the protection of the weak rather than the strengthening of the weak. Both are important, but the latter would draw Swatantra more fully into social intervention, and here the party remains painfully silent. Reliance on trusteeship does more to protect the strong than to protect or to strengthen the weak, and reliance on individual initiative is manifestly insufficient to emancipate the Indian masses from their century-old burdens and afflictions, particularly where the *harijans*, landless labourers, and other particularly depressed groups are concerned. Rajaji certainly does not display any righteous indignation over the glaring inequalities, and those who are sensitive to this situation have not spoken out in positive terms about ways of helping the weak. Masani, certainly no friend of the caste system or of the ethos which underlies it, has also spoken more of the mass of *sudras* which he feels that statism is creating, rather than the *sudras* and untouchables already extant, and the causes responsible for their unhappy state.

This, too, has not escaped attention, in part because of sharp criticism from outside as well as inside the party. In considering various drafts of the 1962 election manifesto, Latchanna, the highly regarded untouchable leader in Andhra, and Basant Singh of the Punjab, among other Swatantra state leaders, criticized the inadequate provisions concerning the untouchables and the depressed classes generally.[36] So, too, after the 1962 elections, Masani insisted that attention to this problem 'is a moral and political imperative'.[37] Thus far, however, the concern has not borne any fruit, in terms of a substantial critique of the old order; there has been no detailed statement concerning mass welfare; and the difficulties generated by the emphasis on trusteeship have not been resolved. Admittedly, the problem is not an easy one to solve, but Swatantra cannot escape some blame for neglecting it, as Masani, Latchanna and Basant Singh, at least are willing to admit.

There is one obvious reason for Swatantra's reticence: its virtual obsession with the task 'of opposing statism, which is the greatest enemy of freedom'.[38] In the same vein, Rajaji declared in 1950 (speaking to the CPI members of the Madras assembly), 'I am your enemy Number One...May I say you are my enemy Number One? That is my policy from A to Z.'[39] Given this prevailing attitude, which is reflected in the widespread but by no means universal insistence among Swatantra leaders that the CPI should be banned,[40] it is not particularly surprising that the party does not speak out against the many suffocating influences of the old order or against the obstacles and dangers to freedom which lie on the right. It is partly for this reason that the critique of traditionalism which is implicit in the party's fundamental principles is muted to the point of inaudibility.[41]

In the case of the Congress movement itself, there was a subordination of social issues in the interests of the largely negative political goal of ousting the British; and there were a variety of points of view within the Congress concerning the post-British course of policy. Many felt that the attainment of independence was virtually the end of the struggle and that little remained to be done thereafter. Obviously men like Nehru had vastly different conceptions of future agendas. Swatantra in many ways presents a parallel case. Its primary goal, its very *raison d'être*, is to oppose statism, and, as in the Congress, there are divergent points of view of future policy.

From the earlier analyses it is easy to see that for many Swatantrites, too, the battle would be over if only statism could be defeated. For many, the more conservative elements in the party, the effort ends there. For others, however, there is a bigger agenda of tasks that have to be undertaken. It is uncontestable, however, that the people tending toward the former position outnumber those who tend toward the latter. The social composition and attitudes of much of the leadership reinforces the conclusion that there is a marked tendency to fight the left only, leaving the weight of tradition and the threat of a right authoritarianism outside the pale of relevant concerns. Moreover, if the pressure from the left remains, as it almost surely will in one form or another, it is unlikely that Swatantra will ever articulate a serious challenge to the old order. One may take some solace from the fact that, in such a dialectical situation, the interplay of forces may produce a not unhappy result; but this does not make Swatantra a 'progressive, liberal party'. Swatantra is, in short, in a very difficult historical position, and much of one's assessment of the party will depend on how one reads history, Indian and otherwise. Yet as long as Swatantra attacks only the left and as long as its own more progressive elements remain subdued, it will represent at best a drastically truncated form of liberalism. It is not necessary to go as far as Swatantra's adamant critics—who argue that no one in the party has any progressive ideas— for there to be very legitimate apprehension on this point.[42]

NON-FUNDAMENTAL POSITIONS

Just as Swatantra has been obliged to respond to the prevailing socialist rhetoric, so also has it been obliged to deal with many subjects which lie beyond the bounds of the fundamental principles. The party's leaders do this with some reluctance, of course, because their aim is to develop Indian political consciousness along new, i.e. statist-anti-statist, lines, and they do not want to divert attention from this to issues which it regards as of lesser importance. Thus, Rajaji, in a statement deploring the tendency for proliferation of political parties in India, has said:

> For parliamentary democracy to work satisfactorily, we need two clearly distinguishable political parties, based on two clearly understandable systems of national economy...Questions which affect particular groups adversely or favourably should not be party issues, but should be treated as ethical issues to be dealt with irrespective of party cleavages. Party cleavages should only be on issues affecting the national economy, and so it is necessary to polarize all-India politics on the single question, 'Do you want the State to dominate over the economy and reduce the

citizen to a regulation-ridden slave-worker, or do you stand for maximum free economy with minimum State-controls in the interest of the general welfare...?'[43]

Just as social issues were glossed over in the interest of opposing statism, so all other issues which are not directly related to questions of political economy must also be subordinated.

The fundamental principles offer some hope, however, that the party will be able to address itself 'unofficially' to a host of these 'lesser' issues and thus to accommodate India's diversity and local interests within its framework. The last of the twenty-one points allows party members to adopt any positions they may choose 'on all questions not falling within the scope of the Principles stated above', which Rajaji had explained in the following way: 'This party of freedom is further making a novel experiment in restricting disciplinary control over party members to essential issues, giving freedom in all other matters to vote according to individual opinion. This is not mere strategy to "net in" discordant miscellaneous elements as first might appear.'[44] Without denying that a principled commitment to democratic procedures plays a part in this formulation, it is none the less clear that many 'discordant miscellaneous elements' can be brought into the party, as long as they ostensibly adhere to the basic, anti-statist fundamental principles. Thus, pro-Hindi Swatantrites in the north can co-exist with pro-English Swatantrites in the south; supporters of linguistic states can co-exist with opponents thereof; social reformers can co-exist with steadfast conservatives; pacifists can co-exist with sabre-rattlers; local groups can stress strictly local issues, and so on—as long as they are able to subordinate their passions on these issues in order to consolidate the anti-statist front.

Among the many unofficial matters which have received attention, the question of national language is particularly revealing, because virtually all Swatantra notables argue that English should be retained until such time as all Indians agree voluntarily to use Hindi as the official or 'link' language.[45] They have openly proclaimed that English was one of the two great sources of 'national consciousness', the other being the independence struggle itself; and they bemoan the decline in the 'leadership of the English-educated minority' and regret that 'the psychological and social unity of educated men and women...is being undermined' by ill-considered decisions in linguistic matters.[46] This view has not found favour with many Swatantrites, especially those from UP and Bihar, and Swatantra ranks reveal considerable disarray and friction during consideration of linguistic matters.[47] This is one view which infuriates the Jan Sangh and other pro-Hindi militants, whose spokesmen repeatedly deplore the fact that Indians are still created in Macaulay's image.[48] The late President of the Jan Sangh, Raghuvira, referred to a bill to extend the period in which English could be used 'anti-democratic, anti-Gandhian, and anti-national ...a continuation of colonialism'. He added that 'all opportunities in the high sectors of life are reserved for those who have mastered English' and he referred to the English-knowing people as a 'giant monopoly' in India. Suggestive of the passions aroused here is the fact that on more than one occasion in the Hindi areas Rajaji has been obliged to abandon an address when the crowd heckled him for failing to speak in Hindi, or at least another indigenous tongue.[49] The pro-English stand also offends many other groups which are pressing for exclusive use of indigenous tongues for all government business and as the medium of instruction in all schools, at all levels. Also this stand reflects the more moderate, upper-class temperament which is widespread in the national élite of the party.[50]

In the linguistically related Punjabi *suba* agitation and the recently terminated DMK demand for an independent Dravidian state, i.e. for secession, Swatantra ran afoul of one of the most vexing issues of post-independence Indian politics. Outright endorsement of such agitations would infuriate the militant nationalists once more; but it would also offend more moderate nationalists, as, for example, the party's language position does not. Outright condemnation of these agitations would, however, deprive Swatantra of some possible local support in its battle against the Congress. Swatantra, not very successfully, has tried to have it both ways: it frequently defends these movements as legitimate expressions of democratic rights (i.e. to organize and to plead one's case), but it insists that it is not thereby endorsing the *ends* of these agitations. The situation was particularly vexing in the case of the DMK, because of the demand for secession; and throughout, Rajaji and others willing to seek a common front with the DMK had to insist that this party did not seriously intend to secede—a view which gained some credence during and after the Chinese invasion of 1962.[51]

As we have already seen, Rajaji and Munshi differ very sharply on such problems, about which more will be said in the discussion of electoral alliances. For the time, a brief review of some of Rajaji's pronouncements will suggest the delicacy of this issue.

Rajaji has throughout steadfastly insisted that the party as such has no official position on any but fundamental principles. None the less, he said that he personally did not consider the demand for a Punjabi *suba* improper, given the prevailing pattern of linguistic states, to which he also said he was personally opposed![52] Further, Rajaji pointed to the Swatantra report on the government's handling of the agitation, in which the action against the Akalis was termed 'excessive and indiscriminate', and to a later charge that this action constituted 'a ridiculous exercise of arbitrary power, a provocative move on the part of the Punjab Government, with some sinister design, and a flagrant defiance of the Constitution with no precedent even in the worst period of British terrorism'.[53] The latter referred to the detention of Akali leaders under the preventive detention act, which Rajaji, who was instrumental in its passage (to curb the Communists), said justified the worst fears of its opponents.[54] So, too, when Tara Singh undertook a fast unto death on behalf of the Punjabi *suba* demand, Rajaji asked him to keep a limited fast and also asked the government to respond to it in the same generous way as the British responded to Gandhi's Poona fast (1932) on behalf of the untouchables. Finally, at the end of the fast, Rajaji said: 'I hope the distress gone through will bear some fruit and in adequate measure.'[55]

The Swatantra leaders, Munshi excepted, responded in much the same way to the demands of the DMK. There is, on the one hand, great stress on government repression in dealing with demonstrations; and, for example, in Ranga's by-election campaign in Chittoor (Andhra, August 1962), DMK men supported him and frequently displayed bruises, cuts, etc., which were attributed to police brutality during Madras demonstrations. On the other hand, with respect to the demand for secession, the matter has been dealt with by denying that the DMK is serious about this. Thus, Rajaji called the hope for a separate Dravidistan 'chimerical' and he deplored efforts 'to besmirch the name of the DMK'.[56] Throughout, the leaders insisted that there was no official position on either issue and that by defending the *right* to protest they were not thereby defending the professed *goals* of the protest.

This sort of equivocal or ambivalent approach is designed to provide some basis for anti-Congress activity in concert with the Akali Dal and the DMK,[57] and may appear attractive to those for whom the linguistic or 'secessionist' issue does not bulk large, but it cannot help but offend those for whom these are *the* issues. Thus, while Rajaji has emphasized that the party is not 'governed by its founder-leader's personal views on the official language issue and on the Punjabi *suba* claim'[58] this has not satisfied much of Indian critical opinion, nor has it pleased all Swatantrites. The *Times of India* complained of Rajaji's 'sophistry' in linguistic matters,[59] and Munshi, who is vehemently opposed to both the Akali Dal and the DMK, has made known his distress over Swatantra approaches to these groups.[60] On the other hand, many Akalis in the Punjab felt that Swatantra did not permit sufficient scope for advancing the Punjabi *suba* claim and many felt that the party could have gone further in supporting the Akali efforts.[61] Some Sikh Swatantrites either resigned from party office or from the party completely, to have greater freedom to speak out on Punjabi *suba*; while one disgruntled Swatantrite in the Punjab has stated: 'We do not agree with Mr Rajagopalachari's view on Punjabi *suba*. His recent utterances have shaken our confidence in the principles of the organization...They are trying to appease the Akalis and the Hindus simultaneously on the eve of the general election.'[62] Such are the difficulties involved in trying to establish anti-statism as the pivotal consideration in politics, in areas where people's pre-occupations lie elsewhere, and such are some of the problems involved in trying to build an all-India opposition out of the diverse interests of the sub-continent.

The fundamental principles of the Swatantra Party are also silent on foreign policy, and here, too, individual members are privileged to adopt whatever personal positions they may choose.[63] Both historically and in recent years, there have been sharp differences in the leaders' approaches to international events. Rajaji, for example, has a very strong element of pacifism in his outlook, made his first trip out of India (at the age of 83) to plead with the nuclear powers to cease nuclear testing, and has been inclined to be conciliatory towards communists who seem to believe in peaceful co-existence (just as he was happy when the CPI ostensibly reconciled itself to parliamentarism). Munshi, by contrast, shares many Jan Sangh views, while Masani, in particular, is a vehement anti-communist ideologian, wholeheartedly pro-western in foreign affairs, and determined to sustain a remorseless battle to turn back communists. Not surprisingly, one of Masani's principal efforts was to persuade Rajaji to be less 'soft on communists', and his efforts, coupled with the Chinese invasion, have apparently succeeded.

Such differences are, however, less significant than the high degree of agreement which has prevailed, especially with respect to the challenge of Communist China and the means of combating it. Long before the Chinese invasion in late 1962, Swatantra had insisted that at least towards Communist China the principles of non-alinement, *panch sheel*, and others pillars of Indian foreign policy would have to be replaced. While acknowledging, perhaps for reasons of expediency, that under 'normal' conditions these might be appropriate principles, Swatantra leaders insisted that with the 'rape of Tibet' and Chinese border incursions (including the construction of the Aksai Chin road, which connects Sinkiang with Tibet, across Indian territory) the old notions had been rendered meaningless, if not suicidal. Demanding a more determined posture, Swatantra opposed all gestures of 'appeasement'[64] and condemned the 'Krishna Menon pattern of politics', which was considered to be pro-communist 'neutralism'.[65] Supporting Masani's very tough anti-communist stance, Swatantra has endorsed recommendations that India (1) sever diplomatic relations with Communist China; (2) terminate all trade between the two countries; (3) refuse to sponsor her admission to the UN; (4) recognize a Tibetan refugee government; and (5) attempt to negotiate joint defence agreements against China with other Asian nations, including Pakistan, and more recently with Japan. Both before and, especially, after the Chinese invasion, the party was very emphatic that India seek a *détente* with Pakistan, putting Kashmir in the 'freezer', and, if necessary, that India should aline more closely with the non-communist West. Few have supported Masani's private view that Chiang Kai-Shek might be encouraged to attack mainland China, even at the risk of broadening the scope of military activities to involve the great powers in a potential nuclear war.[66]

This 'tough' foreign policy line against China provides a basis for co-operation among many parties, including not only the rightists, but also the PSP and Socialists. However, Swatantra's rather generous approach to Pakistan and its Kashmir stand have certainly alienated many of the more militant Hindus. Very importantly, however, Swatantra alone of the major Indian parties censured the government for the seizure of Goa, claiming that it was a diversionary action designed to deflect attention from the failings of the ruling party and to enhance the prestige of the then Defence Minister, Krishna Menon.[67] Thus, on a matter which elicited the enthusiastic support of both the extreme left and the extreme right in Indian politics, Swatantra chose to stand apart.[68]

Swatantra's formulations concerning the Punjabi *suba* and DMK agitations undoubtedly have a 'Machiavellian' dimension,[69] but both here and elsewhere the party's views are more principled and ideologically based than many critics admit. Retention of English has some support, especially in non-Hindi areas, but only in a small minority of the population; and especially when Swatantra leaders emphasize English as the medium of instruction in colleges and universities (as many leaders do), they antagonize many ardent supporters of regional languages, as well as the proponents of Hindi. The same is true when the issue of 'linguistic states' versus 'zonal divisions' arises.[70] Its insistence that India take the lead in effecting a *détente* or settlement with Pakistan is similarly not calculated for mass appeal, for in so far as *strong* feelings in the country are concerned, these tend to be decidedly hostile towards Pakistan.[71] The Goa issue did not bulk very large, but Swatantra stood virtually alone in its adverse reaction. Finally, the ambivalent approach to the Akalis and the DMK has tended to isolate the party from the prevailing passions in these areas.

That Swatantra has ultimately addressed itself to issues not directly related to statism is by no means surprising; but the party's insistence that all such views are unofficial and the fact that many of these views are devoid of mass appeal reflect certain biases and preoccupations of the leadership. To be sure, the party has found some resonance among the mass of the voters through its opposition to enhanced taxation and through other anti-statist positions, and it has used other appeals to good effect. But its official doctrine and many unofficial views still seem relatively remote from popular interests and passions. In fact, the liberal tone of the fundamental principles; the stress on such matters as constitutional propriety, administrative efficiency, and judicial review; the penchant for adopting rather unpopular positions, all suggest the moderate, middle- and upper-class sentiments of much of the party's leadership and the debt which Swatantra owes to the early 'Moderate' leaders of the Congress.[72]

This raises, however remotely, the question of the ways in which Swatantra, like the Moderates (and their descendants, the Liberals), might be out of the mainstream of Indian political life;[73] and this is a question to which some Swatantra leaders have also addressed themselves. For example, many Swatantra leaders, particularly in the north, have argued that the party is at a disadvantage *vis-à-vis* the Jan Sangh, because of the latter's more militant posture and because of what is regarded as the Sangh's intrinsically more appealing ideology.[74] Many Swatantrites echo the words of Lobo Prabhu who argued that

> there is a little despondency in some quarters that while the Swatantra Party has convinced those who can think, it has still to reach the masses, less disposed to question their conditions. This idea has been vigorously spread by the Congress in order to emphasize the weakness of the Swatantra Party. But surely, if a Party's principles appeal to the educated and thinking classes, it is a demonstration of the party being in the right.[75]

The same feeling of intellectual superiority (not to say arrogance) was touched upon earlier in discussing the dislike for universal suffrage and intrudes in a different fashion in Rajaji's reference to the 'incredible degree of gullibility in the electorate'.[76]

This sort of sentiment calls into question once again the commitment of certain leaders to democracy based on universal suffrage, which would, for example, be important to gauge if a right-wing authoritarian régime became a possibility in India. It also evokes memories of the early Congress Moderates and their lineal descendants, the Liberals, who came to feel isolated from (emerging) mass politics.

Parallels between the Liberals and Swatantra are worth pursuing, not only for reasons of historical curiosity, but also to sharpen our understanding of Swatantra. Lobo Prabhu's statement provides such a parallel, because it is little more than a rephrasing of a statement by Sir Sivaswamy Aiyar, a prominent Moderate:

> Our party, many of us feel, is in the minority in the country...[but] Sobriety and judgement are bound in the long run to rule the world. It may be that we feel discouraged at times by the fact that we are not able

to muster in thousands as the members of the other party [the Congress 'Extremists'] can claim, but let not that depress us in the least...We are bound to succeed.[77]

In the same spirit, Srinivasa Sastri declared that

I may be a heretic, but I do maintain that that it is no disgrace to a party not to win success at elections...We still are elders knowing life somewhat deeper than other people...such men have a value and I am confident that we should continue to perform our most necessary, though often neglected task;

and Venkataram Sastri declared that

we know as liberals we are a handful in a vast country—we who have courage and are not ashamed to own ourselves to be liberals.[78]

Many Swatantrites share some of these basic perspectives, viz. that they are older, wiser, and more responsible people than those who dominate the political scene, and that it is no disgrace that Swatantra has received such a small percentage of the popular vote. The explicit aversion, in many quarters, to universal suffrage indicates further that some leading Swatantrites doubt that the party can get its message across in a context of mass politics. They also seem to feel that they must continue to fight their battle, even against heavy odds.

One Swatantra leader argued that many of the retired administrators and professionals, in particular, would withdraw from Swatantra if it became 'just another political party', indulging in communal appeals and the like to maximize its strength.[79] Some doubtless would do so, and in this respect they would also parallel the earlier Moderate-Liberal position. Most, however, are determined not to suffer the same fate which befell these early Congress leaders, i.e. almost total eclipse, and do not seem prepared to go down with colours flying.

This determination has led many Swatantrites to turn their backs on a broader liberalism, in the interests of anti-statism and the development of the broadest possible anti-Congress front. One form that this 'compromise' has taken is the willingness to derive aid and comfort from people both inside and outside the party who are anything but liberal and for whom the liberal aspects of the fundamental principles are utterly meaningless, save in the very truncated, anti-statist sense. The Swatantra dilemma here was aptly portrayed by one MP from the party, when he was asked about the extent to which the liberal aspects of party doctrine animated those who supported the party. His response was terse: 'Swatantra is like a parasite plant. It attaches itself to anything which can give it nourishment, but has no roots of its own.'[80]

Another aspect of the party's departure from a broadly liberal stand is the nature of its electoral appeals in many areas. Swatantra candidates almost universally emphasized certain of the fundamental principles, such as opposition to heavy taxes, to deficit financing, and to land ceilings. Save on a very limited scale, however, the emphasis was on the anti-statist issues, not on a set of broadly liberal ideas.

Furthermore, in many areas, even basic anti-statist positions were subordinated to other appeals. Party files contain numerous, detailed studies of the religious and caste composition of certain areas, with recommendations as to how communal factors may be exploited in the selection of candidates, in electoral appeals, and the like.[81] In some districts in Gujarat, religious appeals were made and old Rajput war cries were so widely prevalent that even party leaders admitted that nothing could save certain candidates whose elections had been challenged on the grounds of use of such appeals.[82] By almost universal assent of those immediately involved, a declaration against prohibition was one of the most widely heard from Swatantra platforms in Gujarat; and it was apparently one of the more effective.[83] In the Punjab, Swatantra sought to capitalize on the land question and on opposition to the Hindu Succession Act (particularly the provision which gave inheritance rights to women), and leaders in that state were frank to admit that the latter was very important in their campaign effort.[84] In Madras, Ganesan, the very devout state President, cited chapter and verse from the *Vedas* to show the identity of Swatantra doctrine and classic doctrines; and he threatened to organize a *satyagraha* in protest against the inclusion of *mutt* and temple lands under the Madras land ceiling legislation.[85] This is, however, one area where the public ideology was invoked, for some Swatantra leaders, as well as the press, deplored the fact that Ganesan's efforts were not directed against land ceilings *per se* but against this specific provision, which had obviously religious overtones. More recently, however, the Gujarat state convention of the party had as its keynote speaker a Hindu holy man who was about to embark on a fast over the question of cow-slaughter; and the state party passed a resolution favouring a ban on cow-slaughter at the same convention. Such concessions to religious sentiment, as well as the necessity to cultivate caste loyalties and to respond to parochial concerns (such as boundary issues in Bihar and Orissa), indicate the difficulties confronting Swatantra in this realm.

Many of these issues can, of course, be linked in some fashion to the general issue of statism, but usually this was not done. Even more rarely was an effort made to link these issues to any broadly liberal stance. This is not surprising but it does indicate that a broadly liberal approach was not deemed relevant in most areas. At best, Swatantra emphasized anti-statism, which, to repeat, is not synonymous with liberalism.

The future of Swatantra as a progressive party depends to a great extent on its ability to reach supporters on the basis of a more rounded liberalism, not the drastically circumscribed liberalism-as-anti-statism. This, in turn, depends on other factors, including the balance of power within the Swatantra élites, the existence and/or development of potentially liberal classes, the nature of the challenge from the left, among others. Thus far, however, in the contest between the proponents of ideological purity and those who adopt a victory-at-any-cost posture, the centre of gravity lies with the latter. Swatantra's formal doctrinal pronouncements, which *are* generally liberal in temper and which have exerted some disciplinary pressure, must be read with these other considerations in mind.[86]

CHAPTER 9

ELECTORAL ADJUSTMENTS

INTRODUCTION

Swatantra leaders have always felt that multi-cornered contests had contributed substantially to Congress victories over the disorganized opposition in 1951–2 and 1957. With this in mind, the party supplemented its efforts to build itself up through mergers and grass roots organization with a determined campaign to make electoral adjustments with non-merging parties. Some of the parties whom Swatantra approached were not considered likely prospects for merger under any circumstances, while in other cases, Swatantra hoped for merger, but had to settle for second best.

Broadly speaking, the governing principle of Swatantra's efforts was 'my enemy's enemy is my friend'—at least temporarily. This opened up a very wide field, the only salient exception being that no negotiations were to be undertaken with the CPI.[1] Neither Swatantra nor the CPI saw much advantage in such moves, and the CPI remained well outside the range of Swatantra's actual and potential allies. None the less, both direct and indirect adjustments with the CPI were in some cases made; and Rajaji's remark that he would ally with the devil himself if this would help defeat the Congress seemed to sanction such adjustments.[2] In particular, some Swatantra candidates in Andhra came to direct, explicit understandings with local CPI units; and, elsewhere, Swatantra often negotiated understandings with parties which in turn had made adjustments with the CPI, thus bringing Swatantra into some indirect relations with the CPI.[3]

In confronting the non-Communist opposition, Masani expressed concern over indiscriminate alliances. He preferred that Swatantra contest only 'on its own platform and in furtherance of its own policies without entering into any alliance with other parties'. Yet he was 'painfully aware' that 'a policy of electoral understandings and adjustments' was indispensable, if the Congress majority were to be weakened.[4] The policy ultimately favoured, reflecting Masani's distinction between an 'alliance' and an 'understanding', was that of 'reciprocal courtesy', where Swatantra and other 'democratic' opposition parties would defer to one another according to local strength, without necessarily speaking on behalf of or supporting financially each other's candidates.[5] Swatantra leaders made it clear that even if other opposition parties declined to co-operate widely in such a venture, it was still likely that Swatantra would act unilaterally, and stand aside in favour of another party, if this would weaken the Congress/Communist position. Moreover, party leaders also stated that they would by no means feel compelled to contest against the CPI in all areas, especially where the latter was strong, because this would involve a wasting of resources. Finally, Swatantra leaders also insisted that their party would not feel bound by any understandings reached by their 'allies' with the CPI. If, for example, the DMK and CPI came to an understanding, and if Swatantra and the DMK also came to an understanding, Swatantra reserved the right to set up candidates in those districts in which the DMK had deferred to the CPI. Such a declaration was felt to be necessary, because the DMK and the Akali Dal in particular were negotiating with the CPI and with Swatantra, and Swatantra did not want to find itself in the potentially embarrassing position of being indirectly alined with the Communists. In fact, the latter principle proved to be rather difficult to apply in some instances, as we shall see in due course.[6]

Many negotiations were undertaken at the very highest level—e.g. between Rajaji, Ranga, Masani, *et al.*, with their counterparts in the various opposition groups with which Swatantra considered working out electoral adjustments. In some cases (e.g. Rajasthan), state leaders declined to enter into discussions until they were provided with some guidelines by the national leadership, on the basis of such negotiations.[7] For the most part, however, the relevant discussions ultimately took place at the state or district level (although in some of these cases, Swatantra national leaders still spoke for the party), on the sound assumption that local conditions would prove to be the decisive factor. Most important were the talks with the Jan Sangh, both nationally and in Rajasthan, the Punjab, UP, Madhya Pradesh, and, to a lesser extent, elsewhere; with the RRP nationally and in Rajasthan, UP, and Madhya Pradesh; with the Akali Dal in the Punjab; and with the DMK in Madras.[8]

As in the case of Swatantra's efforts to build its own strength and to induce other parties to merge, the negotiation of understandings involved serious problems. Rajaji argued that 'over and above the desire of every party to maintain its own importance, there is considerable difficulty in appraising the strength of the parties in order to reach electoral adjustments. It is these difficulties that have stood in the way of coming to agreed adjustments so far.'[9] In this he was quite correct, on both counts. Even obviously weak and declining parties seemed reluctant to compromise their own independent standing, while the more vital ones were reluctant to concede much to a new, untested party. In some cases, we can see with the advantage of hindsight that there was a substantial misreading of political strength. Swatantra proved much stronger than imagined in some areas, while elsewhere, other opposition groups proved surprisingly strong. For example, shortly before the elections of 1962, leading newspapers seriously underestimated DMK and Jan Sangh possibilities in Madras and UP, respectively, and exaggerated Swatantra strength.[10] Quite apart from other factors which worked against co-operation among opposition parties, this difficulty in appraising strength was a serious obstacle; and here, as in the effort to induce mergers, Swatantra's limited success must be weighed against the difficulties encountered. But Rajaji was certainly over-optimistic when he stated that 'I expect in the course of time, necessary accommodations will be made and triangular contests avoided'.[11]

In some important respects, Swatantra's problems with the Jan Sangh and the DMK were similar. Both were older parties and both had fairly strong, dedicated cadres, at least in some areas. Both prided themselves on their dynamism and their militancy, which generally took a markedly 'populist' form and which gave them a 'mass' party image. Both tended to regard Swatantra as a presumptuous interloper which should approach them somewhat as supplicants and both tended to portray Swatantra as a tired, moderate, rich man's party. The buoyant confidence of both, coupled with modest electoral successes in 1952 and 1957, helped to keep Swatantra at arm's length, at least until it had proved itself a significant political force. Both felt that for an untried party Swatantra was certainly asking too much, but it was by no means clear that they would respond any better if Swatantra were successful. Given their general 'style' of political action, both the Jan

Sangh and the DMK were not likely to be particularly chastened by Swatantra victories. By and large, these considerations were less important in dealing with the Akali Dal, the RRP and the Mahasabha.[12]

On the other hand, these opposition parties realized that Swatantra did have some distinguished national and state leaders, that it did have the ear of some monied interests, that it shared a desire to oust the Congress, and that full-scale internecine warfare among opposition parties was not the way to achieve this goal.[13] Thus, happily or not, elaborate negotiations were undertaken by the opposition parties; but the Jan Sangh and DMK approached them with the proverbial chip on their shoulders.

THE DMK

Because Rajaji came from Madras, a determined effort was made by Swatantra to ensure a reasonably good showing in that state. After Swatantra absorbed the INDC, the DMK was the principal opposition group in Madras, and Swatantra had to decide how to come to grips with it. There were, however, some very knotty problems, in addition to those just mentioned. The DMK was an offshoot of the virulently anti-Brahmin Dravida Kazagham, and it was not clear to what extent Swatantra's Brahmins could reconcile themselves to working out adjustments with a party with this background.[14] In addition, the DMK, as we have seen, openly preached secession, and as part of its electoral plans it favoured adjustments with the CPI. Both within Swatantra itself and among certain segments of the electorate, these issues could not easily be dodged.

On the communal question, Rajaji himself insisted that a distinction had to be made between the DK and the DMK, even though in the mid-1950s he had accused both of 'openly preaching a creed of hatred based on ethnological conjectures and unrecorded and unproved historical conflicts...', at which time he also added the comment: 'Is it not remarkable that this hatred-mongering is going on, with little disapproval or discouragement from those in authority?'[15] In more recent remarks, the DK was still said to be vehemently anti-Brahmin and communal, according to Rajaji; but by contrast the DMK had abandoned its communal bias and was a party with which Brahmins need not feel uncomfortable. One source argued that it was on Rajaji's advice that Anandorai, the

DMK leader, had broken away from Naicker and the DK, and the same source speculated that Rajaji stood a good chance of persuading the DMK to follow the Ganatantra Parishad into Swatantra.[16] Others have given Rajaji somewhat less credit in these matters but have argued that he did try to persuade Annadorai to temper the communal and secessionist appeals, in the interest of maximizing anti-Congress support behind the DMK. Certainly, some of Rajaji's colleagues in the Madras unit of Swatantra (as well as some in Andhra and Mysore) were either former Justiceites or non-Brahmin Congressmen who had been in the forefront of efforts to oust Rajaji as Chief Minister of the state, which suggests that some old animosities have been overcome under the pressure of new conditions and needs. This, however, would seem insufficient evidence to think that a Swatantra-DMK merger was likely, because the 'communal' question seems less relevant here than broader social and economic considerations.

On the DMK plea for 'Dravidistan', Rajaji simply insisted, as we have seen, that it should not be taken seriously and that DMK leaders had a tiger by the tail without knowing how to let it go. The demand was at worst an exaggerated reaction against north Indian 'imperialism', and at best a legitimate, if also exaggerated reaction against 'statism'. Thus, Rajaji tried once again to make the DMK a respectable party, in this instance in the eyes of the nationalists (both militant and moderate) who looked upon the 'Dravidistan' demand as a menace to the integrity of India.[17]

Swatantra tried to dispose summarily of the CPI-DMK issue by restating its principles concerning understandings: the party would not consider itself bound to stand aside in favour of a CPI candidate, even if the DMK chose to do so. In this fashion, the leadership tried to counter some of the charges of political opportunism levelled against Swatantra when it announced its own talks with the DMK.

There were some plausible reasons for possible DMK interest in reaching an understanding, apart from the desire to avoid any self-defeating triangular contests. Swatantra was a national party; it might provide some help financially, if it turned out to be a 'rich man's party'; it could help to make the DMK more respectable among upper caste voters; and it unofficially supported English as the official language of India. As discussions proceeded, however, it became evident that Swatantra had relatively little to contribute, financially or otherwise. For the DMK, the disadvantages of associating with a 'rich man's party' which was not actually rich outweighed more remote advantages which might accrue.

Whatever differences might have kept them apart, the negotiations were certainly sustained and intense. The result, at one stage, was the preparation of two lists of seats, one in which final adjustments for dividing constituencies had been reached, the second which required further negotiations and which also would have required the DMK leadership to secure the withdrawal of some of its own candidates. It became clear that Swatantra asked too much of the DMK, particularly in the matter of prestige *Lok Sabha* seats which both wanted to contest but in which the DMK felt it could make a much better showing. When it became clear that the difficulties on the second list could not be resolved, Annadorai insisted on reconsidering both lists afresh, and with this, the talks broke down on a state-wide basis.[18] Rajaji was obliged to announce that 'the Swatantra Party will have to face the elections without the advantage which we had hoped to secure. Perhaps it is all for the good that we are forced to stand on our own legs.'[19] Annadorai spoke of the 'unattainability of an agreement' and of the futility of any further state-wide talks, and he attributed the failure of the talks to 'acute differences of opinion about certain constituencies'.[20] Thus they abandoned 'the joint expedition to the Congress mountain', which Rajaji termed 'our eve-of-the-election gift to the Congress'; but as Annadorai stated, 'though a pact has become impossible...the area of agreement wherein there will be no contest between the DMK and Swatantra Party will naturally be fairly large, and triangular contests will be only for a small number of places'.[21] In this, Annadorai was quite right, and, for example, a full and harmonious agreement was reached for the entire Madurai district.[22]

The failure to achieve a general understanding with the DMK was in small part responsible for what Rajaji himself termed 'a great defeat amounting to a rout' in Madras state, as Swatantra did not win a single *Lok Sabha* seat and secured only nine assembly seats, as opposed to seven and fifty, respectively, for the DMK. The DMK's successes in 1962 naturally heightened the party's confidence and led to plans to contest virtually every *Lok Sabha* and assembly seat in 1967, which did not leave much room for negotiations with Swatantra![23]

In addition to limited co-operation in 1962, as in Madurai district, the DMK showed some willingness to work with Swatantra on a limited basis, in spite of Swatantra's 1962 electoral débâcle in Madras.[24] In return for Swatantra support in a key Madras by-election, the DMK supported Ranga's successful candidacy in the Chittoor by-election, thus helping the Swatantra President to return to the *Lok Sabha*, after his defeat in the February 1962 general elections.[25] The DMK also helped to send Ruthnaswamy and Mariswamy to the *Rajya Sabha* from Madras, which suggests that all may not yet be lost, and that the DMK might have had some debts to repay. Now that the DMK has formally abandoned its secessionist pleas, and with recurrent difficulties in the linguistic situation, there is still a distinct possibility that a *modus vivendi* may be worked out for 1967, in which Swatantra would probably hope to barter support for DMK assembly candidates in return for the opportunity to contest for the *Lok Sabha*.[26]

THE JAN SANGH

Negotiations between Swatantra and the Jan Sangh have ranged from discussions of all-India merger to modest efforts at local electoral adjustments. The parties never seem to have come close to merger, although the idea has been mooted repeatedly since very shortly after Swatantra was formed.[27] Even a general 'non-aggression' pact proved to be beyond their grasp in 1962, as Swatantra and the Jan Sangh fought each other bitterly in many areas. Many local adjustments were, however, worked out in 1962, and at the present time (1966) talk of a merger—still very unlikely—can still be heard.

The major 'public' issue that had to be faced in dealing with the Jan Sangh was its *de facto* communalism. Among other reasons given, this *de facto* communalism of the Sangh was cited by leaders of the Ganatantra Parishad and of the Gujarat *kshatrya mahasabha* to explain why they did not join or aline with the Sangh; and most leading Swatantrites echoed this sentiment.[28] For a party which set itself before the electorate as a secular body, as Swatantra did, close association with 'communalists' would be a liability in some quarters. Moreover, the Sangh's association with Hindi imperialism, a key component of its militant nationalism, also smacked of intolerance.

Swatantra dealt with the problem primarily by ignoring it, or by white-washing the Sangh. Proclaiming its own secular basis, Swatantra insisted that association with the Sangh did not constitute endorsement of any of its views and Swatantrites were not permitted to speak from Sangh platforms in support of Sangh candidates. In addition, Masani, among other leaders, has listed it among the 'democratic' opposition parties, and Rajaji has simply denied that the Jan Sangh could be called communal. At a Jan Sangh convention which he addressed he is reported to have called the delegates 'fellow workers for individual freedom and confirmed opponents of the totalitarian tendencies of the Congress'.[29] While this writer, among many others, remains unconvinced when confronting such pro-Sangh statements, these remarks suggest not only Swatantra's concern about the Sangh 'image' but also the way in which it sought to justify its association with that party.

Leaders of both parties have always contended that the points of difference are few, but they have not always agreed on what the critical differences are. For some, economic issues bulk large; for others, it will be linguistic problems or foreign policy, or some non-doctrinal matter (such as Sangh discipline), that will be decisively divisive. For example, leaders of both parties usually assert that economic issues do not separate them; and many point to 'an identical programme on the question of nationalization and co-operative farming' as evidence of this proximity.[30] They often make common cause on these and other economic questions,[31] but it remains true that the Sangh is less solicitous of the interests of large property holders (both urban-industrial and rural) than is Swatantra. This is suggested by the Sangh charge that Swatantra is a 'rich man's party' and was underscored in Rajasthan, where the Sangh joined *all* other parties against Swatantra, in supporting land reform legislation which would further weaken the position of the princes and big *jagirdars*. This reflects the long-standing conflict between 'big' and 'little' Rajputs, and indicates that in some areas, economic issues may continue to divide the two parties, although national leaders underplay them.[32]

Ranga, emphasizing non-economic factors, said that it was foreign policy which kept the two parties from merging,[33] and certainly with respect to Pakistan and Kashmir, there have been and are today some very serious differences. Thus, while Swatantra was emphasizing the need for a *détente* with Pakistan and closer ties with the non-Communist West, the Sangh stressed forcible liberation of all Indian territory held by both Pakistan and China, and withdrawal from the British Commonwealth.[34] However, balancing this is the fact that Red China provides a common foreign policy focus, which even Jan Sanghis are inclined now to take more seriously than Pakistan; while, contrariwise, many Swatantrites are as hostile towards Pakistan as are the most militant Jan Sanghis.[35] Thus, there are ties that bind as well as points of difference in the area of economics and of foreign affairs.

There is one subject, however, which generates considerable friction and which is likely to persist—the question of national language and the linguistically related issue of regionalism. The Sangh has had some non-Hindi speaking Presidents in recent years, but the party continues to favour an immediate shift to Hindi at the national level and to regional tongues for state government and educational purposes.[36] From its militant nationalist perspective, the Sangh is also severely critical of 'fissiparous' forces in India, including the DMK and the Akali Dal. Jan Sanghis were among those in Banaras who so badly heckled Rajaji for speaking in English that he could not complete a scheduled address; and Swatantra is roundly abused for its association with the DMK and the Akalis.[37] Clearly, the relations between the two parties will depend in large measure on the issues which animate the country. Serious pressure from the left at home and/or from Red China abroad would seem to provide the bases for closest co-operation between the two, but it is clear from the Rajasthan case that some manifestations of domestic 'radicalism' are acceptable to the Sangh but not to Swatantra. On balance, the differences—both actual and potential—seem serious enough to preclude complete merger. Even so, a Swatantra leader in Rajasthan, with no love lost for the Sangh, has none the less said that close co-operation, if not merger, between the two, 'will be a great step forward for democracy, individual liberty and general well-being of the country'.[38]

Prior to the 1962 elections, the Sangh, like the DMK, was critical of Swatantra not only on doctrinal grounds but also because it demanded so much for a new, untested party. In this instance, the Sangh could point with undisguised glee to a *Lok Sabha* by-election in Delhi, in which a Swatantra candidate was entered, against the better judgment of the party inner circle which finally yielded to pressure from the local organization. The candidate, one of the many ex-Congressmen who gravitated to Swatantra in Delhi in the early months, lost her security deposit, as the Sangh candidate was victorious. This was widely used as an example of Swatantra overconfidence, when the Sangh was approached in connection with electoral understandings.[39]

The state in which the most serious effort was made to reach an agreement with the Jan Sangh was Rajasthan. The Sangh was by no means a great power in the state, nor did it contain any great local notables upon whom it could count for derivative support, but in some areas it was well organized and its dedicated workers were highly regarded by other political leaders. Moreover, it had scored well in some municipal elections, giving it greater confidence.[40]

Relations in Rajasthan might have been less close than they ultimately were had the Maharani of Jaipur not entered Swatantra; but her presence did much to convince some Sangh leaders that Swatantra was a potential power in the state, a power with which they could not afford to be too cavalier and high-handed. Swatantra on its part sought to implement its general policy of avoiding all multi-cornered fights which could redound to the advantage of the Congress, and elaborate negotiations were undertaken, especially by Dungarpur and the Jaipur family for Swatantra and by the very able and energetic Jan Sangh leader, Bhairon Singh, although national leaders of both parties were involved at various stages.[41]

At least as early as May 1961, Dungarpur said that final decisions depended on the views of the national leadership. However, he said that the state unit of Swatantra hoped to come to some understanding with the Jan Sangh, which he called a 'progressive' party, though he criticized its anti-Pakistan position quite strongly.[42] In November 1961 it was reported that 'an electoral adjustment between the Swatantra Party and the Jana Sangh is now almost certain' as a result of the labours of Dungarpur and both the Maharaja and Maharani of Jaipur, with Bhairon Singh.[43] Particularly with the full grant of power to the Maharani to organize the electoral campaign and arrange adjustments in four major districts around Jaipur, prospects for these areas, at least, looked bright. In commenting on this situation, Rajaji insisted that a final decision would depend on the precise lists of candidates nominated and on their prospects for success: until these points were clear, the matter could not be settled but, pending this, negotiations continued.[44]

As in the case of the DMK, however, state-wide talks ultimately broke down. Although the agreement had been reached 'in principle', Dungarpur refused to concede Bhairon Singh's demands for seats, which were to be split '50–50', with any other adjustments made by Swatantra having to come from its own half.[45] There were also reports that the Jan Sangh had insisted on financial assistance in some areas as a *quid pro quo* for an understanding, which Swatantra leaders also found unacceptable.[46] With only eighty-eight seats to claim as their own and to use in bargaining with the other opposition groups, under the Sangh formula, Swatantra leaders were forced to announce that 'an overall settlement with the Jana Sangh is something we do not approve of'. As usual, however, there was an important addition: 'The door is wide open for local adjustments.'[47]

In the last weeks before the elections, many local adjustments were, in fact, worked out, but in Jaipur City itself there was a curious spectacle. In some assembly contests, Jan Sangh and Swatantra candidates opposed each other, and the Maharaja of Jaipur made speeches supporting the Sangh![48] Elsewhere, a number of Swatantra-Sangh contests took place, indicating that even between these two parties, in a state where a concerted effort might have borne ample fruit for them, much remained to be done before the Congress would confront a reasonably cohesive challenge from the right-wing opposition.

The results of the Rajasthan election were disastrous for the Congress, as most of the state ministers were defeated and Congress' percentage of assembly seats slipped to 50 per cent. Taken together, the Swatantra, Sangh, and other rightist forces netted at least fifty seats, to eighty-seven for the Congress, and internal bickering in the ruling party suggested considerable instability. It was in this context that the Jan Sangh, at the national level, considered authorizing its Rajasthan unit to form an alliance with Swatantra;[49] while on its part, Swatantra for a time toyed with the idea of attempting to form a coalition ministry (if the opportunity arose) with the Sangh, some independents, and some Congressmen whose support was to be secured by offering the chief ministership to the late Jai Narain Vyas, a former Congress Chief Minister whose power had waned considerably. A variety of circumstances combined to preclude such a possibility: Masani opposed such a move if its success would depend on 'buying off' dissident Congressmen; other Swatantra leaders felt that even if such a ministry could be formed it could be squeezed from office by the central government because of the state's precarious financial position; some Swatantra leaders were fearful that their party would be overwhelmed by the more energetic Sangh MLAs; some sharp conflicts arose between the two parties (as on the question of further land reform and the constitutional amendment creating Nagaland);[50] the Congress ministry did not collapse, and Vyas died! Still, it is evident that, under certain circumstances, the Jan Sangh is willing to consider alliances and coalitions, at least in some states.[51] By contrast, in UP, where Swatantra is weak and has become weaker with the resignation of Paliwal and the death of Mankapur, there have been rumours of a possible merger of the Swatantra unit in that state with the Jan Sangh; and here the language issue plays a part.[52]

There was a widespread feeling in Swatantra circles that the Sangh would be a bit chastened after Swatantra had demonstrated some strength in the 1962 elections. This seems not to have been the case to any significant extent. In the main, Sangh leaders concede that Swatantra did better than Mrs Sehgal's disaster in Delhi would have suggested, and for this reason they have been somewhat more cordial in their relations with the new party. Until his death, Dr Raghuvira, Jan Sangh President, met recurrently with Masani and other Swatantra leaders, to discuss merger proposals, legislative fronts, etc., and as we have seen there was a willingness to co-operate in Rajasthan, and to a lesser extent elsewhere. But Jan Sangh sentiment still runs fairly strong against close association with Swatantra, and the Sangh shows signs of resenting the Swatantra successes. It feels that the latter's organization is weak and derivative and, thus, of uncertain staying power. Moreover, smaller Jan Sangh contingents consistently outperform Swatantra's forces, as in Rajasthan, where Bhairon Singh repeatedly dominates the right-wing effort.[53]

As in the case of the DMK, there have been some encouraging signs for Swatantra in its dealings with the Sangh. In the series of prestige by-elections in 1963—Farrukhabad, Amroha, Jaunpur, and Rajkot—many opposition parties joined together in supporting one candidate against the Congress, and, as we have seen, Vajpayee, a leading Sangh parliamentarian, and the Sangh cadres joined in Masani's successful campaign in Rajkot. In addition, the President

(1964) of the Jan Sangh, D. P. Ghosh, announced that Masani and Sangh General-Secretary Upadhyaya had reached an accord for electoral adjustments between the two parties. Against this, however, we must balance Upadhyaya's assertion that no alliances or fronts have been agreed upon and that 'ordinarily we are not for election adjustments'. So, too, we must note the announcement that the Sangh at one point planned to contest the Rajkot *Lok Sabha* seat against Masani, whom it supported in the 1963 by-election. In this area, however, the hard decisions of 1966–7 alone will indicate the degree to which the parties can co-operate. Most probably, however, the Sangh will be willing to work closely with Swatantra only where the latter is overwhelmingly strong or where both parties are weak; there is no evidence to suggest that the Sangh will be co-operative where it itself is fairly strong.[54]

The departure of Ramgarh and the possible decline of Swatantra in Rajasthan have hurt Swatantra once more, because it now looks decidedly less like a prospective national opposition than it did after the 1962 elections. Under the prevailing circumstances, no Swatantra-Sangh merger is likely to occur, at least on terms presently acceptable to Swatantra. Swatantra leaders made this clear, in commenting on a press report that merger talks were in progress.[55] However, many people have taken note of a lead article in the *Statesman*, which called for a merger of the Sangh and Swatantra, because both were 'unfinished structures'—the Sangh with a base but no apex, Swatantra with an apex but no base.[56] Swatantrites are certainly envious of the Sangh's dedicated cadres, if not excited about the issues which animate them. The Sangh, while publicly scornful of the 'rich man's party', is, for its part, aware that big business prefers Swatantra to the Sangh among available opposition parties; and Vajpayee noted, but not with any particular sadness or distress, that Tatas had given Rs. 200,000 (cf. our figures) to Swatantra but 'did not give a *pie* to the Sangh'.[57] Also, there are some signs that in order to expand its activities into non-Hindi regions, the Sangh has had to reconsider its thus far rather virulent stand in favour of Hindi; and any retrenchment here would narrow the doctrinal gap between the two parties.[58] Such matters are important but are not likely to prove decisive, for there are other barriers—such as the power factor—which will continue to keep the parties apart. Discussions at all levels will certainly continue, and there will doubtless be a number of local adjustments, A coalition ministry in Rajasthan is not out of the question, either. But a full union of the two parties, or even some sort of 'federation' as Rajaji once discussed, seems remote, indeed.[59]

THE AKALI DAL

One state in which relations with the Jan Sangh have not been particularly cordial is the Punjab, where Swatantra has decided, for the time at least, to aline itself with the Akali Dal, a Sikh communal organization, sometime partner of the Congress, and spearhead of the drive for a separate Punjabi-speaking state, which would—not incidentally either—be a Sikh-majority state.[60] Neither Swatantra's proximity to the Akalis, nor the Sangh's displeasure is at all surprising. The late Udham Singh Nagoke and Basant Singh, Swatantra state President and General-Secretary respectively, were formerly closely alined with the Akalis, and the early support for Swatantra from members of the Sikh ruling family of Patiala reinforced this proclivity. The Sangh on its part was unequivocally opposed to the demand for a division of the Punjab, and hence to the Akalis and to those who gave them aid and comfort.[61] Moreover, given the tendency to aline with the Akali Dal, it then followed that some triangular contests involving the Congress, the Sangh, and Swatantra-Akali Dal could actually be advantageous to Swatantra. At least it was hoped in some quarters that the Sangh and Congress would split the Hindu vote, enabling the Sikh-oriented Swatantra-Akali forces to capture some seats. However, Swatantra did not rush headlong into this association with the Akalis, nor has the association been without its very serious problems.

In principle, Swatantra hoped to break the Punjabi *suba* 'complex' by appealing to the electorate on non-communal issues, i.e. by opposing the proposals for joint co-operative farming, by rallying both Hindu and Sikh in opposition to new inheritance laws and other social reforms, by stressing tax burdens, corruption, and the like. In dealing with the Punjabi *suba* demand specifically, it was the Swatantra view that proponents of a divided Punjab were politically short-sighted: with the menace of 'statism' flowing from New Delhi, the creation of a separate Punjabi-speaking state would be of no consequence, because the centre would continue to enforce its will against all states. Only if statism were checked, in other words, would it become relevant to worry about the issue of a united versus a divided Punjab. On the principle of 'first things first', Akalis were encouraged to concentrate on defeating the Congress and to co-operate with others who were striving for that goal.

The efforts to use anti-statism as the solvent for communal-linguistic problems were generally unsuccessful. As we have seen, within the Swatantra Party itself there were tensions between Hindu and Sikh interests: Judge Gurnam Singh, an outspoken defender of the Akali cause, was first expelled by the Chandigarh unit of Swatantra because his 'recent activities were communal in nature and detrimental to the interests of the Swatantra Party'.[62] After being reinstated at the insistence of Nagoke, Gurnam Singh finally withdrew from Swatantra, under some pressure, in order to be free to advocate the Akali cause, although there have been reports that he retains his party membership and consults frequently with his erstwhile colleagues. As we have also seen, within the state Swatantra Party there were recurrent complaints by the Sikhs that the party was too generous towards Hindus, and vice versa—a point which is illustrated by the written charge by a Hindu Swatantrite in the Punjab that Basant Singh, a Sikh, 'has betrayed the party and become an Akali'.[63] Even the Swatantra committee of inquiry into alleged repression of Akalis in the Punjab became bound up with the pro- and anti-*suba* positions.[64]

Consistent with its goal of minimizing internecine strife among non-Communist, anti-Congress forces, Swatantra none the less tried hard to find a *modus vivendi* with the Akalis. This effort was complicated by the fact that in the tangle of Punjab politics, the Akalis were also striving for electoral adjustments with the local Communist Party organization, and the latter proved to be very demanding in its terms for co-operation. Swatantra had hoped to forge an anti-Congress front, excluding the CPI, recommending that 'non-party' candidates be selected for the prestige seats which each component of the front would probably want to contest itself.[65] Yet the CPI intended to put up a rather large number of candidates under its own banner, announced some of the names rather early, and declined to consider withdrawing candidates so named. The Akalis themselves had to reduce the number of candidates they would put up, so as to avoid wholesale conflicts with the CPI, and, as a result, the Akalis had relatively few seats over which they could bargain with Swatantra.[66] Moreover, the CPI was violently opposed to Akali support for Nagoke, and in the final outcome Nagoke was withdrawn as a candidate for the *Lok Sabha* in the interests of broader co-operation among opposition parties.[67] Swatantra was thus being ground away between the Akalis and the CPI and found itself obliged to settle for only a scattering of seats —unless it wanted to 'go it alone'—instead of the hundred or so assembly and *Lok Sabha* candidates it had hoped to put up.[68] Very distressing from the standpoint of the national party leaders, particularly Masani, was the fact that some Swatantra candidates choose to contest on the Akali 'hand' symbol or jointly under the 'hand' and the Swatantra 'star', rather than with the Swatantra 'star' alone.[69]

These complicated manoeuvrings did not result in very many 'straight fights', and even the Akalis and the CPI fought one another in many constituencies.[70] Yet in the February 1962 elections, no Swatantrites contested against Akalis for the *Lok Sabha* seats (while in five of the state's twenty-two *Lok Sabha* contests Swatantra fought the Jan Sangh); Swatantra itself often ran Sikhs as its assembly candidates in the Punjabi-speaking regions; and Akali candidates for the *Lok Sabha* received financial support from the Swatantra Party, on the condition that those who were elected join the Swatantra parliamentary group as 'associate' members.[71]

Such close ties as those prevailing in the *Lok Sabha*, coupled with the widespread belief that the social and economic views of Swatantra and the Akali Dal 'are more or less identical'[72] have given rise to recurrent post-election reports of a possible merger. Occasionally, a high-ranking Akali has joined Swatantra, and one Akali-Swatantra MP called for a merger and said that his two colleagues also favoured such a move.[73] Rajaji himself noted this possibility much earlier, but he also argued that even a close alliance would require as a *quid pro quo* on Swatantra's part a reasonably full and open endorsement of the Punjabi *suba* demand; and this was not forthcoming in a manner acceptable to most Akali leaders.[74] Somewhat paradoxically, Swatantra and the Akalis were likely to have made common cause particularly if the Punjabi *suba* issue remained unresolved, yet it appeared that if political temperatures ran high over this issue, Swatantra could not have supported the Akalis to the extent necessary for close co-operation, let alone merger.[75] In this context it is understandable that Swatantra continued in its efforts to find non-communal, non-linguistic common ground and that it continued to argue that the 'statist' policies of the government would render illusory the greater autonomy involved in a separate, Punjabi-speaking state.

In early 1963, Sant Fateh Singh, one of the two pre-eminent Akali leaders, ruled out the possibility of a merger between his group and Swatantra and indicated that the three Akalis might be asked to dissociate themselves from the Swatantra *Lok Sabha* group, although nothing was done on this score at the time.[76] It has also been announced that the Sant-led Akalis would ally with the CPI (Right) in the 1967 elections.[77] Finally, in 1965, the three Akali MPs were asked to dissociate themselves from the Swatantra group, but they and the Akali leadership were prevailed upon to permit their continued association with Swatantra. Master Tara Singh, a declining and somewhat discredited Akali leader, attempted to make something of a political comeback; and he talked extensively with Rajaji, Ranga, and other Swatantra leaders about the Sikh–Punjabi question and about relations with Swatantra. Rajaji insisted on first things first, i.e. defeat the Congress and then worry about the Sikh–Punjabi question; but some of the Akalis were not inclined to be restrained and patient. Sardar Kapur Singh, an Akali-Swatantra MP in the *Lok Sabha* (Oxford-educated, ex-ICS), complained that the Sikhs had been ignored and not given their rightful place in free India. Tara Singh disregarded Rajaji's advice about the need for 'putting smaller issues aside now' and for having the Sikhs take 'full part in saving the country from the Congress Party and its ruinous economic policies': Tara Singh declared strongly for an autonomous *Sikh* state within India, by contrast with the earlier, linguistically based Punjabi *suba* appeal. In this he was seconded by Judge Gurnam Singh who demanded a 'self-determined political status for the Sikhs', a demand which was repudiated by Fateh Singh, the Maharaja of Patiala, and other Sikh leaders.[78] At the time of the bifurcation of the Punjab (1966), Swatantra leaders were rethinking their approach to that state, i.e. a heavy reliance on the Akalis, especially the Tara Singh group. The latter appeared to be losing ground and a commitment to self-determination for the Sikhs would have been most difficult to reconcile with Swatantra's own internal politics and its desire to be a national party which must work co-operatively with the Jan Sangh. For the moment, the parliamentary alliance remains, and Tara Singh and Rajaji have been in close contact; but it appears unlikely that Swatantra will maintain its close proximity to a section of the Akalis, or that if it does it will do either much good.[79]

At the present juncture, it appears most unlikely that any mergers involving the Jan Sangh, DMK, or the Akalis will take place, and Swatantra will confront much the same range of problems in the future. It will, however, confront them as a tested party with somewhat better financial support, which will help in its dealings with these other groups. Neither the Jan Sangh nor the DMK seems anxious to get too close to the 'rich man's party', although well-filled Swatantra coffers would exert considerable appeal. Moreover, the departure of Ramgarh and the apparent demise of Swatantra in Bihar casts some doubt on the viability of Swatantra, which will further reduce the likelihood of important mergers.

Within the Swatantra Party itself, there is by no means universal assent to a policy of indiscriminate alliance and efforts at merger. For example, Raja Anand Chand of Bilaspur, Dungarpur, and many another aristocrat, complained of Jan Sangh electoral tactics towards Swatantra; Dungarpur also expressed concern at the 'socialism' of the Sangh and said that too many of its stalwarts were 'fanatical'; members of the Jaipur family censured it for its 'militancy' and its anti-Muslim stance; Pasricha termed it 'communal and fascist'; and a Bombay businessman called the Sangh a 'subsidiary owned outright' by the RSS, and said that Swatantra should have minimal relations with the party for this reason. Many Swatantrites are, in short, upset about the Sangh's communal tendencies, its fanaticism, and what many consider an undercurrent of anti-property sentiment.[80] Others, more sympathetic to the Sangh (like Munshi and Vaidya) are troubled, on the other hand, by the Akali and DMK demands and their anti-national implications. This has generated considerable strain within Swatantra, as questionnaire and interview data bear out.[81] Respondents run the gamut from 'go-it-alone' purists to 'victory-at-any-cost' compromisers; and evident throughout are the many currents and cross-currents which have made the creation of a reasonably unified, all-India opposition an extraordinarily difficult task. But within Swatantra, the question of alliances has generally been handled in a manner analogous to the question of the role of the aristocracy: maximization of anti-Congress strength is the principal *desideratum* and real trouble is generated only where local power considerations bulk large. For all his complaints about the Sangh,

Dungarpur wants to work closely with that party, at least under prevailing conditions; and the Maharani of Jaipur is similarly disposed. Paliwal, certainly no sympathizer of the militant Hindus after their abuse of his Muslim wife and their criticism of his own allegedly pro-Muslim sympathies, still explained his willingness to co-operate by reference to the Hitler–Stalin pact; and Ruthnaswamy was almost equally blunt about political 'imperatives'.[82] Masani and a handful of others among the top leaders do, however, seem genuinely concerned about the consequences of excessive political 'pragmatism'.

Swatantra did not limit its negotiations to those parties discussed in detail above. However, in other cases, either the party in question or the negotiations were virtually inconsequential. For example, Ranga mentioned the Peasants' and Workers' Party of Maharashtra as a potential ally, but almost nothing was done along these lines, in part because Swatantra itself could not get off the ground in that state. In Bihar, the Jharkand Party was locally potent in the Hazaribagh plateau region, where Ramgarh's strength also lay; and between them, these two parties almost completely routed the Congress in the region. At one point, there were rather serious talks of merger between Swatantra and Jharkand, and Ramgarh claimed that there was no serious bar—save the question of Jharkand leader Jaipal Singh's position in the Swatantra hierarchy. Jharkand ultimately merged with the Congress but has latterly dissociated itself, to resume its independent identity. At present, however, Jharkand shows no signs of leaning toward what remains of Swatantra in Bihar.[83]

In a few instances, Swatantra and local PSP units entered into negotiations. Apart from random reports of some PSP entrants into Swatantra (e.g. Imam), there was a feeling that with the apparent decline of the PSP, its more Gandhian elements were vulnerable to appeals. Pasricha, among others, insisted that few PSPers were genuine socialists of a type that Swatantra need shun, and they carried on sporadic negotiations to win some of them over. One Swatantra leader from Bombay City laboured long to win over *en bloc* the PSP units in Saurashtra and claimed to be on the verge of success—when, he said, Masani insisted on joining the negotiations and alienated the would-be recruits. Devgadh-Baria, to name only one Swatantra leader in Gujarat, insists that relations between the

PSP and Swatantra in that state are good, that a merger would not be out of the question, and that for the time, the true test 'is whether they walk out when we walk out'—which has been the case, according to him. H. V. Kamath, a leading PSP man from Mysore, was at one point reported to be 'very close' to Swatantra and efforts were made to work out a strictly personal understanding with him, as a prelude to broader efforts to recruit among the Mysore PSP. There is little evidence to indicate that many in the PSP share Swatantra's confidence about future relations; and many leaders on both sides are adamantly opposed to close co-operation. Yet there are many Swatantra leaders, at least, for whom the socialism of the PSP holds no terrors; and they will doubtless continue to work quietly to bring the parties closer together. Given the demoralization evident in PSP ranks, it is not difficult to visualize some defectors to Swatantra, particularly in the non-aristocratic areas.[84]

Negotiations with the RRP were carried on for some time at the national and state levels, particularly in Rajasthan, where Swatantra was, in effect, the heir of the RRP. At one point, it was reported that the RRP leadership had agreed to merge with Swatantra on a national basis but that a last-minute appeal from the Jan Sangh prevented this. The RRP was involved in a variety of conferences among opposition parties in Rajasthan, the Punjab, UP, Madhya Pradesh, and elsewhere, as part of the effort to secure more straight fights with the Congress. Agreements were reached with the remnants of the RRP in Rajasthan, in which Swatantra was asked for and conceded too much, judging from the RRP's 1962 electoral performance; and Swatantra will doubtless virtually ignore the RRP henceforth, save in a few constituencies. To some extent this may be an academic question in view of the RRP's weakness and in light of the fact that the RRP man elected in 1962 to the *Lok Sabha* from Rajasthan has joined the Swatantra group.[85]

A recent and inconclusive development of potentially great interest flowed from a decision on the part of Swatantra's top leaders to nominate as many scheduled caste men as seemed feasible, for the *Lok Sabha* and the assemblies. This suggests that Swatantra may have decided to make a move to rally the largely inarticulate untouchable vote; and to this end, Masani undertook negotiations with the Republican Party of India (the successor to Ambedkar's Scheduled Caste Federation), to discuss electoral alliances or adjustments.[86] It seems unlikely that Swatantra will put up large numbers of scheduled caste men (in part for financial reasons already discussed), but it may well try to work something out with the Republicans and to display its own *bona fides* by running a few scheduled caste men on its own, outside of the reserved constituencies. Masani and a few others feel that such a move might be politically opportune, but they also feel that it is not only consonant with but required by the party's commitment to equality for all. This commitment is not sufficiently well received by very many in the party, to the extent that caste Hindus would stand aside in non-reserved constituencies; and the unspeakable condescension with which *harijan* MLAs are treated by most of the Swatantra leadership in the Rajasthan assembly (and the extent to which they are excluded from the normal functioning of the party there) reflects the problems in this area. Yet in areas where Swatantra has not been able to gain a foothold through other caste groups, a turn to the scheduled castes (and to the Republican Party) may yield some results. Swatantra already has in its ranks a few intelligent and highly respected scheduled caste men and its legislative contingents, both nationally and in the states, contain a high proportion of scheduled caste and tribe representatives. If—and this is a very big if—it could build upon this base to some extent, come to treat the scheduled caste legislators as equals and prepare them for effective legislative performance, the Swatantra Party might broaden its social base and improve its position as a party of equality and of the common man. Much depends here on the extent to which Swatantra successfully converts the aristocrats, in particular, into Tory democrats and persuades them to be trustees for and educators of the lower classes. It would be foolish to expect much to come of this, but once again political imperatives seem to coincide with certain Swatantra principles, at least as understood by Masani and a few others. Efforts along these lines will certainly bear watching. They could conceivably presage a bold move to link the old élites with the lowest classes, against the broad, middle peasantry which is thus far political dominant, inside the Congress and in many other parties, too. This, to speculate further and even more wildly, could help to generate an Indian variant of Tory democracy, if only on a modest scale.

SWATANTRA AND LOCAL PARTIES

The negotiations with the Akali Dal point up Paliwal's early suggestion that Swatantra be a 'federal' party, existing primarily at the national parliamentary level as a 'holding company' for local parties. Swatantra support for the Akali *Lok Sabha* candidates, on the condition that they become 'associate' members of the Swatantra parliamentary group is an apt illustration of Paliwal's 'federal' notion. Beyond this, however, Swatantra was in many ways 'federal' in a *de facto* sense, if not *de jure*. Ramgarh retained the bicycle symbol of his Janata Party for the 1962 elections, even though his party had officially merged with Swatantra. The Ganatantra Parishad was denied the right to use its bow-and-arrow, if it merged with Swatantra before the February 1962 elections, and it decided to postpone the merger until after the general elections. In both cases, retention of the old symbol and stress on local issues put these parties in a good position to resume an independent position. Akin to this was the request by certain Swatantrites in the Punjab to the party office that they be permitted to contest under the Akali hand symbol, or jointly under the hand and Swatantra star. So, too, J. Mohammed Imam asked party permission to contest either as an independent or under the PSP symbol, and many others similarly asked to contest as independents. In all such cases, there was considerable strain between Masani and the local units and the individuals involved, because Masani desired to build a strong and disciplined Swatantra Party, using its own symbol and its own programme, as opposed to the tendencies toward parochialism and uncertain commitment implicit in the federal scheme.

As the Akali case indicates, this bears on the question of understandings and alliances in an important way. It has been suggested periodically that given Swatantra's determination to challenge the Congress at the centre, it should sacrifice assembly seats, for which it would support local parties, on the condition that these local parties would in turn support Swatantra candidates for the *Lok Sabha*. This is a variant on the Akali theme; it formed the basis for talks with the DMK at one juncture; and it is an intriguing technique for reconciling Indian diversity with national political life.

It is probable that the pluralism of the Indian subcontinent will force recurrent attention to this technique by would-be consolidators of the party system, and it suggests one possible approach to coalition-building. Masani is inclined to resist this doggedly, but recalcitrant 'raw materials' have obliged him to yield, but not without protest. However, the half-way house represented by the division of assembly seats (to the local party) and *Lok Sabha* seats (to Swatantra) is not likely to bear much fruit in the rigorous Indian political environment. To defer wholly to local parties for *Lok Sabha* support would put Swatantra at the mercy of these parties. In rejecting this, Masani has a good deal of company. If, however, Swatantra develops its own ranks to provide cadres for *Lok Sabha* elections, these local units will not want to forego local power for the possible advantage of capturing some *Lok Sabha* seats. Similarly, the local parties with which Swatantra deals in such situations are not willing to forego national politics in order to accommodate Swatantra, particularly where the basic perspectives of the latter diverge from their own. The Akalis wanted to be free to press for Punjabi *suba* and the DMK for retention of English, neither of which Swatantra was willing to endorse as formal party policy at the legislative level.

Furthermore, such a system would complicate the electoral campaign, if Swatantra insisted on putting up its own candidate for the *Lok Sabha*, while supporting those of other parties for the assemblies. With a largely illiterate electorate, the principal means of identifying a party and its candidates is the electoral symbol, the importance of which has already been suggested at many junctures. If the Swatantra scheme were to be tried, Swatantra and the local party with which it was allied would have different symbols with which to designate their candidates; and it would be quite confusing to tell the same voter to vote for symbol 'x' on the white ballot and symbol 'y' on the pink ballot. At least it would be much simpler if the voter had to worry about only one symbol. It would appear that either a more strenuous effort to develop a 'unitary' party, which Masani obviously wants, or a greater willingness to accept a radically 'federal' scheme as proposed by Paliwal and as illustrated by the Akali case, would seem more feasible than the hybrid we have just examined. Of course, this is not simply an 'either-or' proposition, because Swatantra can combine all three techniques as circumstances may require. But it is clear from this discussion that power, doctrine, and electoral complications work against the hybrid solution to the multi-party problem with which

Swatantra has been wrestling; and Swatantra's electoral predicament, both in terms of its own internal situation and in its relationships with other parties, reveals only too clearly the barriers which stand in the way of a would-be national party in India. Once again, leadership, ample finances, and some organizational stability bulk large in any assessment of present achievements and future prospects.

SWATANTRA AND THE CONGRESS RIGHT

In an earlier chapter, we saw that Swatantra's efforts to recruit 'old warriors' who were actually still in the Congress went largely unrewarded. Still, no one doubted that there was much pro-Swatantra sentiment within the Congress, and there were many ways in which this was manifested. Thus far, defection has been more spiritual than physical, and there is no likelihood that Swatantra ranks will be flooded with Congress defectors, particularly with Nehru gone. Here as elsewhere Congress hegemony and the Congress name, organization, and finances inhibit a more rational alinement of political forces in India; and once again, Swatantra is at a serious disadvantage because of its own organizational and financial problems. In addition, in many northern states many conservative Congressmen are by no means fully reconciled to co-operating with the aristocrats, and vice versa. This also hurts Swatantra's chances somewhat.

The existence of a 'Swatantra lobby' in the Congress has received ample attention. *Link*, for example, has adverted to the 'thinly disguised Swatantras on the Congress benches', the 'creation of a Swatantra lobby in the Congress Parliamentary Party', 'the growth of reactionary lobbies in the Congress' generally, and, in connection with the Punjab, it has observed that 'inside the Congress...especially in its dissident wing, the Swatantra outlook is gaining ground'.[87] A UP Congressman, Govind Sahay, in launching a general broadside against Swatantra and against the *pot pourri* that is the Congress, stated that 'the Congress has a good number of Swatantrites in its fold'.[88] Sanjivva Reddy, when Congress President, announced what everyone already knew, namely that there are many Congressmen who 'do not believe in the policies we are trying to implement';[89] and of course Nehru himself often enjoined the acknowledged dissidents to remove themselves from the party. This is what some leading figures, including some prominent Swatantrites, did, but no one can doubt that far more remained than opted out.

This pro-Swatantra sentiment has many channels through which to express itself. It is common knowledge that two former Congress Chief Ministers in Rajasthan—the late Jai Narayan Vyas and Hiralal Shastri—were consulted about Swatantra candidates prior to the 1962 elections and that they gave aid and comfort to Swatantra, while retaining their Congress labels. It is also no secret around Jaipur that some Swatantrites wanted to offer Vyas the chief ministership in a Swatantra-Jan Sangh-independent coalition which seemed a remote possibility.[90] Swatantra leaders in Gujarat gratefully acknowledge in private the help received from some Congressmen who abused Swatantra in public but who worked behind the scenes on behalf of its candidates.[91] So, too, in parts of Andhra some Reddy landlords, nominally Congressmen, worked for Swatantra in the same *sub rosa* fashion. Many of these insisted that they would join Swatantra were it not for possible Congress reprisals and they insisted that if ever Swatantra mounted a well-financed challenge to the Congress they would shed their timidity and come into open opposition.

Further evidence of support for Swatantra within the Congress is provided by the *Rajya Sabha* elections, where the selection devolves upon MLAs, whose party affiliation is, of course, known. Prior to the 1962 elections, Swatantra had only a small scattering of MLAs, and the Swatantra contingents had little hope of sending a fellow party man to the *Rajya Sabha*, without support from other parties or independents. However, in UP *Rajya Sabha* elections in 1960, Swatantra industrialist Ram Gopal Gupta (whose brother was a prominent Congressman) was elected to the upper house, with the help of Congress MLAs, who defied the party whip to vote for him. Similarly, in the Punjab, Swatantra leader Nagoke lost his bid for election to the *Rajya Sabha*, in part because the CPI instructed its MLAs to vote for Congressmen, rather than to allow Nagoke to be elected with the aid of Congress votes. It was also reported that in Andhra, eighteen Congressmen defied the party whip to help elect another Swatantrite to the *Rajya Sabha*, and such activities persist.[92] In Madras, after the 1962 elections, Mariswamy received the highest vote total of any *Rajya Sabha* candidate, even though Swatantra itself had a very small group in the assembly. It is known that the DMK gave some support, but there is evidence that some Congressmen voted for him as well.[93] Actual physical defectors are thus supplemented by spiritual defectors, whose sentiments, extra-parliamentary efforts and occasional *Rajya Sabha* votes lie with Swatantra.

While it would seem that close co-operation with these sympathetic Congress elements would be a major goal from the Swatantra standpoint, some historical animosities stand in the way, particularly in the northern states. For example, a number of Swatantra national leaders have insisted that Sampurnanand, a veteran Congressman who is now Governor of Rajasthan and an acknowledged conservative, is sympathetic to Swatantra. Some Swatantra MLAs in Rajasthan also believe this, although they have not had substantial contact with the Governor. However, as of 1963, Dungarpur had not even paid his respects to the Governor or communicated with him in any way, and he made it very clear he was loath to do so. The reasons for this he also made clear: Dungarpur is fighting the old battles against the Congress. In some of her parliamentary work, the Maharani of Jaipur categorically refused to contact some members of the Congress with whom relations had been far from cordial in the 'good old days', even though Swatantra leaders strongly urged her to do so. Ramgarh, Dungarpur, the Maharani and many of their aristocratic colleagues still bitterly resent Congress abuse, and even conservative Congressmen are steadfastly shunned. The aristocrat/non-aristocrat split which plagued Swatantra internally in UP and elsewhere also works against Swatantra in its relations with other groups and individuals, as in Rajasthan. This is a real problem for those who would seek to unify the conservative forces in the country, and Swatantra is no exception.[94]

The feeling for support in the Congress, and the aristocrat/non-aristocrat split were examined through questionnaires, and the findings support the preceding arguments. Swatantrites who had been in the Congress, and the 'old warriors' in particular, almost invariably argued that 'in their heart of hearts' virtually all older Congressmen were sympathetic to Swatantra. On the other hand, those Swatantrites who had never been in the Congress, particularly the aristocrats, almost invariably argued that *all* Congressmen were 'socialists' or 'communists'. The old saying has it that politics makes strange bedfellows, which is indisputably true; but in the case of Swatantra, political necessity has not yet been sufficiently felt in some quarters to help overcome some long-standing social conflicts.[95]

No one could seriously expect a sudden, massive defection from the Congress to Swatantra, although there are circumstances under which some Congressmen would join Swatantra. The apparent optimum situation from Swatantra's standpoint would involve a gradual but steady pressure toward the left by the Congress. This would be more likely to drive out smaller groups of Congressmen who would be less able by themselves to constitute a significant political force. Even so, such defectors would prefer to start a 'reformed Congress' or a 'democratic Congress', etc., rather than lose all contact with the Congress name. One high-ranking Congressman sympathetic to Swatantra said that he would in all probability prefer to remain in the Congress and that if he did depart, he would not join Swatantra. He mentioned specifically that he would form a new party, retaining the Congress name in some way, and that he would hope to attract Swatantrites into it.[96]

In the period between 1962 and 1967, this has, in fact, come to pass, as dissident Congressmen have formed such groups in Bengal, Kerala, and Orissa. Orissa is, of course, the most important from the Swatantra standpoint, first because it has some strength there and second because the leader of the Jana Congress is Mahtab, who headed the Congress-Parishad coalition ministry in the late 1950s. Swatantra has sought to work very closely with Mahtab's group, with an eye to a possible coalition ministry; and there was some hope, for a time, that the two parties would contest on the basis of a common manifesto and with a full accord on the division of seats.[97] Whatever the outcome, the widespread entry of such Congressmen into Swatantra is not likely, unless Swatantra makes a strong, national showing.

Throughout all of this, we must remember the tendency of the Congress to shift according to what Kothari has called pressure at the 'margin'.[98] Given its dominant position, Congress has had the capacity to undercut opposition forces by modifying policies, by opening ranks to significant segments of the opposition, and by less ennobling techniques.[99] Swatantra, along with other opposition parties, will have to face this problem; and at least for the moment Swatantra should hope for little more than a few defectors and some marginal help (as in *Rajya Sabha* elections), as well as some co-operation with rump Congresses.

SWATANTRA AND LEGISLATIVE UNITY

Swatantra has endeavoured to achieve greater unity at the legislative level also, and in the *Lok Sabha* and in some states, these efforts have met with modest success. It was noted earlier that Swatantra once tried to enlist the support of leading independents, especially Aney and Prakash Vir Shastri, in a move to strengthen its own legislative group and to consolidate the opposition. Particularly since 1962, the party has sought to forge something of a united front at the legislative level, in terms of a 'minimum programme' or on an *ad hoc* basis. The problem is most important in the *Lok Sabha* and in Rajasthan, because in Bihar, Orissa, and Gujarat, the Jan Sangh and other potentially close allies have been inconsequential. In UP and elsewhere, Swatantra is a very junior partner to the Sangh or another party.

Efforts at legislative unity have been affected by such considerations as the relative size of delegations, the quality of legislative performance and leadership, and the nature of the extra-parliamentary situation prevailing in the respective parties. From 1959 to 1962, Masani and Ranga sat in the *Lok Sabha* and led a small group of MPs who had joined the Swatantra party. The Swatantra performance was good, mainly due to Masani and Ranga, but the group they led was small and the viability of the new party uncertain. Hence, there was little opportunity to rally other parties to the Swatantra cause, even on a very modest basis. When Masani and Ranga failed to return to the *Lok Sabha* in 1962, the position of 'acting leader' was bestowed on Kalahandi, a generally modest, hard-working, but rather unimpressive leader. Under his leadership, the Swatantra *Lok Sabha* group, comprised heavily of newcomers who were reluctant to participate or of members disposed to maintain a high rate of absenteeism, was less impressive than the far smaller group of 1959–62. Yet Kalahandi's leadership had its redeeming features, too. Party meetings were held regularly, and Kalahandi personally maintained quite good relations with the members of the group, being neither oppressive, nor arrogant, nor short-tempered, etc. Kalahandi also tried to encourage wider participation by members of the group, in part because he was not personally disposed to sustain the burden of debate on behalf of his party.

It was during this period, according to one report, that Kalahandi recommended that Aney be approached with a request that he join the Swatantra group and assume leadership of the group. That this effort had proceeded rather far is indicated by Swatantra Party files, in which it is noted that Aney had agreed to join and that, because of his seniority and experience, he would be designated leader of the group.[100]

It also appears that Aney and Shastri were approached for a more general reason, viz. to increase the likelihood of a joint Swatantra-Jan Sangh parliamentary group. On paper, at least, either of these men would have been congenial to the Sangh, itself deprived of certain of its best legislative spokesmen. Aney and Shastri insisted, however, that commitments be secured from other independents, before they would commit themselves; and this was not done. On the other hand, according to one report, Masani was far from enamoured of Shastri and his followers, largely of the militant Hindu variety, vehemently pro-Hindi, virulently anti-Pakistan.[101] These and other factors combined to preclude the recruitment of Aney and Shastri, and in this fashion helped to keep Swatantra and the Jan Sangh from drawing closer together.

After the entry of Ranga in 1963 and of Masani in 1964, Swatantra was certainly much better led in the *Lok Sabha*. Dandekar's even later entry provided yet another very able spokesman. Masani and Dandekar, in particular, have been effective critics of the economic policies of the government of the day.

This larger, better led Swatantra group might have been expected to command greater respect and attention from the other opposition parties, and in many ways it did. However, the presence of Ranga and Masani involved liabilities as well, even for the Swatantra group itself. Ranga's arrival led to the demotion of Kalahandi to the position of deputy leader, which the latter took entirely in stride. In the re-organization of the legislative group, however, Mahida, who had been secretary under Kalahandi and who had got on well with the latter, also found himself demoted, and he did not take this in his stride. Mahida, in fact, wanted even greater recognition in the group and had apparently been satisfied that this was possible under Kalahandi's rather mild leadership, but not under Ranga's. Upset at his demotion, he insisted on a regular election to avoid what he considered the humiliation of a personal rejection by Ranga; and he said he would even leave the party, if he was so unwanted by the party high command. Although this was not the only reason, Mahida did in fact resign from the party and rejoined the Congress.[102]

Another consequence of the entry of Ranga, Masani, and Dandekar, and of the somewhat improved position of C. L. N. Reddy, a friend of Ranga, was the dilution of the heavily Rajput image of the Swatantra group in the *Lok Sabha*. Under Kalahandi, all office bearers in the *Lok Sabha* group were Rajputs, save for Reddy, who was chief whip. All were nominated and approved by the party's parliamentary board, and it was understood, at least by the board, that this arrangement was subject to immediate alteration, upon the entry of Ranga and/or Masani. After Ranga's entry, the preponderance of the office bearers were still Rajputs, but Ranga and Reddy worked closely together, party meetings were less frequent; Ranga, Masani, and Dandekar assumed the principal roles in parliamentary debates; and the relative importance of the Rajputs declined as a consequence. Save in Mahida's case, there is no indication that the Rajputs chafe at this development; but it is a possibility that cannot be overlooked in trying to gauge the condition of the Swatantra *Lok Sabha* group, which remains heavily Rajput.[103]

The post-Ranga situation as regards other parties also has its negative side, from Swatantra's standpoint. None of the Swatantra leaders in the *Lok Sabha* is a Mookerjee, even though some may try to be. In part, this would appear to be a function of the fact that neither Ranga, nor Masani, nor Dandekar articulates views which find much resonance in the great Hindi heartland of north central India. In part, however, it is a function of personality and style. Ranga remains flamboyant and impassioned, occasionally to the point of hysteria, in his public performances; and this appears to mar his image as a legislative leader. Certainly Ranga is less steady, less quietly yet strongly persuasive, and less modest than effective performance of this difficult task would require. Masani, for all of his efforts in this direction, has no appreciable chance of galvanizing the opposition forces either. He is too westernized and pro-western, too quick and imperious, and too little inclined to suffer those he considers fools to rally Jan Sanghis, conservative rural Hindus, and the other groups that would have to be mobilized. If Rajaji were twenty or thirty years younger and were sitting in the *Lok Sabha*, he could do a better job, but there is no one like him at present available. Swatantra's self-estimate in relation to the Jan Sangh points up this problem. There is considerable anxiety on the part of certain leaders that the Sangh, with its more militant posture and more experienced parliamentary group, would come to dominate Swatantra's larger, but less experienced and often less diligent contingent. Some co-operative efforts have been made, however, in large measure through Swatantra's persistence.

Swatantra has not troubled itself excessively with such negligible groups as the Mahasabha and the RRP.[104] At one point, the Mahasabha reportedly pressed for very close ties with Swatantra, at least in Parliament; but Masani rejected the overtures because of the anti-Muslim and anti-Christian approach of the Mahasabha and because of what he considered its policy of appeasement in relations with Communist countries.[105] Not much energy has been expended on the RRP, although, as noted, the RRP member from Rajasthan has joined the Swatantra parliamentary group.

The Jan Sangh is a different matter, because of its far greater strength. There is some evidence, as we have seen, that some leading Swatantrites are wary of the *de facto* communalism of the Sangh and that this was one reason for avoiding close electoral alliances.[106] In so far as Swatantra has kept the Sangh at arm's length, however, it has been for more practical reasons: rather than fear of contamination, it is fear of domination. To state the matter simply, as Masani once did, 'the Jan Sangh tail might start wagging the Swatantra dog'.[107] This was much more serious when Kalahandi was acting leader of the *Lok Sabha* group, but there is still considerable reluctance to formalize a close relationship with the Sangh in the *Lok Sabha*.

In Rajasthan, the situation resembles that which prevailed in the *Lok Sabha* prior to the entry of Ranga, Masani, and Dandekar. Dungarpur, like Kalahandi, is a quiet, dignified speaker, but he and his colleagues are consistently outperformed by the Jan Sangh —and almost single-handedly by Bhairon Singh. Many Swatantra MLAs are disconsolate and demoralized, and the party's MLAs often take their cues from the Sangh rather than from their own ineffectual leadership.[108] Here again the 'feudal' style of Swatantra politics in Rajasthan virtually precludes a substantial change in the situation, although there are some MLAs who have the capacity to improve the party's effort. Thus far, Swatantra has been unable to make its numerical superiority 'pay off' in terms of clear leadership of the opposition, and the younger, better organized, and more aggressive Sangh shows no sign of subordinating itself to Swatantra in the near future.

That Swatantra has not thrown itself into the Sangh's arms, despite much admiration for the latter's dynamism and organization, is worth pondering a moment. A variety of factors underlies this reluctance, but one of them certainly is the unwillingness of most leading Swatantrites to bend to the Sangh's fanaticism on the official language and the Kashmir/Pakistan questions or to yield to its *de facto* communalism. A victory-at-any-cost mentality has not yet emerged in sufficient breadth and depth in Swatantra to cause it to yield on such matters; and from this we may derive some very cautious optimism about the strength of the party's commitment to moderation, if not to a well-rounded liberalism.

Confronting all of these difficulties, Rajaji, Kripalani, and other opposition leaders have attempted to define a minimum programme on which diverse opposition parties could come together, as a first step to fuller co-operation. Rajaji, for example, suggested that the creation of a non-partisan board to grant permits and licences—not a very inspiring issue—could serve as such a rallying point, while Kripalani has been more ambitious.[109] A renewed Chinese Communist challenge would certainly bring the groups closer together, and Swatantra has tried to weld a legislative front regarding the government's China policy specifically and its policy of non-alinement more generally. Serious troubles with Pakistan would not be nearly as effective a cement, and the Sangh could easily take the initiative in such a case, because of Swatantra's moderate and conciliatory stands in this area. None the less, proposals such as those made by Rajaji and Kripalani, electoral co-operation as in north Bombay against Krishna Menon and as in the crucial 1963 by-elections, and co-operation in the 1963 no-confidence motion, bespeak an awareness of the need to work toward greater unity. That these efforts continue is proof that certain party leaders feel the compulsions of the contemporary political situation. That they have not borne much fruit is proof of the very substantial barriers to the creation of a more stable, unified party system, even on the state level.

In its dealing with other opposition parties, Swatantra has been cautiously co-operative. As in the matter of its own internal composition and organization, it is caught between the desire to maximize anti-Congress, anti-Communist strength and the desire to maintain a respectable party. Certain *caveats* aside, most Swatantra leaders are willing to associate with virtually any party, if it will help to weaken the Congress. Thus far, this co-operative spirit has been limited primarily to 'reciprocal courtesy' and has not included more than marginal Swatantra support for such parties as the Jan Sangh. Again as in the case of its own composition, however, Swatantra tends toward an obsessive determination to challenge the Congress effectively, and this pushes it to a victory-at-any-cost position towards the right-wing opposition. Masani's rejection of Mahasabha overtures and the worries about close association with the Sangh must be viewed cautiously. If the Mahasabha should merge with the Sangh, would Swatantra assume that the former had been purified and had become a more acceptable ally thereby? If Swatantra and the Sangh should be able to form a coalition in Rajasthan, how far would Swatantra yield to the Sangh to bring this about? If difficulties with Pakistan should be intensified, how far would Swatantra yield to the Sangh's intransigence toward Pakistan, if only to keep from being outflanked by the Sangh's more militant posture? The early Congress 'Moderates' withdrew to form the Liberal Party rather than yield widely to the more militant, populist elements which had risen in the nationalist movement. Would many Swatantrites do something comparable, if anti-Congress efforts led to closer contact with a Jan Sangh that retained approximately its present tendencies? Put most simply, the question is: can Swatantra hope to oust the Congress without unholy alliances, if not marriages of convenience, and can it hope to exist as a respectable party if it feels that it must cultivate them? Even though Swatantra has not thus far succumbed to the Sangh, there is room for pessimism here.

CHAPTER 10

SWATANTRA: ACHIEVEMENTS, PROBLEMS AND PROSPECTS

Short as its life has been and uncertain as its future may be, Swatantra deserves close study by students of the political process. Its efforts at building and sustaining an effective coalition and its relationships with other parties etch sharply the problem of interest aggregation in the Indian context. Its efforts in the direction of secularism, its emphasis on matters of political economy, its attempt to reconcile the aristocracy to modern political institutions and processes, and so on, bear on the question of political development, as it is understood by Silvert and others.[1] More traditional approaches, such as Emerson's study of the evolution of nationalist movements[2] or Duverger's study of political parties, are also enriched by an examination of Swatantra.

On the Indian side more specifically, the divergent perspectives within Swatantra and the way in which they interact provide a major case study of what Morris-Jones has termed India's 'political idioms'.[3] So, too, the discussion of the relationships between Swatantra and the Congress Party ties in with Kothari's analysis of the Congress 'system'. Here, however, a detailed examination of the Congress response to Swatantra lay beyond the bounds of the study; and this would have to be available to do justice to Kothari's argument.[4]

The summary which follows is not written with any one of the above approaches in mind, but it, like the arguments on which it is based, bears upon many. Two main themes have, however, been stressed in the preceding analyses and will be stressed here: (1) Swatantra's capacity to perform the function of interest aggregation *on any basis*, and (2) the qualitative aspects of its performance, most specifically in terms of conservatism and liberalism.

SWATANTRA AND INTEREST AGGREGATION

The task of interest aggregation in India has always been difficult, because of social heterogeneity and fragmentation. Weber made much of this point, and such contemporary writers as Harrison and Shils have underscored one or more of Weber's points.[5] Much of the argument here pointed in the same direction.

None the less, history affords examples of effective political groupings which have been wrought out of disparate materials, and the Congress itself is one such case. Certainly the Indian historical evidence must not be read so as to preclude further developments along these lines. Indeed, a number of recent studies have shown that under the prevailing conditions of competitive party politics in India, much social fragmentation is being overcome, at least to the extent that broader caste federations are replacing narrowly parochial castes, in the interests of greater electoral effectiveness.[6]

Opposition parties in India not only confronted obstacles imposed by social heterogeneity. In addition, the very heterogeneity of the Congress, the importance of the Congress name and organization, and the party's hegemony and flexibility have combined to inhibit a substantial, more 'rational' alinement of political forces among either rightists or leftists. Kothari rightly stresses this point, but fails to set his argument against the backdrop (1) of the general problems of interest aggregation in India and (2) of the way in which the Congress surmounted this problem. Moreover, the rightist parties confronted distinctive obstacles, which Kothari again does not properly stress.[7] These would include, for example, aristocratic reluctance to join parties (at least if the aristocrats themselves did not control them); Nehru's savage attacks on the right wing particularly; and the prevalence of socialist rhetoric, which helped to suppress explicitly rightist positions. Under such circumstances, the creation of a cohesive, explicitly rightist, national party has been an extremely difficult task.

How has Swatantra fared against this backdrop? Swatantra, with its distinguished (if generally superannuated) leadership, with one general issue on which it tried to capitalize, with some prospect of financial support, and with an approach to party-building which Morris-Jones has rightly termed 'certainly the most flexible and realistically power-oriented' of the rightist parties,[8] was able to rally a wide array of parties, groups, interests, and individuals (many of them erstwhile enemies) to an extent that surpassed earlier efforts by Mookerjee and others. Largely through the residual appeal of the aristocrats, but also through the entry of such groups as the Gujarat *kshatrya mahasabha*, Swatantra was able to achieve some semblance of mass support. While it was unable to forge a massive, anti-Congress front, it managed to work out many local adjustments with other opposition parties, reflecting the compulsions of the electoral system and the need to co-ordinate opposition efforts in order to *transform* the Congress 'system'. In one stride, it moved well up on the list of Indian parties, and to have become the leading opposition in four states and eventually in the *Lok Sabha* was a major accomplishment. For reasons given in chapter 6, this has to be judged a significant but obviously not an irreversible step in the political development of India on the party level.

Against this must be weighed the following facts. Swatantra was non-existent in many states; it was very weak in India's 'advanced' cities; and it was overwhelmingly dependent on the aristocracy for its electoral support. The truly stupendous majorities secured by Gayatri Devi and Devgadh-Baria, among others, and the heavily Rajput *Lok Sabha* contingent on the one hand, and, on the other hand, the difficulties of Masani, Dandekar, *et al.*, in getting elected at all, point up some of the problems here.

For this reason, even Swatantra's strong showing in four states must be viewed cautiously, because questions of viability and effectiveness are also involved, as the Ramgarh affair (among other less cataclysmic events) makes clear. All things considered, Gujarat, of the major Swatantra strongholds, must be adjudged the most satisfactory from the party's standpoint, because of a more socially diverse, better organized, and generally better-led party—though even this unit is not free of the problems already noted. It is for reasons such as these that some Swatantra leaders were quite pleased with the poorer electoral performance in Mysore and Andhra and that the size alone of a legislative contingent is not necessarily a source of satisfaction or a sign of strength.

Given the limitations of the Swatantra coalition, its internal strains, and its vulnerability to virtual decimation if a few aristocrats become slothful or defect, Swatantra's performance, good as it was, cannot be taken to presage the coming amalgamation of all forces to the right of the 'Nehruites' or a decisive confrontation with the Congress in the near future. The party's achievements do not, for that matter, even guarantee an overall reduction in the number of political parties in India. Apart from Swatantra's own internal problems, a major reason for this questioning of the party's 'staying power' is the nature of the Congress 'system'. Swatantra, as we have seen, is in many respects a holding company for local dissident groups which were brought together for a variety of reasons, one of which was the feeling that some degree of unity had to be achieved to provide an effective opposition to the Congress *in New Delhi*. (To say that many who joined Swatantra were not animated by such considerations is true enough but misses a major point: Swatantra would not have come into existence had it not been for the fact that many of its founding fathers were animated by precisely these considerations.) A weakening of the position of New Delhi *vis-à-vis* the states and/or a more 'pragmatic' Congress could markedly undermine Swatantra's position and could frustrate its efforts—in part by eliminating the need—to build a viable, national opposition. Judicious use of carrots and sticks, conciliatory gestures toward offended interests—characteristics of the Congress 'system'—could well take much of the wind out of Swatantra's sails.

Even sizeable defections from the Congress are not likely to redound to Swatantra's advantage, partly because of the dissidents' desire to retain the Congress name in some form (which was, however, also true of the INDC and the Bihar Jan Congress at the outset), but also because of Swatantra's position and vulnerability. Only if Swatantra seems strong and viable in a few states at least, if Rajaji or another leader of stature (not presently on the horizon) is at the helm, and if there is a strong *national* focus in Indian political life would Swatantra seem to stand much chance of benefiting markedly from the emergence of rump Congresses. A broader Congress right-Swatantra merger—not an unhappy outcome for many Swatantrites in any event—would mean a more rational alinement of political forces but it would probably mean the virtual demise of Swatantra as an independent political force, even though not everyone in Swatantra could be accommodated by such a coalition or reconciled to its formation. Had Nehru lived longer, sustained gradual pressure on the right-wing elements, driven out small groups of dissidents, while resisting counter-pressures from the 'margin', Swatantra's future would have been more promising than it now seems. Here, the party's future becomes bound up with major questions of national leadership in India, of centre-state relations, and so on, which cannot be examined here. But if Harrison (among others) is correct about pressures toward devolution of leadership and political power,[9] and if the Congress becomes more conservative in its social and economic engineering, then a large part of Swatantra's *raison d'être* will evaporate.

SWATANTRA'S QUALITATIVE PERFORMANCE

Given this generally pessimistic assessment of Swatantra's capacity to survive and to thrive in the Indian environment, it may seem superfluous to consider its qualitative performance. However, even if Swatantra is inevitably relegated to the 'margin', this question is still worth considering. Constitutional-democratic politics are still far from securely rooted in the new nations, and exponents of liberal doctrines are few and far between. *Assuming that these are desirable*, any significant political force which takes a decisive stand in favour of such institutions, processes, and values and which acts to strengthen them would be serving a useful function. Even a party on the 'margin' can help or hinder here. How does Swatantra fare on this score?

In some respects, Swatantra fares very well, indeed. The party has certainly made strenuous exertions to caution India about totalitarianism of the left, the forestalling of which Swatantra has set as its main task. But to be opposed to totalitarianism of the left is not necessarily to be constitutional-democratic, let alone liberal. Does the party have anything else to offer?

At its best, Swatantra has a good deal more to offer, with respect to constitutionalism. In striving to develop a strong alternative to the Congress, Swatantra has set before the Indian public the familiar rationale for a competitive two-party system.[10] In its effort to instutionalize the opposition of the aristocrats, as part of this party-building process, it has tried to reconcile this important social group to the institutions and processes of constitutional-democratic politics. The fact that the party strives for a national opposition which transcends the parochial pulls of Indian society is also important, if the maintenance of a national system of politics is a *desideratum*.

Also on the credit side of the ledger is Swatantra's attitude toward constitutional-democratic procedures. By and large, the party has eschewed walk-outs and disruptive tactics in legislatures, threats of *satyagraha* and of fasting unto death, and of chauvinistic demagoguery as legitimate political techniques. It has, for the most part, stressed the parliamentary arena and strictly constitutionalist procedures; and even where its leadership has been inept (as in the Rajasthan assembly), its legislative behaviour has been dignified. In terms of its manifest political behaviour, Swatantra is not a party of constitution wreckers, and we may hope that Swatantrites will heed Rajaji's injunction that no matter how dim the party's prospects may be, it would not be desirable to 'turn our thoughts from peace and democracy to force and revolution'.[11]

Still further evidence is available on the question of Swatantra and constitutionalism. The party's 'public advice committee', its Punjab inquiry commission, and its detailed attention to many constitutional questions,[12] have all underscored precise political and constitutional issues in a significant fashion. Needless to say, the relationship between the Planning Commission and the Cabinet and Parliament has also received sustained attention. The party's outspoken criticism of the economic and foreign policies of the government has certainly contributed to the sometimes halting and one-sided political dialogue in India. On many of these questions, the party has published useful analyses, however limited the audience for these might be.[13] Given the assumption that constitutional-democratic procedures and values are important and that sound policy will emerge from a confrontation of alternatives, Swatantra deserves ample credit in these respects.

It is necessary, however, to take note of some lapses from grace. There is within the party leadership a strong strain of anti-democratic élitism (aristocratic, administrative and professional) and frequent criticism of universal suffrage. There have been *some* threats of *satyagraha*, there have been some walk-outs, etc. There are certainly some Swatantrites, including some who are highly placed, who would not mourn the passing of constitutional democracy, provided the 'right' people assumed control.

Thus far, these summary remarks have been confined to issues of constitutional-democratic politics and of alternative policies within that framework, where, generally, Swatantra fares well. In confronting its substantitive policy recommendations and Swatantra's place in the political spectrum from that vantage point, we face certain difficulties. For one thing, one's judgment here depends in large measure on the perception of the dialectical nature of competitive party politics. If we concede the Swatantra contention that the Congress and other major parties have swung far to the left (or else do not appreciate the threat from the left), then we will be less critical if we find that Swatantra lies much to the right, because a balance *may* be struck in the interaction of the contending forces. Similarly, if we concede the argument that statism is the greatest enemy to personal freedom and that its triumph is approaching in India, then we will be less critical if we find that Swatantra tends toward a victory-at-any-cost approach towards the Congress.

A second major difficulty relates to the divergent perspectives within Swatantra itself, the balance among which is by no means firmly settled.[14] There is the related problem of ideological shifts on the part of individuals and groups, as they participate in the political process. An accurate assessment of Swatantra's qualitative performance depends on a reasonably precise understanding of these ambiguities.

The simplest matters to dispose of concern formal party doctrine and the question of secularism. For all its lacunae and ambiguities, formal party doctrine is predominantly liberal in tone; and even after due allowances are made for non-believers, for lapses from grace, and for the consequences of Morris-Jones' diverse 'idioms',[15] this, too, ought not be lightly dismissed. A major Indian political party is publicly committed to such a doctrine, which is poles apart from the views of the RRP, Hindu Mahasabha, and the Jan Sangh. Related to this is the fact that at the highest levels, at least, Swatantra has set forth a moderate, secular, nationalist approach to public life, to which people of diverse religions have been willing to subscribe and with which most feel comfortable. It is incontestable that of all political parties which may with any justice be placed to the right of the political spectrum, Swatantra is the most secular, and this, too, ought not be lightly dismissed.[16]

Other factors are relevant, however, in defining the position of the party, and among these are the social backgrounds and the perspectives of those who comprise the party. Rajaji, by all odds Swatantra's stellar attraction, looks upon the party as a conservative one and he has explicitly referred to it as a party of the right. So did Menon, and most of the aristocrats would concur. Some have been quite outspoken in their view that Swatantra should appeal to aristocrats, non-aristocratic landed classes, businessmen, and other groups of 'haves', because the party will protect these vested interests. To this extent, the problem of defining what Swatantra stands for is answered by some Swatantra leaders in emphatic language: for privilege and for conservatism in one or another entirely recognizable form. Rajaji was even willing to call his party the 'Conservative Party', but he was apparently convinced that this would be a distinct political liability.[17]

We have also seen that within Swatantra there are people of a more liberal temper and that both explicitly and implicitly they pose a challenge to the more conservative elements in the party. Certainly a liberal party in the classical European sense would also generate 'dislocation, disturbance, and distress' of the type that Rajaji opposes. This is obvious from Rajaji's assessment of western individualism, social reform movements based thereon, and industrialization; and Rajaji is, in this sense, conservative not only towards the statists but also to the liberals. In short, Swatantra contains both conservative and liberal elements, albeit in unequal measure; and in many respects it contains in microcosm the classic battle between these two perspectives.

A central problem, therefore, is the way in which the balance has been struck between these points of view, and we must see this without being seduced by those who insist that such distinctions as we have been making are utterly meaningless. That the analytical waters have been amply muddied is immediately obvious. At one point prior to the creation of Swatantra, it was argued that 'every day that passes makes the need for a conservative party in this country to check the tide of statism increasingly urgent'. The argument continued by saying that 'a conservative party in the context of Indian politics is not a party of reaction'—which may be accepted without qualm—but to say, then, that 'it will be a progressive liberal party, which will have its roots in basic democratic principles and in the cherished traditions of the country' simply does not follow.[18] Admitting that it is difficult to use parts of the political vocabulary with precision, we still cannot permit this statement to pass unchallenged. It is one thing to say that conservatives and liberals can join hands in opposing statism, but it is quite another thing—and quite incorrect—to argue that they are identical.

Masani has done little to clarify the picture. On one occasion he said:

I do not much care what label such a party adopts. Rajaji would like to call it a conservative party. Being myself a liberal and one of the Patrons of the Liberal International, I would prefer another title. But whether it is called a Democratic Party, People's Party, or Centre Party, it is not important. What is important is that it should present a clear democratic alternative to the policies of the ruling party, so that the people of India may be given an opportunity to exercise an effective choice. In my view, the new party should be what may be broadly called a middle-of-the-road party or centre party which would eschew dogma and extreme of any kind.[19]

This characterization would obviously permit both liberals and conservatives to join hands against the statists, but it still does not settle the question of the interaction between them.

Elsewhere, too, Masani has been of little help, as he has sought to free Swatantra from the label of 'rightist', even though Rajaji does not seem to mind this characterization:

While large sections of the press both in India and abroad have described the Swatantra Party as a 'Rightist' party, coupling it in this respect with the Jan Sangh, every serious student of political science knows that the terms 'Left' and 'Right' have lost all meaning in recent decades. There can be nothing more reactionary than the Communist ideology, with its belief in totalitarian control...and yet it is labelled 'Leftist' along with the democratic socialist elements. *There can be nothing more progressive and radical* than the philosophy of the Swatantra Party with its stress on individual liberty, the dignity of the human personality and the assertion of the Fundamental Rights in the Constitution, and yet it is often described as 'Rightist!'[20]

This is a variant on the theme of who is a true socialist, as is evident from the remark that Nehru was 'a pre-Revolution Marxist; we are post-Revolution Marxists'.[21] In the second extended quotation, Masani stresses the individualistic, progressive aspects of Swatantra, but by contrast to the statists, not to the conservatives.

The problem is not only one of contending groups within Swatantra, but it is also one which is visible within a single individual, as we have seen in the case of Rajaji himself. He is fundamentally a Burkean conservative, of that there can be no doubt. Yet recently, Rajaji has come to talk more in terms of liberal individualism than in terms of conservatism, without clearly facing the implicit contradictions himself; and he has explicitly rejected any 'back-to-the-village' programme. Some Swatantrites, confronted by the massive challenge of socialism and by the massive verbal challenge to the old order, have, indeed, shifted toward more liberal positions, as Rajaji has done.[22] Over wide areas, however, no real fusion of the two perspectives is evident, and the conflict between conservative and liberal elements remains, even though it is often suppressed. There are some indications, however, that the pressure of the competitive situation is, in fact, moving Swatantra generally away from conservative positions.

If we approach this problem in terms of the party which has been built so far—its élites, composition, formal doctrine, the pattern of electoral support and of electoral understandings—the prospects of a well-rounded liberal position, as distinct from a constitutionalist or technologically progressive role, are not good. The liberal element is, in the first place, numerically small, even within the élites, and there is an obvious weakening of liberal commitment as one moves down the party hierarchy. This is to be expected in terms of Morris-Jones' arguments about India's political idioms. Secondly, there is the problem of reaching the electorate in terms of broadly based, liberal programmes. Thirdly, there is the related problem of the extreme dependence on aristocrats who are (1) not fully reconciled in many cases to modern, democratic politics, (2) quite conservative on the whole, and (3) not disposed to put their residual, traditional appeal at the disposal of the more liberal elements in the party. Even when aristocratic commitment to modern industry is taken into account, when occasional cases of Tory democracy are acknowledged, and when Masani's efforts to assert the position of the more modern, liberal elements are noted, the general situation is still quite depressing from the standpoint of Swatantra's modern men—not all of whom are, in any event, liberals. Moreover, the Masani-led effort runs afoul of much non-aristocratic conservatism and parochialism as well. It will be only with the greatest difficulty that Swatantra's more modern and liberal men will make appreciable headway.

The obstacles confronting Swatantra in this respect are clear enough. With limited time and resources, coupled with a feeling among many that it is 'now or never', Swatantra sought aid and comfort wherever it could be found. Many less than edifying local notables were welcomed into the fold and these proved to be largely responsible for the party's electoral successes. Given Swatantra's estimate of the present political scene, it is inconceivable that the party would consider a major 'purge' in order to put its organization on a more modern and liberal footing. Local notables have the appeal, and Swatantra, by and large, had to take whatever it got, and it is likely to continue to do so.

Masani, as usual, has been able to specify the central issues, even if he has not been able to implement pertinent policies. At one juncture he told his party that 'we should be careful not to depend on dubious elements. Our enthusiasm and eagerness to see the Party grow should not lead us to welcome people into our fold without due discrimination'.[23] In addition, in surveying the 'lessons' of the general elections of 1962, Masani insisted that 'the moral is simple':

> The Swatantra Party has to build its own structure on a sound and more broad-based social basis. It has, in particular, to devote specific attention to massive sections of the people, like Harijans, Adivasis, small farmers, industrial and agricultural labour, shopkeepers, youth and women. Specific attention to the needs of these classes of our people, many of whom are under-privileged in social and economic terms, is called for. For a Party which has put the needs of the Common Man in the forefront of its programme and Manifesto, such a task is a moral and political imperative.[24]

These are unexceptionable positions, action upon which seems unlikely, if, by it, Masani means to circumvent the local notables upon whom Swatantra has been so dependent. In the absence of a conversion of the aristocracy, such circumvention is essential if Swatantra is to become the spokesman for the middle class, let alone for the 'common man'. This, however, would involve virtually the total reconstruction of the party precisely in those areas where it has made some of its most impressive showings. Even such verbally gifted people as Masani or Rajaji could not convince a sensible person that the party in Bihar or Rajasthan was a party of the common man, and Rajaji admitted as much in the case of Ramgarh. Masani may have soothed some personal guilt feelings but should have confused no one when he said that 'our inability to reach large sections of the electorate also meant that the Big Lie about the Swatantra Party being a party of maharajas and capitalists remained unanswered in so far as large numbers of voters were concerned'.[25] Until the pattern of electoral support and the composition, or at least the outlook of most of the northern cadres, change rather markedly, the question will remain largely unanswered—and, in so far as it is answered partially, it will not be to Swatantra's advantage.

If Swatantra's reliance on the aristocracy raises some doubts about the party's liberal future, its relations with other opposition groups raise still more. Masani again provided a useful approach to the problem when he said that while Swatantra 'is a National Democratic Party of all elements and communities in India' which 'could not agree' with the Jan Sangh, Hindu Mahasabha, DMK, and Akali Dal, 'insofar as they are sectarian parties', most, if not all non-Communist opposition parties were, in his view, acceptable electoral allies: 'That is the choice of evils we have to make. The total evil is the communist evil, whether it is in the Communist Party or whether it has infiltrated the Congress.'[26] Thus, the Swatantra perception of the Indian situation as well as objective aspects of that situation (such as the multiplicity of parties, Swatantra's poor finances, etc.) leads it toward positions, both in terms of its own membership and organization and in terms of its electoral and legislative understandings and alliances, which seriously prejudice its chances for liberal respectability. Swatantra will have a most difficult time, in the prevailing Indian context, without considerable reliance on 'dubious elements' both inside and outside the party ranks. The fault is not entirely due to a uniform lack of will in Swatantra; but wherever the fault lies, the party faces a steep ascent, if it is to establish itself not only as a constitutional-democratic party but as a modernizing, liberal one as well.[27]

At this point in time, then, it would seem fair to characterize Swatantra as a predominantly conservative party which embraces, in particular, aristocratic conservatism, non-aristocratic landed conservatism, and the conservatism of the idealized village. Its modernizing potential would seem to be greatest in the political realm, i.e. through its willingness to function through contemporary national political institutions and organized parties, with the economic sector ranking next in this respect, as a result of the presence of some urban, industrial interests, plus some technologically progressive aristocrats. Weakest of all thus far is an open, aggressive commitment to social modernization, which is, of course, intimately related to the question of liberalism. A more modern and in some cases more liberal element is certainly present, and it has tried to assert its position through its involvement in formal doctrinal matters and through judicious use of the rupee; but thus far it has tended to exist toward the 'margin' of a party itself at the 'margin' of the Congress system.

These considerations are, of course, related to certain of our introductory remarks about conservatism. Huntington and others have noted the two-directional battle of the French middle classes, and many have noted the retreat of the liberals in nineteenth-century Germany, in the face of a rising socialist challenge. The problems inherent in this 'middling' position are abundantly evident in the Swatantra case.[28] To a modest degree, liberal ideas are being articulated against the *ancien régime* elements in Swatantra, but for the most part, as we have seen over and over again, the threat from the left is considered to be so serious that this critique is muted to the point of inaudibility. It is for such reasons that analysts who easily characterize Swatantra as a nineteenth-century liberal party (largely due to misplaced emphasis on formal ideology) miss a key point. The fact is that twentieth-century India is not eighteenth- or nineteenth-century Europe, and even the liberals in Swatantra are not liberals in the classical European sense. The Swatantra liberals have consistently emphasized the statist threat and have understated or completely ignored the weight of tradition and the dangers which lie to the right; and, in so far as they continue to do so, they will represent at best a very truncated form of liberalism. Masani would do well to consider the nineteenth-century German case, as part of his world-historical analyses.

THE FUTURE OF THE INDIAN RIGHT

The future of Swatantra as the principal vehicle for either Indian conservatism or for Indian liberalism (or some combination of the two) would not seem promising. This does not mean that the Indian right is in eclipse or that it is inconsequential in the Indian political system. The bases of Indian rightism are ample, but the major components have been disorganized and somewhat beneath the surface of overtly conservative party political life.

The poor electoral performance of the explicitly rightist parties prior to Swatantra's arrival justifies only modest conclusions. It indicates only that the most venturesome exponents of various right-wing positions have thus far been devoid of substantial mass appeal as independent forces. It says little about the (latent) strength of such views within the Congress itself, particularly about moderate conservatism, as opposed to the views of the RRP, Hindu Mahasabha, or the Jan Sangh. Swatantra, for reasons suggested by Kothari's analysis, as we have amended it here, may well suffer serious setbacks and recede in importance, particularly if Congress hegemony is sustained and if the ruling party responds to pressure at the 'margin'.

A most obvious fact is that there is more to Indian rightism than meets the eye—at least the eye which scans only electoral data and official party propaganda. In the future, there should be ample scope for both moderate and militant rightism (if not for aristocratic conservatism or for RRP-style obscurantism), although it is impossible to specify what the balance will be.[29] What may safely be said is that the social forces which have supported various rightist positions will continue to work through diverse channels, some of which will surely be more explicitly rightist now that Nehru has passed from the scene. Whether Swatantra and the Jan Sangh merge, or whether Swatantra and the Congress right merge, or whether some other pattern evolves (e.g. one based on a drastic disintegration of national politics), the underlying social forces, and their interaction, must receive greater attention than has thus far been the case, if Indian political development is to be properly understood.

It is most likely that India's rightist forces will remain reasonably disorganized and will seem somewhat less strong and less explicitly rightist than they in fact are. These are virtually inescapable aspects of rightist activity in India today and are likely to remain so for some time. The prevailing disorder may seem to be a luxury that the right can ill-afford, but we must remember that there are substantial conflicts within the rightist camp on major issues. There is certainly no compelling reason for all rightist forces to unite, and there is certainly little likelihood that they will do so in the absence of a sustained and serious attack from the left. In this writer's view, the latter has thus far not been forthcoming and is not likely in the near future, Swatantra charges of statism and incipient totalitarianism notwithstanding. There is also considerable historical evidence to suggest that even in the face of a serious challenge the rightist groups would not heed the maxim, 'we had best hang together, else we shall hang separately', but, in so far as this situation persists today, Swatantra cannot be blamed for it.

The pattern of Indian public life in the mid-1960s suggests that Congress reformism is unlikely to 'get that huge country moving' widely and swiftly. Persistent problems, domestic and foreign, *could* generate a sense of frustration and already seem to have generated a more cautious approach on the part of the Congress, as the suggestions for a plan 'holiday' and/or more modest development programmes testify. If this should be the case, and if the failures of earlier policy be traced to Nehru and his 'western' ideas, then a renaissance of more 'Indian' ideas could come increasingly to permeate public life. Such a renaissance along militant Hindu lines would probably be disastrous in terms of communal relations (i.e. Hindu *v.* Muslim), although it would hold out the hope for industrial and some social advance, within the framework of a strong, more centralized nation-state. A re-emphasis along the lines of the idealized village would doubtless be disastrous on almost all counts, although many Indians could announce their revolutionary intent and could console themselves with the thought that they were being true to Gandhi.

In this context, a Swatantra Party which aggressively propagated a liberal and moderate nationalist line, maintaining a firm commitment to industrialization and to national political institutions, could perform a valuable function in Indian public life. And there are some modestly hopeful signs. The present evidence suggests, however, that Swatantra will not be equal to the task of a two-front war, critical of rightist dangers to freedom as well as of the leftist threat. Again, we must emphasize that this is not due entirely to a uniform lack of will. Broadly liberal classes simply do not exist in India, and the impact of colonialism and of world-wide Marxism have probably thrown India into a situation in which classical liberalism is not likely to flourish. Even if we agree with Swatantra that the principal threat flows from totalitarianism of the left, we must yet insist (with Brecher, for one)[30] that the Indian right poses serious problems as well. Here many western observers join hands in irresponsibility with all too many Swatantrites: by steadfastly ignoring the substantial, if often latent or untapped or disorganized reservoirs of right-wing strength in India, or by blithely assuring us that anti-statism is equivalent to liberalism or that a conservative party in India is not really conservative, but liberal, they avoid coming to grips with one of the fundamental problems of Indian public life. But neither in intellectual nor in practical terms will the many problems posed by the Indian right be solved by denying that they exist.

APPENDIX I

A NOTE ON THE 1967 ELECTIONS

The months prior to the 1967 elections were ones of intense excitement and interest. The new and unproved ministry of Indira Gandhi was increasingly viewed as representing a deterioration of national political power (both in governmental and party terms) in India. Famine conditions, inflation, a host of strikes, riots, and fasts, seemed to many to symbolize not only the deterioration of incumbent political leadership but also of the Indian nation and its democratic system. Stern warnings from home and abroad were heard that Indian democracy was in danger.[1]

Opposition parties, looking to the first election in which Nehru was not at the helm of the Congress, sensed the opportunity for marked gains; many of them, after carefully stocking the pond, proceeded to fish in the inviting waters. Of the rightist parties, Swatantra and Jan Sangh talked enthusiastically of controlling some states (individually or in coalition) and of substantially reducing the Congress majority at the Centre. The right-wing elements within the Congress itself also felt that the tide was running in their favour.

There was some basis for right-wing optimism. All the misfortunes which had befallen India could be laid at the door of the ruling party in one way or another; and, where they were well organized, the right-wing elements could hope to capitalize on the discontent. The Jan Sangh in particular responded eagerly to the bifurcation of the Punjab and to the demand—accompanied by assorted fasts of dubious integrity—for a ban on cow-slaughter. A host of essentially local issues were also assiduously exploited by the opposition parties.[2]

Especially important in the context of this book was the upsurge in overt, anti-Congress activity on the part of the aristocracy and the business communities. Much of the previously latent right-wing sentiment was swiftly and energetically coming to the surface.[3] With the prospect of more potent candidates (i.e. aristocrats) and better finance, the right-wing opposition saw better days ahead.

Related to this, but complicating the political picture for the right-wing opposition was the emergence of a spate of rump Congresses, under assorted designations.[4] On the one hand, the emergence of such groups, some of which were rightist, suggested further fragmentation of the anti-Congress vote. Hence, there was much wailing in many opposition quarters. On the other hand, certain elements had come out of the Congress,[5] and if electoral adjustments and agreements on the formation of coalition ministries could be worked out with them, this development could work to the advantage of the opposition collectively, although it might frustrate the ambitions and aspirations of an individual party. The opportunities and problems here led to strenuous efforts by opposition parties to minimize undesirable fragmentation of the vote, by achieving at least state-wide electoral agreements.[6]

More specifically, the Swatantra Party confronted the elections with a combination of anxiety and hope, in varying proportions over time and space. Deprived of the large group of Bihar legislators who followed Ramgarh on his seemingly endless political meanderings, Swatantra's numerical strength and territorial impact were reduced.[7] Although there were some important entrants into the party (mostly outside of the legislative arenas), notably in Gujarat, these did not compensate for the quantitative loss in Bihar.

Organizationally, too, Swatantra had cause for concern. Masani detailed numerous deficiencies in his report to the 1966 convention in Delhi, and they boiled down to the fact that, in too many cases, Swatantra had no organization and no cadres worthy of the name, even in states where it had considerable legislative strength. In Gujarat, already organizationally better than most states in which Swatantra had some strength, the situation was encouraging. There, H. M. Patel, a retired ICS officer, sought to develop and to regularize the party's organization; and in this effort he was aided by some prominent ex-Congressmen who brought with them an appreciation of good grass-roots organization and of sustained contact with the electorate. On the other hand, there was little sign of progress in Rajasthan, where an ex-IAS officer took the post of state General-Secretary; and in Orissa, Swatantra influence continued to be confined almost entirely to the princely influenced highlands, where the erstwhile Ganatantra Parishad had held sway.

Illustrative of one of the central problems discussed in this book was the charge made by Swatantrites in coastal Orissa that the aristocratic leadership was intentionally neglecting organizational matters, so that power would remain firmly in aristocratic hands. Even Gujarat was not immune to this problem. In fact, it became worse as the election approached, because a number of aristocrats came into the party (or stood as Swatantra-supported independents) and started to assert themselves in a more vigorous fashion than was true of earlier years in Gujarat. Even with H. M. Patel's efforts, the Gujarat unit came to display some of the characteristics of aristocrat-influenced units in other northern states. (Also notable on the Gujarat scene was the not-unrelated struggle between *kshatryas* and Patidars.[8]) In both Orissa and Gujarat, there were open rebellions against local aristocratic leadership; and in some cases these dissident Swatantrites openly fought the official nominees of the party.[9] But here, as elsewhere, the party's dependence on aristocratic support made it most difficult to achieve a *modus vivendi*.[10]

Swatantra had some basis for hope, too. Many of the businessmen and aristocrats who came out openly against the Congress turned to the Swatantra party. Swatantra benefited primarily in Gujarat and Rajasthan, and, to a far lesser extent, in UP. For example, the Saurashtra region of Gujarat, which gave negligible support to Swatantra in 1962, looked quite promising as the 1967 elections approached, in large part because of aristocratic support; and the entry of a number of prominent Birla men bolstered Swatantra hopes in Rajasthan. In terms of finance, Swatantra was certainly in a much better position than in 1962, although, as expected, its aspirations outran its resources and there was great reliance on self-financing candidates again.[11]

Relations with other opposition parties also produced mixed reactions. The emergence of the rump Congresses was bemoaned by Masani, among others, who were upset over the entry of yet more aspirants in the political arena. Yet in Orissa, after much pulling and hauling, Swatantra and the Mahtab-led Jana Congress worked out an agreement quite favourable to Swatantra; and there was some co-operation between the Congress dissidents in Rajasthan and the Swatantra unit in that state.[12] In both of these cases, there was considerable optimism that Swatantra-led governments might be formed with the help of such dissident elements.

On the whole, relations with other opposition parties were more orderly prior to the 1967 elections than they were in 1962. Swaantra and the Jan Sangh reached a reasonably firm accord in Rajasthan, where Swatantra's superior position was recognized. In return for Jan Sangh support for Masani in Rajkot, the Gujarat unit was obliged to concede far more to the Sangh than the latter's strength would have warranted; and while it required persistent effort, relations remained tolerably good.[13] In Madras, Swatantra acknowledged its weakness and joined as a minor, but effective partner in a broad, anti-Congress front dominated by the DMK. Elsewhere, informal or formal understandings were reached with a wide range of parties, including, in some cases, the two wings of the Communist Party.[14] In some cases (as in Madras), this resulted in a quantitatively reduced but qualitatively better effort on the part of the Swatantra Party.

In the matter of electoral understandings and, more broadly, in confronting the electorate, Swatantra leaders frankly admit that they often yielded to the pressure of necessity, defined in terms of how best to defeat the Congress. As before, the propaganda which emanated from the central office remained overwhelmingly oriented toward economic problems and was scrupulously secular; and party leaders tried to project Swatantra's image as a responsible, constitutional-democratic party. Still, it was only after a frequently bitter debate that the national party refrained from including a demand for a ban on cow-slaughter in its election manifesto; and many state units and individual candidates were side by side with the Jan Sangh in exploiting the cow-slaughter issue.[15] Masani and other secular leaders were dismayed at this, and even Rajaji decried the fact that cow-slaughter seemed to dominate the political scene for so long, but they all admitted that necessity led down other paths. The boycott of the Andhra legislature over a steel-plant location issue, the electoral understandings with the Communists, and other actions were similarly tolerated.[16]

In the immediate pre-election period, the scoring of electoral successes was obviously uppermost in the minds of the party leaders; but many of the underlying problems analysed in the main part of this book were obviously not far below the surface. Organizational and ideological deficiencies were clearly recognized in many quarters, and, for example, many national and state leaders were frankly apprehensive at the prospect of Swatantra(-led) ministries in Gujarat and Rajasthan.[17] The highly educated and extremely able group of candidates put up for the *Lok Sabha* provided some consolation at that level of politics, but the situation at the state level left many Swatantra leaders very much depressed. It was still not clear that the more modern elements (in both organizational and ideological terms) could satisfactorily assert themselves, either within the Swatantra Party itself or within the broader political context.

In this connection, it is important to note that the central office of the party again made its primary effort in elections to the *Lok Sabha*.[18] Here, the most notable development was the support rendered to more modern Swatantrites by the aristocrats, particularly in Gujarat and Rajasthan.[19] Whether this support stemmed more from indifference to sitting in the *Lok Sabha* (as opposed to the state assemblies) or other factors is not yet clear. It is even less clear that such support will be forthcoming in the future. But whatever the cause and whatever the future of such co-operation between aristocratic and industrial elements, there can be no doubt that Swatantra's modern men benefited greatly in the 1967 elections for the *Lok Sabha*.[20]

In general, the results of the 1967 elections represent a substantial, although not irreversible step forward for the Swatantra Party. As against eighteen *Lok Sabha* members elected on the Party symbol in 1962 (or twenty-two, if the Ganatantra Parishad be added), Swatantra secured forty-four seats in 1967 (and it must be remembered that of the eighteen seats in 1962, seven were lost in Bihar upon Ramgarh's defection). There was a marked improvement in its more established strongholds—Gujarat, Orissa and Rajasthan—and there were gains also in Mysore, Madras, and Andhra.[21] In Gujarat, Orissa, and Madras, Swatantra gained more *Lok Sabha* seats than the Congress, while in Rajasthan, Mysore and Andhra it occupied second place (although in Andhra it was a very, very poor second). Only in Bihar and UP did it lose strength in the *Lok Sabha*.[22]

In the state legislatures, Swatantra also improved its position (although here, by contrast with the *Lok Sabha*, it lost second place to the Jan Sangh in terms of total seats). It was the largest single party in Orissa, and it appeared destined to form a reasonably stable coalition ministry with the Jana Congress. It moved into a very strong opposition position in Gujarat, and it improved its position in Rajasthan as well; and in the latter, there was a possibility of a broad coalition ministry, including Swatantra, Jan Sangh, SSP, and independents. Its strength increased in Madras,

Andhra, and Mysore, while Bihar and UP recorded losses of seats (although Swatantra's performance in the latter was not much inferior to its 1962 performance).[23]

What does the pattern of support suggest about Swatantra's viability and future prospects? First, in some important cases, Swatantra's *Lok Sabha* performance was relatively better than its *Vidhan Sabha* performance. This would seem to be due partly to the centre's emphasis on *Lok Sabha* seats and to the extremely well-financed campaigns mounted in key *Lok Sabha* constituencies. In addition, this pattern of support suggests that Swatantra's local roots and organization in many areas still leave much to be desired. Secondly, taking 1962 and 1967 results together, Swatantra has established itself quite firmly in Gujarat, on a reasonably broad and stable social basis. Its strength in Rajasthan and Orissa—which, in 1967, fell below expectations—still owes too much to the influence of a few key aristocrats and remains vulnerable to defections.[24] Of the remaining states, Mysore is the most promising from the Swatantra standpoint, as neither prestigious local notables, nor lavishly financed campaigns, nor firm electoral alliances played a significant part in Swatantra successes.[25] By contrast, the substantial gains in Madras are due much more to the carefully engineered, DMK-led united front (in the building of which Rajaji played a major part, however) than to any great strength of Swatantra *per se*.[26]

The 1967 elections thus broaden Swatantra's areas of significant representation to include the southern states. A combination of south Indian MPs and the large number of industrialist MPs from the north substantially modify the social composition of the *Lok Sabha* group, which had been heavily Rajput after the 1962 elections. (The debts owed by some industrialists to Rajput aristocrats must not be forgotten, however.) The Swatantra Party in the *Lok Sabha* will be a formidable group, and the dominance of that group by industrial and professional elements will lead to a more well-defined modern image and to a great emphasis on economic matters, where Swatantra's principal spokesmen may be counted upon for a superlative performance. This means, however, that the *Lok Sabha* group (deprived, at least for the moment, of Ranga's presence)[27] lacks a strong, middle-class, rural component; and the party will have to struggle even harder than before to persuade people that it is primarily a rural peoples' party. (The peasant component is more in evidence at the state level, particularly in Gujarat, and, to a lesser extent, in the south.)

On balance, the 1967 elections indicate somewhat greater viability for Swatantra and an improvement in the position of the more modern component of the party, particularly in the *Lok Sabha*. The failure of certain aristocrats to retain their own seats, and the poorer-than-expected performance in Rajasthan, Orissa, and UP, may also persuade party leaders that this source of support has reached its maximum and that future improvements will require conscious effort to overcome the organizational and social limitations of the aristocracy.[28]

It would still be premature to predict a healthy future for Swatantra, but its future looks brighter than it did in 1962. Much still depends on relations with the Congress right and with other opposition parties, particularly the Jan Sangh, which made striking gains in the north and which has intensified its efforts (largely unrewarded in 1967) in non-Hindi speaking areas.[29] The role of the rump Congresses will also be important here. It is also premature to announce the ascendancy of the modernists in the Swatantra Party, although here, too, the prospects seem to have improved somewhat.

Given a relatively stable political environment, Swatantra may be expected to perform responsibly and well at the national level and in most states. But it will face some stern tests, with respect to its secular, constitutional-democratic commitments. The Rajasthan unit behaved very poorly during the post-election, ministry-forming crisis in that state; and the argument that Swatantra irresponsibility was forced upon the party to avoid being outflanked by the Jan Sangh is scarcely an encouraging sign.[30] Rather it raises the question: what else will Swatantra be willing to do to avoid being surpassed by the Sangh?

There are other major questions as well. How will Swatantra respond to the leftist(-dominated) ministries which have been, or are likely to be formed in some states? How will Swatantra respond to delicate law-and-order situations, particularly where demonstrations, etc., may be organized by leftist elements? Will its *Lok Sabha* spokesmen (and its assembly spokesmen, too) support those measures which not only protect the rich, the wise, and the well-born, but which strengthen, educate, and lift up those who are not? More broadly, will Swatantra be able to curb the élitist, anti-democratic elements in its ranks, in the event of signs of political instability?

The next few years are likely to be decisive in terms of the course which India will take. As before, a technologically progressive, secular, and constitutionalist party has much to recommend it; and Swatantra has made some significant strides along these lines. It will face the stern tests of the next years as a stronger, more broadly based party than it was after the 1962 elections. We have raised some of the major questions, for which time alone can provide the answers; but, judging from the general conditions prevailing in India, some answers, at least, should not be too long in coming.

APPENDIX II

Note. Tables I–IV are reproduced from Morris-Jones' *Government and Politics of India*, pp. 163–6. Tables V and VI are based on the official election returns of 1962 and give a more detailed, state-by-state picture of Swatantra's performance. The following abbreviations are used in Morris-Jones' tables:

Tables I and II

CPI	Communist Party of India
PSP	Praja Socialist Party.
SP	Socialist Party (Narayan)
KMP	Kisan Mazdoor Praja Party (Kripalani).
SP	Socialist Party (Lohia)
JS	Jan Sangh
HM	Hindu Mahasabha
RPI	Republican Party of India
RRP	Ram Rajya Parishad

Tables III and IV

DMK	Dravida Munnetra Kazagham
GP	Ganatantra Parishad
ML	Muslim League
PWP	Peasants' and Workers' Party
PDF	Peoples' Democratic Front

Tables V–VIII use the same abbreviations as those for Tables I and II with the addition of:

CON	Congress
SWA	Swatantra Party

Appendix II

Table I. *All India parties—Lok Sabha*

Parties	Candi-dates	Seats gained	% seats	Votes polled	% votes	Votes per candidate
			1952			
Congress	472	364	74·4	47,665,875	45·0	100,987
Swatantra	—	—	—	—	—	—
CPI	49	16	3·3	3,484,401	3·3	71,110
PSP { SP	256	12	2·5	11,216,779	10·6	43,816
PSP { KMP	145	9	1·8	6,156,558	5·8	42,459
SP	—	—	—	—	—	—
JS	93	3	0·6	3,246,288	3·1	34,906
HM	31	4	0·8	1,003,034	0·95	32,356
RPI	27	2	0·4	2,501,964	2·36	92,665
RRP	55	3	0·6	2,151,603	2·03	39,120
Other parties	215	35	7·2	11,739,244	11·1	54,601
Independents	521	41	8·4	16,778,749	15·8	32,205
Total	—	489	—	105,944,495	—	—
			1957			
Congress	490	371	75·1	57,579,593	47·78	117,509
Swatantra	—	—	—	—	—	—
CPI	108	27	5·4	10,754,075	8·92	99,575
PSP { SP	189	19	3·8	12,542,666	10·41	66,363
PSP { KMP	—	—	—	—	—	—
SP	—	—	—	—	—	—
JS	130	4	0·8	7,149,824	5·93	54,999
HM	19	1	0·2	1,032,322	0·86	54,333
RPI	19	4	0·8	1,812,919	1·5	95,417
RRP	15	—		460,838	0·38	30,723
Other parties	73	29	5·9	5,805,873	4·81	79,519
Independents	475	39	7·9	23,377,805	19·39	49,216
Total	—	494	—	120,513,915	—	—
			1962			
Congress	488	361	73·1	51,512,243	46·02	105,558
Swatantra	172	18	3·6	7,784,495	6·80	45,259
CPI	137	29	5·9	11,399,268	9·96	83,206
PSP { SP	166	12	2·4	7,829,997	6·84	47,169
PSP { KMP	—	—	—	—	—	—
SP	107	6	1·2	2,812,795	2·49	26,288
JS	198	14	2·8	7,363,772	6·44	37,191
HM	32	1	0·2	502,115	0·44	15,691
RPI	69	3	0·6	3,185,168	2·78	46,162
RRP	35	2	0·4	629,823	0·55	17,995
Other parties	82	21	4·3	7,251,066	6·33	88,428
Independents	497	27	5·5	14,154,805	12·27	28,481
Total	—	494	—	114,425,547	—	—

Appendix II

Table II. *All-India parties—State assemblies*

Parties	Candi-dates	Seats gained	% seats	Votes polled	% votes	Votes per candidate
			1952			
Congress	3,153	2,246	68·4	43,802,546	42·2	13,892
Swatantra	—	—	—	—	—	—
CPI	465	106	3·2	4,552,537	4·38	9,790
PSP {SP	1,799	125	3·8	10,071,211	9·7	5,598
PSP {KMP	1,005	77	2·3	5,306,219	5·11	5,280
SP	—	—	—	—	—	—
JS	717	35	1·1	2,866,566	2·76	3,998
HM	194	14	0·4	848,415	0·82	4,373
RPI	171	3	0·1	1,751,294	1·68	10,241
RRP	314	31	0·9	1,260,049	1·21	4,013
Other parties	—	—	—	10,776,136	10·4	—
Independents	7,492	635	19·3	22,566,226	21·74	4,405
Total	—	3,283	—	103,801,199	—	—
			1957			
Congress	3,027	2,012	64·9	54,794,454	44·97	18,102
Swatantra	—	—	—	—	—	—
CPI	812	176	5·7	11,407,192	9·36	14,048
PSP {SP KMP	1,154	208	6·7	11,881,094	9·75	10,296
SP	—	—	—	—	—	—
JS	584	46	1·5	4,380,638	3·60	7,501
HM	87	6	0·2	614,754	0·5	7,066
RPI	99	21	0·7	1,603,578	1·31	16,198
RRP	146	22	0·7	842,956	0·69	5,774
Other parties Independents	4,863	611	19·7	36,317,487	29·81	7,468
Total	—	3,102	—	121,842,153	—	—
			1962			
Congress	3,062	1,984	60·2	51,801,965	43·53	16,918
Swatantra	1,012	170	5·2	7,721,870	6·49	7,630
CPI	975	197	6·0	12,403,703	10·42	12,722
PSP {SP KMP	1,149	179	5·4	9,153,193	7·69	7,966
SP	632	64	1·9	2,828,409	2·38	4,475
JS	1,135	116	3·5	6,436,784	5·40	5,671
HM	75	8	0·2	287,777	0·34	3,847
RPI	99	11	0·3	673,680	0·56	6,805
RRP	99	13	0·4	348,536	0·29	3,521
Other parties Independents	5,313	242 313	7·3 9·5	27,357,469	23·0	5,149
Total	—	3,297	—	119,013,386	—	—

Appendix II

Table III. *One-state parties—Lok Sabha*

Parties	Candi-dates	Seats gained	% seats	Votes polled	% votes	Votes per candidate
			1952			
DMK (Madras)	—	—	—	—	—	—
Akali Dal (Punjab)	8	2	0·4	569,973	0·53	71,247
GP (Orissa)	12	4	0·8	959,749	0·91	79,979
ML (Kerala)	1	1	0·2	79,470	0·08	—
Jharkhand (Bihar)	6	2	0·4	601,865	0·57	100,311
Forward Bloc (W. Bengal)	8	—	—	425,971	0·40	53,246
PWP (Maharashtra)	12	—	—	899,489	0·8	74,957
Janta (Bihar)	6	1	0·2	236,094	0·22	39,349
PDF (Andhra)	12	7	1·4	1,367,404	1·29	113,950
			1957			
DMK (Madras)	—	—	—	—	—	—
Akali Dal (Punjab)	—	—	—	—	—	—
GP (Orissa)	15	7	1·4	1,291,141	1·07	86,076
ML (Kerala)	—	—	—	—	—	—
Jharkhand (Bihar)	12	5	1·0	751,830	0·62	62,653
Forward Bloc (W. Bengal)	5	2	0·4	665,341	0·55	133,068
PWP (Maharashtra)	6	4	0·8	868,344	0·72	144,724
Janta (Bihar)	11	3	0·6	501,269	0·42	45,570
PDF (Andhra)	8	2	0·4	1,044,032	0·87	130,504
			1962			
DMK (Madras)	18	7	1·4	2,315,610	2·02	128,645
Akali Dal (Punjab)	7	3	0·6	829,129	0·72	118,447
GP (Orissa)	10	4	0·8	342,970	0·30	34,297
ML (Kerala)	4	—	0·4	419,761	0·37	104,940
Jharkhand (Bihar)	11	3	0·6	499,950	0·44	45,450
Forward Bloc (W. Bengal)	6	1	0·2	615,395	0·54	102,566
PWP (Maharashtra)	10	—	—	703,582	0·61	70,358
Janta (Bihar)	—	—	—	—	—	—
PDF (Andhra)	—	—	—	—	—	—

Table IV. *One-state parties—state assembly*

Parties	Candi-dates	Seats gained	% seats	Votes polled	% votes	Votes per candidate
			1952			
DMK (Madras)	—	—	—	—	—	—
Akali Dal (Punjab)	88	33	17·7	922,268	14·6	10,480
		(186)		(6,333,058)		
GP (Orissa)	38	31	22·1	741,887	20·2	19,523
		(140)		(3,677,046)		
ML (Kerala)	13	5	1·3	186,546	1·0	14,350
		(375)		(19,997,256)		
Jharkhand (Bihar)	53	33	10·0	765,272	8·0	14,439
		(330)		(9,548,840)		
Forward Bloc (W. Bengal)	77	10	4·2	506,274	6·8	6,575
		(238)		(7,444,225)		
PWP (Maharashtra)	87	14	4·4	717,963	6·5	8,252
		(315)		(11,123,242)		
Janta (Bihar)	38	11	3·3	301,691	3·2	7,939
		(330)		(9,548,840)		
PDF (Andhra)	78	42	23·0	1,096,112	21·2	14,053
		(175)		(5,178,593)		
			1957			
DMK (Madras)	—	—	—	—	—	—
Akali Dal (Punjab)	—	—	—	—	—	—
GP (Orissa)	109	51	36·4	1,221,794	28·7	11,209
		(140)		(4,255,915)		
ML (Kerala)	—	—	—	—	—	—
Jharkhand (Bihar)	70	31	9·7	726,983	6·9	10,386
		(318)		(10,585,421)		
Forward Bloc (W. Bengal)	26	8	3·2	425,318	4·1	16,358
		(252)		(10,469,803)		
PWP (Maharashtra)	60	33	8·3	1,186,169	7·1	19,770
		(396)		(16,712,160)		
Janta (Bihar)	122	22	6·9	831,273	7·9	6,814
		(318)		(10,585,421)		
PDF (Andhra)	63	23	21·9	914,335	25·4	14,513
		(105)		(3,603,585)		
			1962			
DMK (Madras)	142	50	24·3	3,406,804	27·0	23,992
		(206)		(12,620,995)		
Akali Dal (Punjab)	46	19	12·3	798,925	11·9	17,368
		(154)		(6,701,171)		
GP (Orissa)	121	37	26·4	655,099	22·3	5,414
		(140)		(2,932,285)		
ML (Kerala)	12	11	8·7	401,925	5·0	33,494
		(126)		(8,104,077)		
Jharkhand (Bihar)	84	20	6·3	458,244	4·7	5,455
		(318)		(9,848,995)		
Forward Bloc (W. Bengal)	34	13	5·2	441,098	4·6	12,974
		(252)		(9,571,091)		
PWP (Maharashtra)	79	15	5·7	818,801	7·5	10,366
		(264)		(10,965,394)		
Janta (Bihar)	—	—	—	—	—	—
PDF (Andhra)	—	—	—	—	—	—

Appendix II

Table V. *1962 elections, seats according to parties, Lok Sabha*

N.B. The three figures in each entry are in order, the number of candidates sponsored by the party who (i) contested, (ii) were elected, and (iii) forfeited their security deposits.

States and territories	No. of seats	CON	CPI	SWA	PSP	JS	RPI
Andhra Pradesh	43	43-34-0	20-7-0	28-1-11	1-0-1	8-0-8	3-0-3
Assam	12	12-9-0	4-0-1	Nil	8-2-2	Nil	Nil
Bihar	53	53-39-0	16-1-6	43-7-17	32-2-15	13-0-11	Nil
Gujarat	22	22-16-0	Nil	14-4-1	6-1-3	5-0-5	1-0-0
Kerala	18	14-6-0	14-6-0	1-0-1	4-0-0	4-0-4	Nil
Madhya Pradesh	36	35-24-1	3-0-3	5-0-5	19-3-6	28-3-13	7-0-7
Madras	40	40-30-0	14-2-1	16-0-2	5-0-4	1-0-1	2-0-0
Maharashtra	44	44-41-0	6-0-0	3-0-3	13-1-5	17-0-13	20-0-4
Mysore	26	26-25-0	3-0-2	7-0-1	12-0-2	7-0-6	4-0-1
Orissa	19	19-13-0	2-0-0	1-0-0	5-1-0	Nil	Nil
Punjab	22	22-14-0	4-0-0	6-0-4	Nil	17-3-10	7-0-4
Rajasthan	22	21-14-1	5-0-3	10-3-1	Nil	11-1-4	Nil
Uttar Pradesh	85	85-61-1	18-2-8	33-2-26	48-2-23	74-7-33	22-3-15
West Bengal	36	36-22-0	24-9-0	4-0-3	12-0-5	4-0-4	Nil
Delhi	5	5-5-0	1-0-1	Nil	1-0-1	5-0-0	1-0-1
Himachal Pradesh	4	4-4-0	Nil	2-0-0	Nil	2-0-2	1-0-0
Manipur	2	2-1-0	1-0-1	Nil	1-0-1	Nil	Nil
Tripura	2	2-0-0	2-2-0	Nil	1-0-1	Nil	Nil
Total	491	485-358-3	137-29-26	173-18-75	168-12-69	196-14-114	68-3-35

States and territories	No. of seats	SP	HM	RRP	Other recognized parties	Un-recognized parties	Inde-pendents
Andhra Pradesh	43	Nil	Nil	Nil	Nil	Nil	44-1-28
Assam	12	2-0-1	Nil	Nil	Nil	2-1-1	13-0-7
Bihar	53	24-1-19	3-0-3	3-0-3	11-3-3[a]	Nil	35-0-31
Gujarat	22	1-0-1	2-0-2	Nil	Nil	3-1-1[b]	14-0-8
Kerala	18	Nil	Nil	Nil	3-2-0[c]	1-1-0	9-3-6
Madhya Pradesh	36	14-1-10	7-0-4	14-1-9	Nil	1-0-0[d]	26-4-15
Madras	40	2-0-2	Nil	Nil	18-7-1[e]	7-1-3	46-0-42
Maharashtra	44	Nil	3-0-2	2-0-2	10-0-1[f]	Nil	50-2-39
Mysore	26	Nil	Nil	Nil	Nil	3-1-1[g]	26-0-20
Orissa	19	3-1-2	Nil	Nil	10-4-0[h]	Nil	8-0-8
Punjab	22	1-1-0	Nil	3-0-3	7-3-1[i]	1-1-0	39-0-36
Rajasthan	22	6-0-4	2-0-2	7-1-5	Nil	Nil	49-3-40
Uttar Pradesh	85	51-1-35	13-1-11	12-0-12	Nil	Nil	86-5-70
West Bengal	36	1-0-1	7-0-6	Nil	6-1-1	4-2-0[d]	14-2-10
Delhi	5	Nil	1-0-1	Nil	Nil	Nil	14-0-13
Himachal Pradesh	4	Nil	Nil	Nil	Nil	Nil	2-0-1
Manipur	2	2-1-0	Nil	Nil	Nil	Nil	5-0-5
Tripura	2	Nil	Nil	Nil	Nil	2-0-2	Nil
Total	491	107-6-75	38-1-31	41-2-34	65-20-7	24-8-8	480-20-379

[a] Jharkhand. [b] Nutan Mahagujarat Janata Parishad. [c] Muslim League. [d] Forward Bloc. [e] DMK. [f] PWP. [g] Lok Sevak Sangh. [h] Ganatantra Parishad. [i] Akali Dal.

Table VI. *1962 elections, percentage of votes for Lok Sabha*

Based on official election returns.

States and territories	CON	CPI	SWA	PSP	JS	RPI	SP	HM	RRP	Other recognized parties	Un-recognized parties	Inde-pendents
Andhra	47·96	21·04	14·91	0·07	1·17	0·96	—	—	—	—	—	13·89
Assam	45·16	7·05	—	19·16	—	—	2·88	—	—	—	5·02	20·71
Bihar	43·89	6·38	18·21	12·69	2·34	—	6·12	0·24	0·20	4·70[a]	—	5·23
Gujarat	52·56	—	25·00	7·10	1·44	0·89	0·05	0·38	—	—	3·71[b]	8·87
Kerala	34·28	35·46	0·17	9·89	0·68	—	—	—	—	4·49[c]	3·60	11·43
Madhya Pradesh	39·55	0·90	0·73	12·30	17·87	1·84	5·29	3·80	4·83	—	0·53[d]	12·36
Madras	45·26	10·24	10·47	1·68	0·04	1·54	0·36	—	—	18·64[e]	4·26	7·51
Maharashtra	52·89	4·05	0·28	5·36	4·40	11·66	—	0·74	0·08	6·31[f]	—	14·23
Mysore	52·67	1·53	7·81	14·49	2·68	3·86	—	—	—	—	3·33[g]	13·63
Orissa	55·53	5·11	1·15	15·50	—	—	2·67	—	—	17·42[h]	—	2·62
Punjab	41·30	4·73	4·28	—	15·18	6·25	2·25	—	0·22	12·22[i]	1·75	11·82
Rajasthan	37·58	2·99	18·10	—	9·28	—	3·69	0·22	3·69	—	—	24·44
Uttar Pradesh	38·20	3·63	5·04	10·35	17·57	4·27	8·64	1·39	0·72	—	—	10·19
West Bengal	46·78	29·38	1·02	4·54	1·05	—	0·04	1·04	—	6·32[d]	3·76	6·06
Delhi	50·68	2·14	—	0·12	32·66	3·14	—	0·49	—	—	—	10·77
Himachal Pradesh	68·65	—	12·78	—	4·49	6·56	—	—	—	—	—	7·52
Manipur	30·93	8·13	—	4·12	—	—	26·30	—	—	—	—	30·52
Tripura	42·81	51·27	—	1·98	—	—	—	—	—	—	3·94	—
Total	44·72	9·94	7·89	6·81	6·44	2·83	2·69	0·65	0·60	4·79	1·56	11·08

[a] Jharkhand. [b] Nutan Mahagujarat Janata Parishad. [c] Muslim League. [d] Forward Bloc. [e] Dravida Munnetra Kazhagam. [f] PWP. [g] Lok Sevak Sangh. [h] Ganatantra Parishad. [i] Akali Dal.

Table VII. *1962 elections, seats according to parties, assemblies*

N.B. The three figures in each entry are in order, the number of candidates sponsored by the party who (i) contested, (ii) were elected, and (iii) forfeited their security deposits.

Seats	No. of seats	CON	CPI	SWA	PSP	JS	RPI
Andhra Pradesh	294	294-171-1	136-51-8	141-19-70	6-0-4	70-069	18-0-17
Assam	105	103-79-2	31-0-12	—	53-6-21	4-0-4	—
Bihar	318	318-185-10	84-12-38	259-50-123	199-29-102	75-3-61	—
Gujarat	154	154-113-2	1-0-0	105-26-20	53-7-25	26-0-23	13-0-12
Kerala[c]	—	—	—	—	—	—	—
Madhya Pradesh	285	285-139-12	42-1-34	43-2-39	140-33-64	195-41-91	33-0-27
Madras	206	206-139-0	68-2-26	94-6-59	21-0-15	4-0-4	6-0-1
Maharashtra	264	264-215-1	56-6-13	9-0-5	101-9-47	127-0-100	66-3-27
Mysore	206	206-136-0	31-3-23	59-9-23	84-20-15	63-0-56	19-0-14
Orissa[c]	—	—	—	—	—	—	—
Punjab	154	154-90-1	47-9-23	42-3-30	10-0-5	80-8-47	5-0-16
Rajasthan	175	175-87-4	45-5-25	93-36-33	22-2-14	94-15-55	—
Uttar Pradesh	430	429-249-15	147-14-101	169-15-125	288-38-164	377-49-192	123-8-97
West Bengal	251	251-156-1	145-50-8	24-0-19	87-5-52	25-0-24	—
Total	2,842	2839-1759-49	833-153-311	1038-155-546	1064-149-528	1140-116-726	301-11-211

States	No. of seats	SP	HM	RRP	Other recognized parties	Unrecognized parties	Independents
Andhra Pradesh	294	15-2-11	—	—	—	—	302-51-173
Assam	105	14-0-9	—	—	—	27-19-9	177-8-121
Bihar	318	132-7-96	3-0-3	17-0-17	75-20-36[a]	—	367-12-325
Gujarat	154	2-0-2	12-0-11	2-0-2	—	20-1-11[b]	131-7-81
Kerala[c]	—	—	—	—	—	—	—
Madhya Pradesh	285	86-14-55	50-6-31	76-10-46	—	9-0-8[d]	374-39-279
Madras	206	7-1-6	—	—	143-50-11[e]	44-3-25	207-5-189
Maharashtra	264	14-1-12	5-0-5	3-0-3	79-15-30[f]	—	437-15-347
Mysore	206	9-1-5	—	—	—	27-10-8	179-27-107
Orissa[c]	—	—	—	—	—	—	—
Punjab	154	8-4-4	1-0-1	4-0-4	46-19-3[g]	9-3-1	330-18-285
Rajasthan	175	40-5-25	7-0-6	23-3-13	—	—	390-22-323
Uttar Pradesh	430	273-24-203	73-2-69	41-0-40	—	—	700-31-608
West Bengal	251	7-0-7	25-0-20	—	35-13-10[d]	67-16-34	294-11-236
Total	2,842	607-59-435	176-8-146	166-13-125	378-117-90	230-45-96	3888-246-3074

[a] Jharkhand. [b] Nutan Mahagujarat Janata Parishad. [c] No elections in 1962. [d] Forward Bloc. [e] Dravida Munnetra Kazhagam.
[f] Peasants' and Workers. [g] Akali Dal.

Table VIII. *1962 elections, percentage of votes for assemblies*

Based on official election returns.

States	CON	CPI	SWA	PSP	JS	RPI	SP	HM	RRP	Other recognized parties	Un-recognized parties	Inde-pendence
Andhra	47·25	19·53	10·40	0·30	1·04	0·40	0·61	—	—	—	—	20·47
Assam	48·25	6·39	—	12·69	0·45	—	1·50	—	—	—	6·91	23·82
Bihar	41·35	6·23	17·25	14·17	2·77	—	5·23	0·03	0·18	4·39[a]	—	8·40
Gujarat	50·84	0·18	24·43	7·74	1·33	0·41	0·03	0·49	0·02	—	2·51[b]	12·02
Kerala[c]	—	—	—	—	—	—	—	—	—	—	—	—
Madhya Pradesh	38·54	2·02	1·23	10·72	16·66	1·26	4·73	3·23	3·79	—	0·26[d]	17·56
Madras	46·14	7·72	7·72	1·26	0·08	0·45	0·38	—	—	27·10[e]	3·70	5·34
Maharashtra	51·22	5·90	0·44	7·23	5·00	5·38	0·50	0·11	0·01	7·46[f]	—	16·75
Mysore	50·22	2·28	7·15	14·08	2·29	0·82	1·00	—	—	—	4·84	17·32
Orissa[c]	—	—	—	—	—	—	—	—	—	—	—	—
Punjab	43·72	7·10	3·88	0·90	9·72	2·15	1·39	0·01	0·05	11·87[g]	2·04	17·17
Rajasthan	40·02	5·40	17·11	1·46	9·15	—	3·68	0·34	2·01	—	—	20·88
Uttar Pradesh	36·33	5·08	4·68	11·52	16·46	3·74	8·21	1·06	0·29	—	—	12·63
West Bengal	47·29	24·96	0·57	4·99	0·45	—	0·03	0·80	—	4·61[d]	5·30	10·98
Totals	44·38	8·59	7·42	7·01	6·07	1·58	2·71	0·51	0·41	5·65	1·65	4·02

[a] Jharkhand. [b] Nutan Mahagujarat Janata Parishda. [c] No elections in 1962. [d] Forward Bloc. [e] DMK. [f] PWP. [g] Akali Dal.

NOTES

ABBREVIATIONS

At various points in the notes, abbreviations have been used to refer to certain sources. In every case, the first reference is given in full and the abbreviation to be used subsequently has been noted. However, for the reader's convenience, the following list of frequently used abbreviations is provided.

AS	*Asian Survey* (monthly)
HT	*Hindustan Times* (daily)
HWR	*Hindu Weekly Review* (overseas edition)
JAS	*Journal of Asian Studies* (quarterly)
OHT	*Overseas Hindustan Times* (weekly)
PA	*Pacific Affairs* (quarterly)
SN	*Swatantra Newsletter* (more or less monthly)
TI	*Times of India* (daily)

CHAPTER 1, pp. 1–9

1 Gabriel Almond and James Coleman (eds.), *The Politics of the Developing Areas* (Princeton, Princeton University Press, 1960), Introduction.
2 For example, K. M. Munshi, a Swatantra leader, suggested that the author entitle this work 'The Swatantra Party: India's Search for a Constitutional Opposition'. Some reasons for the present emphasis (which does not preclude attention to other issues) are found in Howard L. Erdman, 'Conservative Politics in India', *Asian Survey* (*AS*), VI, 6 (June 1966), 338–47.
3 Samuel P. Huntington, 'Conservatism as an Ideology', *American Political Science Review* (*APSR*), LI, 2 (June 1957), 459.
4 See Karl Mannheim, 'Conservative Thought', in his *Essays on Sociology and Social Psychology*, ed. Paul Kecskemeti (New York, Oxford University Press, 1953). See idem, *Ideology and Utopia*, trans. by Louis Wirth and Edward Shils (New York, Harvest Books, n.d.).
5 Roberto Michels, 'Conservatism', *Encyclopedia of the Social Sciences* (*ESS*) (New York, Macmillan, 1937), IV, 230.
6 Carl. J. Friedrich, *Constitutional Government and Democracy* (revised ed. Boston, Ginn, 1950), pp. 425–6.
7 Michael Oakeshott, 'On Being Conservative', in his *Rationalism and Politics* (New York, Basic Books, 1962), pp. 183 and 168.
8 *ESS*, IV, 230.
9 See *Ideology and Utopia*.
10 *ESS*, IV, 230.
11 *Rationalism and Politics*, p. 168.
12 Peter Viereck (ed.), *Conservatism* (Princeton, Van Norstrand, 1956), p. 15.

13 *Ibid.* p. 17.
14 *Constitutional Government*, p. 425.
15 Kalman Silvert, 'Some Psychocultural Factors in the Politics of Conflict and Conciliation', mimeo, read before the American Political Science Association, 8–11 Sept. 1965, p. 14.
16 Barrington Moore, Jr., *Social Origins of Dictatorship and Democracy* (Boston, Beacon Press, 1966), and, for example, Maurice Dobb, *Studies in the Development of Capitalism* (New York, International Publishers, 1963).
17 *APSR*, LI, 466.
18 *Constitutional Government*, p. 426.
19 *Conservatism*, p. 15.
20 *APSR*, LI, 466.
21 *Conservatism*, p. 12.
22 *ESS*, IV, 230.
23 See Eugen Weber's introduction to Hans Rogger and Eugen Weber (eds.), *The European Right* (Berkeley, University of California Press, 1965).
24 See Max Weber, *The Religion of India*, trans. and ed. Hans Gerth and Don Martindale (Glencoe, Free Press, 1958), and idem, *The City*, trans. Don Martindale and Gertrud Neuwirth (New York, Collier, 1962), as well as Edward Shils, *The Intellectual Between Tradition and Modernity: The Indian Case* (The Hague, Mouton, 1961), for major examples. Reinhard Bendix, *Max Weber: An Intellectual Portrait* (Garden City, N.Y., Doubleday, 1960), is also useful here.
25 The term 'sanskritization' refers to the process whereby a lower caste or segment thereof emulates the behaviour pattern of a superior caste, in order to improve its status, usually following an improvement in its economic position. The process is group-based, not individualistic; it often takes generations to come to fruition; it is accompanied by the strictest application of closure towards formerly equal and subordinate castes; and it rarely, if ever, has been successful as a means of mobility for untouchables. For these reasons, the process is obviously a conservative one. For a major statement on this subject, see M. N. Srinivas, 'A Note on Sanskritization and Westernization', in his *Caste in Modern India and Other Essays* (New York, Asia Publishing House, 1962), pp. 42–62.
26 See Moore, *Social Origins.*
27 The fact that many radical Indians look with favour upon the profoundly conservative rebellion of 1857 suggests the problem here. See, for example, P. C. Joshi, 'A Social Revolution', in Ainslie Embree (ed.), *1857 in India* (Boston, D.C., Heath, 1963), pp. 59–61.

CHAPTER 2, pp. 10–45

1 Lloyd I. Rudolph and Susanne Hoeber Rudolph, 'The Political Role of India's Caste Associations', *Pacific Affairs* (*PA*), XXXIII, 1 (March 1960), 5.
2 Hugh Tinker, *India and Pakistan* (New York, Praeger, 1962), p. 121.

3 See Erdman, *AS*, VI, 338–47.

4 From an unsigned article in *Economic Weekly*, Special Number, July 1959, p. 893.

5 The Maharaja of Rewa, *Indian Round Table Conference, First Session, 12 Nov. 1930 to 19 Jan. 1931, Proceedings* (London, HMSO, 1931), p. 57. Hereinafter, *RTC, I*.

6 Nehru, for example, termed the princely states 'sinks of reaction and incompetence' and argued that the native rulers 'stoutly declare their intention of maintaining medieval conditions...such as exist nowhere else in the world...The Indian States represent today probably the extremest type of autocracy existing in the world.' See, respectively, Reginald Coupland, *Indian Politics, 1936–1942* (London, Oxford University Press, 1944), p. 174, and Nehru, *Towards Freedom* (Boston, Beacon Press, 1958), p. 320. See, in general, Michael Brecher, *Nehru: A Political Biography* (New York, Oxford University Press, 1959), ch. 9, 'Hero of the Left', and Nehru, *India's Freedom* (London, Allen and Unwin, 1962), *passim*.

7 Quoted in Coupland, *Indian Politics*, p. 93.

8 The preceding summary is based on numerous books which cannot be cited individually here. Brecher, *Nehru*, at least touches on most of these points and dwells at length on some of them. Citations at certain junctures below will indicate some of the specific sources used.

9 The preceding summary is again based on sources too numerous to cite fully here. For the princes, see V. P. Menon, *The Story of the Integration of the Indian States* (Bombay, Orient Longmans, 1961). For the landed aristocrats and land reform, see Govindlal D. Patel, *The Indian Land Problem and Legislation* (Bombay, N. M. Tripathi, 1954), and H. D. Malaviya, *Land Reforms in India* (New Delhi, All-India Congress Committee, 1954). For village affairs, see the village studies cited in the general bibliography, especially the titles by Bailey, Dube, Epstein, Isaacs, Retzlaff, and Srinivas. For the business communities, see Helen Lamb, 'The Indian Business Communities and the Evolution of an Industrial Class', *PA*, XXVIII, 2 (June 1955) and her 'Business Organization and Leadership in India Today', in Richard L. Park and Irene Tinker (eds.), *Leadership and Political Institutions in India* (Princeton, Princeton University Press, 1959); Gokhale Institute of Politics and Economics, *Notes on the Rise of the Business Communities in India* (New York, Institute of Pacific Relations, 1951); and Myron Weiner, *Politics of Scarcity* (Bombay, Asia Publishing House, 1962). Of a more general nature are Brecher, *Nehru*; Vera M. Dean, *New Patterns of Democracy in India* (Cambridge, Harvard University Press, 1959); H. Venkatasubbiah, *The Indian Economy Since Independence* (New York, Asia Publishing House, 1961); and Taya Zinkin, *India Changes!* (New York, Oxford University Press, 1959).

10 Quoted in Khushwant Singh, *The Fall of the Kingdom of the Punjab* (Bombay, Orient Longmans, 1961), p. 1.

11 A decent summary of these points is found in Menon, *The Story*. For 1857, see Embree (ed.), *1857 in India*, and the bibliography therein.

The constitutional problems of the 1920s and 1930s, from the standpoint of the princes, may be examined through: K. M. Panikkar, *Indian States and the Government of India* (London, Martin Hopkinson, 1932), and his *Indian Princes in Council* (London, Oxford University Press, 1936); Ranbir Singh, *The Indian States Under the Government of India Act, 1935* (Bombay, Taraporevala, n.d.); Coupland, *Indian Politics*; and *RTC, I*, and *Indian Round Table Conference, Second Session, Proceedings* (London, HMSO, 1932). The last title will be, hereinafter, *RTC, II*.

12 See Patel, *Indian Land Problem*; Malaviya, *Land Reforms*; Venkatasubbiah, *Indian Economy*; Brecher, *Nehru*; Dean, *New Patterns*; A. R. Desai, *Social Background of Indian Nationalism* (3rd edn. Bombay, Popular Book Depot, 1959); and R. Palme Dutt, *India Today* (London, Gollanz, 1940). Restricted in scope but useful here is Paul R. Brass, 'Regionalism, Nationalism, and Political Conflict in Utter Pradesh', mimeo, read before the Association of Asian Studies, 2–4 April 1965.

13 This paragraph is based on a mimeo MS on politics in Rajasthan by Susanne H. Rudolph. Specific citations to Rudolph, *MS*, refer to this mimeo text. Lloyd I. and Susanne H. Rudolph, *The Political in Social Change: Princes and Politicians in Rajasthan* (forthcoming) contains all of the mimeo material cited in this book, although the pagination naturally differs.

14 See Erdman, *AS*, VI, 338–47.

15 For Rajput-Jat conflicts, see, for example, Rudolph, *MS*. For Kamma–Reddy conflicts, see Selig Harrison, *India: The Most Dangerous Decades* (Princeton, Princeton University Press, 1960), and Srinivas, *Caste in Modern India*. For *kshatrya*–Patidar conflicts, see Myron Weiner, chapter on Kaira, in *Party Building in a New Nation: The Indian National Congress* (forthcoming), and Rajni Kothari and Rushikesh Maru, 'Caste and Secularism in India', *Journal of Asian Studies* (*JAS*), XXV, 1 (Nov. 1965), 33–50. The Weiner chapter will henceforth be referred to as Weiner, *MS*.

16 See the articles by Lamb, cited in n. 9, above; Gokhale Institute *Notes*; and Weiner, *Politics of Scarcity*. See also Weber, *The City*; Reinhard Bendix, *Max Weber*; and the titles on economic history, the structure of Indian industry, and on specific topics such as the Bombay Plan, in the general bibliography.

17 Briefly, this doctrine held that the rich, the wise, and the well-born should use their advantages for the good of society as a whole, on a voluntary basis. Other leaders who could appeal to the peasantry were often vehemently anti-capitalistic, as were the more socialistic elements in the Congress coalition. The discussion of N. G. Ranga in chapter 5, below, will illustrate this point.

18 Sir Tej Bahadur Sapru, a leading member of the Liberal Party, the lineal descendants of the early Congress 'Moderates', was anxious to bring the aristocracy into the developing political system, to serve as a stabilizing element, but this was a minor element in the Congress itself in these years. See Menon, *The Story*, pp. 27–8, and *RTC, I* and *II*, for some of Sapru's views.

For Rajasthan, see Rudolph, *MS*, and for Madras, see Rudolph and Rudolph, 'Political Role', *PA*, XXXIII, and Lloyd I. Rudolph, 'Urban Life and Populist Radicalism', *JAS*, XX, 3 (May 1961), 283–97. Some of the disaffected elements entered the Swatantra Party and will be discussed further below.

20 See Coupland, *Indian Politics*, pp. 175–6 and 144.

21 Quotations are from the *White Paper on Indian States* (New Delhi, Ministry of States, 1950), pp. 124, 63 and 30, respectively. Sir Kenneth Fitze, *Twilight of the Maharajas* (London, John Murray, 1956), p. 165, terms Patel 'a most able and forceful politician' to whose 'ruthless and resourceful hands' the integration of the states was entrusted. For his efforts here, Patel has been called by some 'the Bismarck of India'. See also Menon, *The Story*.

22 These matters are all discussed in the *White Paper*, and some are covered in Menon, *The Story*. The fact that distinctions between public and personal property were not clear allowed many rulers to retain vast landholdings and other forms of wealth. The fact that princely revenues were often not precisely known also meant that in calculating the privy purses (fixed at some percentage of previous revenues) there was some latitude for princely self-protection. Gandhi, who favoured voluntary abandonment of powers by the princes, in accordance with the trusteeship notion, recommended at one time a maximum privy purse of Rs. 300,000, which is far below many which have actually been paid. See Gandhi, *The Indian States Problem* (Ahmedabad, Navajivan Press, 1941), p. 636 and *passim*, for his views, which were decidedly restrained. The office of *Rajpramukh* was equivalent to that of a governor in a former province of British India and was established in those areas where post-independence federal units largely coincided with one or a group of former princely states. The office was subsequently abolished, although it had been assured at least for the life of the incumbents. Some ex-rulers have, however, continued to serve as governors.

23 Quoted in *White Paper*, p. 124. Menon, *The Story*, pp. 455 ff., argues that the price was small when the value of the states' public cash balances and public properties, which accrued to the Union, is calculated. Needless to say, many people have cavilled at the amount paid.

24 The fragmentary quote is from Zinkin, *India Changes*, p. 209. She observes that for many the purse was 'just sufficient to keep them from bankruptcy'.

25 E.g. even such wealthy rulers as the Maharaja of Jaipur have converted palaces into luxury hotels, museums, etc.

26 Percival Griffiths, *Modern India* (London, Ernest Benn, 1905), p. 105, argues thus, and some supporting evidence is found in Menon, *The Story*.

27 *Census of India, 1951*, II, 'Uttar Pradesh', Part 1a, Report (Allahabad, Government of Uttar Pradesh, 1953), p. 246. Patel, *Indian Land Problem*, p. 246, supports this contention. Naturally the wealthier landed aristocrats were in the best position to do this.

28 Quoted in Malaviya, *Land Reforms*, pp. 20–1. Concerning full compensation, Nehru said, *ibid.* p. 20, that this was 'on the face of it impossible, as we cannot find the enormous amount of money for it'. The Congress election manifesto of 1946 stressed these points and declared for abolition with partial compensation.

29 See Patel, *Indian Land Problem*, p. 373, where he notes that in Hyderabad, *jagirdars* could retain up to 500 acres, acquired via evictions, if necessary. See also *ibid.* p. 395, where he questions whether such acts can be considered 'progressive'. Zinkin, *India Changes*, p. 212, claims that in Hyderabad, 'where the aristocracy is unusually oppressive, more than half the tenants have been evicted.'

30 Patel, *Indian Land Problem*, p. 399. See also *ibid.* pp. 371 ff., 406 ff., 434 ff., and Venkatasubbiah, *Indian Economy*, pp. 67 ff.

31 This is based on a wide range of village studies, for which see the general bibliography. Socio-religious reforms elicited much opposition at the time of introduction, many were watered-down, and most remained a dead letter at the local level. None the less, efforts along these lines, parricularly efforts to improve the position of the most depressed groups, may well be expected to produce a stronger middle caste response, when and if they get off the ground to the extent that a large number of aggressive, self-conscious, and economically more secure untouchables come to challenge caste Hindu domination. Thus far, this has not been the case, save in limited areas; but the caste Hindu response gives a pre-vision of things to come: it seems virtually certain that middle caste conservatism will become more explicit in the future.

32 For the 'red herring', see Dean, *New Patterns*, p. 128. This FBI report was published in 1956. In general, see the titles by Baldwin, Crane, Deshmukh, and Spencer in the general bibliography. Many of these points are best examined through the annual reports of individual enterprises, many of which are available in the *Times of India* (*TI*). It is also pertinent to note that businessmen have played key roles in government, as ministers, governors, members of development councils, of public financial institutions, and of public corporations. See Lamb, 'Business Organization...', in Park and Tinker (eds.), *Leadership*, pp. 264–7.

33 Rajni Kothari, 'The Congress "System" in India', *AS*, IV, 12 (Dec. 1964), 1161–73.

34 See Menon, *The Story*, ch. 21, esp. pp. 410–15. The *Manchester Guardian*, quoted *ibid.* p. 413, observed that the government 'has struck back quickly. It is likely to have no more trouble from the princes. Nobody will risk his comfortable income'. As will be seen, this was a bit premature a judgment on princely politics.

35 For examples, see *TI*, 24 June 1961, and the *Hindu Weekly Review* (*HWR*), 29 May and 28 Aug. 1961. *Link* from April through June 1961 contains numerous references to the carrot-and-stick policy *vis-à-vis* the princes.

36 See Rudolph, *MS*, p. 192, for the first quote, and Zinkin, *India Changes*, p. 210, for the second.

37 In one case, a would-be anti-Congress *jagirdar* was most reluctant to enter politics actively because the government still owed him Rs. 17·5 *lakhs* (Rs. 1,750,000) in compensation as well as irrigated canal lands for personal cultivation. This was publicly noted by the Maharani of Jaipur during the campaign preceding the 1962 elections; and the *jagirdar*, who joined Swatantra with the Maharani, expressed serious doubts that he would ever receive further compensation. From interviews and correspondence.

38 That is, the many religious and caste divisions; reluctance, if not outright refusal to enter competitive politics, because it would be degrading, etc., many aspects of which will be discussed below.

39 The Maharaja of Bikaner, in the introduction to Panikkar, *Princes in Council*, p. v.

40 Quoted in Dutt, *India Today*, p. 212.

41 From *RTC, II*, pp. 152 and 211.

42 From Dutt, *India Today*, p. 212, and *RTC, II*, p. 152, respectively.

43 Quoted in Dutt, *India Today*, p. 212.

44 See Fitze, *Twilight*, p. 163, where he notes their 'shining record of loyal and faithful services...to the Crown' and, in general, pp. 162 ff. See also Sir William Barton, *The Princes of India* (London, Nisbet, 1934), and Sir George McMunn, *The Indian States and Princes* (London, Jarrolds, 1936), for strongly pro-princely views. For British gratitude for princely help in 1857, see Menon, *The Story*, p. 9; *White Paper*, p. 12; and Barton, *Princes of India*, p. 132.

45 Ranbir Singh, *Indian States*, p. 19, and *RTC, I*, p. 59, respectively.

46 *RTC, I*, p. 34 and Ranbir Singh, *Indian States*, pp. 19–20, respectively.

47 *RTC, II*, p. 152.

48 Ranbir Singh, *Indian States*, p. 21.

49 See *RTC, II*, p. 211, and *RTC, I*, p. 78, respectively.

50 See, for example, *RTC, II*, p. 152.

51 For these fragments, see, respectively: *RTC, I*, p. 125; Barton, *Princes of India*, p. 47; McMunn, *Indian States*, p. 232; and Panikkar, *Indian States*, p. xvii. The last three are by the respective authors and are not quotations from aristocrats.

52 *RTC, II*, p. 140.

53 Barton, *Princes of India*, p. 75.

54 McMunn, *Indian States*, p. 238.

55 Barton, *Princes of India*, p. 293. Note here the class factors, discussed in the preceding section of this chapter.

56 The Raja of Ramgarh, quoted in Harrison, *Dangerous Decades*, p. 312. The Raja will be discussed below, in his capacity as the founder-leader of the Janata Party and as a one-time Swatantra luminary.

57 Quoted in G. Morris Carstairs, *The Twice-Born* (Bloomington, Ind., University of Indiana Press, 1958), pp. 58 and 176.

58 *Ibid.* p. 58.

59 See, respectively, Panikkar, *Princes in Council*, p. 13, and Menon, *The Story*, p. 57, the latter stating that 'an important ruler' made the assertion. For comparable statements, see Panikkar, *Princes in Council*, pp. 13 and 119.

60 From an interview in India with a Swatantra Party aristocrat.

61 See, for example, *RTC, I*, pp. 124 ff.

62 Quoted in *Overseas Hindustan Times* (*OHT*), 8 Feb. 1962.

63 See *TI*, 8 Aug. 1961, p. 14.

64 Carstairs, *Twice-Born*, pp. 24–5.

65 Quoted in Philip Woodruff, *The Men Who Ruled India*, I, *The Founders* (London, Jonathan Cape, 1953), p. 343.

66 Of course, in areas where the aristocratic classes were dominant at the village level, this is certainly the case.

67 W. Norman Brown, 'Class and Cultural Traditions in India', in Milton Singer (ed.), *Traditional India: Structure and Change* (Philadelphia, American Folklore Society, 1959), p. 38.

68 See the village studies in Park and Tinker (eds.), *Leadership*, and Srinivas, *Caste in Modern India*, *passim*.

69 S. C. Dube, *India's Changing Villages* (London, Routledge and Kegan Paul, 1958), pp. 216 and 138–9, respectively.

70 *Ibid.* pp. 138–9

71 Zinkin, *India Changes*, pp. 138–40, for quotations and further details.

72 From the party's paper, *The Justice*, quoted in J. H. Hutton, *Caste in India* (Bombay, Oxford University Press, 1961), p. 203.

73 *Harijans Today* (New Delhi, Publications Division, Ministry of Information and Broadcasting (PDMIB), n.d.), pp. 45–6.

74 Many of these points are developed at length in Howard L. Erdman, Ph.D. dissertation, 'The Swatantra Party and Indian Conservatism', Cambridge, Harvard University, 1964, ch. 3.

75 See, for example, Adam B. Ulam, *The Unfinished Revolution* (New York, Random House, 1960), for a splendid analysis of the response to the early stages of industrialization.

76 See, in general, Gandhi, *Economic and Industrial Life and Relations*, ed. V. B. Kher (3 vols. Ahmedabad, Navajivan Press, 1959); Bharatan Kumarappa, *Capitalism, Socialism or Villagism?* (Madras, Shakti Karyalayam, 1946); K. M. Munshi, *Reconstruction of Society Through Trusteeship* (Bombay, Bharatiya Vidya Bhavan, 1960); Susanne H. Rudolph, 'Consensus and Conflict in Indian Politics', *World Politics*, XIII, 3 (April 1961), 385–99; and the writings of Vinobha Bhave, Jayaprakash Narayan, and Shriman Narayan (Agarwal). Parallels to these perspectives are widely found, as in Sukarno's rejection of western 'free-fight' democracy and his defence of the traditional village system of building consensus. See Paul Sigmund (ed.), *The Ideologies of the Developing Nations* (New York, Praeger, 1963), pp. 57 ff.

77 In the case of the princes, Gandhi insisted on the application of the trusteeship principle, 'viz., the plan of princes voluntarily parting with power and becoming real trustees'. He acknowledged that 'very few people have faith in my plan' but insisted that he would advocate it 'as long as I believe in its practical possibility'. He admitted that he would 'not ask for their coercion' if they 'will not listen'. See Gandhi, *Indian States Problem*, pp. 344 and 636. Nehru, *Towards Freedom*, p. 320, complained that Gandhi, following 'a long succession of religious men', was 'always laying stress on the idea of trusteeship of the feudal princes, the big landlord, and the capitalist', and he made it abundantly clear that he was one of those who had little faith in Gandhi's approach.

78 See the extended discussion of Rajaji in chapter 5, below, for illustrations of this and other major points in this paragraph.

79 C. Rajagopalachari, paraphrasing Gandhi, in 'Gandhiji's Teachings and Philosophy', *Swarajya* (Special Number 1963), pp. 41 and 44.

80 The felicitous phrase, 'messiahs of backwardness', is from Panikkar, *The State and the Citizen* (Bombay, Asia Publishing House, 1956), pp. 25–37, 'The Danger of Reaction'.

81 See the conclusions of Srinivas, *Caste in Modern India*, p. 104, and of F. G. Bailey, 'Oriya Hill Village: II', in M. N. Srinivas (ed.), *India's Villages* (2nd edn. Bombay, Asia Publishing House, 1960), p. 145. Many other village studies reach essentially the same conclusion.

82 See the works by Bailey, Dube, and Srinivas, and Erdman, dissertation, ch. 3.

83 See Carstairs, *Twice-Born*; J. A. Curran, *Militant Hinduism in Indian Politics: A Study of the RSS* (New York, Institute of Pacific Relations, 1951); Dhananjay Keer, *Savarkar and His Times* (Bombay, A. V. Keer, 1950); Stanley Wolpert, *Tilak and Gokhale* (Berkeley, University of California Press, 1962); Myron Weiner, *Party Politics in India* (Princeton, Princeton University Press, 1957); and biographies of the other leading figures noted above. The discussion which follows is based primarily on Curran, *Militant Hinduism*, Weiner, *Party Politics*, and Rudolph, *MS*.

84 For the first, see Theodore L. Shay, *The Legacy of the Lokamanya* (London, Oxford University Press, 1956), p. 92, and for the second, see Weiner, *Party Politics*, p. 172. The Shay volume, like the bulk of the biographies of Tilak, is rather a 'white-wash' of this controversial figure. A more balanced account, tending to be quite critical of Tilak, is found in Wolpert, *Tilak and Gokhale*.

85 Weiner, *Party Politics*, pp. 167–8. Because the militant Hindu strand is largely embodied in the Jan Sangh, much detail has been deferred to the following section, and to the point at which Swatantra-Jan Sangh relations are examined.

86 For historical materials pertinent here see Weber, *The City* and *Religion of India*; Bendix, *Max Weber*; A. L. Basham, *The Wonder that was India* (New York, Grove Press, 1959); H. G. Rawlinson, *India: A Short Cultural History* (New York, Praeger, 1965); and Helen Lamb, 'The Indian Merchant', in Singer (ed.), *Traditional India*. In questionnaires, some Swatantra Jains identified themselves as Hindus by religion, Jain by sub-caste.

87 See B. B. Misra, *The Indian Middle Classes* (New York, Oxford University Press, 1961); W. H. Moreland, *India at the Death of Akbar* (London, Macmillan, 1920); and Susanne H. Rudolph, 'The Princely States of Rajputana: Ethic, Authority, and Structure', *Indian Journal of Political Science*, XXIV, 1 (Jan.–March 1963).

88 For a critique of Weber's *Religion of India*, see Milton Singer, 'The

Religion of India: The Sociology of Hinduism and Buddhism (Max Weber)', *American Anthropologist*, LXI, I (Feb. 1961).

89 See Lamb, 'Indian Merchant', in Singer (ed.), *Traditional India* and Harrison, *Dangerous Decades*, ch. 4, under 'The Ubiquitous Marwari'.

90 Based on the various articles by Lamb; Gokhale Institute *Notes*; Misra, *Indian Classes*; and Joan B. Landy, 'Factors in the Rise of the Parsi Community in India', senior honours' thesis, Radcliffe College, 1962.

91 Lamb, 'Indian Business Communities', *PA*, XXVIII, 106.

92 See Harrison, *Dangerous Decades*, ch. 4, under 'The Ubiqitous Marwari'.

93 From Rudolph, *MS*. Many of the leading financial supporters of the Congress were Marwaris.

94 See statements by business representatives in *RTC, I*, p. 158 and in *RTC, II*, pp. 141, 361 and 370.

95 See, for example, Weiner, *Politics of Scarcity*, pp. 123 ff.

96 For the quotations from Birla, see his *In the Shadow of the Mahatma* (Bombay, Orient Longmans, 1953), p. xv. Weiner, *Politics of Scarcity*, p. 133, notes that many business leaders 'frequently criticized Gandhi's "antiquarian" anti-industrial outlook'. For references to Gandhi's 'saintly' qualities, see Birla, *loc. cit.*, and Weiner, *Politics of Scarcity*, p. 123. For recent business criticism of support for cottage industries, see Lamb, 'Business Organization and Leadership', in Park and Tinker (eds.), *Leadership*, p. 261; and the reports of Messrs N. K. Jalan of Elphinstone Spinning and Weaving Mills, and of O. S. Gupta of Sajjan Mills, *TI*, 1 June 1961 and 5 Oct. 1961, respectively. For a statement by the Tamil Nad Mill-Owners Association stating that increased excises (as proposed) on units with more than 49 looms would force many shut-downs, see *HT*, 14 Feb. 1963.

97 For Nehru, see *Toward Freedom*, p. 347, and for Ranga, see Desai, *Social Background*, pp. 173 ff. Ranga has been Swatantra President from the party's inception to the time of writing (1966) and will be discussed further below.

98 See Weiner, *Politics of Scarcity*, p. 123. For the first Birla reference, see *RTC, II*, pp. 361 and 370, and, for the second, see his *Shadow of the Mahatma*, p. 48, from a letter dated 14 March 1932, which was already after some of Nehru's more fiery speeches but well before the Congress Socialist Party emerged as an articulate left wing inside the Congress.

99 See Brecher, *Nehru*, pp. 510 ff., for the 'strike of capital'.

100 See Lamb, 'Business Organization and Leadership', in Park and Tinker (eds.), *Leadership*, p. 260. See also P. A. Wadia and K. T. Merchant, *The Bombay Plan—A Criticism* (Bombay, Popular Book Depot, 1945). The Bombay Plan argued that public utilities and certain key industries could be state-run or state-controlled, that death duties and taxes could be used to redistribute income, etc., but the general conclusion about the thrust of the proposal is still valid.

101 See Weiner, *Politics of Scarcity*, pp. 124 ff., and the several publications of the FFE listed in the bibliography, especially those by A. D.

Shroff and Murarji Vaidya. As a key element in the formation of the Swatantra Party, the FFE is discussed further below.

102 *Politics of Scarcity*, pp. 139–40.

103 This conclusion is based mainly on evidence found in published annual reports of industrial concerns, particularly of textile companies. See Erdman, dissertation, ch. 4, for a fuller account of these.

104 *Nehru*, pp. 510–11, as in the vehement opposition to retention of certain price controls shortly after independence, the 'strike of capital', among others.

105 See, for example, Charles A. Myers, *Labor Problems in the Industrialization of India* (Cambridge, Harvard University Press, 1958). Evidence on this point will be presented below, in discussing the position of business interests in Swatantra.

CHAPTER 3, pp. 46–64

1 Much evidence is found in Rudolph, *MS*, and in S. V. Kogekar and Richard L. Park (eds.), *Reports on the Indian General Elections* (Bombay, Popular Book Depot, 1956).

2 See F. G. Bailey, 'Politics and Society in Contemporary Orissa', in C. H. Philips (ed.), *Politics and Society in India* (New York, Praeger, 1962), pp. 103–4, and Rudolph, *MS*, pp. 183–4. The other side of the coin, noted in Rudolph, *MS*, *loc. cit.*, was revealed by the Congressman who said sadly, 'the people couldn't be shaken out of their slavish frame of mind'. See also the paper by Brass, for the Association of Asian Studies meeting, already cited.

3 See Kogekar and Park, *Reports*, *passim*, for examples of the transformation of some *ad hoc* groups into local political parties.

4 See S. R. Maheshwari, *The General Election in India* (Allahabad, Chaitanya, 1963), chs. 5 and 6.

5 The Jan Sangh has controlled municipalities, but this lies beyond the scope of the present study. Some leaders of these parties have gone in and out of the Congress and in a detailed study one could examine some aspects of this problem through a consideration of their Congress activities.

6 To the extent that caste leaders have widely served as 'vote banks', almost every party draws on traditional loyalties and 'organization'.

7 See Harrison, *Dangerous Decades*, p. 312, and chapter 2 above for some of the Raja's views.

8 Kogekar and Park, *Reports*, p. 20. During the 1951–2 elections, Ramgarh contested against the sponsor of the legislation, K. B. Sahay, in three constituencies, winning in two. Ramgarh also contested in another constituency in which Sahay was not a candidate, and he won here as well, becoming the only person in India to have been victorious in three assembly districts. See *ibid.* p. 21.

9 *Statesman*, 5 Feb. 1962.

10 Based on Harrison, *Dangerous Decades*, p. 312; Kogekar and Park, *Reports*, pp. 19 ff.; Asok Mehta, *The Political Mind of India* (Bombay, Praja Socialist Party, 1952), p. 27; R. V. Krishna Ayyar *et al.* (eds.), *All-*

India Election Guide (Madras, Oriental Publishers, 1956), pp. 32 and 94; and interviews in India with the Raja of Ramgarh and other party leaders in 1962–3. In addition, Mr Noorul Arfin, personal assistant to the Raja, was interviewed in the United States in 1964 and has supplied much valuable information subsequently.

11 F. G. Bailey, 'The Ganatantra Parishad', *Economic Weekly*, 24 Oct. 1959, p. 1469. Harrison, *Dangerous Decades*, p. 312, states that the Janata Party and the Parishad 'can accurately be described as feudal elements', although he does little more than cite some of Ramgarh's more vitriolic pronouncements in support of this contention. Brecher, *Nehru*, p. 477, observed that in 1957 'a group of dispossessed princelings was able to arouse feudal loyalties and almost succeeded in unseating the Congress ministry'. K. P. Karunakaran, in his introduction to S. L. Polpai (ed.), *1962 General Elections in India* (Bombay, Allied Publishers, 1962), p. 13, calls the Parishad 'a conservative party' which included 'vestiges of medievalism and feudalism', and a report in Kogekar and Park, *Reports*, p. 124, insisted that 'the princes were fighting for the restoration of their *gaddis*'. Upon his resignation from the party, Surendra Mahanty censured it for 'being increasingly deployed to maintain conservatism and vested interests'. See *TI*, 6 April 1961.

12 *Economic Weekly*, 24 Oct. 1959, p. 1476 and generally pp. 1469 ff. For Mehta, see his *Political Mind*, pp. 26 and 67, and for Sadiq Ali, *The General Elections 1957* (New Delhi, All-India Congress Committee, 1959), p. 54.

13 For middle-class elements, see Bailey, *Economic Weekly*, 24 Oct. 1959, and Kogekar and Park, *Reports*, p. 128.

14 Kogekar and Park, *Reports*, p. 128.

15 H. H. Patna is very widely respected, and on the basis of the author's interviews and investigations, and on the basis of information supplied by Richard Taub of the Department of Sociology, Brown University, a high estimate of his ability and integrity would be in order.

16 See Krishna Ayyar *et al.* (eds.), *Election Guide*, p. 90.

17 *Ibid.* pp. 89–90.

18 For Ali see his *General Elections*, p. 57. For Morris-Jones, see his *Government and Politics of India* (London, Hutchinson University Library, 1964), p. 160.

19 See his *Political Mind*, pp. 26–7.

20 In addition to the sources cited in these paragraphs, see: Bailey, 'Politics and Society in Contemporary Orissa', in Philips (ed.), *Politics and Society*, and his nine-part series, 'Politics in Orissa', *Economic Weekly*, Aug.–Nov. 1959; P. K. Deo (H. H. Kalahandi), *My Humble Contributions* (Cuttack, Ganatantra Parishad, 1951); *Ganatantra Parishad or Democratic Party: Policy Statement* (Balangir, Ganatantra Parishad, 1951); and the *Election Manifesto of the Ganatantra Parishad* (Balangir, Ganatantra Parishad, 1961). Both the Janata Party and the Ganatantra Parishad merged with the Swatantra Party and will be discussed below.

21 Weiner, *Party Politics*, p. 156 and *passim.* See also Morris-Jones, *Government and Politics*, pp. as cited in the index.

22 The first Hindu *sabha* was formed in 1907, but the All-India Hindu Mahasabha was not established until 1925. It was less a political party than a cultural group and for a long time dual membership in the Congress and the Mahasabha was permitted. For some background and basic Mahasabha perspectives, see Weiner, *Party Politics*, pp. 166 ff.; V. D. Savarkar, *Hindu Rashtra Darshan* (Bombay, L. G. Khare, 1949); and Dhananjay Keer, *Savarkar*, *passim*. Keer, *op. cit.* pp. 274 ff., contains a scathing attack on Rajaji for his views. The Muslims have always borne the brunt of the attack. Savarkar, for example, praised the Parsis because they had no extra-territorial or anti-national loyalties. Weiner, *Party Politics*, p. 167, notes, however, that following independence the Mahasabha turned its guns on 'the Westernized Indian community', which would certainly include many Parsis.

23 Weiner, *Party Politics*, pp. 166 ff.

24 See *ibid.* pp. 170 ff. I would defend this characterization of the RRP as orthodox and conservative, if not reactionary, even though in Rudolph, *MS*, there are assertions that 'right radical' tendencies can be identified in the party, at least in Rajasthan. The fact that the more affluent *jagirdars* seem to have supported the RRP while the 'little' Rajputs supported the Jan Sangh lends some credence to my conclusion. Among the candidates supported by the RRP were Sir Homy Mody, one of India's most westernized and most influential Parsi businessmen-financiers, and Major Thakur Raghubir Singh of Bissau, a sophisticated, Oxford-educated *jagirdar*. Even a brief encounter with either of these men, among other RRP candidates, will indicate that the party programme does not receive universal approbation from its nominal adherents or standard-bearers. This is further reflected in the fact that many RRP supporters turned to the more moderate Swatantra Party after the latter's formation in 1959. This was particularly true in Rajasthan.

25 See Weiner, *Party Politics*, p. 169, for the quotation and some general observations, and see as well Curran, *Militant Hinduism*, for a detailed account of the RSS. The RSS was founded in 1925. The RSS and the Mahasabha, which had been informally linked for some time, were both implicated in Gandhi's assassination and neither was permitted to function for some time. Many felt that the Mahasabha had outlived its political usefulness, while others felt that no new party (i.e. the Jan Sangh) was needed.

26 Tinker, *India and Pakistan*, p. 120. Weiner, *Party Politics*, pp. 177 ff., presents a comparable estimate. Mookerjee was one of the RSS leaders who 'fell under the influence of Savarkar' of the Mahasabha (p. 187) and joined the latter in 1939. He resigned from that party after Gandhi's assassination, urged the Mahasabha to admit Muslims and to confine itself to strictly cultural work. Tinker, *loc. cit.*, calls Mookerjee 'a conservative in the best sense', which probably means that he was something of an Indian 'Tory', in his view.

27 *India and Pakistan*, p. 120. The Sangh's weekly, *The Organiser*, regularly abuses Muslims, Pakistan, and westernized Hindus.

28 Jan Sangh General-Secretary, Deendayal Upadhyaya, quoted in

Poplai (ed.), *1962 Elections*, p. 56. A comparable motto was used by Savarkar and the Mahasabha.

29 Upadhyaya, in Poplai (ed.), *1962 Elections*, pp. 58–9.

30 From the 1962 election manifesto, in *ibid.* p. 144, It is also stated that 'large-scale industries will be given full scope for growth' with 'defence and basic industries' in the public sector.

31 Conversations with leading Jan Sanghis did not clear up this ambiguity. The author's impression is that nationalization of certain industries is fully acceptable but that attacks on smaller property holders find no support. This seems true of property in land as well, i.e. abolition of huge estates is acceptable. On the matter of socialist rhetoric, the Sangh claims to have imbibed Marx's moral revulsion *vis-à-vis* the industrial process but abjures all institutional arrangements commonly associated with Marxism. The Hindu Mahasabha emphasizes 'Hindu socialism' and 'joint co-operative farming' because of the alleged existence of communal ownership of land in ancient India and because of the success of the Israeli *kibbutz*. See *TI*, 24 April 1961; *HWR*, 1 May 1961; and *HWR*, 4 Dec. 1961, for the Mahasabha. *The Organiser* remains the best source for the Sangh.

32 For a brief, comparative analysis of Jan Sangh and Swatantra foreign policy views, see Howard L. Erdman, 'The Foreign Policy Views of the Indian Right', *Pacific Affairs*, XXXIX, 1–2 (spring–summer 1966), pp. 5–18.

33 Upadhyaya in Poplai (ed.), *1962 Elections*, p. 57. Both the Sangh and the Mahasabha refuse to admit that reunification of India and Pakistan is impossible or at least extremely unlikely.

34 In an interview with a leading Jan Sanghi, the author was told that the party invariably received a 'bad press', largely because of the RSS connection. The interviewee claimed that the RSS had done much good work during partition, that it was becoming less militant, and that it would be better if the RSS shed its para-military and vehemently anti-Muslim posture. He made it clear, however, that he would under no circumstances repudiate the support of the RSS, pending such developments. For the most part, Sangh legislators acquit themselves quite well.

35 See the excellent tables and discussion in Morris-Jones, *Government and Politics*, pp. 161–6. The tables are reproduced, by permission, in Appendix II. Generally speaking, the RRP, Ganatantra Parishad and the Janata Party appear to have drawn primarily on rural conservative elements on a largely derivative basis, i.e. through local notables, especially the princely-landlord classes. The Sangh and the Mahasabha seem to have had as their hard core middle and lower-middle class urbanites, and in the early years after partition, among refugees. In Rajasthan, as noted earlier, the RRP drew upon larger landholders, the Jan Sangh on smaller ones and on displaced retainers in some urban areas. As Weiner, *Party Politics*, p. 170, points out, communal party strength 'has shifted into areas where the Western impact has been the weakest', particularly in former princely states. He points out that in 1951–2, 65 of the 84 assembly seats won by the RRP-Mahasabha-Sangh were in former princely areas. Given the dislocations attendant upon industrialization, Weiner quite properly speculates that the urban areas in backward states 'may provide a new basis for Hindu communalism in the years to come'.

36 S. L. Poplai (ed.), *National Politics and the 1957 Elections in India* (Delhi, Metropolitan Book Company, 1957), pp. 32–3, discusses this unity effort but mentions only the RRP, Mahasabha, Sangh and Akalis. Weiner, *Party Politics*, p. 199, mentions all those listed above. Harrison, *Dangerous Decades*, p. 291, similarly notes the inclusion of the southern parties. Poplai (ed.), *1957 Elections*, p. 32, claims that the group totalled 30; Weiner, *Party Politics*, p. 199, puts the figure at 34. For an excellent discussion of the origins of the Commonweal Party and Tamilnad Toilers, see Rudolph and Rudolph, 'Political Role', *PA*, XXXIII.

37 Harrison, *Dangerous Decades*, pp. 291–2. W. H. Morris-Jones, *Parliament in India* (Philadelphia, University of Pennsylvania Press, 1957), pp. 113–14, refers to the situation as follows: 'The communal parties have fallen further since their thorough defeat in 1952, and the death in 1953 of Dr S. P. Mukherjee [Mookerjee], the creator and leader of the Jan Sangh, removed the one man who might have been able to transform these parties into a coherent nationalist conservative party.'

38 Poplai (ed.), *1957 Elections*, p. 35. In dealing with this aspect of right-wing unity efforts, Weiner, *Party Politics*, pp. 199 ff., does not discuss the Ganatantra Parishad.

39 For the quotation, see Weiner, *Party Politics*, p. 203. This entire discussion is based on Weiner's book, pp. 200 ff. He notes, *ibid.* p. 204, that Deshpande took exception to such charges, insisting that all would have been well had not some Jan Sanghis 'indulged in vilifying or misrepresenting the Mahasabha. Statements were issued calling Hindu Mahasabha communal and a body composed of capitalists...I need not answer the baseless charge of Princes, Rajas, jagirdars, being in Hindu Mahasabha.' The evidence in Kogekar and Park, *Reports*, indicates that in some areas the charge was far from 'baseless'.

40 Chatterjee will be discussed further below, in connection with his short romance with Swatantra. He has been somewhat 'rootless' as a politician and on this basis it seems plausible that he would be willing to contemplate the demise of the Mahasabha.

41 See Weiner, *Party Politics*, pp. 210 ff. Other factors, such as the Sangh's aggressiveness and emphasis on discipline, could also be cited.

42 As we shall see, leaders of the Ganatantra Parishad and the Janata Party were willing to contemplate the formation of a national opposition in which their separate identities would be lost. In interviews, leaders of these parties said that after Mookerjee's death, there was simply no one around with sufficient stature to induce them to help form such a party and they also disliked the 'images' of the major right-wing groups. Sangh discipline was also a deterrent in some cases.

43 For the Rajasthan case, see Rudolph, *MS*.

44 Kogekar and Park, *Reports*, and Maheshwari, *General Election*, will indicate satisfactorily the range of co-operation and conflict. The former, p. 75, notes that in Madhya Pradesh, the Sangh, Mahasabha and RRP supported each other; in the Punjab, the Sangh is said to have had some 'understandings' with the Zamindara Party and the Akali Dal (p. 138); in UP, there were 'local agreements' involving the Praja Party and the 'big three' (p. 154). On the other hand, in the now defunct state of Madhya Bharat, the rightists 'fought each other in several constituencies', with sixteen contests between the Sangh and the RRP, six between the RRP and the Mahasabha, and three between the Sangh and the Mahasabha (p. 190). Rudolph, *MS*, p. 204 and *passim*, also contains material on this general issue. This *MS* contains an excellent, detailed study of unity efforts at the state level. According to the *MS*, pp. 329 ff., the so-called 'Sanyutka Dal', which included the RRP, Sangh and independents, fell apart after land reform controversies divided the Rajputs who dominated the front.

45 *India and Pakistan*, pp. 120–1. See also Zinkin, *India Changes*, p. 225, for a reference to Prasad's reaction, which, according to this account, involved a threat of resignation if the bill were not modified drastically. For a detailed study, see Gene D. Overstreet, 'The Hindu Code Bill', in James B. Christoph (ed.), *Cases in Comparative Politics* (Boston, Little Brown, 1965), pp. 413–40. See also Dhananjay Keer, *Dr Ambedkar: His Life and Mission* (Bombay, A. V. Keer, 1954), pp. 396 ff., for an account of this leader's bitter disappointment over the mutilation of this bill.

46 *India and Pakistan*, p. 121.

47 As noted, Tinker was generally impressed by Mookerjee, and Poplai (ed.), *1957 Elections*, pp. 37–8, stated that the Sangh was moving toward 'the position of a Conservative Party in certain respects'. Occasionally, when the Sangh elevates a southerner to a prominent position and *seems*, therefore, to be moderating its pro-Hindi stand, such speculations become more frequent. Interviews in India with top Sangh leaders left little doubt in this writer's mind that no such illusion should be harboured. It is likely to remain adamant on Hindi, alienating at least the south, and its RSS ties will continue to give the party a communal aspect which will not be easily shed.

48 'Congress Ideology', *India Quarterly*, XVI, 1 (Jan.–March 1960), 10.

49 By the leftist periodical *Link*, 20 March 1960.

50 Quoted in *TI*, 13 Oct. 1961.

51 *TI*, 9 Oct. and 28 Nov. 1961.

52 Norman Palmer, 'India Faces a New Decade', *Current History*, XL, 235 (March 1961), 149.

53 William A. Robson, 'India Revisited', *The Political Quarterly*, XXXI, 4 (Oct.–Dec. 1960), p. 428.

54 From *Swarajya*, the 'unofficial' organ of the party, 18 April 1959.

55 From an interview with a pro-Swatantra Indian diplomat posted in the United States.

56 The major Indian newspapers generally followed the same basic line, in assessing Swatantra at the time of its birth. See, for example, *TI*, 8 May 1959; *Hindu*, 11 May 1959; *HT*, 12 May 1959; *Delhi Hindustan Standard*, 13 May 1959; *HT*, 17 May 1959; *HT*, 18 May 1959; *TI*, 18 May 1959; and assessments of the various party conventions, manifestos, and the like.

57 Editorial, 'For Nehru: An Opposition', 16 March 1962.

CHAPTER 4, pp. 65–81

1 K. P. Karunakaran, in Poplai (ed.), *1962 General Elections*, p. 2.

2 From his inaugural address at the Bombay (Preparatory) Convention, August 1959, reprinted in *Swatantra Party Preparatory Convention* (Bombay, Swatantra Party, 1959), p. 18. The Popular Book Depot, Bombay, is cited as the distributor.

3 All three will come in for further attention below, because of their connection with the Swatantra Party. According to Vaidya (in an interview in Bombay, 1962), he gave an address to the All-India Manufacturers' Association of which he was then (1956) President, in which he cautioned against excessive state controls, both in terms of their effects on economic initiative and on political liberty. Nehru, who had agreed for the first time to open the meeting, heard the warning, and, according to Vaidya, he agreed, in general terms, that excessive government controls were to be feared. Shortly thereafter, both Vaidya and Shroff wrote 'anti-statist' articles for a special supplement of the *Times of India*, and upon reading these pieces, Masani arranged for a meeting with Vaidya and Shroff, and the idea of a 'Forum of Free Enterprise' was launched. Vaidya claims to have mentioned the projected group to Nehru, who said that while it was a hopeless venture in the Indian context, it was only fitting that in a democracy such a group should form and propagate its ideas. Vaidya himself insisted that subsequent attacks on the group by Nehru were inspired more by his 'lieutenants' than by Nehru's own personal hostility.

4 The FFE publishes a wide range of anti-statist material, regardless of the party identification of the author. The FFE unit in New Delhi has, at least in the past, been more sympathetic to the Sangh than to Swatantra.

5 From the 'Manifesto' originally published on 18 July 1956, in a pamphlet entitled 'The Forum of Free Enterprise', Bombay, FFE, n.d., p. 4.

6 For the quotation, see the 'Forum of Free Enterprise', p. 1. The literature, very often, consisted of reprints of speeches and articles by business leaders, economists, educators, and others in public life. For a partial list of Forum publications, see the bibliography.

7 See *ibid.*, and Shroff, *Free Enterprise and Democracy* (Bombay, FFE, n.d.), p. 2.

8 *The Road to Serfdom* (Chicago, University of Chicago Press, 1944).

9 *The Communist Party of India* (New York, Macmillan, 1954), p. 240.

10 *Ibid.* p. 229.

11 *Ibid.* pp. 242 and 250–1.

12 *Ibid.* p. 230.

13 From an interview with Ramgarh, in Bombay, 1963.

14 For Masani's statement, see *Modern Review*, CV, 3 (March 1959), 182. In *Hindu*, 15 Feb. 1959, Rajaji condemned the Nagpur Resolution on the grounds that coercion would inevitably be used to bring about joint co-operative farming.

15 For the type of position taken by Masani, see his *A Plea for Realism* (Bombay, Popular Book Depot, n.d.), which is a collection of some speeches delivered in the *Lok Sabha* between May and August 1957. For

the argument he had been advancing about the need for an opposition see his 'Need for a Centre Party', *TI*, 4 June 1959.

16 *Communist Party of India*, p. 242.

17 Based on interviews with Rajaji, Vaidya, and Masani, in 1962–3.

18 Based on interviews with several participants in these meetings.

19 See Weiner, *Politics of Scarcity*, p. 106, and, in general, pp. 105 ff., for a brief and superficial account of the Forum and Swatantra. See also Ranga, 'The Story of the Birth of the Swatantra Party', in Kailash Pati Singh (ed.), *Swatantra Party Souvenir 1960* (no data), pp. 3 ff.

20 Further evidence on this will be presented below, in discussing Swatantra finances.

21 Here, too, Swatantra leaders admit that when B. L. Singh's connection with Swatantra was brought to Nehru's attention, Nehru insisted that no action be taken against him with respect to his official position as adviser to the Planning Commission.

22 This geographical concentration is to some extent reflected in the group's office bearers, who, with the exception of B. L. Singh, were all from South India, as of 1959. Prof. M. Ruthnaswamy, in an interview, supported this contention.

23 Kogekar and Park (eds.), *Reports*, pp. 89, 112, refer to support for candidates by a 'Madras Agriculturalists' Federation' in the 1951–2 elections, which antedates, of course, the formation of the AIAF. According to one source, the Madras group was a component of the AIAF when it came into existence in 1958.

24 For a fragmentary criticism, see Karunakaran, in Poplai (ed.), *1962 General Elections*, p. 16, and, for a rebuttal, see B. L. Singh, 'What All-India Agriculturalists' Federation Stands For', in *Souvenir 1960*, pp. 68 ff.

25 Masani, 'Opening Remarks', in *Preparatory Convention*, p. 9.

26 The latter is noted by B. L. Singh, in *Souvenir 1960*, p. 68. Ranga, 'The Story', in *Souvenir 1960*, p. 5, notes that both he and Rajaji had stressed the *kisan* component when Nehru levelled the charge that Swatantra was a projection of the FFE. Throughout his 'Story', Ranga plays down the role of the FFE, which Masani, Vaidya, and others are happy to stress, at least in private.

27 The AIAF and Swatantra have sponsored meetings jointly, and in 1963, the AIAF office bearers were Ranga (President), B. L. Singh and Gayatri Devi (Vice-Presidents), and C. L. N. Reddy (Secretary). See *TI*, 23 April 1963, and *Express*, 23 April 1963.

28 Based on interviews with Masani and Ramgarh.

29 Based on interviews with Kalahandi, Patna, and Rajaji.

30 Based on a biographical sketch in *Souvenir 1960*.

31 As we shall see, many retired civil servants, judges, educators, and the like were among those who turned to Rajaji, in their first venture into politics. For Kanoongo, see *Souvenir 1960*.

32 From Ranga, 'The Story', in *Souvenir 1960*.

33 *TI*, 23 June 1959.

34 Ranga, 'The Story', in *Souvenir 1960*, notes that on 28 Feb. he and Masani spoke at Belgaum (Maharashtra) and that on 15 May S. K. D.

Paliwal of UP invited Ranga and others to preside over the inaugural of a 'rural peoples' publication.

35 For Munshi, see *Modern Review*, CV, 2 (Feb. 1959), 88. For Paliwal, see Ranga, 'The Story', in *Souvenir 1960*.

36 See Ranga, 'The Story', in *Souvenir 1960*.

37 The INDC was formed shortly before the 1957 elections. The Andhra Democratic Party was formed in February 1959, and then joined with the Andhra Socialist Party (defectors from the Lohia group) to form the Andhra Socialist Democratic Party, as a means to unseat the Communists as the legislative opposition party. For this, see *TI*, 10 July 1959, and the *Hindu*, 1 Aug. 1959.

38 For some of these see: V. V. Prasad, 'New Delhi Diary', *Swatantra*, 3 Nov. 1956; Kongot, 'Rajaji is Rising', *Swatantra*, 10 Nov. 1956; V. S. Krishnaswamy, 'Wanted: An Opposition Party', *Swatantra*, 24 Nov. 1956; 'C.R.: Some Footnotes to His Future Biography', *Swatantra*, 15 Dec. 1956; Sethu, 'Sidelights', *Swatantra*, 22 Dec. 1956; and the exchange of letters between A. S. Karanth and Rajaji in *Swatantra*, 29 Dec. 1956. In his letter, Rajaji said that he wanted an opposition but that he was too old to lead it personally.

39 *Our Democracy and Other Essays* (Madras, B. G. Paul, 1957), p. 3.

40 *Ibid.* p. 3. Cf. *Swarajya*, 8 Sept. 1962, for his criticism of 'left' and 'right' categories.

41 *Our Democracy*, p. 2.

42 From an interview with Rajaji in 1962.

43 The foreign observer, a Harvard professor, has asked to remain nameless here. The interview took place in 1959. In his inaugural speech at the Swatantra national convention in Bangalore, 1 Feb. 1964, Rajaji concluded by saying: 'The Swatantra Party's future is, according to intelligent assessment, bright. Let us gather more and more strength quickly. I cannot wait much longer, friends.' The speech has been printed by the Kalki Press, Madras, publishers of *Swarajya*.

44 See Kabir, 'Congress Ideology', *Indian Quarterly*, XVI, 9–10; Palmer, 'India Faces a New Decade', *Current History*, XL, 149; and Vincent Sheean, *Nehru: The Years of Power* (New York, Random House, 1960), p. 45, respectively.

45 Sheean, *Nehru*, pp. 45 and 56. Palmer, *Current History*, XL, states that Rajaji was 'a close associate of Gandhi, a veteran leader of the independence struggle'.

46 Brecher, *Nehru*, p. 86.

47 *Toward Freedom*, p. 371.

48 Rajaji has by no means escaped criticism. Brecher, *Nehru*, p. 24, speaks of his tendency to indulge in 'Olympian criticism', and Frank Moraes, *India Today* (New York, Macmillan, 1960), p. 230, calls Rajaji 'subtle and subterranean, but clear-headed' and notes that he 'is sometimes referred to maliciously as the Machiavelli of Madras, or after his home district, Salem, as the Savonorola of Salem'.

49 For the curious, B. V. Raman, 'Outlook for Swatantra Party', in *Souvenir 1960*, pp. 79–81.

50 *Our Democracy*, pp. 4–5.
51 *Preparatory Convention*, pp. 9–10.
52 Palmer, *Current History*, XL, 149.
53 Kabir, *India Quarterly*, XVI.
54 For a partial list of those at Madras, see *Preparatory Convention*, p. 5. The major newspapers of 5 June 1959 report this.
55 From interviews with people who naturally want to remain nameless.
56 This discussion is based on interviews. Narayan declined the offer, insisting that he was determined to pursue the goal of a 'partyless' democracy and that, in any event, he was not sufficiently conservative to find the party attractive. He did, however, give Swatantra a modest boost by expressing his admiration for Rajaji and for the emphasis on 'trusteeship' in the tentative manifesto, and by saying that as long as India was *not* a partyless democracy, a strong opposition was needed to check Congress power.
57 *Statesman*, 14 June 1959.
58 *Preparatory Convention*, p. 10. Note that Masani here and elsewhere emphasizes the 4 June date and the role of *non-business* interests.
59 'The Need for a Centre Party', *TI*, 4 June 1959. Note that he explicitly referred again to the middle-class basis for the party. My emphasis.
60 For Shastri, see *TI*, 8 July 1959.
61 The preparatory convention was originally announced for Ahmedabad, on the above days, but the venue was changed. One source (*TI*, 23 June 1959) speculated that Ahmedabad had been chosen for three reasons: first, that the party had elicited considerable enthusiasm from some key members of the Gujarat Khedut Sangh; secondly, that the textile interests in that city were vulnerable to a 'middle of the road' party committed to greater latitude for private enterprise; and thirdly, that Ahmedabad, above all other Indian cities, bore the imprint of the Gandhian notion of 'trusteeship' in its labour-management relations. See also Ranga, 'The Story', *Souvenir 1960*.
62 *TI*, 12 June 1959, and see also *TI*, 30 July 1959. Ranga had participated in a number of Punjab peasant meetings with Nagoke, the leader of the Dehati Janata Party, and at a meeting of the party itself, shortly after Swatantra was born, Ranga induced Nagoke and his colleagues to amend the Dehati Janata constitution, which had originally stated that the group would be non-partisan. See *HT*, 16 June 1959.
63 For Paliwal, see *HT*, 28 June 1959.
64 Particularly vehement were some remarks made by Nehru at a press conference on 7 July, reported in all of the major papers on 8 July. He accused the party of being the political 'projection' of the FFE and said it completely distorted the intent of the Nagpur proposals. In speaking to A. D. Shroff's remark that Nehru had been put in office by an illiterate electorate, Nehru said that such attitudes smacked of fascism. He was reasonably generous and/or restrained in many of his remarks, but the press emphasized the charges relating to the FFE and fascism.
65 *TI*, 11 July 1959.

66 There had been a number of local meetings prior to the preparatory convention, and one state meeting, in Mysore, on 22 July, for a report of which see the *Hindu*, 23 July. A *Hindu* report (7 July) of a meeting in Bombay noted that two men who became Swatantra stalwarts—K. M. Munshi and Sir Homy P. Mody—were present and that the latter had already been designated as 'honorary treasurer'. These figures will be discussed further in the next chapter, while the various local parties which merged with Swatantra will be considered in chapter 6. Press comment on Swatantra's birth was, in broad terms, cautiously optimistic. Most assessments conceded that a liberal/moderate opposition was useful or necessary but warned against excessive negativism, willingness to admit any and all anti-Communist and anti-Congress elements.

CHAPTER 5, pp. 82–108

1 Weiner, *Politics of Scarcity*, p. 105. Biographical data may be found in *Souvenir 1960*, pp. 87 ff., or in almost any *Times of India Directory and Yearbook*, in 'Who's Who'. A close examination of their careers leaves little doubt that the leaders are 'distinguished' rather than 'popular', as we saw in the case of Rajaji, in the preceding chapter.

2 Kabir, *India Quarterly*, XVI, 9, footnote, emphasizes their age. Rajaji was born in 1879; Mody in 1881; Munshi in 1887; Ranga in 1900; and Masani in 1905. Many of the others to be discussed below would also qualify as 'comparatively older men', to say the least.

3 In the early days of Swatantra, this was one of the favourite terms of abuse. Nehru himself often joined in the chorus, for which see *Swarajya*, 10 Oct. 1959. Nehru is reported to have said that the 'medley' which was the Swatantra leadership made it difficult to know what the party stood for or how to characterize it. Rajaji, however, commented (*loc. cit.*) that 'if I have a "medley of companions"...it is not only natural but fair. Our nation is a medley...It is not a good thing that this big country and this large nation should be governed by anything that approaches the homogeneity of a clique. I take the reproach of the new Party being a medley as a compliment.'

4 See Hari Kishore Singh, *History of the Praja Socialist Party* (Lucknow, Narendra Prakashan, 1959), p. 21, where he notes that Masani 'studied at the London School of Economics and was influenced by Fabian thought. Like [Asoka] Mehta he is a good example of the social democratic strand in Indian socialism.'

5 Quoted *ibid.* pp. 29 and 47, respectively.

6 *Ibid.* p. 21. Morris-Jones, *Government and Politics*, p. 212, argues that Masani was not a Gandhian; but he certainly came to admire Gandhi very much, and was accused of 'selling out' to Gandhism by the more orthodox Marxists.

7 See Morris-Jones, *Government and Politics*, p. 156.

8 *Revolutionary Peasants* (Delhi, Amrit Book Co., 1949), p. 64.

9 *Ibid.* pp. 54–5,

10 Quoted in Desai, *Social Background*, p. 173.

11 From a biographical sketch in 1952 by the late Khasa Subba Rao, in *Swatantra*, quoted in N. G. Ranga, *Freedom in Peril* (Hyderabad, The Indian Peasants Institute, 1961), p. 3. In *ibid.* p. 9, there is a statement by Prof. Hiren Mukherjee, a leading Bengali Communist, which praises Ranga's 'spirit of protestantism, a spirit of non-conformism, a spirit of defiance which seem to run in his blood'; and while noting 'serious fundamental differences' with Ranga, Mukherjee added: 'but that does not prevent me from expressing my admiration, or even my appreciation, of the talent which he has brought to bear in the services to the country...'.

12 Harrison, *Dangerous Decades*, p. 218.

13 It is worth noting here that Ranga, *Revolutionary Peasants*, p. 69, cites the existence of considerable friction between the peasant leaders and the CSP, at the time the former were trying to develop the All-India Kisan Sabha. Ranga's outlook was, and remains, decidedly pro-peasant and he certainly distrusted that strand of socialism which wanted to remake India in the image of the great industrial west, at the expense of the peasantry.

14 Munshi, for example, was a close friend of the Brahmin Darbhanga *Raj* and other ruling families, while Rajaji was quite content to apply Madras anti-sedition laws to many anti-prince agitators. For the latter, see Coupland, *Indian Politics*, p. 133, where it is also noted that Gandhi supported Rajaji here, against violent criticism from radical Congressmen.

15 V. Subramanian, 'Bismarck of India', *Swatantra*, 6 March 1948.

16 These fragments are culled from *Rajaji's Speeches* (Bombay, Bharatiya Vidya Bhavan, 1958), I, 159–61.

17 *Ibid.* p. 161.

18 *Loc. cit.* All of these remarks appear to have been taken from an address to the princes themselves, although the precise situation is not clear from the text.

19 Quoted in Malaviya, *Land Reforms in India*, pp. 52–3.

20 For his support for the Karachi Resolution, see *Hindu*, 8 Feb. 1962. Coupland, *Indian Politics*, p. 137, calls the projected land reforms in Madras, 1937–9, 'radical', although no action had been taken on key measures when the ministry was called upon to resign. In commenting on the proposed legislation, Coupland indicates that there was a good deal of opposition within the Congress itself, but Rajaji was apparently willing to countenance some fairly drastic (from the landlords' standpoint) reform proposals. Referring to both of his Madras ministries, Rajaji stated that 'I am reminded...that I got an Act passed to wipe out peasants' debts where they had paid by way of interest double the principal borrowed, that I got tenancy laws passed by which farm tenants and labourers got a much larger share of the produce than ever before in the Tanjore area...that these were revolutionary Socialist measures...' (from *Swarajya*, 31 Oct. 1959). The Tanjore area was one of the very worst in Madras State and was the scene of considerable, and widely successful, Communist agitation—which may have had more to do with Rajaji's reforms than is suggested by his remarks. For Munshi, see J. H. Dave *et al.* (eds.), *Munshi: His Art and Work* (4 vols. Bombay, Munshi 70th Birthday Citizens' Celebration Committee, n.d.), II, 249–51.

21 *RTC, I*, p. 158.
22 It might be noted that Mody resigned from the Viceroy's Council in 1943 in protest against the government's treatment of Gandhi. It is also useful to remember that V. P. Menon, who was one of the Madras founding fathers, was Patel's assistant in the integration of the princely states. The story that one maharaja drew a pistol on Menon when he broached the subject of absorption reminds us that moderate nationalism is not equivalent to extreme reaction along aristocratic lines.
23 See Howard L. Erdman, 'Chakravarty Rajagopalachari and Indian Conservatism', *Journal of Developing Areas*, I, 1 (Oct. 1966), 7–21, for a somewhat different statement of the main arguments presented here.
24 *Nehru*, p. 56.
25 'Gandhiji's Teachings', *Swarajya* (Special Number, 1963), pp. 41 and 44.
26 *Ibid.* p. 44.
27 *Rajaji's Speeches*, I, 108. Here of course, he joins Gandhi and many others, both Indian and non-Indian, in reacting to the problem of alienation and related issues. For those who sympathize with this concern, the question still remains: will any action, predicated on such feelings, in a pre-industrial society generate any significant economic and social movement? There are costs—terrible human costs—involved in stagnation, just as there are costs involved in dislocation and alienation.
28 From Sheean, *Nehru*, pp. 50 ff.
29 *Rajaji's Speeches*, II, 172.
30 See *Rajaji's Speeches*, II, 161, and Sheean, *Nehru*, pp. 45–56, for the first point. I am indebted to material supplied by Prof. Susanne Hoeber Rudolph for the second point.
31 'To Preserve Family Economy', in *Why Swatantra?* (Bombay, Swatantra Party, n.d.), pp. 11–12. Here it should be noted that a resolution to nationalize the rice trade, presented at the 1964 Congress session at Bhubaneshwar, Orissa, was defeated. State-trading in food grains was also included in the Nagpur Resolution. Recall, for example, the 1962 Jan Sangh programme which insisted that a time limit be set, within which the *khadi* industry 'will be required to become self-sufficient' because 'in spite of heavy subventions' it 'has not yet become economic'. Rajaji made his plea at a time when *khadi* was suffering grievously, in the late 1940s.
32 See the anti-power loom article in *Swarajya*, 30 Jan. 1965. Students of American history may want to compare this with Jefferson's view that his country's workshops should remain forever in Europe.
33 *Rajaji's Speeches*, I, 198. Significantly, in his 'Gandhiji's Teachings', *Swarajya* (Special Number, 1963), p. 35, Rajaji drew on this earlier speech but amended the last sentence to read 'coercion, fraud and corruption' rather than simply 'fraud and corruption', which reflects his growing concern for state control of the economy.
34 *Rajaji's Speeches*, II, 131. My emphasis.
35 See *Swarajya*, 19 Dec. 1964.
36 Munshi, *Warnings of History* (Bombay, Bharatiya Vidya Bhavan,

1959), pp. 12–13. He was referring specifically to the Marxists in the latter remark.

37 Munshi, *Reconstruction of Society*, *passim*. The place of the notion of trusteeship in formal Swatantra doctrine will be discussed in chapter 8, below.

38 *Rajaji's Speeches*, II, 177. See also Rajaji, *Our Culture* (Bombay, Bharatiya Vidya Bhavan, 1963), *passim*.

39 *Our Culture*, p. 26.

40 *Ibid.* p. 39. See Rajaji, 'The Value of Traditional Values', *Swarajya*, 26 Dec. 1964.

41 *Our Democracy*, p. 29. See *ibid.* pp. 47–8.

42 *Our Culture*, pp. 27 and 29, for the two quotes.

43 *Ibid.* p. 27.

44 *Ibid.* p. 33. My emphasis.

45 *Ibid.* pp. 31 and 33.

46 Rajaji, *Social and Religious Decay* (Bombay, Swatantra Party, n.d.), p. 6.

47 Rajaji considers the former the Russian approach, the latter the American approach.

48 See *Swarajya*, 21 Feb. 1959, and *Our Culture*, p. 50, for the quotations.

49 Rajaji has also taken a strong stand in defence of slums, against the 'city planners', along familiar lines. He has said that slums are a useful form of 'self-help' which, if anything, 'should be preserved'. See *Link*, 14 Feb. 1960, and *Swatantra*, 29 Nov. 1952.

50 For the *harijan* issue, see Coupland, pp. 144 ff., and *Swarajya*, 31 Oct. 1959. A permissive bill was substituted for one which would have made temple entry mandatory. The former would be akin to a bill which would permit Mississippi racists to use the principal of local option to admit Negroes to public facilities. Rajaji's daughter married Gandhi's son: not a typical inter-caste marriage by any means. For the argument about traditional medicine, see *Rajaji's Speeches*, I, 50, and for the business communities, see *ibid.* pp. 178–81. For his statement about the impossibility of a return to the village economy, see *Swarajya*, 29 Feb. 1963. The author discussed the question of social reform with Rajaji on two separate occasions, and Rajaji's main points were these: (1) no party could turn its back on the processes set in motion by the British and the Congress; and (2) Swatantra would pay primary heed to defence needs, after which rural welfare in general would receive the highest priority.

51 *Rajaji's Speeches*, I, 196.

52 'Gandhiji's Teachings', *Swarajya* (Special Number, 1963), p. 35.

53 Quoted in *Swarajya*, 10 Oct. 1959.

54 *Our Culture*, p. 37.

55 For these two points see, respectively, *HT*, 4 Sept. 1959 and *Swarajya*, 29 Feb. 1964.

56 *Rajaji's Speeches*, II, 180.

57 *Swarajya*, 14 March 1959.

58 *Swarajya*, 21 Dec. 1963. My emphasis.

59 In terms of the earlier argument, that statement that 'to let every person act creatively as he chooses...is the best means of making people work' would encourage the son of the village potter to take up another occupation if he found it more attractive, whereas Rajaji would normally want him to be disciplined by 'culture' and remain on the job. The tension between the two has not yet been resolved, but it would appear that under the pressure of the doctrinal 'dialectic', Rajaji has been obliged to shift somewhat toward more liberal formulations. I think it is fair to say, however, that in a contest between liberalism and conservatism, Rajaji would be very much on the side of the latter.

60 Morris-Jones, *Government and Politics*, p. 156.

61 From the Constituent Assembly Debates (CAD), IV, 544, quoted in Morris-Jones, *Parliament in India*, p. 82, n. 3.

62 Dave, *Munshi*, II, 258–9 and *passim*, ch. 8. See *ibid.* for a discussion of Munshi's admittedly ruthless suppression of communal disturbances during his term as home minister of Bombay, 1937–9.

63 Quoted in *HT*, 23 April 1961.

64 Cf. the dispute between the Congress and the Muslim League prior to independence.

65 Interviews, with Munshi and Swatantra members drawn from these minorities, amply bear out this point.

66 Quoted in *HT*, 5 April 1961.

67 *HT*, 22 July 1961.

68 Quoted in the *Hindu*, 9 Jan. 1961.

69 For Munshi on zones, see the *Hindu*, 9 Jan. 1961; for Rajaji, see *HT*, 11 March 1961. For a relatively recent defence of English by Munshi, see *Swarajya*, 1 Sept. 1962, and in general see Dave, *Munshi*, II, 263–5.

70 *Hindu*, 22 July 1961, and 31 Aug. 1962.

71 See Donald Eugene Smith, *India as a Secular State* (Princeton, Princeton University Press, 1963), p. 241.

72 For the quotation, see Dave, *Munshi*, II, 136–7. See *ibid.* pp. 9–10, for a statement along Arya Samajist lines.

73 Smith, *Secular State*, p. 485, during a debate on the 'Useful Cattle Preservation Bill, 1951'. Nehru was adamantly opposed to a national cow-slaughter prevention bill, an issue which has animated Hindu revivalists from the days of Dayanand Saraswati, founder of the Arya Samaj, through Tilak, Gandhi, and others.

74 Headquarters in Bombay, with branches elsewhere. 'Bharat' is a more secular word for 'India' than is 'Hindustan'. It is pertinent to note here that the full title of the Jan Sangh is 'Bharatiya Jan Sangh'. Also, *vis-à-vis* Pakistan, the Sangh stands for 'Akhand (united) Bharat', while the Mahasabha stands for 'Akhand Hindustan'.

75 From 'What Bharatiya Vidya Bhavan Stands For'. The complete statement is available in the fly-leaf of many Bhavan publications, including Rajaji's retellings of the *Ramayana* and the *Mahabharata* for modern audiences. These are almost perfect examples of what Munshi means by the need to relate old truths to new circumstances. In addition to many works by Rajaji and Munshi, the Bhavan has a lengthy list which is not narrowly parochial, i.e. it has published some of Asok Mehta's writings on socialism.

76 *Loc. cit.* Cf. Rajaji's statements about the relevance of the Vedas, the Gita, etc., for modern times, in light of modern science, notions of citizenship, and the like. See also *Bhavan's Journal*, a periodical published by the Bhavan, and *Hindu*, 10, 11 Jan. and 13 Dec. 1963, for other references to Munshi and the Bhavan.

77 *Dangerous Decades*, p. 313. Rajaji, in his own way, would rank very high here, but Harrison is evidently thinking of the more militant revivalists. He should not overlook the other main group, ably represented by Rajaji.

78 According to some of Munshi's closest associates, he was on more than one occasion offered the presidency of the Jan Sangh, and according to one of these the Sangh considers him 'as one of their own'. From interviews in Bombay, 1962. It is, of course, important to note that Munshi never joined the Sangh. It is also pertinent to note here that Rajaji has been a frequent contributor to the Sangh's *Organiser*, even though he and the Sangh are sharply at odds on Pakistan and the language question.

79 From a questionnaire completed by Munshi. The same view is presented in Dave, *Munshi*, II.

80 *Ibid.* pp. 263–5.

81 'Tradition and Experiment in Forms of Government', in Philips (ed.), *Politics and Society*, pp. 158–9.

82 Sampurnanand was at that time Premier of UP and was not in the constituent assembly. He is now (1966) Governor of Rajasthan. His statement was made at a convocation address at Agra in 1949, quoted by Tinker, in Philips (ed.), *Politics and Society*, p. 159.

83 All from Constituent Assembly debates, quoted in Morris-Jones, *Parliament in India*, p. 88. For Munshi's role, see *ibid.* pp. 73–89, and Dave, *Munshi*, II, ch. 8. For an excellent discussion of political 'styles' which bears on this issue, see Morris-Jones, 'India's Political Idioms', in Philips (ed.), *Politics and Society*, pp. 133–54, or ch. 2 of his *Government and Politics*.

84 From Tinker, in Philips (ed.), *Politics and Society*, pp. 159, 157, and 160, respectively.

85 Dave, *Munshi*, II, 251.

86 See *ibid.* p. 248 and ch. 8, *passim*.

87 Concerning the President, see Munshi, 'Is the President Mere Figurehead', *Tide*, 30 Jan. 1963 and 'The President of India', the *Hindu*, 26 Jan. 1963. Munshi touches on the role of the attorney-general here as well, in arguing that the President needs such a legal adviser, who is not removable at the pleasure of the Cabinet or Prime Minister, as would have been the case under the proposed law minister–attorney-general fusion. In general, Munshi argues for autonomous powers for the President, the supreme court, the attorney-general, and kindred agencies to check the power of the Cabinet. For a roughly comparable argument, but with less attention to the intent of the framers or to general constitutional experience, by Rajaji, see the *Hindu*, 9 Dec. 1962. For general background on the attorney-general–law minister issue, see the *Hindu*, 5 Jan. 1963 and *HT*, 16 Feb. 1963, the latter reporting that the Government had decided to abandon the proposal. This is one specific case in which Swatantra's energetic opposition helped to modify government policy. For a more detailed and semi-official Swatantra statement, see A. P. Jain, 'The Case of the Attorney-General', mimeo (no. 6 of a series of 'position' papers prepared by the Swatantra Parliamentary Office, New Delhi). This document examined precedent in England and in India under the 1935 Act, the 'intent of the framers', and the contemporary issues. The conclusion stresses the need for 'independent legal counsel' to help check abuses of power. The Swatantra Parliamentary Board, on 13 Jan. 1963, passed a resolution condemning the proposal, which would have required an amendment of Article 76 of the constitution.

88 The committee consisted of Munshi, as chairman, and a number of other distinguished former judges and advocates. For a list of the members and the terms of its commission, see the *General-Secretary's Report* to the first national convention (Patna), 1960, pp. 10–11.

89 That is, the demand for a separate Punjabi-speaking state, which would also be a Sikh-majority state. The criticism of Munshi by Sikhs was widespread. See the *Report of the Punjab Enquiry Committee* (Bombay, Swatantra Party, 1960), and the *General-Secretary's Report* to the second national convention (Agra), 1961, p. 18. For press comments on the Punjab report, see *Swatantra Newsletter* (*SN*), no. 11, Nov. 1960.

90 For some other works by Munshi, see the bibliography.

91 *Hindu*, 21 May 1961.

92 *Communist Party of India*, p. 15.

93 Based on interviews, Bombay and Delhi, 1962–3.

94 *HWR*, 28 Aug. 1961.

95 *Government and Politics*, p. 156.

96 Notwithstanding Savarkar's effusive praise for the Parsis (*Hindu Rashtra Darshan*, p. 69), the latter have nothing to gain and a good deal to lose from a marked resurgence of militant Hinduism. In some respects, the contrast between Rajaji and Munshi has been overdrawn, to emphasize the difference in style. In this connection, it is worth noting some aspects of Rajaji's relations with Christians. At one point, Rajaji sent a letter of congratulations to a group of re-converts to Hinduism, which in many eyes—Christian and non-Christian—was tantamount to Hindu communalism. However, two leading Madras Swatantrites, Dr M. Santosham and Prof. M. Ruthnaswamy, both Christians, regard Rajaji very highly and do not feel that the aforementioned action makes him a communalist, and their conclusion seems well taken. Rajaji certainly has a tremendous pride in the Hindu tradition as he understands it, and he is confident that it can be purged of some of its worst defects, without rejecting it completely. In this light, he was naturally gratified when some 'defectors' returned to their spiritual 'home'. This is akin to Gandhi's view of *swadeshi* as applied to religion, viz. that one should remain with one's ancestral religion and reform it where it is deficient. Such a view is not, however, equivalent to the militant demand for aggressive efforts at reconversion, which is a high-priority item. On this score, Rajaji would seem to escape censure, as his Christian colleagues argue.

97 It is worth restating that Savarkar, *Hindu Rashtra*, p. 122, said that many non-Hindu minorities, but especially the Parsis, are 'too allied to us in culture and too patriotic' to be anti-national or out of the national mainstream. Still, the westernized Bombay Parsi is quite isolated from the dominant 'political culture' of India.

98 Brecher, *Nehru*, p. 86.

99 For the Swaraj Party, see H. K. Singh, *Praja Socialist Party*, pp. 1–4.

100 See the introduction to vol. I of Dave, *Munshi*, and vol. II, *passim*, for these points. Both Munshi and Rajaji were further isolated after the death of Sardar Patel.

101 See Harrison, *Dangerous Decades*, pp. 207 ff. He notes (p. 207) that 'at the end of the war' Ranga 'was on the far fringes of the Andhra Congress power structure', in large measure because he was a Kamma in the Reddy-dominated Congress. In 1945–6 (p. 218), Ranga tried to organize 'a compact political striking force, bent upon increasing Kamma influence in the Congress while at the same time fighting the Communists by reciting the story of Stalin and the peasant'. His fortunes from 1945 to 1951 'went first upward and then to rock bottom' and he formed the KLP, which, with the CPI, was one of the 'champions of the delta' in Andhra (then still part of Madras). See *ibid.* pp. 226–8. For the electoral performance of the KLP see Poplai (ed.), *1957 Elections*; Mehta, *Political Mind*, pp. 10–12, 23 and 27; and Kogekar and Park, *Reports*, chapter on Madras. The KLP had some strength among the Jats of Rajasthan, particularly in Bharatpur district, in Gujarat, and elsewhere. For the association with the Congress, see *TI*, 23 Aug. 1957, where it is noted that there were 31 members of the APCC executive, 'but no room has been found in such a large body for Mr N. G. Ranga'. See Harrison, *Dangerous Decades*, pp. 283 ff., and Weiner, *Party Politics*, p. 260, for somewhat conflicting statements on the precise relationship between the KLP and the Congress. Upon his resignation from the Congress in 1959, Ranga was confronted with a demand that he resign from the *Lok Sabha* as well, at which point Ranga insisted that he was not formally a Congressman when he was elected, even though in 1959 he was Secretary of the Congress parliamentary party.

102 For his letter of resignation and other pertinent material see Ranga, *Freedom in Peril*, pp. 148–59 and *passim*. The long and turbulent career of this man provides an excellent case study in the role of caste, ideology, and power factors, and their interaction, in Indian politics, although this cannot be gone into here.

103 This is irrelevant in the sense that it does not tell us very much about critical aspects of Swatantra's contribution to Indian political life. It is not irrelevant to the extent that the quest for power is held in very low esteem in India. Such charges against Swatantra could remotely affect its political fortunes.

104 Recall here the appeal to Narayan to assume the leadership of the party. Even the more moderate Swatantra leaders did not drag their heels as much as did the aristocrats, who were not prominent in the early days of the party. As we shall see, however, the aristocrats are of crucial importance to Swatantra. An important aspect of this important issue is the fact that the princes in particular have considerable residual appeal but are often not attuned to competitive party politics. The following chapters develop this point at great length.
105 Based on interviews in Bombay, 1962.

CHAPTER 6, pp. 109–146

1 The last of the party's twenty-one 'fundamental principles' gives members complete freedom on all issues not covered in the preceding twenty principles. See chapter 8.
2 E. P. W. daCosta, 'Indian Politics Today and Tomorrow—Assessment and Prophecy', *Far Eastern Economic Review*, XXVII, 5 (4 Feb. 1960), 161.
3 The Tamilnad Democratic Party to which daCosta referred is presumably the INDC, previously known as the Congress Reform Committee (CRC).
4 *Preparatory Convention*, p. 27.
5 *TI*, 28 July 1959, reported that the INDC had voted unanimously to merge.
6 As late as *HWR*, 17 April 1961, it was reported only that the INDC 'has practically identified itself with...Swatantra'. By this time, many INDC men had already dissociated themselves from Swatantra, citing the reactionary views of Rajaji and the party generally. See *Link*, 24 April 1960. Biographical sketches of some leading INDC-Swatantra men are found in *Souvenir 1960*, pp. 100 and 107.
7 George Rosen, *Democracy and Economic Change in India* (Berkeley, University of California Press, 1965) and André Beteille, *Caste, Class, and Power* (Berkeley, University of California Press, 1965), both refer to Rajaji's appeal to and support for Swatantra from Brahmins.
8 *Link*, 30 Dec. 1962. For the discussion of the INDC, I am indebted to L. I. Rudolph, who has provided me with much information, much of which appears in his 'Urban Life', *JAS*, XX.
9 For the quotation, see *Link*, 31 Jan. 1960. This account notes that the Toilers Party is based largely on 'the backward Vanniya community'.
10 See L. I. Rudolph, 'Urban Life', *JAS*, XX, and Rudolph and Rudolph, 'Political Role', *PA*, XXXIII. According to the former, p. 294, both parties had merged with the Congress after Rajaji's departure and the subsequent 'democratization' of the Congress under Kamaraj. According to information supplied by L. I. Rudolph, the Toilers split, with part going to Swatantra, part to the Congress, and part to the CPI. This is a most important development, because only very shortly before, both Toilers and Commonweal were fairly compact action arms of the Vanniyars. For Padayachi, see also *SN*, no. 6, April–May 1960.

11 Rajaji mentioned the possibility of a merger at one point but it never came about. After Thevar's death, Swatantra and the Forward Bloc combined against the Congress in the by-election but were defeated.
12 *Statesman*, 5 Feb. 1962.
13 *Preparatory Convention*, p. 28.
14 According to *Hindu*, 21 Sept. 1959, Janata formally voted to merge on 20 September.
15 Darbhanga was also a leader of the effort to have *zamindari* abolition legislation invalidated in the courts, and he opposed the Hindu Code reforms. He himself did not join Swatantra or openly support it, about which more will be said below. For the Jan Congress, see *Souvenir 1960*, p. 112, and *SN*, no. 3, Jan. 1960.
16 From an interview with Paliwal in Agra, 1962. This discussion is based almost entirely on that interview.
17 *Ibid.*
18 As early as *HT*, 28 June 1959, Paliwal was reported to have been co-opted to the Swatantra executive bodies. For the Gram Raj merger, see *SN*, no. 1, Oct. 1959. According to *SN*, no. 6, April–May 1960, Paliwal led a group of twenty-three MLAs in the UP legislature.
19 For Nagoke's letter of resignation see *SN*, no. 1, Oct. 1959.
20 See Ranga, 'The Story', *Souvenir 1960.*
21 *Delhi Hindustan Standard*, 15 July 1959.
22 *TI*, 25 Feb. 1962.
23 Nagoke served with Munshi, Prof. M. Ruthnaswamy, and Maharani Gayatri Devi of Jaipur as Vice-Presidents.
24 *HWR*, 20 Nov. 1961.
25 See above, chapter 4.
26 See *Link*, 7 Feb. 1960, where it was stated that Ramgarh was negotiating with Orissa princes; *Link*, 18 April 1961, for a report of later talks; and *HWR*, 25 Jan. 1960, where Kalahandi is quoted as saying that talk of merger was 'baseless' and that there were no discussions whatever concerning a merger.
27 For a discussion of the advantages of coalition from the Parishad-Swatantra standpoint see *TI*, 19 May 1960. The writer of the account suggested that the coalition would be maintained (as far as the Parishad and Swatantra were concerned) until the eve of the 1962 general elections, at which time the Parishad might be more willing to consider a merger with Swatantra.
28 For the quotation, see *TI*, 3 April 1961. See also *Link*, 16 April 1961.
29 This was Harihar Das, son of a former Congress Chief Minister.
30 See *TI*, 18 April 1961, for a condemnation of the proposed accord by Sanjiva Reddy, who said that this proved that the Parishad was truly reactionary; *TI*, 19 April 1961, noted that no accord was reached and that Ramgarh was engaged in further talks; *TI*, 26 April 1961, for a report that the state Swatantra unit wanted to contest the elections but would under no circumstances fight the Parishad. For another statement on co-operation in the mid-term elections, see *HT*, 6 April 1961.

31 Based on interviews with Kalahandi, Patna, and Lokanath Misra (MP, *Rajya Sabha*), New Delhi, 1963.

32 For a preliminary report on the talks see *TI*, 12 Oct. 1961. For the latter, see *HWR*, 20 Nov. 1961. The discussions dwelt on many organizational and policy matters, such as the relationship between the infant Swatantra organization in Orissa and that of the Parishad and the extent to which the Parishad could continue to emphasize local issues.

33 *HWR*, 20 Nov. 1961. The statement announced that details would be discussed by Masani and Ranga for Swatantra and by Dr Ram Prasad Misra (President), Kalahandi and Patna, for the Parishad. The actual merger was postponed until after the 1962 elections, because of the problem with respect to the electoral symbol. Had the merger taken place in 1961, the Parishad-Swatantra candidates would have been obliged to use the Swatantra star symbol, rather than the familiar Parishad bow-and-arrow. The Election Commission could have made an exception but it refused, in part because it had already made an exception for Ramgarh who asked to use the Janata bicycle symbol instead of the star.

34 From an interview with a Parishad leader who has asked to remain nameless here.

35 From Swatantra Party files.

36 From an interview with Kalahandi, New Delhi, 1963.

37 *Ibid.* The reference to the umbrella was prompted by talks, after the Chinese invasion in 1962, of a US–UK 'air umbrella' to protect India against air attack. With respect to funds, the Parishad received at least Rs. 250,000 from Swatantra for the 1962 elections.

38 See *HWR*, 7 March 1960, and *SN*, no. 6, April–May 1960.

39 See Morris-Jones, *Government and Politics*, p. 160, and chapters 4 and 5 above for some points on Ranga, the KLP, and the Democratic Party. See also *SN*, no. 2, Nov. 1959; *HT*, 13 Feb. 1962; and *Hindu*, 14 Feb. 1962.

40 For Gujarat, see Kirtidev Desai, 'Emergence of the Swatantra Party in Gujarat', *Journal of the Gujarat Research Society* (*JGRS*), XXV, 2 (April 1963), 143–51, and Devavrat Pathak, M. G. Parekh and Kirtidev Desai, *Three General Elections in Gujarat* (Ahmedabad, Gujarat University, 1966), *passim.*

41 There were also some defections from some of these parties, about which more will be said below.

42 See *Link*, 14 Feb. 1960; and *SN*, no. 8, July 1960, no. 11, Oct. 1960, no. 21, Aug. 1961, and no. 17, April 1961. These groups were not of uniformly high status.

43 See *SN*, no. 7, June 1960, and *Link*, 14 Feb. 1960.

44 For Gujarat *kshatryas* see Kothari and Maru, 'Caste and Secularism', *JAS*, XXV, 35–50; Weiner, *MS*; Desai, *JGRS*, XXV, 143–51; and Pathak *et al. Three General Elections*, *passim.*

45 *Ibid.*

46 Certain Gujarat Rajputs, in particular, cited 'external' influence.

47 E.g. Kamma and Reddy landed interests.

48 Based in part on biographical data in *Souvenir 1960* and on information supplied by Miss Carolyn Elliot, who did field work in Andhra for two years (1962–4) as a Fulbright grantee.

49 See the list in *Preparatory Convention*, pp. 36–40.

50 Paul Brass, *Factional Politics in an Indian State* (Berkeley, University of California Press 1965), ch. 4, 'Gonda'.

51 See *SN*, no. 3, Jan. 1960, for the Punjab and Bhinai; and no. 7, June 1960, for Dungarpur. For Bhalindra Singh see *HT*, 16 Sept. 1959, and for the later entry of Banswara see *SN*, no. 21, Aug. 1961, and *TI*, 25 Oct. 1961.

52 For Bhadawar, *Statesman*, 14 Feb. 1962. He had joined the party much earlier than the date of this report, however. For further material on Mankapur, *Statesman*, 29 Jan. 1962.

53 For Kaluhera, *SN*, no. 6, April–May 1960. The statement by Zamindar is from party files.

54 See *HT*, 29 Jan. 1961, for her entry. One such reluctant *jagirdar* was Major Thakur Raghubir Singh of Bissau, to whom the government still owed substantial compensation payments. A successful RRP candidate for the assembly in 1952, Bissau joined Congress prior to the 1957 elections (though he was not given a Congress ticket), and then lost interest in active politics until the Maharani brought her pressure to bear on him and other *jagirdars*.

55 See *Statesman*, 7 May 1961, for a statement by Gayatri Devi about her husband's political career.

56 See *HT*, 29 Jan. 1961, and *Link*, 12 March 1961, for some remarks about the *durbar* and for Ranga's remark that it was 'silly'. For *Lok Sabha* comment, *Link*, 5 March 1961.

57 Jodhpur's death in an airplane crash immediately after the elections contributed to the collapse of the front, which was precarious, in any event, due to the split between 'big' and 'little' Rajputs.

58 *Link*, 5 Feb. 1961. See also *Statesman*, 22 Oct. 1961.

59 For Congress consideration of this question, see *HWR*, 29 May and 28 Aug. 1961, and *Link*, 21 May 1961.

60 *Statesman*, 22 Oct. 1961.

61 See *Link*, 21 Feb. 1960, and *HT*, 12 May 1960. The early date suggests a healthy respect for the possibility of an anti-Congress Rajput resurgence, before the Maharani's entry. According to the former report, Sukhadia, 'in his anxiety to gain supporters, seems to have overlooked the fact that most of the new entrants to his cabinet are not ideologically at one with him. Ex-ruler Harishchandra often sounds like a Swatantri.' The former Chief Minister, Jai Narain Vyas, had built up his power in part by cultivating Rajput support.

62 *Statesman*, 22 Oct. 1961. In a wise move, Vyas did not in fact contest against the Maharani, whose majority was so great that all other candidates forfeited their security deposits. Vyas would have been wiser still had he not stood against Maharajkumar Jai Singh of Jaipur, one of the Maharaja's sons by a previous marriage—as he lost this contest for an assembly seat.

63 Based on party files.

64 Devgadh-Baria had married a daughter of the Jaipur family, but he and his wife had separated.
65 Based on party files.
66 See *Link*, 13 and 20 March and 17 April 1960, for these points.
67 E.g. M. A. Sreenivasan, to be discussed below, and B. V. Narayana Reddy, once a joint treasurer with Mody. Reddy had been with the State Bank of Mysore.
68 See, for example, *Link*, 31 July 1960.
69 *Link*, 15 Jan. 1961. Bastar was finally deposed.
70 Based on interviews. In a major party split, some state leaders of Swatantra supported an independent candidate against the Maharaja, over the decision of the local unit. Baroda's brother was scheduled to contest an assembly seat for Swatantra in the 1967 elections.
71 *Link*, 5 Feb. 1961, reported that Bikaner had 'apparently' joined Swatantra and other sources reported the same news.
72 See *TI*, 25 Oct. 1961, where it is noted that she would campaign with Gayatri Devi and the two Maharanis of Banswara. See *Statesman*, 22 Nov. 1961, for a statement by Rajaji to the effect that she would only endorse a slate of candidates but would neither contest herself nor campaign for her endorsed slate.
73 *Link*, 28 May 1961.
74 The Maharani of Jaipur, Himmatsinhji of Kutch, Dungarpur, and Devgadh-Baria also campaigned for Masani. At least the *Yuvarajes* of Wankaner and Jasdan have since openly joined Swatantra, along with a number of other Saurashtra aristocrats.
75 See *Statesman*, 13 Feb. 1962, and *TI*, 16 Feb. 1962. In late 1966 it was announced that Bharatpur would stand as an independent against Congress.
76 *HT*, 14 and 22 Jan. 1962, and *Statesman*, 30 Jan. 1962.
77 From an interview in 1962.
78 For Sukhadia's remark, *Link*, 25 Jan. 1961.
79 Swatantra was most worried about the Maharani's ability to fight an energetic campaign, but she has declared her intention to do so. There have also been reports that Jaipur would resign his ambassadorial post prior to the 1967 elections.
80 *TI*, 15 and 16 Jan. 1961, for the quotations.
81 *Link* delights in pointing out 'feudal' elements in Swatantra (as does *SN*, but without the same flourish, or bias). See *Link*, 13 and 20 March, 10 and 17 April, 25 Sept., 10 Oct. and 18 Dec. 1960; 15 Jan., 5, 12 and 26 Feb., 9 April, 28 May and 22 Aug. 1961, for some salient examples.
82 From an interview, Delhi, 1962.
83 From an interview, Delhi, 1963.
84 From an interview, Delhi, 1963.
85 From a questionnaire.
86 From an interview, Jaipur, 1962. In interviews, virtually every Swatantra aristocrat made substantially the same comment.
87 This was quoted in chapter 2.
88 From a report on the 1962 elections in Bihar, submitted to the

central office by Ramgarh. These words were widely quoted in the press and *SN*.

89 *My Humble Contributions*, p. 148. For other statements by Kalahandi which suggest his 'resilient' outlook, see *ibid.* pp. 39–41, 61–2, 74–5, 103, 107, 146–8 and 264.

90 Lloyd I. and Susanne H. Rudolph, mimeo on political development in Rajasthan. (This is *not* the same as Susanne Rudolph, *MS*, from which we have quoted above.) This material will appear in their *The Modernity of Tradition: Political Development in India* (Chicago, University of Chicago Press, 1967).

91 They make the argument particularly with respect to the Jaipur family.

92 The questionnaire asked which Congressmen at the national or state level were sympathetic to the Swatantra point of view.

93 Based on an interview, Bombay, 1962.

94 Quoted in *Modern Review*, CV, 6 (June 1959), 438. See also *Hindu*, 15 Sept. 1959, for a comparable statement.

95 From an interview, Bombay, 1962.

96 E.g. Vasantrao Oak and Mrs Manmohini Sehgal in the Delhi unit were political itinerants who inspired little confidence.

97 *HT*, 26 June 1961. Mahtab was Chief Minister in the Congress-Parishad coalition ministry.

98 During 1962–3 there were frequent press reports of statements by Mahtab and Hanumanthaya, along these lines.

99 From an interview, Delhi, 1962. See his privately printed volume *The Second Phase*, a collection of speeches made in the Rajya Sabha. Much of Dahyabhai's distress flows from the fact that the Congress failed to honour his father's memory properly. This bitterness notwithstanding, his *Rajya Sabha* performance has been quite good.

100 Based on a questionnaire. See also *TI*, 16 July 1959, for Patel and Joshi.

101 See Pathak *et al. Three General Elections*; Desai, *JGRS*, XXV; *Dr Bhailalbhai Patel 75th Birthday Souvenir* (Vallabh Vidyanagar, Charutar Vidyamandal, 1963), and *Shri Bhailalbhai Patel 70th Birthday Souvenir* (Vallabh Vidyanagar, Charutar Vidyamandal, 1958). The last two volumes contain material in both English and Gujarati.

102 *Link*, 6 March 1960. E. M. S. Nambudiripad, CPI leader in Kerala, asked Chatterjee to conduct an inquiry into conditions in that state. See also chapter 3, above, and *TI*, 11 July 1959 (for the Sangh's interest in Chatterjee).

103 Based on an interview, Madras, 1962.

104 Based on a questionnaire, to which he appended a lengthy, unsolicited statement about the Indian party system.

105 The *Lok Sabha Who's Who* (New Delhi, Lok Sabha Secretariat, 1962), will provide pertinent biographical data. For Aney, see *Sunday Standard*, 28 April 1963. The above account is based on interviews and party files.

106 Based on interviews and party files.

107 Based on an interview, Bombay, 1963. Lobo Prabhu held high posts in Madras and at the centre. See his weekly publication *Insight* (Mangalore) and his frequent contributions to *Swarajya.* See also his *New Thinking* (Bombay, India Book House, 1959), which is an analysis of the second five-year plan; his *Third-Plan X-Rayed* (n.d.), reprinted from *Commerce,* 24 Sept. and 1, 8, 15 and 29 Oct. 1960; and his *Industrial Policy* (Calcutta, Society for the Propagation of Democratic Truth, 1963), for more elaborate statements on economic affairs.
108 Based on questionnaires. Sreenivasan is associated with a number of the premier textile and plantation industries in South India.
109 For V. N. Rao, see *Swarajya,* 29 Aug. 1959, and for a later discussion of the function of his office, see V. T. Sreenivasan, 'Can the Comptroller and Auditor-General Make Himself Felt?', *Swarajya* (Special Number, 1963). pp. 117–20. For Pasricha, see 'Our Stuporous Society', *Quest* (April–June 1962), pp. 32–3, and 'Free Economy and the Wealth of Nations' (Delhi, Swatantra Party, 1963), the latter being adapted from *Swarajya* (Special Number, 1963). Menon's 'Planning Commission and State Autonomy', *Swarajya* (Special Number, 1962), pp. 98–9, is also useful here.
110 See *Shri H. M. Patel 60th Birthday Commemoration Volume* (Vallabh Vidyanagar, Charutar Vidyamandal, 1964), with material in both English and Gujarati. Patel was secretary in the finance ministry during the Mundhra scandal but was cleared after an inquiry. He resigned, however, and soon took up work with Bhailalbhai Patel, whom he eventually replaced as head of some Vallabh Vidyanagar activities. There was also some pressure in 1966 to have H. M. Patel replace Bhaikaka as leader of Swatantra in Gujarat, but thus far, H. M. Patel has contented himself with a major re-organization of the state party apparatus, which has placed the Gujarat unit on much sounder footing.
111 The business recruits will be discussed separately below.
112 For mention of ICS distress see S. H. Rudolph, 'Consensus and Conflict', *World Politics,* XIII; Zinkin, *India Changes,* where the ICS men are listed with the princes, landlords, and some businessmen as the 'dispossessed' of post-independence India; and Nehru, *The Discovery of India,* ed. and abridged by R. Crane (Garden City, Anchor Books, 1959), pp. 297 ff., for the ICS between 1937 and 1939.
113 See, for example, A. D. Gorwala, 'The Administration Today', *Swarajya* (Special Number, 1962), pp. 51–2.
114 Patel was quite popular among ICS men because they felt that he tried to protect the services against erosion, demoralization, meddling, etc.
115 Quoted in Harrison, *Dangerous Decades,* pp. 3 and 91.
116 From a questionnaire, where this opinion was volunteered, i.e. no question raised this issue or anything close to it.
117 From an interview in Bombay, 1963.
118 *Swarajya,* 4 Sept. and 24 July 1965, respectively.
119 *Swarajya,* 24 July 1965.
120 From an interview, Jaipur, 1963.

121 See *TI*, 8 July 1959, and *Delhi Hindustan Standard*, 9 July 1959.
122 See *Swarajya*, 8 and 25 May 1965.
123 Aristocrats, administrators, and other professionals joined in this view, but it is important to note that the aristocrats are very likely to succeed in the battle for votes (even where they find the competitive party system distasteful), whereas administrators are not.
124 Quoted *SN*, no. 18, May 1961.
125 *Swarajya*, 9 Jan. 1965.
126 'Where Ministers Accumulate and Administration Decays', *Swarajya* (Special Number, 1962), p. 57.
127 'Swatantra Party's Contribution to Democracy', *Souvenir 1961*, p. 36, and, in general, pp. 36–8.
128 See the discussion of business ideology, chapter 2, above.
129 The suffering may be more psychological than material, although prohibition in Bombay hurt Parsis economically. A number of Parsi and Christian leaders interviewed in India emphasized the fact that they felt 'at sea' since the British left and that they had turned to Swatantra because of the latter's more moderate, tolerant perspectives.
130 See the discussion of Rajaji in chapter 5 above.
131 See the discussion of Masani in chapter 5 above.
132 An intentionally vague question was asked about the respondent's feelings about the Hindu Code. This does not mean that all supporters of the Code are *ipso facto* liberal or modern or that all opponents are *ipso facto* conservative or reactionary; but in the context of social background, etc., of the respondents, the responses become very significant.
133 See the titles cited in the discussion of Lobo Prabhu, in the preceding section of this chapter.
134 'Fifteen Years of Democracy', *Swarajya* (Special Number, 1962), p. 36. Cf. Rajaji's 'Gandhiji's Teachings', *Swarajya* (Special Number, 1963).
135 'Our Stuporous Society', *Quest* (April–June 1962), pp. 23–38, is the source for all of these remarks by Pasricha.
136 Some of these limitations are discussed below; others will be evident from an examination of the electoral data in the tables in Appendix II.
137 Latchanna, state President in Andhra, is the most notable *harijan* office bearer.
138 This will be discussed further in the next chapter. At the national level, we have already noted the presence of two Parsis in the inner circle. For a time, two Hindus (Munshi and Gayatri Devi) served with a Christian (Ruthnaswamy) and a Sikh (Nagoke) as Vice-Presidents. In Madras, Ruthnaswamy and Dr M. Santosham, a Christian doctor, are prominent, although most leaders are high caste Hindus. In Mysore, we find a Jain (Hegde), a Lingayat (Rao Bahadur B. L. Patil), a Christian (Lobo Prabhu) and a Muslim (Imam), among the top leaders.
139 See the tables in Appendix II.
140 *Ibid.*
141 The state of Rajasthan was divided into zones, for electoral and

organizational purposes, and all three Swatantra MPs came from the Maharani's zone. This zonal division will be discussed further in the next chapter.

142 See *Hindu*, 14 May 1960, for Reddiar's defection and *HWR*, 7 March 1960, for the return to Congress of ten MLAs who had followed Ranga.

143 R. P. Misra, once Parishad President, entered the Congress, as did Rani Nabakumari Devi, also of the Parishad. S. Supakar, another former President, responded to the merger by declaring that he would not himself stand as a candidate and that he would not support the party's candidates actively. See *HT*, 12 Feb. and 22 April 1962, for Supakar, Misra, and the Rani. Swatantra leaders were adamant after Misra entered the Congress, claiming that Patnaik had engaged in unethical practices to weaken opposition parties.

CHAPTER 7, pp. 147–187

1 See chapter 8 for Swatantra's formal doctrine.

2 Not all 'modern' men are liberal, but the emphasis here will be on those in Swatantra who are inclined to be both.

3 See above, chapter 5, for details of Rajaji's views.

4 Based on interviews, Delhi, 1962 and 1963.

5 Based on party files.

6 Based on interviews and on *Link*, 31 July 1960 and 12 Nov. 1961. Morris-Jones, *Government and Politics*, p. 156, also refers to the use of religious appeals by Swatantra. See also chapter 8, below, for this point.

7 For a discussion of this general issue, see *TI*, 24 Oct. 1966.

8 Based on questionnaire data.

9 *Communist Party of India*, p. 231.

10 See the statement by B. Madhok, *OHT*, 13 May 1965. *SN*, no. 4, Feb. 1960, refers to the inclusion of Hindu, Muslim, Parsi, and Christian prayers, hymns, etc., at Bombay City meetings.

11 Based on interviews, party files, and correspondence.

12 Based on extended interviews with all major Swatantra leaders in Rajasthan, Jaipur, 1962 and 1963. The Gujarat case was discussed in chapter 6, above.

13 Based on interviews and correspondence.

14 Based on interviews, Jaipur, 1962 and 1963.

15 Based on interviews and party files. Man Singh has since resigned.

16 Based on interviews, Jaipur, 1962 and 1963.

17 Based on correspondence. Padayachi has founded a new, strictly local party once again.

18 Based on party files and correspondence.

19 Bhailalbhai Patel's death would also encourage aristocrats in Gujarat to assert their position.

20 *Government and Politics*, p. 160.

21 From a questionnaire. Other Orissa respondents made much the same comment.

22 *Statesman*, 7 May 1961. Dungarpur is reported to have admitted the existence of considerable bitterness between Rajputs and Jats, but he did not elaborate on what he meant by 'unusual' concessions. Little has been done, to this date, to gain the confidence of the Jats.
23 Based on party files and interviews.
24 Based on party files.
25 From a questionnaire.
26 Translated for the author from the Hindi weekly *Chetana*, 17 April 1962, from a copy in Swatantra files.
27 Translated from *Chetana*, 15 May 1962. In this article, many leading Swatantrites (in UP and elsewhere) were mentioned by name.
28 See *OHT*, 12 Sept. 1963.
29 *Hindu*, 14 Sept. 1959.
30 'The National Appeal of the Swatantra Party', *Souvenir 1961*, p. 40.
31 *Ibid.*
32 *Ibid.* For an important study which bears upon the matter of the respectability of party, see Harvey Mansfield, Jr., *Statesmanship and Party Government* (Chicago, University of Chicago Press, 1965).
33 'National Appeal', *Souvenir 1961*, p. 40.
34 *Ibid.* pp. 40–1.
35 Based on interviews, Bombay, 1962.
36 From an interview. In a lighter vein, another Swatantra leader said, 'Ramgarh has an inferiority complex...he thinks he's Napoleon!'
37 From an interview, Agra, 1962.
38 Based on interviews, 1962 and 1963.
39 Based on interviews.
40 *Swarajya*, 19 Sept. 1964.
41 This will be discussed in detail shortly.
42 This will be discussed in detail shortly.
43 E.g. opposition to major public sector 'display' projects, acceptance of a 'Gandhian' approach to India's problems, etc. Some of these points are discussed in the next chapter.
44 The General Council was originally an appointed body, whose maximum size was 250. It was intended to embrace a cross-section of the national and state leadership. The COC was a smaller body which included the pivotal national and state figures. Under the revised party constitution of 1964, the COC became the 'national executive' and was to be elected by the General Council, with some provision for co-operation.
45 Only one party election has thus far been held, well after the 1962 elections. The Chinese invasion in 1962 in part frustrated plans for party elections. Internal difficulties also played a part here.
46 Based on interviews and party files.
47 The absence of a cohesive aristocracy bears on this problem and can cut both ways in organizational terms. On the one hand, it means that the defection of even a major aristocrat will not necessarily lead all others out of the party. On the other hand, it means that Swatantra cannot even count on aristocratic solidarity as a substitute for a more formal party organization.

48 Based on interviews, Baroda and Ahmedabad, 1966.

49 Based on interviews and personal observation at party meetings. Devi Singh has since been replaced as state General-Secretary by a retired IAS officer, Mandhata Singh. Devi Singh is now an MP (*Rajya Sabha*).

50 Based on interviews, Jaipur, 1963.

51 *Ibid.*

52 The author was present at at least two meetings at which Dungarpur made such a statement.

53 Based on interviews, 1962 and 1963.

54 Based on interviews, party files, and personal observation at party meetings, 1962 and 1963.

55 Based on interviews and party files.

56 Based on an appeal from the Bihar unit to the General Council and on rejoinders submitted by the central office, made available to the author by the central office.

57 The author was in Bombay when the General Council considered the Bihar appeal and all major figures were interviewed.

58 Based on correspondence with close associates of the Raja. The loan is discussed by Rajaji, *Swarajya*, 19 Sept. 1964.

59 Based on *OHT*, 6 and 27 Aug. 1964, and on correspondence.

60 Based on *OHT*, 27 Aug. 1964, and on correspondence.

61 *OHT*, 24 Sept. 1964. The decision was announced on 12 Sept. at which time it was said that 'only details of the merger remain to be worked out...'.

62 Based on *Swarajya*, 19 Sept. 1964, a news statement issued by the central office (dated 1 Oct.), and correspondence.

63 E.g. after the 1963 appeal from Bihar was withdrawn and Ramgarh was instructed to reconstitute the state executive along lines defined by the central office, a number of papers expressed satisfaction that Swatantra rejected Ramgarh's demand for unfettered powers. For further details on Ramgarh, Swatantra, and Congress, see: *TI*, 9 and 10 Sept 1964, and *HT*, 10 and 11 Sept. 1964; *Statesman*, 17 and 25 May 1965, and *Indian Nation* (Bihar), 24 May 1965. After remaining in limbo for an extended period, Ramgarh contemplated the restoration of Janata and a merger with Jharkand, which had latterly left the Congress. However, Ramgarh and almost all of his followers finally entered the Congress.

64 *OHT*, 24 Sept. 1964.

65 See Maurice Duverger, *Political Parties*, trans. Barbara and Robert North (London, Methuen, 1954), p. 359, notes that 'cadre parties, which have no strong financial backing and live in perpetual money difficulties, are always soft-hearted towards candidates willing to cover the costs of the campaign and in practice investiture is obtained without any difficulty'. On the other hand, he points out, p. 59, that if the central office receives a substantial proportion of the funds available to fight elections, this can be used to discipline local units, candidates, etc., which is precisely what Masani has tried to do.

66 There have been efforts to deny tickets to Congress 'rejects', as well as those from other parties; but while most parties agree to this in principle, they depart from it by a wide margin in practice.

67 For Rajaji, *Swarajya*, 19 Sept. 1959, and for Mody, *SN*, no. 1, Oct. 1959. See also 'Which is the Rich Man's Party?', *Swarajya*, 4 Sept. 1959. *SN*, no. 5, March 1960, quotes Rajaji as saying that 'the heart of the rich is with us but their money is with the Congress because of compulsion'.

68 For Birla, *Link*, 31 Jan. 1960. For the second remark, by Karunakaran, see his introduction to Poplai (ed.), *1962 Elections*, p. 18.

69 For the proposed ban, *HWR*, 15 Aug. 1960, *Link*, 21 Aug. 1960, and *HWR*, 7 Aug. 1961. For Masani's statement, see *HWR*, 7 Aug. 1961, or *TI*, 2 Aug. 1961. Under the then existing company law, a joint stock company could contribute Rs. 25,000 or 5 per cent of its net profits, whichever was higher.

70 Tata was head of the great Tata empire. Khatau was head of Associated Cement Companies and was also on the board of the Central Bank of India (the 'Tata bank'), of which Mody was then chairman. Dandekar was once a director of Associated Cement. For one reference to the appeal, *Hindu*, 2 Aug. 1961. This entire discussion is, however, based on party files and on interviews.

71 Based on party files, interviews, and a limited amount of public information. For some financial data see the *General Secretary's Report* to the second national convention (Agra), pp. 6–7. See also *Swarajya*, 20 April 1963, for a discussion of the Tata-Khatau contributions to Swatantra and to the Congress. *Link*, 17 Sept. 1961, refers to a 'great capitalist house' which had decided to give a substantial sum to Swatantra but more to the Congress. *Link*, 6 Aug. 1961, notes that a Madras textile man had given both Swatantra and the Congress Rs. 16,000. *TI*, 6 Sept. 1961, noted that Sir Biren Mookerjee, chairman of the board of Indian Iron and Steel had announced prospective contributions to Congress and to an opposition party—the latter in the interests of strengthening democracy in India. The anonymous gifts were discussed with Swatantra leaders who insisted that the same people had given more to the Congress, openly. The Ahmedabad case was discussed with Patel, Bombay, 1962. Also, Rajaji received many large gifts, as personal tributes, and these were presumably turned over to the party. See, for example, *TI*, 7 April 1960, for a report of a purse of Rs. 100,000 from textile men in Kanpur. State units also received contributions, too, but no records of these were made available to the author. However, in 1966, Masani was most upset that leaders in Gujarat had solicited funds for the state unit from people whom he had planned to approach for central office funds. Masani accused these Gujarat leaders of ignoring the needs of the national party in financing campaigns in poor states (such as Orissa), but it is clear, too, that he wanted to have these funds to use as a lever in controlling state units and individual candidates. See below for a full discussion of this point.

72 The official minutes of the COC note a shortfall of Rs. 1,000,000 with respect to the goal set for the national fund.

73 Based in part on party files. One source stated that certain Akali Dal candidates for the *Lok Sabha* each received Rs. 30,000 from Swatantra, which suggests that this amount was generally provided to aspiring MPs who were endorsed by the national party.

74 Based on interviews, Jaipur, 1963.
75 From the *General Secretary's Report*, to the third national convention (Bangalore), 1 and 2 Feb. 1964, p. 14.
76 Based on interviews, 1963 and 1966, and on correspondence. The financial picture of the Gujarat unit had brightened considerably by 1966, and many major industrialists were themselves planning to contest for the *Lok Sabha* from Gujarat, on Swatantra tickets.
77 E.g. in 1964, at the Bhubaneshwar session of the Congress, a resolution urging nationalization of all banking and of food grain trade was turned down.
78 Based on party files.
79 Based on party files and on interviews. Most Swatantra leaders in Gujarat felt that they had contested too many seats in that state, for the assembly at least.
80 Based on party files.
81 *Political Parties*, p. 359.
82 Based on party files. See *Hindu*, 2 Nov. 1961, for a report of the resignation.
83 Based on party files.
84 Based on interviews with Masani and Rajasthan leaders, 1963.
85 Based on the Bihar unit's appeal and the rejoinder thereto. Masani would have insisted on using the Swatantra star symbol and on otherwise identifying himself as a Swatantrite.
86 From the central office rejoinder to the Bihar appeal.
87 See *HT*, 6 Jan. 1962, for a statement by Masani to the effect that he would not contest a *Lok Sabha* seat in 1962.
88 Based on interviews, correspondence, and party files. The record of Swatantra MPs from Bihar was, to say the most, dismal.
89 See *Statesman*, 24 May and 1 June 1963; *Patriot*, 29 May 1963; and *Amrit Bazar Patrika*, 3 June 1963.
90 To some extent, the problem is a personal one, because Masani is often brusque, impatient, etc., but much resentment among state and local leaders is due to the pressure that Masani applies to further the cause of the modern wing of the party.
91 See, for example, *Statesman*, 29 Jan. 1962.
92 Based on interviews, Bombay and Baroda, 1966.
93 E.g. Lobo Prabhu might have been returned in this fashion, although there is no indication that he wanted to sit in the *Rajya Sabha*, let alone from Rajasthan.
94 Based on party files and on correspondence.
95 From questionnaires and follow-up interviews.
96 This is discussed in the next chapter.
97 See the party constitution, as revised 2 Feb. 1964, at the third national convention (Bangalore), clauses 4, 5, and 5*a*. The party is divided into life workers, who must pay a minimum of Rs. 100 for life membership; workers, who must pay Rs. 3 per annum, and members, who pay nothing but must sign a statement supporting the fundamental principles of the party. Only the first two groups are eligible to vote in

party elections. Enrolment of workers does not technically require the approval of the national organization, although its advice, where sought, is binding. On the other hand, the national executive may expel a worker entirely on its own authority.

98 Based on correspondence and on interviews in India, 1966.

99 Based on interviews, correspondence, and party files.

100 Based on interviews and party files.

101 Based on interviews and party files. A number of other businessmen, including some quite young ones, also joined Swatantra in Gujarat and were planning to contest for public office in 1967.

102 Based on interviews. See C. Rai, 'Why I Took to Politics', a Rotary Club speech reprinted by the Swatantra party.

103 Based on correspondence with Swatantra leaders in Rajasthan.

104 Most businessmen, that is, are more concerned with protecting free enterprise from state controls rather than with pushing broadly liberal programmes. However, as questionnaire data on the Hindu Code measures suggest, there is a more broadly liberal dimension present as well. How aggressively it is, or can be propagated is another matter.

CHAPTER 8, pp. 188–211

1 *Towards Doom?* (Bombay, Swatantra Party, n.d.), pp. 7–8.

2 The emphasis on political affiliation is based on the party's contention that preferential treatment in all sectors is accorded to those who either belong to the Congress or help it financially.

3 These fragments are from the twenty-one points (fundamental principles). The last fragment, among others, suggests the 'constitutionalist' background of many leaders.

4 See Rajaji, 'To Save Freedom', in *Why Swatantra?* (Bombay, Swatantra Party, n.d.), p. 3. This publication contains short statements by Rajaji, Ranga, Munshi, and Masani on the general topic of 'why Swatantra?' See the manifesto 'To Prosperity Through Freedom', para. 7 of part IV.

5 *HT*, 27 Oct. 1959.

6 For the proposal that the Congress resign from office six months prior to a general election, see *HT*, 16 March 1962. For the permit-licence board recommendation, advanced strongly at the 1964 Bangalore convention, see *HWR*, 17 Feb. 1964; *HWR*, 10 Feb. 1964; and *Swarajya*, 15 Feb. 1964. See also A. P. Jain (ed.), *Lawless Legislation* (New Delhi, Swatantra Party Parliamentary Office, 1963), which is an attack on the 17th Amendment (prior to its passage); M. R. Masani, *The Fraud of Gold Control* (Bombay, Swatantra Party, 1964); M. R. Masani *et al.*, *The Budget versus The People* (Bombay, Swatantra Party, n.d.); N. Dandekar and Kapur Singh, *A Fair Deal for Public Servants* (Bombay, Swatantra Party, n.d.); M. R. Masani and N. Dandekar, *Judgment Reserved* (Bombay, Swatantra Party, n.d.), concerning a proposed motion of no-confidence. In 1966, an administrative reforms committee under Morarji Desai recommended the creation of an office like that of the *Ombudsman*; the gold control order was relaxed; abolition of land revenue was recommended by the Madras Congress and the cry was taken up elsewhere; licensing laws were eased; there was talk of 'plan holidays' and more modest plans; and the like, suggesting that the Swatantra critique was having some impact.

7 Rajaji, *Towards Doom?*, p. 9. See also the discussion of Rajaji, chapter 5.

8 From a questionnaire submitted by a Brahmin legislator.

9 See chapter 6.

10 'To Preserve Freedom', *Why Swatantra?* p. 5. Many Swatantrites do not, of course, reject legislative 'compulsion' and Rajaji himself, as noted in the preceding chapter, was associated with remedial legislation in the area of rents and interest on debts. Many of those who would be willing in some cases to countenance legislative 'coercion' are of the opinion that no such measures are required in the present context. Thus, anti-control positions are advanced for both 'moral' and 'practical' reasons.

11 See, for example, Munshi, *Reconstruction of Society*. Jayaprakash Narayan, former Communist and Socialist and now a Bhoodan leader, noted ('On Rajaji', in *Swarajya*, Special Number, 1962, p. 114) that trusteeship was a key notion for Rajaji 'which I am afraid is not shared by his colleagues'. He adds (*loc. cit.*) that 'the Swatantra Party has reconciled itself to that idea only as a token of regard for its great leader'. Narayan feels that trusteeship alone raises Swatantra conservatism to a respectable level.

12 For an 18-point manifesto, see *TI*, 28 June 1959, and for a 19-point manifesto, see *Statesman*, 16 June 1959. Masani, Munshi, Ranga, and Ruthnaswamy, in addition to Rajaji, are those most deeply involved in doctrinal matters. Drafts of various resolutions, etc., are also presented to various party organs, such as the Central Organizing Committee, the General Council, and to state leaders, about which something further will be said subsequently.

13 See chapter 5, above.

14 For a discussion which includes material on many industries, see Vithaldas Kothari (ed.), *Why Khadi and Village Industries?* (Ahmedabad, Navajivan Press, 1957).

15 Except as otherwise noted, all of the fragments quoted above come from the fundamental principles of 21 points.

16 See *Statesman*, 6 June 1960, for one of the numerous statements against the Planning Commission, as a 'super-cabinet', by Masani. He is reported here to have said, 'if the Swatantra Party had a chance, its first act would be to liquidate the Planning Commission'. See also *Delhi Hindustan Standard*, 19 May 1960, for the same argument.

17 See *HWR*, 28 Aug. 1961, and chapter 5, above. The anti-plan votes were recorded by those sitting MPs who joined Swatantra after its creation, and the battle has been carried on by its contingent in the present *Lok Sabha*.

18 From party files. Among those who asked to contest as independents was the head of the Madras FFE who had been a member of the Jan

Sangh until Swatantra was founded; a number of prospective *Lok Sabha* candidates from Mysore; J. Mohammed Imam, also from Mysore, who wanted to contest either as a PSP man or as an independent; Yashpal Singh of UP, who did contest as an independent, was opposed by a Swatantra candidate, won, and then joined the party! These are only a few of the many cases. Some did not mind the 'rich man' image, but were deterred by other factors, e.g. Rajaji's defence of English was held to be a liability in UP, as will be discussed below.

19 *OHT*, 5 Jan. 1961.

20 *HWR*, 30 May 1960, *TI*, 24 May 1960, and *HT*, 28 May 1960, for the statement by Hutheesing. The latter two also contain rejoinders by Vaidya. In words almost identical to those used by Paliwal much later, Hutheesing said that his 'instinct' made him apprehensive from the outset but that he wanted to make sure Swatantra was as bad as it seemed before resigning.

21 From party files. The author was permitted to examine all of the drafts of the party manifesto, with comments thereon from national and state leaders.

22 To some extent, all situations require a balance of the external and internal restraints, but the rejection of legislation as an instrument of policy goes a bit far in the voluntary direction!

23 From an editorial in the PSP weekly *Janata*, 9 Aug. 1959.

24 For the source, and the full quotation, see chapter 2, under the discussion of business ideology. Cf. Shroff's comment that the Congress had been put in office by an illiterate electorate with these remarks about 'the dynamic urge of democratic ideals'.

25 See, for example, Ranga's presidential address at the Patna Convention; his *Freedom in Peril*, pp. 115–47 ('Planning in India'); and his 'Swatantra and the Plan', *Swarajya* (Special Number, 1962), pp. 169–72. Also relevant is the Swatantra Manifesto, 'To Prosperity Through Freedom'. Munshi on one occasion asserted that 'Parliament, in fact does not govern the country...The nominated super-cabinet, the Planning Commission, does the supervision, control and direction of the Government of India, and owes no responsibility to Parliament' (quoted in Norman D. Palmer, *The Indian Political System* [Boston, Houghton Mifflin, 1961, p. 172]). Munshi advanced the same argument in 'To Restore Fundamental Rights', *Why Swatantra?*, p. 14: 'The Parliament is dominated by the Congress, the Party by its leader...And the super-Cabinet of the country—the nominated Planning Commission—is always there to bring errant ministers to heel. The National Development Council of ministers...has also arrogated to itself equal powers of a super-Cabinet.'

26 From a *Lok Sabha* address by Ranga, reprinted under the title 'No Truck with the Plan', in *What's Wrong with the Third Plan* (Bombay, Swatantra Party, n.d.), p. 27.

27 See, for example, the articles by Ruthnaswamy in *Swarajya*, 24 Aug. and 9 Nov. 1963.

28 *Indian Finance*, 8 Sept. 1962, p. 429. Those engaged in drafting the alternative plan are economics Professor B. R. Shenoy, J. M. Lobo Prabhu, Dandekar, Masani and a few others. Lobo Prabhu has prepared a variety of drafts, ranging in length from a dozen or so pages to close to one hundred, indicating some of the major contours of a possible Swatantra plan. To this writer's knowledge, none of these have been published in any form, but some of Lobo Prabhu's personal views may be found in the English-language weekly, *Insight*, which he has founded, and in *Swarajya*.

29 *Swarajya*, 4 July 1959, where Rajaji quotes Lenin to the effect that socialist agriculture would require decades to bring about and that the *kulak* must be relied upon.

30 *HT*, 12 April 1960, for Masani, and *Swarajya*, 17 Oct. 1959, for Rajaji.

31 See *ibid.* for many of these specifics. See *HWR*, 18 March 1960, for Ceylon, and 13 June 1960 for Great Britain.

32 See 'Who is Outdated? German Social Democrats Echo Swatantra' (Bombay, Swatantra Party, n.d.), and 'Socialism: an Ism that has become a Wasm' (Bombay, Swatantra Party, n.d.).

33 'To Provide a Democratic Alternative', in *Why Swatantra?*, p. 29.

34 See *TI*, 6 Jan. 1962; *HWR*, 13 June 1960; and *Preparatory Convention*, p. 8, for references to this. In the latter, Masani argues that Congress socialism 'is more accurately described as State Capitalism'.

35 This range of discourse reflects Masani's involvement in the Liberal International, the Congress for Cultural Freedom, and associated causes. Needless to say, this argument is addressed to the tiny intellectual stratum, while more accessible fare is served to the 'common man'.

36 The author was permitted to examine various drafts of the programme. Masani and Munshi worked on one draft, while other drafts were prepared by Rajaji and Ruthnaswamy. The final manifesto followed closely the Masani-Munshi version.

37 From the *General-Secretary's Report* to the Swatantra party candidates' convention, Bombay, 7 and 8 April 1962, p. 6.

38 From a party resolution on 'national integration', excerpted in *HWR*, 7 Aug. 1961.

39 Quoted in Frank Moraes, *Jawarharlal Nehru* (Bombay, Jaico, 1959), p. 417.

40 Based on questionnaires.

41 Here, too, men of different perspectives are brought together. Rajaji clearly does not believe that the 'old order' involves many oppressions, as he suggested when he argued that 'feudal' oppression had largely been overcome and that statism was now the principal—if not the only—source of mass distress. Men like Masani, Pasricha, *et al.*, are prepared to concede that the old order has abundant evils but that these are clearly secondary to those flowing from 'statist' politics. For Rajaji, see *Towards Doom?*, pp. 10–11. For Masani see, for example, 'The Congress Path to Communism', speech in Bombay, 2 Aug. 1961, reprinted by the Swatantra Party, pp. 10–11.

42 Cf. the history of the German liberals in the nineteenth century.

43 *Swarajya*, 8 May 1965.

44 'To Save Freedom', in *Why Swatantra?*, p. 4. This, of course, is in keeping with the broader Swatantra attack against the Congress, which is accused of unwarranted imposition of the legislative whip, as part of its prevailing 'authoritarian' tendencies.

45 Rajaji once supported compulsory study of Hindi in the south but is now a vehement defender of English. Much of the party's support for English is due to the intensity of Rajaji's feelings on this issue. See Rajaji's pamphlet, 'My Inconsistencies', and 'English for Unity', *Swarajya*, 20 Feb. 1965.

46 See *HWR*, 7 Aug. 1961, for these quotations from the statement on 'national integration'. See also Pasricha's 'Our Stuporous Society', *Quest* (April–June 1962), for a comparable view; and Munshi's 'Language and Literature as Integrating Forces', *Illustrated Weekly of India*, 12 Aug. 1962, pp. 54–5. Recall, however, Munshi's views, quoted above (chapter 5), which criticize leadership which is 'remote' from the masses. For a representative statement by Rajaji, see *HWR*, 9 May 1961. Naturally the southerners, and the many Parsis for whom English is the 'native' tongue, would be expected to take this position.

47 E.g. during the *Lok Sabha* debate on the language bill in the spring of 1963 feelings ran very high and two Swatantra MPs—Yashpal Singh of UP and C. L. N. Reddy of Andhra—found themselves heatedly on different sides of the fence. Elsewhere tension is evident. As far as the author could ascertain, Yashpal Singh refused to speak in English to his southern colleagues (e.g. C. L. N. Reddy) even though he knew English well while the latter did not know Hindi at all. This pro-English view is naturally not well received in the great Hindi heartland, and Swatantra leaders in UP and elsewhere reported to the author their belief that the language position, although 'unofficial', hurt the party's efforts in the 1962 elections.

48 For the Macaulay reference, see above, ch. 3.

49 For Raghuvira, see *TI*, 22 April 1963. For one report of such heckling, see *Delhi Hindustan Standard*, 15 April 1960. The Jan Sangh/RSS and Lohia Socialist elements are most frequently charged with such behaviour.

50 Also widely supported in the national élite was a 'zonal' rather than a 'linguistic' division of India. A large majority of respondents to questionnaires opposed the principle of linguistic states, although obviously not always for the same reasons. Many of these admitted that they originally had supported the linguistic principle.

51 That is, the DMK set aside its demand for secession during the invasion, and when confronted with a constitutional amendment prohibiting demands for secession, C. N. Annadurai, the leader of the DMK, publicly abjured this goal for his party.

52 *OHT*, 11 Aug. 1960.

53 See *TI*, 19 Oct. 1960, and *HWR*, 26 June 1961.

54 *HWR*, 6 June 1960.

55 See *HWR*, 14 Aug. 1961; *HWR*, 11 Sept. 1961; and *TI*, 2 Oct. 1961. For a time it was suggested that Rajaji investigate the case and present

his findings before a commission of enquiry (*TI*, 4 Oct. 1961; *HWR*, 2 Oct. 1961), but Rajaji repeatedly insisted (e.g. *HWR*, 6 June 1960) that he could not do so, because of 'acute arthritis'. For other references, see *HWR*, 4 April 1960, and *HWR*, 2 Jan. 1961—both of which contain 'unofficial' endorsements of the Punjabi *suba* demand by Rajaji.

56 See *Swarajya*, 31 March 1962 and 13 Jan. 1962, respectively. See also *Swarajya*, 29 April 1961, and, for some of Masani's views, *TI*, 10 and 19 Aug. 1961.

57 See the next chapter for a discussion of electoral alliances.

58 *Swarajya*, 22 March 1961.

59 Editorial, 17 May 1961.

60 See, for example, *The Hindu*, 1 Sept. 1962. Munshi favoured the constitutional amendment to ban secessionist agitation and in the report on the situation in the Punjab he was, as noted earlier, quite critical of both the Government and the Akalis.

61 E.g. Nagoke, one-time leader of the Akali Dal and Swatantra leader in the Punjab, was reportedly upset at the reluctance of the national leaders to take a 'positive' stand for Punjabi *suba* and at excessive attention to Hindu Swatantrites. See *Link*, 22 Jan. and 23 July 1961. The latter reports that Masani was obliged to visit the Punjab to pacify Nagoke, but that he emphasized that the fundamental principles did not cover this issue and that the party would not take a binding stand.

62 Mahabir Singh Kalra, secretary of a local unit of the party, quoted in *TI*, 14 Sept. 1961. For reported defections as a result of Rajaji's stand on Punjabi *suba*, see *HT*, 1 Jan. 1961. As will be discussed in the next chapter, there was a good deal of difficulty keeping both sides happy in this respect. For one strong statement by a Sikh Swatantrite who resigned from the party (after being expelled, then reinstated) to press for Punjabi *suba*, see Sardar Gurnam Singh, *A Unilingual Punjabi State and the Sikh Unrest* (Dehli, the author, n.d.), It is not absolutely certain that Gurnam Singh is the author of this, but a reliable source has reported that if it is not Gurnam Singh, then it is another Sikh Swatantrite.

63 See Erdman, *PA*, XXXIX, 5–18.

64 E.g. Nehru's invitation to Chou En-Lai to discuss problems, for which see *HWR*, 22 Feb. 1960.

65 See *TI*, 2 Nov. 1961.

66 See *loc. cit*. The last view is *not* even 'unofficial' party policy. For further references to joint defence proposals and views on Pakistan, see: the Manifesto, 'To Prosperity Through Freedom'; Ranga's Presidential Address at the Patna Convention (where he noted that he and many others had originally favoured non-alinement in order to allow the country to concentrate on domestic problems); *OHT*, 22 Sept. 1960 (where Masani urged disengagement in Kashmir to free Indian troops for the China frontier) and 29 Sept. 1960 (where Rajaji urged a Nehru-Ayub Khan gentlemen's agreement on a Kashmir truce line); and *HWR*, 25 Jan. 1960, 14 and 28 March 1960, 18 April 1960 (where Rajaji urged a suspension of non-alinement and expressed his desire that the Kashmir issue be put in the 'freezer'); 8 Aug. 1960, 2 Jan., 13 March, 6 Nov. 1961. At the Patna Convention some spokesmen expressed the view that 'we should accept military aid from friendly countries on honourable terms befitting the dignity of our Nation' (see *Patna Report*, p. 82, and also pp. 62–3). In a post-invasion address in Jaipur, Masani said that India should take western military aid, because there was no prospect that India could, by herself, build up adequate defence against China and that all such efforts would lead to intolerable taxation. After some western aid was accepted, Swatantra insisted that the Government of India had not shown proper appreciation, had not publicized it sufficiently within India and had been grudging in its thanks. For further views of Rajaji, Ranga, Munshi, Masani, Mody, and Dandekar, on a wide range of matters, see *Swatantra Answer to the Chinese Communist Challenge* (Bombay, Swatantra Party, 1963). Masani, and to a lesser extent Ranga, are the exponents of the 'tough' line, while Rajaji originally was much 'softer' on Communism generally, especially with respect to the USSR. (It is widely agreed in Swatantra circles that Masani has succeeded in convincing Rajaji that a harder line against Communism generally is necessary.) In the columns of *Swarajya* and elsewhere, Rajaji has frequently inveighed against the attitudes of both the US and the USSR in the cold war, has occasionally spoken against excessive preoccupation with defence and military affairs in India, and has been vehement in his denunciation of all nuclear testing and weaponry. See, for example, *HWR*, 6 Nov. 1961, for a reference to Soviet testing as a 'wicked act' and a 'colossal crime'. He wanted India and other nations to take (unspecified) steps to show the USSR that it had placed itself 'outside' the pale of humanity by continuation of nuclear testing. For a statement on the atomic bomb, which argues that India should aline with the west to secure its nuclear deterrent against China, see Masani, *India's Answer to the Chinese Bomb* (Bombay, Swatantra Party, n.d.).

67 See *OHT*, 30 Nov. 1961.

68 For many years prior to the seizure of Goa and the other Portuguese enclaves, both the extreme left and extreme right had been recommending a take-over, for 'anti-imperialist' and 'nationalist' reasons respectively. Nehru and others had evidently hoped that a peaceful resolution (such as that which obtained in the case of the French enclaves) would be possible, but when the Congress finally yielded to a variety of pressures, articulate Indian opinion was *almost* unanimous. Here, as elsewhere, Swatantra demonstrated its willingness to stand 'above the struggle' and the passions which animate many other Indian parties.

69 I.e. in connection with electoral alliances, which will be discussed in the following chapter.

70 Almost all Swatantra leaders who were interviewed or who returned questionnaires were opposed to linguistic states now, although many had favoured their creation earlier.

71 There are many Swatantrites for whom Masani, Rajaji and others go much too far in the direction of 'sweet reasonableness' toward Pakistan.

72 For the latter, see, for example, V. N. Naik, *Indian Liberalism*

(Bombay, Padma, 1945), *passim*. The author notes (p. 3) that the Moderate leaders displayed 'animated moderation' and (p. 4) a 'fine blend of historic sense, culture and courage'. He quotes (p. 16) a speech by Gokhale, in which the latter said 'I want our men and women, without distinction of caste and creed, to have opportunities to grow to the full height of their stature, unhampered by cramping and unnatural distinctions.' These and similar thoughts abound in the speeches of Naoroji, Mehta, Gokhale, Ranade, *et al.*

73 See Kabir, *India Quarterly*, XVI, for some discussion of the place of Swatantra ideology in the Indian political tradition.

74 Based on interviews. Most of the UP and Rajasthan leaders adverted to this issue, when asked about the prospects for Swatantra and the Sangh, as well as relations between the two.

75 *Swarajya*, 16 Sept. 1961.

76 *Swarajya*, 8 May 1965.

77 Naik, *Indian Liberalism*, p. 63.

78 *Ibid.* pp. 260 and 267.

79 From an interview with a Bombay professional man.

80 From an interview in New Delhi, 1962.

81 As noted at various points above, the author had access to all party files.

82 Based on interviews.

83 Based on interviews and on personal observation at election tribunal proceedings in Baroda.

84 See, for example, *HT*, 26 Oct. 1959, *Statesman*, 28 May and 1 June 1960.

85 *HT*, 18 July 1960.

86 It should be quite clear, even from this brief survey, that a considerable gap separates Swatantra doctrine from that of the Jan Sangh and the RRP, discussed in chapter 3. This is not to say that some of Rajaji's formulations would not elicit the approval of either (or both), or that they have no common points, in both domestic and foreign policy. The overall 'tone' and most important specifics are different, however. This will become somewhat clearer in the subsequent discussion.

CHAPTER 9, pp. 212–244

1 Masani in particular was adamant on this point. See *HWR*, 22 May 1961.

2 See *Link*, 9 July 1961. However, in *TI*, 10 Oct. 1960, Rajaji listed acceptable allies—including the Sangh, RRP, DMK, and Akali Dal—but did not mention the CPI. Recall also that while Rajaji termed the CPI his 'enemy number one', he also said he would not favour a ban on it, as long as it refrained from insurrectionary activity.

3 For Andhra, see *Hindu*, 14 Feb. 1962. Party files record this as one of the serious breaches of discipline in the 1962 elections. The indirect relations with the CPI occurred primarily in Madras, via the DMK, and in the Punjab, via the Akalis, and these will be discussed below.

4 *TI*, 29 July 1961. Masani included the PSP and the Socialist Party among those with whom adjustments would be sought.

5 *HWR*, 22 May 1961.

6 For a lengthy statement concerning understandings, see *Hindu*, 13 Jan. 1961, and *HT*, 23 Jan. 1961.

7 Dungarpur, in dealing with the Jan Sangh in Rajasthan, initially held back, pending advice from the national leaders, who had been talking with Sangh leaders (*Statesman*, 14 April 1961).

8 There were others, of course: the Jharkand Party (Bihar); the Forward Bloc (Madras); the Hindu Mahasabha (UP and Madhya Pradesh), as well as the socialist parties. In terms of rightist politics specifically, however, talks with the Sangh, RRP, and Mahasabha were the most important, while in terms of serious contenders for power, the Sangh, DMK, and the Akali Dal bulked largest. At some junctures, leading independents were also approached.

9 *HT*, 23 Nov. 1961.

10 See, for example, *HT*, 31 Jan. 1962, for the DMK, and the *Statesman*, 10 May 1960, for the Jan Sangh in UP.

11 *HT*, 23 Nov. 1961.

12 See, for example, the statement by T. G. Gehani of the Jan Sangh, *TI*, 3 Aug. 1961, in which he claims that Sangh strength is often underestimated by others.

13 This, of course, was a point which Swatantra never failed to emphasize. With respect to Swatantra's entry as one among many opposition groups, one Swatantra leader compared the party's position to that of a merchant who seeks to set up a new shop in an old bazaar district. Other merchants view the newcomer with suspicion, if not hostility, as a competitor; they wait to see how well business will go; and they will seek some agreements with respect to trade, if circumstances seem to require it, i.e. if the new party establishes itself as a worthy competitor. The analogy, while far from perfect, is none the less useful.

14 Questionnaires returned by Brahmins from Madras, Andhra, and Mysore generally opposed electoral understandings with the DMK and some of them explicitly mentioned anti-Brahmin 'communalism' as the reason for the position taken.

15 Harrison, *Dangerous Decades*.

16 The Rajaji-Annadorai link is claimed by *Economic Weekly*, 8 Sept. 1962, p. 1439. See also the *Hindu*, 18 Feb. 1962.

17 See *TI*, 2 Jan. 1962, *Hindu*, 16 Feb. 1962, and 'The Meaning of Chittoor', *Economic Weekly*, 8 Sept. 1962, p. 1439. Harrison, *Dangerous Decades*, speculated that the DMK might exploit strained international relations to further its secessionist cause, which proved to be wrong.

18 For details on the negotiations, see *HT*, 26 June 1961; *TI*, 5 Aug. 1961; *HWR*, 6 Nov. 1961; as well as *TI*, 19 April and 13 June 1961. In an interview in Madras, Aug. 1962, Mr V. K. Narasimhan, associate editor of the *Hindu*, stressed Swatantra's image in explaining the breakdown of negotiations, while most Swatantra and DMK leaders interviewed in

Madras stressed Swatantra's demands for some prestige seats, as well as for a relatively large number of seats, as the principal factor. For the question of the lists, see *Statesman*, 4 and 9 Jan. 1962.

19 *Statesman*, 4 Jan. 1961.

20 *Loc. cit.*

21 See, respectively, *Statesman*, 9 Jan. 1962, *TI*, 31 Jan. 1962, and *Statesman*, 4 Jan. 1962, for these fragments.

22 *Hindu*, 9 Feb. 1962.

23 One DMK leader interviewed said that his party would certainly contest almost every seat, avoiding only a few where some well-established figure was virtually unbeatable. Swatantra did not come out of Madras completely empty-handed: the late U. M. Thevar, popular leader of the Thevar-based Madras Forward Bloc, received Swatantra support and became an associate member of the Swatantra parliamentary party, although to the knowledge of Swatantra leaders in the *Lok Sabha* he never once appeared at a group meeting and, as far as they knew, he never appeared in New Delhi. Thevar died in 1964, and in the by-election to fill this seat, the Swatantra-Forward Bloc forces were defeated by the Congress candidate.

24 There were a number of contests for both the *Lok Sabha* and assembly where Swatantra candidates were narrowly defeated.

25 At Tiruchengode, in August 1962, where the DMK won a seat vacated by a Congressman. The Chittoor by-election was held in late August 1962, shortly after that in Tiruchengode. Chittoor is in Andhra but is close to the Madras–Andhra line, and the DMK has some influence in the district. In pre-election activity, the DMK and Swatantra shared the same platform quite frequently, while the Congress and CPI held separate meetings in support of the Congress candidate. The DMK brought in many people from Madras City where there had recently been very serious disturbances involving the DMK and a frequently heard electoral message was that concerning Congress brutality in suppressing DMK activities. As expected, the DMK claimed credit for Ranga's margin of victory, which was very slight. The *Hindu* and the *Express* (Chittoor edition) for August 1962 provide detailed coverage of this important by-election.

26 The latter point will be considered more fully below. Munshi, and some other Swatantrites (particularly in UP, but generally in the north), are still extremely hostile to the DMK and to Rajaji for courting it. For other criticism of Swatantra on this score, see *TI*, 10, 18 and 19 Aug. 1961.

27 See *TI*, 11 July 1959.

28 See Weiner, *MS*, for the Gujarat case.

29 Quoted in *Link*, 31 Jan. 1960. According to a letter in *Link*, 3 Dec. 1961, Rajaji at one point explicitly denied that the Sangh can be called communal.

30 From a statement by a Sangh leader in Andhra, cited *TI*, 16 May 1961. Recall also that Murarji Vaidya, now a Swatantra leader in Bombay, helped to draft the 1957 Jan Sangh economic programme.

31 See, for example, *Link*, 24 Jan. 1960, for reference to concerted opposition efforts among the 'tax-burdened peasantry' of the Punjab.

32 Most Jan Sangh leaders who were interviewed felt that differences on economic issues were more apparent than real. The Sangh's defence of land ceilings was lightly dismissed by one leader who said it was simply a matter of accepting a *fait accompli* and of associating with a measure widely considered 'progressive'. He argued that Swatantra's opposition would do absolutely no good, and that in the last analysis, both parties would have to learn to live with land ceilings. He denied, however, that the Sangh was at all enthused about such 'attacks' on property, and in passing he condemned the Lohia Socialists because they were 'real Socialists'. Many Swatantra party men feel, however, that many Jan Sanghis are also 'real Socialists'—a view which is also held widely about the DMK.

33 *TI*, 29 July 1961.

34 For the Sangh positions, see *TI*, 15 Sept. 1961, and *OHT*, 21 Sept. 1961.

35 Significantly, the late Jan Sangh President, Dr Raghuvira, was reportedly 'gagged' because too many of his public pronouncements were conciliatory towards Pakistan. See Erdman, *PA*, XXXIX, 5–18, for a comparison of Swatantra and Jan Sangh foreign policy views.

36 See chapter 3, above, for Upadhyaya's statement about education in 'Macaulay's mould'.

37 For the first point, see *HWR*, 11 April 1960. For the second, see *TI*, 16 May and 15 Sept. 1961. On all counts, the Sangh's criticism finds some resonance in Swatantra itself, particularly in Munshi, of the national leaders, and in UP. In terms of culture and tradition more broadly conceived, the Sangh finds little fault with Rajaji. M. R. Malkani, editor of *The Organiser*, emphasized the language division. In an interview in Cambridge, Mass., Dec. 1961.

38 From a report on the 1962 elections in Rajasthan, sent by the state unit to the central office. Here, as elsewhere, the author is grateful to Swatantra authorities for having made the party's files available to him.

39 *TI*, 3 Aug. 1961.

40 *Statesman*, 4 Jan. 1962.

41 E.g. Masani held a number of meetings with the late Dr Raghuvira, Jan Sangh President at one stage, concerning both nationwide and state-by-state adjustments.

42 *Statesman*, 7 May 1961. Dungarpur is reported to have criticized the Sangh aim of 'Akhand Hindustan' and to have favoured the canal water treaty with Pakistan which the Sangh had condemned. Dungarpur insisted that harmonious relations with Pakistan had to be cultivated and that Sangh positions worked counter to this goal.

43 *TI*, 20 Nov. 1961. The report notes that the Maharaja met twice with Bhairon Singh, leader of the Jan Sangh group in the state assembly; they had arrived 'at some sort of a working arrangement on the distribution of assembly constituencies to avert a direct clash between the two parties'; and that final arrangements would be made in discussion between Masani and Bhairon Singh.

44 *Statesman*, 22 Nov. 1961. *TI*, 24 Nov. 1961, reports a tour of some districts by both the Maharaja and Maharani of Jaipur in the course of which the latter was supposed to meet with opposition leaders.

45 See *HT*, 12 Dec. 1961, and *Statesman*, 13 Dec. 1961, for some accounts of these developments.

46 From interviews in Rajasthan, 1962 and 1963.

47 *Statesman*, 13 Dec. 1961. See also *Statesman*, 4 Jan. 1962, for a further reference, to the effect that 'the breakdown of talks...has destroyed the image, sought to be built up, of these Opposition parties as an alternative to the Congress. Local adjustments are still contemplated...'.

48 *HT*, 19 Feb. 1962.

49 *TI*, 4 March 1962.

50 *HT*, 23 Oct. 1962.

51 During one time of troubles for the Congress in Rajasthan, Dungrapur intimated that he would be willing to enter a coalition with a wing of the Congress and support Sukhadia as the Chief Minister. See *HT*, 8 Aug. 1962.

52 See *OHT*, 14 May 1964, for a report of the rumoured merger and a denial by the Swatantra state unit.

53 *HT*, 24 April 1962, refers to Bhairon Singh as the Sangh's 'astute and alert leader' who 'has not allowed the spotlight to wander far away from him, or for too long. He is the sleuth of the opposition, and knows the location of every grievance in the administration, or outside'. For press charges about Swatantra's poor performance in Rajasthan, see: *Express*, 12 April 1962; *New Age*, 15 April 1962; *HT*, 24 April 1962; and *Statesman*, 30 April 1962. Dungarpur submitted a rebuttal to these charges and this document is in Swatantra Party files, Bombay.

54 See *OHT*, 14 May 1964; *TI*, 19 July 1965; and *TI*, 20 July 1965, respectively.

55 *SN*, no. 41, Jan.–Feb. 1964.

56 *Statesman*, 8 June 1965, reproduced in the *Organiser*, 14 June 1965, and discussed in *Swarajya*, 3 July 1965.

57 From an interview.

58 In mid-1965, there were numerous reports that Sangh units in Gujarat, Mysore, and other non-Hindi-speaking states insisted on a more restrained language policy and that the leadership did yield some ground.

59 The death of Raghuvira seems to have hurt relations between the two parties. Masani and other Swatantra leaders got on well with Raghuvira, who, among other things, was reportedly 'muzzled' by the Sangh because of a relatively moderate stance towards Pakistan.

60 See *TI*, 15 March 1960, for an announcement that the Akali Dal had decided to abrogate its alliance with the Congress, coupled with a request that all MPs and MLAs elected on the joint Congress-Akali ticket move from the government benches to the opposition benches. The decision was taken because of the failure of the Congress to respond to Akali demands concerning the linguistic issue and related matters.

61 *TI*, 26 Sept. 1959, reports that the Punjab unit of the Jan Sangh (like the national organization) demanded that Nehru unequivocally reiterate his stand that there would be no division of the Punjab.

62 *Statesman*, 16 July 1960. The resolution, passed by general meeting of the Chandigarh unit against Gurnam Singh, who was its chairman, specifically referred to his close association with the Akali Dal. Gurnam Singh and Harbans Singh Gujral had been serving as counsel to Master Tara Singh of the Akali Dal.

63 From party files.

64 See the discussion of Munshi in chapter 5 and of Swatantra doctrine in chapter 8.

65 *TI*, 24 June 1961.

66 *Statesman*, 2 Jan. 1962.

67 See *ibid.*, where it is noted that Nagoke was supposed to contest against a Communist candidate who would under no circumstances be withdrawn. Thus Akali support for Nagoke would have obliged them to oppose the CPI, prejudicing chances for broader Akali-CPI co-operation. *HT*, 1 Jan. 1962, notes that representatives of the Akalis, CPI, Swatantra, PSP and the Republican Party met together to consider electoral adjustments but had been successful in only a very few cases. The *Statesman*, 20 Jan. 1962, reports Nagoke's withdrawal.

68 *HT*, 28 April 1961, reports a Swatantra announcement that it hoped to contest about 100 out of 154 assembly seats. In *HT*, 1 Jan. 1962, and *Statesman*, 2 Jan. 1962. There are reports of Swatantra displeasure over the small number of seats which they were 'conceded' by the other opposition parties. *TI*, 3 Jan. 1962, reported that Swatantra finally announced a list of 39 assembly and 7 *Lok Sabha* candidates but many of these were withdrawn, too, at the last minute. Nagoke was among the latter, as was Raja Bhalindra Singh, who refused to contest for the Patiala *Lok Sabha* seat after his brother, the Maharaja, had declined to support him.

69 *Statesman*, 20 Jan. 1962. Basant Singh, the state General-Secretary, was reported to be among those who would use the Akali symbol alone. In a report to the Central Organizing Committee of the Swatantra Party, Masani listed the use of the Akali symbol as one of the serious breaches of discipline evident in the 1962 elections.

70 See *Statesman*, 20 Jan. 1962, and, for further information on Akali-CPI negotiations, *TI*, 3 and 5 Jan. 1962.

71 According to very reliable sources, Swatantra provided Rs. 30,000 to each Akali candidate for the *Lok Sabha*, and the three victorious Akalis became, in fact, associate members of the Swatantra group in Parliament. One of these, Sardar Kapur Singh, has been an office-holder in the Swatantra parliamentary organization, which suggests rather complete amalgamation at the *Lok Sabha* level. None the less the two remain organizationally distinct outside of Parliament and Akalis are far from convinced that Swatantra is a satisfactory vehicle through which they can advance their interests. The question of Akali-Swatantra candidacies remains a bit obscure because some Swatantra candidates did use the Akali symbol.

72 *Statesman*, 7 Feb. 1963. Rajaji said much the same thing, *HWR*, 4 April 1960.
73 For the statement by the MP (Buta Singh), see *TI*, 13 Feb. 1963. For the entry of one high-ranking Akali, see either *HT* or *TI*, 20 Sept. 1962. Also see *Statesman*, 7 Feb. 1963, and *TI*, 14 Feb. 1963, for reports of possible merger.
74 *OHT*, 7 April 1960.
75 *HT*, 3 Jan. 1961, argues that Nagoke had played a key role in efforts to have the Akali Dal reject *in toto* an appeal from Nehru to reduce tension over the Punjabi *suba* issue. According to this report, Nagoke took part in the formal Akali discussions, by special invitation.
76 See *TI*, 14 Feb. 1963, for Fateh Singh's statement.
77 *HT*, 28 April 1965.
78 Based on correspondence and on the following newspaper accounts: *HT*, 28 April 1965 (Kapur Singh); *Patriot*, 8 July 1965 (Akali meeting to decide future); *HT Weekly*, 11 July 1965, and *Patriot*, 11 July 1965 (Gurnam Singh and the opposition of Patiala and Fateh Singh); *TI*, 21 July 1965 (Sant-Master reconciliation effort); *Pioneer*, 25 July 1965 (Tara Singh-Rajaji); *Express*, 29 July 1965 (split among Akali legislators in Punjab assembly and Gurnam Singh's role); *ibid.* (Rajaji-Ranga-Tara Singh talks); *Organiser*, 1 Aug. 1965 (Sikh state demand); *Express*, 4 Aug. 1965 (Tara Singh decline, relations with Swatantra); *TI*, 11 Aug. 1965 (Rajaji quote).
79 A resolution of the Punjabi *suba* issue might conceivably allow the Akalis to turn their attention to the type of issue which Swatantra prefers to emphasize; but at least at the present time, it would appear that under such conditions an Akali-Congress *entente* would be more likely.
80 To be sure, the Sangh does admit non-Hindus and is therefore officially non-communal, which may make it sufficiently respectable as a close ally or even for purposes of merger. The fusion of the ranks of the two parties would be very difficult for a variety of reasons, among them Swatantra's non-Hindu appeal in some states.
81 P. S. Krishnaswamy, a founder of Swatantra in Coimbatore district, resigned, complaining about a policy of indiscriminate alliances undertaken by Swatantra. Munshi's distress is evident in *Swarajya*, 25 Sept. 1962.
82 Based on interviews.
83 Based on correspondence and newspaper accounts cited in the discussion of Ramgarh in chapter 7.
84 Based on interviews.
85 Based on interviews and on the following accounts: *Indian Affairs Record*, Jan. 1960 (Swatantra-RRP merger talks); *Link*, 14 Feb. 1960 (merger talks); *Link*, 25 Sept. 1960 (merger effort by the late Bhinai, then a Swantantrite, formerly a member of the RRP and Sangh, at a Rajasthan Rajput meeting); *TI*, 3 Aug. 1961 (unity conference, including RRP, Swatantra, Jan Sangh, Hindu Mahasabha, and the Ganatantra Parishad, called by Karapatri of RRP).
86 Based on *TI*, 8 Aug. 1965, and correspondence.

87 *Link*, 4 Sept. 1960; 8 May 1961; 5 June 1960; and 27 March 1960, respectively, for these fragments.
88 *Link*, 22 May 1960.
89 *Link*, 17 Jan. 1960.
90 Based on a wide variety of interviews with interested parties and on personal observation at meetings where the matter was discussed. The attention to Vyas as a possible Chief Minister stemmed in part from Dungarpur's insistence that he had 'had his innings' as a serious politician and that under no circumstances would he assume the chief ministership.
91 Based on interviews.
92 See *Link*, 3 April 1960, for the first two cases, and *Link*, 3 July 1960, for the last.
93 Based on correspondence with Swatantra leaders in Madras. This is not a one-way street, as we have seen. In Bihar, in 1964, the first Swatantra nominee for the *Rajya Sabha* did not get elected, even though the party had ample strength in the assembly.
94 This discussion is based on interviews and on discussions at Swatantra Party meetings which the author was permitted to attend. Masani was at his most persuasive best in trying to get Dungarpur to visit Sampurnanand, and Dungarpur finally acquiesced, reluctantly. I have not yet received a report that Dungarpur has actually paid such a visit. We have already seen that in the south, the Brahmin/non-Brahmin split is involved in Swatantra relations with the DMK; but it should also be noted that many historic cleavages have been overcome, e.g. as between some of the Justiceites and the Brahmins. Even in Rajasthan, the situation was not completely hopeless. Swatantra did work with Vyas and Shastri to a limited extent, and Dungarpur has said upon occasion that he would not be averse to supporting Sukhadia in some sort of coalition ministry.
95 Questionnaires were returned by almost all leading Swatantrites, both national and state. In some cases where they were not returned, interviews elicited much the same information; and in some cases, follow-up interviews were used to explore certain points. Not very surprisingly, when asked in the questionnaire which leading Congressmen were closest to Swatantra in outlook, S. K. Patil was named most often, with Hanumanthaya and Mahtab next. These three were mentioned very frequently, with little variations in terms of the state from which the respondent came. The others mentioned were generally lesser Congressmen and were very heavily weighted in terms of the state from which the respondent came. In very few cases was anyone at a loss to name at least two or three state ministers among the 'fellow-travelling' Swatantrites. Patil is very much pro-private enterprise, Hanumanthaya and Mahtab more 'old warriors' who look upon themselves as Gandhians.
96 Based on interviews on 1962.
97 Based on correspondence and in interviews, 1966.
98 Kothari, *AS*, IV, 1161–73.
99 A number of examples of such efforts have been noted already, and in the pre-1967 election period there was strenuous activity along these lines.

100 Based on party files, interviews, and correspondence.
101 Based on interviews and correspondence.
102 Based on interviews and correspondence.
103 Based on interviews and correspondence.
104 Where these parties have any support, Swatantra has negotiated with them, as with the RRP in Rajasthan. One MP and some MLAs from the RRP in Rajasthan have joined Swatantra.
105 *SN*, no. 20, 9 July 1961. This was, of course, prior to the first general elections in which Swatantra contested.
106 See *Link*, 6 March 1960. As far as I have been able to ascertain, Swatantra gave no help to Jan Sangh General-Secretary Upadhyaya in the Jaunpur by-election in 1963. There was, in any event, serious opposition among top Swatantra leaders to the giving of such help.
107 From an interview.
108 Based on interviews and on observation of assembly and Swatantra Party meetings in Rajasthan.
109 Rajaji made his suggestion at the Bangalore convention of Swatantra in 1964. For Kripalani, see *Swarajya*, 6, 13 and 20 July 1963, and for a comparable effort by Munshi, see *HT*, 3 June 1963.

CHAPTER 10, pp. 245–260

1 Kalman Silvert (ed.), *Expectant Peoples* (New York, Random House, 1963), introduction.
2 Rupert Emerson, *From Empire to Nation* (Cambridge, Harvard University Press, 1960).
3 *Government and Politics*, ch. 2.
4 *AS*, IV, 1116–73.
5 Harrison, *Dangerous Decades*, and Shils, *The Intellectual Between Tradition and Modernity*.
6 As in the work of the Rudolphs, Morris-Jones, Weiner, and Kothari and Maru, among others.
7 *AS*, IV, 1161–73.
8 *Government and Politics*, p. 160. See also Weiner, *MS*.
9 For Harrison, see *Dangerous Decades*.
10 Implicity rejecting Kothari's contention that the Congress 'system' is satisfactorily democratic.
11 *Swarajya*, 22 May 1965.
12 These include the position of the president *vis-à-vis* Cabinet and Parliament, the proposed amalgamation of the offices of law minister and attorney-general, the use of preventive detention, the continuation of the state of emergency after the Chinese invasion in 1962, the possible role of an Ombudsman, and the utilization of a non-partisan board to assign permits and licence to private enterprise.
13 These were published by both the central office and the parliamentary office, almost exclusively in English.
14 The question of balance is inherent in Morris-Jones' approach, *Government and Politics*, ch. 2.

15 *Ibid.*
16 See Silvert (ed.) *Expectant Peoples*, introduction.
17 *Modern Review*, CV, 6 (June 1959), 434, and *OHT*, 11 June 1959, both claim that Rajaji wanted to call the party 'conservative'. The PSP periodical *Janata*, 17 Jan. 1960, refers to the formation of a 'Conservative Party' under Rajaji's leadership, although by that time, of course, the name Swatantra had been firmly fixed. Kabir, *India Quarterly*, XVI, 8, argues that 'conservative' would have been disastrous. We have already quoted Rajaji's view that a 'party on the right' is necessary to give expression to 'the pain involved' in the 'dislocation, disturbance, and distress' which every change 'necessarily' produces.
18 *Swarajya*, 18 April 1959.
19 *TI*, 4 June 1959. See also *Modern Review*, CV, 6 (June 1959), 434.
20 From the *General Secretary's Report*, Swatantra Party candidate's convention, Bombay, 7 and 8 April 1962, p. 5. My emphasis.
21 *Modern Review*, CV, 6 (June 1959), 435.
22 See above, chapter 5.
23 *Party Politics in India* (Ahmedabad, Harold Laski Institute, 1962), p. 19. The statement was originally made at a party convention and was repeated in an address at the Harold Laski Institute, which published the address under the above title.
24 From his *Report*, candidates' convention, 1962, p. 6.
25 *Ibid.* p. 5.
26 *The Congress Path to Communism*, pp. 10–11.
27 For some fairly typical partisan views, see H. D. Malaviya, *The Swatantra Party: Its Real Character and Designs* (New Delhi, Socialist Congressman, n.d.), and N. C. Zamindar, *Congress Refuted* (Indore, Sahityalaya, 1962). Zamindar is not the most able spokesman, but he is earnest. For more sober fare, see *Why Swatantra?*
28 Vincent Starzinger, *Middlingness* (Charlottesville, Va., University of Virginia Press, 1966), provides an analysis of nineteenth-century French and British developments.
29 Weiner, *Party Politics*, argues, for example, that the radical right has a future, based largely on uprooted rural people, displaced artisans, and others adversely affected by the process of social change. The Rudolphs, 'Political Role', *PA*, XXXIII, 5, argue that conflict in India 'has generally been dealt with less by confrontation of adversaries, struggle and decision, than by compartmentalization, absorption, and synthesis'. The configuration of right-wing forces depends very much on arguments such as these, on international developments, and on so many imponderables that speculation on the subject would be little more than a very lengthy catalogue of 'if...then' propositions.
30 *Nehru*, conclusion.

APPENDIX I, pp. 261–268

1 President Radhakrishnan's 1967 Republic Day address is a good case in point.

2 E.g. the language issue in Madras, ground-nut policy in Gujarat.

3 In addition to those who entered active politics for the first time, there were others who abandoned the Congress. The once-faithful Birla family allegedly divided its politicial contributions equally among the Congress, Swatantra and the Jan Sangh. Among the aristocrats, the Rajmata of Gwalior (Madhya Pradesh) left the Congress and spearheaded the complete rout of the Congress in the former Gwalior region of Madhya Pradesh; and the Maharaja of Bharatpur, whose ambitions were similarly frustrated by the state (Rajasthan) Congress unit, contested for the *Lok Sabha* as an independent and won an overwhelming victory. Other examples could easily be cited.

4 E.g. the Jana Congress (Orissa), the Bangla Congress (Bengal), the Kerala Congress (Kerala), among others.

5 There was, as usual, the possibility that some would rejoin the parent body.

6 Swatantra, although a leader in this effort, was by no means alone. There were very broad and stable anti-Congress fronts in Kerala, Bengal, and Madras, in particular.

7 Ramgarh, having been admitted into the Congress, was dissatisfied with the treatment he and his followers received in candidate selection and defected. With some dissident Congressmen, he helped to form the Jan Kranti Dal (Peoples' Revolutionary Party), which is now a partner in the coalition ministry in Bihar. Swatantra tried to carry on in Bihar but was completely routed.

8 This was evident both in candidate selection and in the premature consideration of the constitution of the Gujarat ministry.

9 Some Orissa dissidents formed a rump Swatantra party, while in Gujarat, dissidents generally fought as independents. The Gujarat dissidents came primarily from aristocratic-dominated areas of Kutch, Saurashtra, and Panchmahals.

10 E.g. Piloo Mody's candidacy from Panchmahals in Gujarat was largely in the hands of H. H. Devgadh-Baria; Dandekar's campaign in Jamnagar owed much to the support of the Thakur of Dhrol; etc. In the first case, most observers and party leaders agreed that the dissidents did not demand much—only considerate treatment and some consultation before major decisions were taken; but even this was not readily forthcoming.

11 In terms of the problems of finance, as discussed in the main part of the book, there were other important issues. The Birla money was specifically earmarked for Birla candidates in Rajasthan, and much money was given directly to the state units, rather than being funnelled through the central office. This made it more difficult to finance resource-poor state units and it weakened Masani's position somewhat as he confronted state units.

12 There was a more restricted and informal understanding with the Janata Paksha in Mysore.

13 There was persistent fear that the Jan Sangh would work *sub rosa* to subvert Masani's position and to keep him out of the *Lok Sabha.* During the campaign, the charge was also made that Masani was a beef-eater and many Swatantra leaders felt that this was raised primarily by the RSS men in Rajkot, who were allegedly working on Masani's behalf. Elsewhere in Gujarat, the feeling was that the understanding with the Jan Sangh did Swatantra more harm than good.

14 The Andhra unit was particularly active in reaching understandings with the Communists.

15 Kalahandi was the leader of the group in favour of the demand for a ban on cow-slaughter. The opposition was led by the Bombay City representatives but they had much support from other regions. The Gujarat and Madras units were foremost in their advocacy of a ban on cow-slaughter, and even many people who had no sympathy for such a move felt that it was an exploitable issue. Hence, there was great disappointment in many quarters when the cow-slaughter fasts-unto-death were terminated.

16 Representatives of the central office uniformly deplored these actions but felt they were absolutely indispensable for electoral success.

17 Many national leaders quietly expressed the hope that Swatantra would not form ministries in these states, and, for example, most pro-Swatantra businessmen in Baroda hoped for a Congress ministry in that state.

18 Candidates were generally very closely screened; central office contributions were made contingent upon the submission of periodic reports of work and adequate accounting of expenditures; and the *Lok Sabha* candidates were authorized to arrange disbursement of funds to their assembly candidates as they saw fit.

19 The Gujarat case is notable in that many of the businessmen were outsiders.

20 As noted, Mody in Panchmahals and Dandekar in Jamnagar received much help, as did Masani in Rajkot and most of the *Lok Sabha* candidates in Rajasthan.

21 This is in terms of seats gained. In terms of percentage of total vote for *Lok Sabha* candidates by state, Swatantra recorded losses in Bihar, UP, Andhra and Madras, although in the last two states the number of seats increased (which discrepancy is to be explained in terms of more limited efforts). In terms of votes per contested seat, Swatantra recorded a significant improvement in aggregate terms. In terms of its major states, its votes per contested seat dropped only in Bihar and remained constant in UP. By this last index, notable gains were recorded in Gujarat, Rajasthan, Orissa, Andhra, Madras, and Mysore.

22 The losses in Bihar were expected—no *Lok Sabha* seats and only four assembly seats—although with greater concentration of effort, one or two *Lok Sabha* seats might have been gained. UP, where a major effort was made, was the biggest disappointment, as one sitting MP declined to stand and another lost his deposit, as part of a general rout.

23 This again is in terms of seats gained. As before, there is considerable

variation in terms of percentage of vote and votes per contested seat. Thus, in Gujarat and Rajasthan, Swatantra showed increases in number of seats, percentage of votes, and votes per contested seat; while in Madras and Mysore, its percentage of the vote declined but there were marked gains in the other two respects. According to available figures, its poll percentage in Andhra remained nearly constant, but it gained more seats and nearly doubled its votes per contested seat. Only a detailed analysis using all of these indices, together with factors such as regional concentration of seats, votes, etc., would provide an accurate measure of Swatantra's quantitative and qualitative performance.

24 E.g. approximately half of Swatantra's MLAs in Rajasthan come from Jaipur division.

25 As noted, there was a limited and informal understanding with the Janata Paksha, which, according to Swatantra national leaders, played some role in Swatantra's victories.

26 Relations between Rajaji and Annadorai, the DMK leader, have been quite cordial; and, according to one report, Rajaji said 'leave Madras to me; the last act of my life will be to convert the DMK into the Madras unit of the Swatantra Party'. A proposed Swatantra-DMK bloc in the *Lok Sabha* nearly came to fruition; but difficulties at the state level have, for the moment, laid this to rest.

27 Ranga was defeated in the general election but is standing in a by-election.

28 E.g. the Maharani of Jaipur was defeated in her assembly contest, although she won her *Lok Sabha* seat comfortably; and Himmatsinhji of Kutch lost his *Lok Sabha* seat. In the weeks following the 1967 elections there has already been much talk of developing a Swatantra counterpart to the RSS cadres, which sounds a bit far-fetched. However there is widespread realization that if Swatantra is to hold its own, it must develop some cadres. But as one Swatantra leader put it, in discussing this need: 'What do we substitute for the emotional issues which give strength to the RSS and the Jan Sangh?' Others feel that the party does not require a band of zealous workers, such as the RSS, but needs only to put its conventional party apparatus on a sounder footing. Even this will be difficult to achieve in many areas, but it will be easier to accomplish than to build an RSS counterpart.

29 In addition to huge gains in UP and Madhya Pradesh, the Jan Sangh improved its position in Rajasthan and made a good start in Bihar. It also did extremely well in Delhi. Most Jan Sangh leaders obviously want the party to develop on its own and to make an even stronger effort in 1972, without undue attention to the Swatantra Party. However, talks of a united front in Parliament and of complete merger have taken place, and Balraj Madhok seems quite responsive to the idea of a merger. The united front in the *Lok Sabha* was discussed immediately after the elections, but Swatantra's terms were unacceptable to the Jan Sangh. Swatantra insisted, for example, that the leader and chief whip of the group be from the largest party in any front, and that on all issues on which the members of the front could not agree, everyone should have a free vote (i.e. individual parties could not issue whips to their own members). In the negotiations, the DMK was also involved, and together the three parties would have formed a group of approximately one hundred members.

30 In Rajasthan, the Congress was by far the largest single party but it still fell a few seats short of an absolute majority. Both the Congress and the united opposition claimed a majority, including independents, defectors from the others' ranks, etc. When, after some rather inept efforts to ascertain who should be invited to form the ministry, Governor Sampurnanand turned to the Congress, there were serious public disturbances in Jaipur, including several deaths and much destruction of property Swatantra leaders in Rajasthan claim that they did not want to get involved in the public demonstrations but that they had to, to avoid leaving the field to the Jan Sangh and the SSP, both of which were very happy to take to the streets. Anticipating new elections in Rajasthan within a short time, Swatantra leaders felt that they had to involve themselves in the 'democratic protest' against Sampurnanand's decision. Finally, President's Rule was declared, although the assembly was only suspended, not dissolved.

BIBLIOGRAPHY

This bibliography is primarily a list of materials used in the preparation of the book, with several additions to provide further background on some points, etc. The listing is divided into six parts: (1) general background—works used in connection with discussions of conservatism and political development; (2) Indian background; (3) post-independence politics, with the emphasis on parties and elections; (4) Swatantra bibliography, mainly works by or about Swatantra leaders; (5) publications of the Swatantra Party; and (6) publications of the Forum of Free Enterprise. A note on interviews and questionnaire respondents appears at the end.

Three points should be noted. First, books and articles have been listed together. Secondly, the inclusion of an item in one section rather than another has in some cases been quite arbitrary; and, for example, pieces authored by Masani appear in parts 4, 5, and 6, due to circumstances of publication. Thirdly, Indian editions of some works have been used, and, as in the case of Weiner's *Politics of Scarcity*, pagination differs from English and American editions.

1. GENERAL BACKGROUND

Almond, Gabriel, and James Coleman (eds.) *The Politics of the Developing Areas*. Princeton, Princeton University Press, 1960.

Dobb, Maurice. *Studies in the Development of Capitalism*. New York, International Publishers, 1963.

Duverger, Maurice. *Political Parties*. Trans. Robert and Barbara North. London, Methuen, 1954.

Emerson, Rupert. *From Empire to Nation*. Cambridge, Harvard University Press, 1960.

Friedrich, Carl J. *Constitutional Government and Democracy*. Revised edn. Boston, Ginn and Co., 1950.

Huntington, Samuel P. 'Conservatism as an Ideology', *American Political Science Review*, LI, 2 (June 1957).

Mannheim, Karl. *Essays on Sociology and Social Psychology*. Ed. Paul Kecskemeti. New York, Oxford University Press, 1953.

—— *Ideology and Utopia*. Trans. Louis Wirth and Edward Shils. New York, Harvest Books, n.d.

Mansfield, Harvey, Jr. *Statesmanship and Party Government*. Chicago, University of Chicago Press, 1965.

Michels, Roberto. 'Conservatism', *Encyclopaedia of the Social Sciences*, IV. New York, Macmillan, 1937.

Moore, Barrington, Jr. *Social Origins of Dictatorship and Democracy*. Boston, Beacon Press, 1966.

Oakeshott, Michael. *Rationalism and Politics*. New York, Basic Books, 1962.

Rogger, Hans, and Eugen Weber (eds.). *The European Right.* Berkeley, University of California Press, 1965.

Silvert, Kalman (ed.). *Expectant Peoples.* New York, Random House, 1963.

—— 'Some Psychocultural Factors in the Politics of Conflict and Conciliation', mimeo, read before the American Political Science Association, 8–11 Sept. 1965.

Starzinger, Vincent. *Middlingness.* Charlottesville, University of Virginia Press, 1965.

Ulam, Adam B. *The Unfinished Revolution.* New York, Random House, 1960.

Viereck, Peter (ed.). *Conservatism.* Princeton, Van Norstrand, 1956.

2. INDIAN BACKGROUND

Alexandrowicz, Charles H. *Constitutional Developments in India.* London, Oxford University Press, 1957.

Anstey, Vera. *The Economic Development of India.* 4th edn. London, Longmans, Green, 1957.

Baden-Powell, B. H. *The Origin and Growth of Village Communities in India.* London, Swan, Sonnenschein, 1908.

Bailey, F. G. *Caste and the Economic Frontier.* Manchester, University of Manchester Press, 1957.

—— *Tribe, Caste, and Nation.* Manchester, University of Manchester Press, 1960.

Baldwin, George B. *Industrial Growth in South India.* Glencoe, Ill., Free Press, 1959.

Barton, Sir William. *The Princes of India.* London, Nisbet, 1934.

Basham, A. L. *The Wonder that was India.* New York, Grove Press, 1949.

Basu, Durga Das. *Commentary on the Constitution of India.* 3rd edn. 2 vols. Calcutta, Sarkar, 1955.

Basu, Saroj Kumar. *Industrial Finance in India.* Calcutta, University of Calcutta, 1940.

Beidelman, Thomas O. *A Comparative Analysis of the Jajmani System.* Locust Valley, N.Y., J. J. Augustin, 1959.

Bendix, Reinhard. *Max Weber: An Intellectual Portrait.* Garden City, N.Y., Doubleday, 1960.

Birla, G. D. *In the Shadow of the Mahatma.* Bombay, Orient Longmans, 1953.

Buchanan, Daniel. *The Development of Capitalist Enterprise in India.* New York, Macmillan, 1934.

Carstairs, G. Morris. *The Twice-Born.* Bloomington, University of Indiana Press, 1958.

Chatterjee, Rabindranath. *Indian Economics.* 7th edn. revised Krishna Ch. Roy Chowdhury. Calcutta, Chatterjee and Co., 1959.

Chaudhuri, S. B. *Civil Rebellion in the Indian Mutinies.* Calcutta, World Press, 1957.

Coupland, Reginald. *India: A Restatement.* London, Oxford University Press, 1945.

—— *The Indian Problem.* 3 vols in 1, London, Oxford University Press, 1944. Originally published as (1) *The Indian Problem 1833–1935*; (2) *Indian Politics 1936–1942;* (3) *The Future of India.*

Crane, Robert I. *Aspects of Economic Development in South Asia.* New York, Institute of Pacific Relations, 1954.

Curran, J. A. *Militant Hinduism in Indian Politics: A Study of the R.S.S.* New York, Institute of Pacific Relations, 1951.

Darling, Sir Malcolm. *The Punjab Peasant in Prosperity and Debt.* 4th edn. London, Oxford University Press, 1947.

Das, Nagbopal. *Industrial Enterprise in India.* London, Oxford University Press, 1938.

Desai, A. R. *Recent Trends in Indian Nationalism.* Bombay, Popular Book Depot, 1960.

—— *Social Background of Indian Nationalism.* 3rd edn. Bombay, Popular Book Depot, 1959.

Deshmukh, C. D. *Economic Developments in India 1946–1956.* Bombay, Asia Publishing House, 1957.

Drekmeier, Charles. *Kingship and Community in Ancient India.* Stanford, Stanford University Press, 1962.

Dube, S. C. *India's Changing Villages.* London, Routledge and Kegan Paul, 1958.

Dutt, R. Palme. *India Today.* London, Gollancz, 1940.

—— *India Today and Tomorrow.* London, Lawrence and Wishart, 1955.

Embree, Ainslie (ed.). *1857 in India.* Boston, D.C., Heath, 1963.

Epstein, T. Scarlett. *Economic Development and Social Change in South India.* New York, Oxford University Press, 1962.

Fitze, Sir Kenneth. *Twilight of the Maharajas.* London, John Murray, 1956.

Gadgil, D. R. *The Industrial Evolution of India in Recent Times.* 4th edn. London, Oxford University Press, 1944.

—— *Origins of the Modern Indian Business Class.* New York, Institute of Pacific Relations, 1959.

Gandhi, M. K. *Economic and Industrial Life and Relations,* ed. V. B. Kher. 3 vols. Ahmedabad, Navajivan Press, 1957.

—— *The Indian States Problem.* Ahmedabad, Navajivan Press, 1941.

Gokhale Institute of Politics and Economics. *Notes on the Rise of the Business Communities in India.* New York, Institute of Pacific Relations, 1951.

Griffiths, Sir Percival. *Modern India.* London, Ernest Benn, 1957.

Harijans Today. Delhi, Publications Division, Ministry of Information and Broadcasting, 1955.

Hutton, J. H. *Caste in India.* Bombay, Oxford University Press, 1961.

Indian Round Table Conference, First and Second Sessions: Proceedings. London, His Majesty's Stationery Office, 1931 and 1932.

Isaacs, Harold. *India's Ex-Untouchables.* New York, John Day, 1965.

Karunakaran, K. P. (ed.). *Modern Indian Political Tradition.* New Delhi, Allied Publishers, 1962.

Keer, Dhananjay. *Dr Ambedkar: His Life and Mission.* Bombay, A. V. Keer, 1954.

—— *Savarkar and His Times.* Bombay, A. V. Keer, 1950.

Kothari, Vithaldas (ed.). *Why Khadi and Village Industries?* Ahmedabad, Navajivan Press, 1957.

Kumarappa, Bharatan. *Capitalism, Socialism, or Villagism?* Madras, Shakti Karyalayam, 1946.

Lamb, Helen. 'The Indian Business Communities and the Evolution of an Industrial Class', *Pacific Affairs*, XXVIII, 2 (June 1955).

Landy, Joan B. 'Factors in the Rise of the Parsi Community in India', unpublished B.A. honours' thesis. Cambridge, Radcliffe College, 1962.

McMunn, Sir George. *The Indian States and Princes.* London, Jarrolds, 1936.

Malaviya, H. D. *Land Reforms in India.* New Delhi, All-India Congress Committee, 1954.

Marriott, McKim (ed.). *Village India.* Chicago, University of Chicago Press, 1955.

Mehta, M. M. *Combination Movement in Indian Industry.* Allahabad, Friends' Book Depot, 1952.

Misra, B. B. *The Indian Middle Classes.* New York, Oxford University Press, 1961.

Moreland, W. H. *The Agrarian System of Moslem India.* Cambridge, Heffer, 1929.

—— *India at the Death of Akbar.* London, Macmillan, 1920.

Naik, V. N. *Indian Liberalism.* Bombay, Padma, 1945.

Nair, Kusum. *Blossoms in the Dust.* New York, Praeger, 1962.

Nanavati, Manilal, and C. N. Vakil (eds.). *Group Prejudices in India.* Bombay, Vora, 1951.

Nanda, B. R. *Mahatma Gandhi.* London, George Allen and Unwin, 1959.

Narain, Brij. *Charkha Marxism: Indian Socialism.* Lahore, Rama Krishna, 1941.

Nehru, Jawaharlal. *Towards Freedom.* Boston, Beacon Press, 1958.

O'Malley, L. S. S. *India's Social Heritage.* London, Oxford University Press, 1934.

—— *Popular Hinduism: The Religion of the Masses.* New York, Macmillan, 1935.

Panikkar, K. M. *Common Sense About India.* London, Gollancz, 1960.

—— *Indian Princes in Council.* London, Oxford University Press, 1936.

—— *Indian States and the Government of India.* London, Martin Hopkinson, 1932.

—— *The State and the Citizen.* Bombay, Asia Publishing House, 1956.

Panjabi, Kewal L. *The Indomitable Sardar.* Bombay, Bharatiya Vidya Bhavan, 1964.

Parikh, Narhari D. *Sardar Vallabhbhai Patel.* 2 vols. Trans. not named. Ahmedabad, Navajivan Press, 1953 and 1956.

Patel, Govindlal D. *The Indian Land Problem and Legislation.* Bombay, N. M. Tripathi, 1954.

Patel, Surendra J. *Agricultural Labourers in Modern India and Pakistan*. Bombay, Current Book House, 1952.

Rao, Baditha Srinivasa. *Surveys of Indian Industries*. 2 vols. London, Oxford University Press, 1957.

Retzlaff, Ralph. *Village Government in India*. New York, Asia Publishing House, 1962.

Savarkar, V. D. *Hindu Rashtra Darshan*. Bombay, L. G. Khare, 1949.

Schuster, George, and Guy Wint. *India and Democracy*. London, Macmillan, 1951.

Sen, Surendra Nath. *Eighteen-Fifty-Seven*. Delhi, Publications Division, Ministry of Information and Broadcasting, 1957.

Shils, Edward. *The Intellectual Between Tradition and Modernity: The Indian Case*. The Hague, Mouton, 1961.

Singer, Milton, 'The Religion of India: The Sociology of Hinduism and Buddhism (Max Weber)', *American Anthropologist*, LXI, 1 (Feb. 1961).

—— (ed.). *Traditional India: Structure and Change*. Philadelphia, American Folklore Society, 1959.

Singh, Ranbir. *The Indian States Under the Government of India Act, 1935*. Bombay, Taraporevala, n.d.

Sitaramayya, B. Pattabhi. *The History of the Indian National Congress*. Ahmedabad, Congress Working Committee, 1935.

Spencer, Daniel. *India: Mixed Enterprise and Western Business*. The Hague, Martinus Nijhoff, 1959.

Srinivas, M. N. *Caste in Modern India and Other Essays*. New York, Asia Publishing House, 1962.

—— (ed.). *India's Villages*. 2nd edn. Bombay, Asia Publishing House, 1960.

Stokes, Eric. *The English Utilitarians in India*. London, Oxford University Press, 1959.

Thorner, Daniel. *The Agrarian Prospect in India*. Delhi, Delhi University, 1956.

Tod, James. *Annals and Antiquities of Rajasthan*. 2 vols. London, Routledge and Kegan Paul, 1957.

Venkatasubbiah, H. *Indian Economy Since Independence*. New York, Asia Publishing House, 1961.

Wadia, P. A., and K. T. Merchant. *The Bombay Plan—A Criticism*. Bombay, Popular Book Depot, 1945.

Weber, Max. *The City*. Trans. Don Martindale and Gertrud Neuwirth. New York, Collier, 1962.

—— *The Religion of India: The Sociology of Hinduism and Buddhism*. Trans. and ed. Hans Gerth and Don Martindale. Glencoe, Ill., Free Press, 1958.

Wiser, William E. *The Hindu Jajmani System*. Lucknow, Lucknow Publishing House, 1936.

Woodruff, Philip. *The Men Who Ruled India*. 2 vols. London, Jonathan Cape, 1953 and 1954.

Zinkin, Taya. *Caste Today*. New York, Oxford University Press, 1958.

—— *India Changes!* New York, Oxford University Press, 1958.

3. POST-INDEPENDENCE PARTY POLITICS

Ali, Sadiq. *The General Elections 1957*. New Delhi, All-India Congress Committee, 1959.

Ayyar, R. V. Krishna, *et al.* (eds.). *All-India Election Guide*. Madras, Oriental Publishers, 1956.

Bailey, F. G. *Politics and Social Change: Orissa 1959*. London, Oxford University Press, 1963.

—— 'Politics in Orissa.' Nine parts. *Economic Weekly* (Aug.–Nov. 1959).

Beteille, Andre. *Caste, Class, and Power*. Berkeley, University of California Press, 1965.

Brass, Paul. *Factional Politics in an Indian State*. Berkeley, University of California Press, 1965.

Brecher, Michael. *Nehru: A Political Biography*. New York, Oxford University Press, 1959.

—— *Succession in India*. London, Oxford University Press, 1966.

daCosta, E. P. W. 'Indian Politics Today and Tomorrow—Assessment and Prophecy', *Far Eastern Economic Review*, XXVII, 5 (4 Feb. 1960).

Dean, Vera M. *New Patterns of Democracy in India*. Cambridge, Harvard University Press, 1959.

Election Commission (India). *Report on the First General Elections in India 1951–1952*. 2 vols. Delhi, Manager of Publications, Government of India, 1955.

—— *Report on the Second General Elections in India 1957*. 2 vols. Delhi, Manager of Publications, Government of India, 1959.

—— *Report on the Third General Elections in India 1962*. 2 vols. Delhi, Manager of Publications, Government of India, 1963.

Harrison, Selig. *India: The Most Dangerous Decades*. Princeton, Princeton University Press, 1960.

Kabir, Humayun. 'Congress Ideology', *India Quarterly*, XVI, 1 (Jan.–March 1960).

Karaka, D. F. *Morarji*. Bombay, Times of India Press, 1965.

Kogekar, S. V., and Richard Park (eds.). *Reports on the Indian General Elections 1951–52*. Bombay, Popular Book Depot, 1956.

Kothari, Rajni. 'The Congress "System" in India', *Asian Survey*, IV, 12 (Dec. 1964).

—— and Rushikesh Maru. 'Caste and Secularism in India', *Journal of Asian Studies*, XXV, 1 (Nov. 1965).

Maheshwari, Shri Ram. *The General Election in India*. Allahabad, Chaitanya, 1963.

Mehta, Asok. *The Political Mind of India*. Bombay, Praja Socialist Party, 1952.

Menon, V. P. *The Story of the Integration of the Indian States*. Bombay, Orient Longmans, 1961.

Ministry of States (India). *White Paper on Indian States*. Delhi, Government of India, 1950.

Mookerjee, H. C. *Congress and the Masses*. Calcutta, Book House, n.d.

Moraes, Frank. *India Today*. New York, Macmillan, 1960.

Moraes, Frank. *Jawarharlal Nehru*. Bombay, Jaico, 1959.

Morris-Jones, W. H. *Government and Politics of India*. London, Hutchinson University Library, 1964.

—— *Parliament in India*. Philadelphia, University of Pennsylvania Press, 1957.

Overstreet, Gene D. 'The Hindu Code Bill', *Cases in Comparative Politics*, ed. James B. Christoph. Boston, Little, Brown, 1965.

Palmer, Norman. 'India Faces a New Decade', *Current History*, XL, 235 (March 1961).

—— *The Indian Political System*. Boston, Houghton Mifflin, 1961.

Park, Richard L., and Irene Tinker (eds.). *Leadership and Political Institutions in India*. Princeton, Princeton University Press, 1959.

Pathak, Devavrat, M. G. Parekh and Kirtidev Desai. *Three General Elections in Gujarat*. Ahmedabad, Gujarat University, 1966.

Philips, C. H. (ed.). *Politics and Society in India*. New York, Praeger, 1962.

Poplai, S. L. (ed.). *National Politics and the 1957 Elections in India*. Delhi, Metropolitan Book Co., 1957.

—— (ed.). *1962 General Elections in India*. Bombay, Allied Publishers, 1962.

Robson, William A. 'India Revisited', *The Political Quarterly*, XXXI, 4 (Oct.–Dec. 1960).

Rosen, George. *Democracy and Economic Change in India*. Berkeley, University of California Press, 1965.

Rudolph, Lloyd I. 'Urban Life and Populist Radicalism', *Journal of Asian Studies*, XX, 3 (May 1961).

Rudolph, Susanne H. 'Consensus and Conflict in Indian Politics', *World Politics*, XIII, 3 (April 1961).

—— 'The Princely States of Rajputana: Ethic, Authority and Structure', *Indian Journal of Political Science*, XXIV, 1 (Jan.–March 1963).

—— *Some Aspects of Congress Land Reform Policy*. Cambridge, Massachusetts Institute of Technology, Center for International Studies, 1957. Mimeo.

—— *MS* on Rajasthan. Mimeo. Revised and forthcoming as in second entry following.

Rudolph, Lloyd I. and Susanne H. *The Modernity of Tradition: Political Development in India*. Chicago, University of Chicago Press, 1967.

—— *The Political in Social Change: Princes and Politicians in Rajasthan*. Forthcoming.

—— 'The Political Role of India's Caste Associations', *Pacific Affairs*, XXXIII, 1 (March 1960).

—— 'Toward Political Stability in Underdeveloped Countries: The Case of India', *Public Policy*, no. 9, ed. Carl J. Friedrich and Seymour Harris. Cambridge, Harvard University Graduate School of Public Administration, 1959.

Sheean, Vincent. *Nehru: The Years of Power*. New York, Random House, 1960.

Singh, Hari Kishore. *A History of the Praja Socialist Party*. Lucknow, Narendra Prakashan, 1959.

'Third General Elections', *Asian Recorder* (30 April–6 May 1962).
Tinker, Hugh. *India and Pakistan.* New York, Praeger, 1962.
Weiner, Myron. 'India's Third General Elections', *Asian Survey*, II, 5 (May 1962).
—— *Party Building in a New Nation: The Indian National Congress.* Forthcoming.
—— *Party Politics in India.* Princeton, Princeton University Press, 1957.
—— *Politics of Scarcity.* Bombay, Asia Publishing House, 1962.
—— 'Traditional Role Performance and the Development of Modern Political Parties: The Indian Case', *Journal of Politics*, XXVI, 4 (Nov. 1964).

4. SWATANTRA BIBLIOGRAPHY

Bhailalbhai Patel 70th Birthday Souvenir. Vallabh Vidyanagar, Charutar Vidyamandal, 1958.
Bhailalbhai Patel 75th Birthday Souvenir. Vallabh Vidyanagar, Charutar Vidyamandal, 1963.
Dave, J. H. *et al.* (eds.). *Munshi: His Art and Work.* 4 vols. Bombay, Munshi 70th Birthday Citizens' Celebration Committee, n.d.
Deo, P. K. (Maharaja of Kalahandi). *My Humble Contributions.* Cuttack, Ganatantra Parishad, 1961.
Desai, Kirtidev. 'Emergence of the Swatantra Party in Gujarat', *Journal of the Gujarat Research Society*, XXV, 3 (April 1963).
Erdman, Howard L. 'Chakravarty Rajagopalachari and Indian Conservatism', *Journal of Developing Areas*, I, 1 (Oct. 1966).
—— 'Conservative Politics in India', *Asian Survey*, VI, 6 (June 1966).
—— 'The Foreign Policy Views of the Indian "Right",' *Pacific Affairs*, XXXIX, 1–2 (Spring–Summer 1966).
—— 'India's Swatantra Party', *Pacific Affairs*, XXXVI, 4 (winter 1963–4).
—— 'The Swatantra Party and Indian Conservatism', Ph.D. dissertation. Cambridge, Harvard University, 1964.
Felton, Monica. *I Meet Rajaji.* London, Macmillan, 1962.
H. M. Patel 60th Birthday Commemoration Volume. Vallabh Vidyanagar, Charutar Vidyamandal, 1964.
Lobo Prabhu, J. M. *Draft Third Plan X-Rayed.* n.d.
—— *Industrial Policy.* Calcutta, Society for the Propagation of Democratic Truth, 1963.
—— *New Thinking.* Bombay, India Book House, 1959.
Malaviya, H. D. *The Swatantra Party: Its Real Character and Designs.* New Delhi, Socialist Congressman, n.d.
Masani, M. R. *The Communist Party of India.* New York, Macmillan, 1954.
—— *Party Politics in India.* Ahmedabad, Harold Laski Institute, 1962.
—— *A Plea for Realism.* Bombay, Popular Book Depot, 1957.
—— *Workers' Participation in Management.* Bombay, n.p., 1955.
Munshi, K. M. *Foundations of Indian Culture.* Bombay, Bharatiya Vidya Bhavan, 1965.

Munshi, K. M. *New Outlook*. Lahore, Indian Book Co., 1947.
—— *Reconstruction of Society Through Trusteeship*. Bombay, Bharatiya Vidya Bhavan, 1960.
—— *The Ruin that Britain Wrought*. Bombay, Padma, 1946.
—— *Warnings of History*. Bombay, Bharatiya Vidya Bhavan, 1959.
—— *Zonal Divisions of India*. Bombay, Vora, 1945.
Pasricha, Col. H. R. 'Our Stuporous Society', *Quest* (April–June 1962).
Patel, Dahyabhai V. *The Second Phase*. Bombay, author, n.d.
Rajagopalachari, C. *Ambedkar Refuted*. Bombay, Hind Kitabs, 1946.
—— *The Defense of India*. Madras, Rochouse, n.d.
—— *Hinduism: Doctrine and Way of Life*. Bombay, Bharatiya Vidya Bhavan, 1964.
—— *Our Culture*. Bombay, Bharatiya Vidya Bhavan, 1963.
—— *Our Democracy and Other Essays*. Madras, B. G. Paul, 1957.
—— *Plighted Word*. Delhi, Servants of Untouchables Society, n.d.
—— *Prohibition*. Madras, Kamala Prachuralayam, 1943.
Rajaji's Speeches. 2 vols. Bombay, Bharatiya Vidya Bhavan, 1960.
Ranga, N. G. *Freedom in Peril*. Hyderabad, Indian Peasants' Institute, 1961.
—— *Kisan Speaks*. Madras, Kisan Publications, n.d.
—— *Outlines of National Revolutionary Path*. Bombay, Hind Kitabs, 1945.
—— *Revolutionary Peasants*. New Delhi, Amrit Book Co., 1949.
Ruthnaswamy, M. *Vote for Swatantra: Why?* Palamcottah, Madras, n.d.
Singh, Gurnam. *A Unilingual Punjabi State and the Sikh Unrest*. New Delhi, author, 1960.
Srinivasan, C. M. *Nehru Discovered*. Madras, Aiyar, 1961.
Zamindar, N. C. *Congress Refuted*. Indore, Sahityalaya, 1962.
(See also parts 5 and 6)

5. SWATANTRA PARTY PUBLICATIONS

REPORTS AND OFFICIAL DOCUMENTS

Swatantra Party Preparatory Convention. Bombay, Swatantra Party-Popular Book Depot, 1959.
First National Convention (Patna). 1960.
Second National Convention (Agra). 1962.
Third National Convention (Bangalore). 1964.
General-Secretary's Report to the Candidates' Convention. Bombay, Swatantra Party, 1962.
General-Secretary's Report on Organisation (for internal circulation only). Bombay, Swatantra Party, 1966.
Swatantra Party Constitution, as revised 1964.
Swatantra Party Souvenir 1960. n.d.
Swatantra Party Souvenir 1961. Bombay, Swatantra Party, 1961.
Munshi, K. M. *et al. Report of the Swatantra Party Punjab Enquiry Committee*. Bombay, Swatantra Party, 1960.
Swatantra Newsletter (more or less monthly, for internal circulation only). Bombay, Swatantra Party.

Swatantra in Parliament (erratic, for internal circulation only). Bombay, Swatantra Party.

ELECTION AND GENERAL PROPAGANDA (roughly chronological)

To Prosperity Through Freedom (1962 election manifesto).
Towards Doom? (Rajaji).
Why Swatantra? (Rajaji, Ranga, Munshi, Masani).
Labour's Friend—Congress or Swatantra?
What's Wrong With the Third Plan?
Co-operation or Coercion?
Social and Religious Decay (Rajaji).
Who is Outdated? German Social Democrats Echo Swatantra.
Inflation: Your Personal Enemy.
The Fight Against Inflation.
Inflation—Your Hidden Enemy.
Socialism—An Ism That is Now a Wasm.
Congress Path to Communism.
Swatantra Answer to the Chinese Communist Challenge.
The Fraud of Gold Control.
Swatantra Alternative to the Third Plan (Ranga, Masani).
India's Answer to the Chinese Bomb (Masani).
Swatantra Demands Fair Deal for Public Servants (Dandekar, Kapur Singh).
Lawless Legislation (ed. A. P. Jain).
17th Amendment vs. Farm, Family, Freedom.
Judgment Reserved (Masani, Dandekar).
The Voice of the People (Masani, Dandekar).
First Swatantra Budget (Masani). Calcutta, Swatantra Forum, 1965.
Can India Escape Bankruptcy? (Masani).
We Accuse! (Deo, Dandekar).
The Congress Path to National Disaster (Ranga, Gayatri Devi).
Why I Took To Politics (C. Rai).
Yet Another Bad Budget (Ranga, Masani, Patel).
Foreign Capital? Yes! Govt.-to-Govt. Loans? No! (Masani).
Devaluation—What Next? (Masani).
Devaluation—The Guilty Men (Masani, Dandekar).
Why Swatantra Supports Tashkent Agreement? (Patel, Deo).

MIMEO DOCUMENTS BY A. P. JAIN, SWANTATRA PARLIAMENTARY OFFICE

'Prohibition: Should It Be Put Into Reverse Gear?'
'Sino-Indian Relations: A Résumé of Latest Developments.'
'Colombo Peace-Makers.'
'Gold Control.'
'The Case of the Attorney-General.'
'The Railway Budget.'
'Emergency Outstretched.'
'Swatantra Party in Parliament: Report of Speeches.' (Now superseded by formal publication noted above.)

GANATANTRA PARISHAD PUBLICATIONS

Policy Statement, parts I and II. Cuttack, Ganatantra Parishad, 1951.
Election Manifesto 1961. Bolangir, Ganatantra Parishad, 1961.

6. FORUM OF FREE ENTERPRISE PUBLICATIONS
(all Bombay, n.d.)

Antia, J. M. *Sales Tax.*
Bhaba, C. H. *The Cult of State Capitalism in India.*
Fazalbhoy, Y. A. *The Case for Sponsored Radio.*
Hayek, F. A. *Two Essays on Free Enterprise.*
Lobo Prabhu, J. M. *Democracy in India.*
Masani, M. R. *Economics of Freedom.*
Mathew, T. *A Socialist Society Cannot be Democratic.*
Matthai, J. *Limits of Nationalisation.*
'An Observer.' *Problems of Free Enterprise in India.*
Palkhivala, N. A. *A Review of the Finance (No. 2) Bill, 1962.*
Panandikar, S. G. *et al. State Trading in a Democracy.*
Rao, B. G. *Community Development.*
Ruthnaswamy, M. *Towards an Economical Administration in India.*
Shenoy, B. R. *Indian Planning and the Common Man.*
—— *The Food Situation and the Common Man.*
—— *Prune the Plan.*
Shroff, A. D. *Desperate Proposals.*
—— *An Economic Review—1957.*
—— *Free Enterprise and Democracy.*
—— *Free Enterprise in India.*
—— *Free Enterprise in India—A Call for Leadership.*
—— *Planning in India.*
—— *The Transport Bottleneck.*
—— *et al. Private Enterprise and Politics.*
Taraporevala, R. J. *Wealth and Expenditure Taxes.*
Vaidya, J. *Free Enterprise and Freedom.*

PERIODICALS

The Hindu (Madras), daily.
The Hindu Weekly Review (Madras).
The Hindustan Times (Delhi), daily.
The Overseas Hindustan Times (Delhi), weekly.
The Indian Express, daily.
The Times of India (Bombay and New Delhi), daily.
Blitz (Bombay), weekly.
The Current (Bombay), weekly.
Economic Weekly (Bombay).
Link (Delhi), weekly.
Insight (Mangalore), weekly.
Swarajya (Madras), weekly and annual numbers.
Swatantra (Madras), weekly, predecessor of *Swarajya*.

7. INTERVIEWS AND QUESTIONNAIRES

Except where stated to the contrary, all of the interviews listed below took place in India between August 1962 to May 1963. Where the person in question was interviewed more than once, the number of more or less formal interviews is noted; and those with whom the author spent much time, over extended periods, have their names in CAPITALS. As it would be too cumbersome to indicate in each case the various national and state offices held, it will suffice here to note that virtually every major national and state office-bearer was interviewed or responded to very detailed questionnaires. (By 'national office-bearer' I do not mean members of the Central Organizing Committee/National Executive or the General Council, but President, Vice-President, etc.)

NATIONAL OFFICE-BEARERS

C. Rajagopalachari (3); N. G. Ranga (3); M. R. MASANI (7, including 1966); K. M. Munshi; S. K. D. Paliwal; Raja Kamakhya Narain Singh of Ramgarh; Maharani Gayatri Devi of Jaipur (2); Professor M. Ruthnaswamy (2); Jathedar Udham Singh Nagoke (through an interpreter); Sir Homy Mody (3, including 1966).

STATE OFFICE-BEARERS, *et al.* (by state)

Andhra. T. Krishnamma Choudhuri (2); C. L. N. Reddy (2); N. Ranga Reddy; N. Sankara Reddy; S. N. Reddy.

Assam. John Deng (2); Professor Martin Narayan (2).

Bihar. Raja J. K. P. N. Singh of Maksoodpur; N. Bakshi; P. K. Ghosh (2); S. A. Matin.

Bombay City. Piloo Mody (2); R. V. Murthy (2); Murarji Vaidya; Madhu Mehta (4).

Delhi Pradesh: Col. H. R. PASRICHA (4); A. C. Basiaria.

Gujarat: Bhailalbhai Patel; Maharaja Jaideepsinhji of Devgadh-Baria (3); Maharajkumar Himmatsinhji of Kutch (4); Dahyabhai Patel (2); H. M. Patel (1966); Pravinsinh Solanki (4); Narendrasingh Mahida (3); NANU B. AMIN (7, including 1966); P. C. Hathi.

Madhya Pradesh: R. Agnibhoj; N. C. Zamindar.

Madras: Saw Ganesan; S. S. MARISWAMY (5): M. SANTOSHAM (over 6); T. Sadasivam.

Mysore: J. M. Lobo Prabhu; V. T. Srinivasan; M. A. Sreenivasan.

Orissa: Maharaja R. N. Singh Deo of Patna; Maharaja P. K. DEO OF KALAHANDI (7, including 1965); Lokanath Misra; Raghunath Misra; Harihar Patel; Ghasiram Majhi; G. C. Roy.

Punjab: Sardar Basant Singh; Sardar Kapur Singh (3); Buta Singh.

Rajasthan: Maharawal Laxman Singh of Dungarpur (4); Maharajkumar Jai Singh of Jaipur (2); Raja Man Singh of Bharatpur (3); Devi Singh of Mandawa (3, including 1966); Major Thakur RAGHUBIR SINGH OF BISSAU (many times, including 1966); Kesri Singh of Pali (3); Ayuwan Singh; Lt. Gen. Thakur Nathu Singh of Gumanpura (5, including 1966).

Uttar Pradesh: Thakur Yashpal Singh.

Bibliography

NON-PARTY INTERVIEWEES

Professor R. Bhaskaran (University of Madras); Dr S. P. Aiyar (University of Bombay); V. K. Narasimhan (*The Hindu*); M. R. Malkani (*The Organiser*, 1961); A. B. Vajpayee (MP, Jan Sangh); Hem Barua and S. N. Dwivedy (MPs, PSP); K. Manoharan (MP, DMK); Harekrushna Mahtab (MP, Congress); Maharaja P. K. Deo Bhanj of Daspalla (MP, Congress, 2, including 1965); C. M. Srinivasan (Madras Forum of Free Enterprise); among other MPs, journalists, etc.

QUESTIONNAIRE RESPONDENTS

Andhra. B. Ramachandra Reddy; C. L. N. Reddy; N. Sankara Reddy; P. V. K. Reddy; K. M. Reddy; K. Narasimha Reddy; Y. C. Veerabhadra Goud; D. Ramachandra Rao; Lakkaraju Subba Rao.

Assam. John Deng.

Bihar. Jaleshwar Prasad; T. P. Bakshi; K. J. N. S. Deo; U. S. Prasad; J. Chowdhary; Michael Kujim; Chhatu Turi; P. C. Mahato.

Bombay City. M. R. Masani; K. M. Munshi; R. V. Murthy; Murarji Vaidya.

Gujarat. Maharajkumar Himmatsinhji of Kutch; Narendrasingh Mahida; Hamirsinhji Jaysinhji Solanki; Lalitmohan Chunilal Gandhi; Maganlal B. Joshi.

Himachal Pradesh. Bishan Singh, Bhagmall Sauhta.

Kerala. S. S. Koder.

Madhya Pradesh. H. S. Dwivedy, N. C. Zamindar.

Madras. M. Ruthnaswamy; K. Sundaram; M. Santosham; S. Narayanaswamy.

Maharashtra. B. B. Walvekar; K. R. Koshti; R. D. Kulkarni.

Mysore. K. B. Jinraja Hegde; J. M. Lobo Prabhu; J. Mohammed Imam; M. A. Sreenivasan; G. D. Patil; B. L. Patil.

Orissa. Raghunath Misra; Harihar Patel; B. K. Deo; K. Panigrahy; P. Bhagat; A. Sahoo; Anchal Majhi; Ghasiram Majhi; C. S. S. Bhoi.

Punjab. Jathedar Udham Singh Nagoke; Sardar Basant Singh; Col. Rajadhiraj Maheshindra Singh of Patiala; Karan Singh Malik; Ram Singh; Dhanna Singh Ghulshan.

Rajasthan. Maharani Gayatri Devi of Jaipur; Professor Madan Singh.

Uttar Pradesh. Raja Raghavendra Singh of Mankapur; Raja Ram Singh of Gangawal; Raja Mahendra Singh of Bhadawar; Wahidur Rahman; Sant Saran Shukla; N. R. Sharma; Munnu Singh.

West Bengal. R. P. Patodia.

INDEX

Index

Index